UNIX and Windows 2000 Integration Toolkit

UNIX and Windows 2000 Integration Toolkit

A Complete Guide for Systems Administrators

Rawn Shah

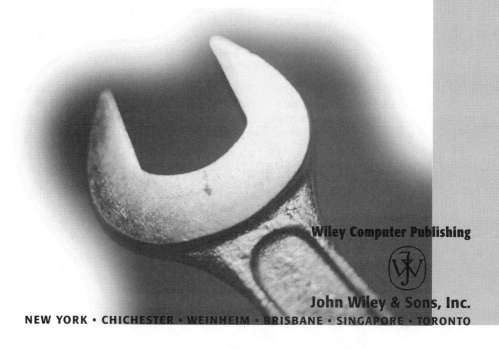

Wiley Computer Publishing

John Wiley & Sons, Inc.

NEW YORK · CHICHESTER · WEINHEIM · BRISBANE · SINGAPORE · TORONTO

Publisher: Robert Ipsen

Editor: Robert M. Elliott

Managing Editor: Micheline Frederick

Associate New Media Editor: Brian Snapp

Text Design & Composition: North Market Street Graphics

ISBN 0-471-29354-7

For W. Richard Stevens,
may he find rest in UNIX heaven.

CONTENTS

ACKNOWLEDGMENTS

In any endeavor, small or large, there are always others providing the support at the very root. I cannot go without acknowledging their effect on me, and their help with my work on this book, with my career, and with my life.

I would like to thank my best friend, Tom Duff, for helping with the book. I know you didn't have the time to help out more, but what you did certainly put me ahead. I have to thank Deborah Bonkoski for putting up with my temperament, stress-outs, and busy schedule while writing the book. I would certainly like to thank my parents, who worried when I took my first job as a network administrator way back when I was still in college.

I'd certainly like to thank Bob Elliott, Emile Herman, Micheline Frederick, and all those over at John Wiley & Sons. They have made sure that we have a strong focus in the book and have helped me work out the details of approach and continuity on too many occasions.

I would also like to thank the editors at the various magazines that I write for, for their patience in not harrying me about the time spent writing this book. Thanks to Tom Young, Carolyn Wong, Nora Mikes, Kane Scarlett, and everyone else at the division formerly known as Web Publishing, Inc., at IDH. Definitely a big hand to all those involved in *SunWorld* magazine, which has run my "Connectivity" column in *Advanced Systems* and *SunWorld Online.* And thanks, of course, to Mark Cappel and Mac McCarthy for giving my the break into writing in the first place, all those years ago.

Finally, to all the readers who wrote commentaries on my various published works, thank you for beating me into shape with your precise, caring bludgeons of truth.

How do you marry the desktop personal computer (PC) systems that most of your users have with the UNIX server systems that run the critical functions of the business? It never ceases to amaze me that a problem that has been in existence for almost 15 years is still one of the top problems that information technology (IT) managers and administrators face every day.

Since the dawn of networking for PC systems, one of the holy grails has been to find a way to allow PC users to take advantage of the resources of UNIX systems and vice versa. It started in the mid-1980s with the development of Transmission Control Protocol/Internet Protocol (TCP/IP) software for PCs, followed by Network File Sharing (NFS) and X Windows.

At that time, the PC was woefully underpowered compared to UNIX systems, and thus most of the resource sharing went in one direction, from UNIX to PC. Today's systems are more equal, although at the high-end UNIX systems still hold the flag. However, with the cost-effectiveness of PC servers today, the resource sharing has become more bidirectional.

In the years since I have written about connectivity between PC and UNIX systems, many different solutions have emerged, although there has never been anything close to a single cure-all product. While some vendors have attempted to cram every possible common TCP/IP-based application into a package for the PC, this isn't how solutions are found. Other vendors have followed Microsoft's lead and have built NetBIOS applications that run over TCP/IP. This way they have had to make few changes to the dynamics of their software and have been able to follow the compatibility road. Unfortunately, most UNIX systems do not willingly speak NetBIOS.

Most of these come from third-party vendors, and not directly from the vendors of the UNIX or PC operating systems. The good thing for the industry is that this means that there are lots of niches and nooks for helpful products that an aspiring start-up can tackle. However, without total support from the original vendors, this means that the brunt of the integration work—finding a solution that works and implementing that solution—lies in the hands of IT managers and administrators, respectively. Some operating systems vendors have tried to create such integration products on their own, but the general belief is that there is not enough money in it for them or that the work takes too much support. Even with the help of vendors, the designs of UNIX network systems are different than those of PC network operating systems. Although they are getting closer and closer together, the devil is in the details.

I am grateful to see that PC operating systems such as Windows are finally growing up and being designed for the enterprise computer network rather than for pockets of independent local-area networks (LANs). Windows 2000 takes a step in a new direction to help combine larger networks of PC systems. With a proven background based on Windows NT, it takes the next step toward bringing features for management and access to all the systems on the network. Although several companies have had success with deploying NT systems supporting tens of thousands of users, most have achieved it with hardship and overkill. The new features of Windows 2000, particularly Active Directory, make it faster and easier to manage and use, on everything from a 5-machine LAN to a 50,000-station multinational network.

On the integration front, there are improvements that make it both easier and harder to integrate with UNIX systems. Possibly the biggest benefit to users is the move away from outdated NetBIOS technology for applications. Microsoft has had to put in too many duct-tape applications to allow NetBIOS to run in large networks. The move toward all-TCP/IP-based system applications acknowledges that IP is now the foremost network protocol for just about any type of network, and that most users now demand IP as the protocol for communicating with others or using applications. Furthermore, Microsoft is taking the brave step of implementing a number of new IP features that are radically innovative but necessary, such as the IP Security Protocol, certificate services, directory services, and quality of service features.

On the downside, Microsoft still employs its "Embrace and Extend" philosophy, which is basically an excuse for making more proprietary extensions to standards. This, of course, ends up making the software nonstandard. And so, some of these same features, particularly the Active Directory system, have become somewhat nonstandard. Again, the great thing for third-party vendors is that this gives them a niche to develop new products, and some vendors have done just that.

In preparing this book, I have gone over many of the existing technologies that work between Windows NT and UNIX and examined how they work under Windows 2000. Most of them work flawlessly, or with minor glitches that can be ignored. However, with the changes in Windows 2000, you really need to look for those products that have been improved to take advantage of the new features.

Overview of the Book and Technology

The field of Windows and UNIX integration has gone from the obscure to the relevant. In many companies today, you will find lots of systems of both kinds. The general trend has been to keep both systems operational and to use networking and application standards to communicate between the two. There has been an acknowledgment that Windows servers are necessary in the enterprise, and a realization that, in spite of Microsoft's promises, they are not as robust as most UNIX systems.

The most pertinent of the applications involved in this cross-platform integration provide end-user connectivity between the two systems, such as:

- Windows Terminal Server, X Windows, or Telnet
- Disk and printer resource sharing between the two using NFS, the Common Internet File System (CIFS), or other protocols
- Foreign application execution using system emulation or remote application access

- Cross-platform user management with protocols and applications such as directory services, network logins, and remote access

This book thus falls to the task of helping to discover or solve these details. Unlike the general "just show me" approach taken in other books, the concept here is to give you a thorough understanding of the basic problems and help you discover your own solution to your own network integration problems. I don't expect that everyone will run the same products, or that everyone implements their network in the same way. Furthermore, it is not possible to always keep up with every new development in technology. So I go the route to find the root of the problem and suggest what products may work for that problem and how they can solve it.

This book covers some technologies that are very different internally; however, the role of the book is not to discuss intricately how this internal structure of the integration software works but, rather, to explain how it behaves externally to the user and the network manager. In fact, most of the internal details are beyond the scope of information that network managers need to know, and some even span into topics in advanced computer science.

How This Book Is Organized

This book is split up into four parts: *Know Your NT Systems*, *Planning for Integration*, *System Integration*, and *Management Strategies*. Each part focuses on one aspect of integrating the two platforms together. The book begins with an overview of the operating systems involved and how they work. With this working base of knowledge, you can move on to determining a plan for integration and investigating the factors that affect this step. Once you have a plan at hand, you can begin performing the integration steps to unite the systems. Finally, with the system deployed, you can look at methods for making your job of managing this combined system easier.

The chapters are structured as follows:

- Chapter 1, *The UNIX Operating System*, presents an overview of the state of UNIX systems. Since this book is targeted at UNIX system administrators, you probably already know a lot of this material. The idea, however, is to provide a level platform from which you can compare and contrast similar concepts presented in the next few chapters, covering Windows 2000.

- Chapter 2, *The Windows 2000 Operating System*, presents a general description of how the operating system is structured, the major components of Windows 2000, the kernel and process model, and a quick overview of the major system controls.

- Chapter 3, *Windows 2000 File Systems*, explains all the different file systems that are natively supported by the operating system. These includes the NT File System (NTFS), the file allocation table (FAT) for DOS and Windows, and the variations thereof.

- Chapter 4, *Windows 2000 Networking*, shows all the networking services built into Windows 2000. Topics include all the different network protocols it supports, the naming systems, routing and remote access, and compatibility issues between different implementations in Windows and UNIX.

- Chapter 5, *Windows 2000 Active Directory Services*, presents a detailed description of Active Directory. This new core component of systems services in the operating system affects nearly all other areas of the system. This chapter explains how Active Directory works and how it interfaces with other directory services.

- Chapter 6, *Windows 2000 Security*, provides details on the internal security architecture of the operating system and an external view of how users and administrators are affected by it.

- Chapter 7, *The Windows 2000 User Interface*, discusses the user interface of the Windows environment, including interesting lesser-known and not-so-obvious items that make working on the system much simpler.

- Chapter 8, *Selecting System Hardware*, covers the background of Intel-based PC computers on which Windows 2000 runs. This chapter describes the major features of workstation and server platforms that you should look for or avoid, and is designed to help you make a purchasing decision based on various hardware and vendor-service features.

- Chapter 9, *Selecting Integration Packages*, shows the considerations you have to take into account before choosing a cross-platform integration package, based on usage, cost effectiveness, management control, and security.

- Chapter 10, *Developing an Integration Strategy*, shows how to develop a plan for integrating the two environments. It illustrates the administrative procedures of deployment—the steps you need to take, the information you need to gather, the people you need to talk to, the vendor selection process, and the effects on your budget.

- Chapter 11, *Integrating Network Services*, is the first of the hands-on chapters on building cross-platform services. Starting at the lowest level of network communications, it examines the different aspects of network services, the hidden compatibility issues, and the ways to circumvent these problems

- Chapter 12, *Managing Users and Domains*, describes how to manage dual sets of users on different platforms and how to integrate them together. It focuses on implementing the directory services model to create the necessary infrastructure to support the enterprise domain of users.

- Chapter 13, *Disk and Printer Sharing*, describes how to distribute the available resources on each platform using built-in methods and add on packages that implement complementary protocols used by each platform.

- Chapter 14, *Integrating Server Applications*, describes the high-level application services that are affected by the differences in the platforms and how they can be united—in particular, e-mail services, Web services, file transfer services, and remote script execution.

- Chapter 15, *Client Station Integration*, describes how the two platforms can support a base of client desktops and workstations on both a small and large scale. It describes methods for managing and administratively controlling all these desktops centrally so as to reduce time and costs.

- Chapter 16, *Establishing Integrated Management Policies*, discusses methods for better management of a cross-platform environment, the different types of policies you should implement in your network environment, and how you can develop a training program to bring your users to the new integrated environment.

- Chapter 17, *System and Security Management*, describes the major management interfaces in the platforms and the types of system and security management tools available that you will likely need to deploy to support your network.

- Chapter 18, *Success with Integration*, wraps up the book by giving management advice on determining whether the integration project has been successful.

Who Should Read This Book

If you are trying to understand the fundamental issues of integrating UNIX and Windows 2000 systems, this is the book for you. The book is written for an audience of information technology managers and system administrators. It focuses on those who are currently familiar with the UNIX platform but have to integrate Windows 2000 systems into their network environment. It doesn't matter if you have 10 machines or 10,000 machines. If you are planning on making these two platforms work together, you should delve through the chapters and familiarize yourself with the intricacies of integration.

The book is arranged in a sequential order, so reading it from cover to cover will be beneficial. Managers will be interested in Parts Two, Three, and Four of this book, which cover planning, integration, and management issues regarding the two platforms. Part One covers background technical information about the operating systems. System administrators will want to read Parts One, Three, and Four in particular, but may also want to read about planning issues in Part Two.

Tools You Will Need

You shouldn't need any special tools to use this book other than the operating systems concerned. To view the CD-ROM, however, you will need at least a common Web browser, such as Microsoft Internet Explorer or Netscape Navigator.

What's on the CD-ROM and Web Site

The CD-ROM and Web site conjoined form an important repository of scripts, worksheets, and information that will be helpful to your integration project. Since information and systems are constantly changing, especially in light of the fact that Windows 2000 itself is new, do visit the

Web site to follow up on the topics covered in the book. You will find a lot more details on the Web site, which will attempt to keep up with the churning flow of information generated by our industry.

Within the text you will find key referencing material that may be found on either the Web site or CD-ROM.

 Indicates that additional information may be found on the book's Web site.

 Indicates additional material that may be found on the CD-ROM.

Together CD-ROM and Web site contain details on commercial and free-ware products for integration, comparisons of some of these products, links to other resources on the Internet for regular news and reviews, free helpful scripts and programs to perform specific tasks detailed in the book, and frequently asked questions about these technologies.

Where We Go from Here

Now, prepare yourself for a journey to the next great integration project. It takes a strong mind to keep up with the various pressures of a system administrator or network manager's job. We constantly have to grow in knowledge while at the same time solving all our users' problems for them and planning to improve services for the future. But take heart in the knowledge that many have gone ahead of you and come out of it alive and better than before. I hope that this book will both educate you about the variations in the nature of UNIX and Windows systems and make you appreciate the realities of working with both systems. Your journey begins first with knowledge, then with practice, and ends, I hope, with understanding and wisdom.

## PART ONE

Know Your NT System

## CHAPTER 1

The UNIX Operating System

A nd on the 6.9th day, He created UNIX.

Before we jump onto the *trampoline of delights* that is the process of integrating UNIX and Windows 2000, we first need a stable position to jump from. In this respect, we begin by a succinct introduction to UNIX. It's not that we don't think you already know all there is to know about it, but we want to give comparable concepts between the two operating systems, so that when we begin talking about Windows 2000, you will understand what we mean.

This isn't an utter, complete, comprehensive, all-encompassing, every-bit-about-everything review of UNIX, only most of the basic ideas on how the system works and runs. It tries not to go too much into the programming depths of the operating system (OS), but then if you were interested in that, you'd be reading a hardcore book on the internals of UNIX instead. It also cannot cover every tool and command that is available in UNIX across all the versions because of the years of variations between them. What's more, we expect that you may have a bit of experience with UNIX as it is. What this book will give you is a working understanding of how UNIX runs so that you can compare it against the Windows 2000 architecture.

UNIX Alive!

UNIX is undoubtedly one of the most resilient operating systems ever. It is also the only operating system still in wide commercial use that's almost 30 years old. It has evolved over the years to take advantage of new ideas in computer science as well as new hardware technology. Yet, there are ideas and concepts in UNIX that its progenitors could point to and see similarities in since its first inception. Today, UNIX can be seen running in the largest massively parallel computers in the world, as well as some of the smallest handheld devices. What we really see is not one operating system but a whole family of them, running on different processor types and system motherboards, and with different capabilities. And all it took to start the whole shebang was one idle programmer who wanted to play a game of Space Travel. . . .

UNIX Operating System Layers

The UNIX operating system is layered like most others and was one of the first to introduce a separation between the kernel and the user space (see Figure 1.1). Essentially, the model is like a cross-section of a peanut. At the very center is the *kernel*, which constitutes the core components of

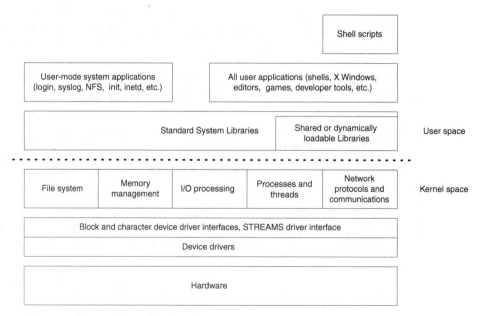

Figure 1.1   The UNIX operating system layers, generalized.

UNIX in Retrovision

In the summer of 1969 when Ken Thompson's wife was away for vacation at her parents' place, he sat down to build a toy on a Digital Equipment Corporation PDP-7. He had been working on the large computer development effort at Bell Labs known as the Multiplexed Information and Computing Service (MULTICS), which had recently been put to bed as a misadvised technical nightmare. But thankfully, our hero found better use of his time, working on his own pet operating systems project, known amusingly as UNICS. Soon others at Bell Labs, like Dennis Ritchie, who thought it a surprisingly impressive toy, joined in the project and began expanding it and bringing it to more modern machines like the PDP-11 series, and in the process created another little gem known as the C programming language.

In 1974, when Thompson and Ritchie published their paper on UNIX in the professional journal *Communications of the ACM*, they received a great deal of attention from universities across the United States that also had PDP-11 series computers. AT&T soon licensed copies of this new OS to most of them for a fee. The first standard version came out as UNIX V6, named after the sixth edition of the *UNIX Programmer's Manual*.

This is where it begins to break up. The popularity was so overwhelming that several academic groups decided to enhance it with their own versions. The first two derivatives were XENIX and BSD. The former eventually went on to become SCO UNIX, and the latter can still be seen in FreeBSD, NetBSD, and all its derivatives.

The University of California at Berkeley was primarily responsible for the Berkeley Systems Design (BSD) version. Other UNIX legendaries like Bill Joy, Kirk McKusick, and Rob Kolstad joined the BSD group over time to develop several versions. The BSD group also was the first introduce the TCP/IP protocol into UNIX, and created the standard communications model known as sockets. For the longest time this had stabilized into version 4.2 and then 4.3, and several companies licensed this code to make their own operating systems, including Digital Ultrix and Sun Microsystems' SunOS.

On the commercial front, AT&T still owned the license and continued to develop its version of the standard, which split off after Version 8 and rejoined with several of the other UNIX efforts to eventually become System V Release 3. The last improvement to this was released as UNIX System Version 4. Today, commercial and noncommercial UNIX operating systems such as Sun Solaris, SGI IRIX, IBM AIX, Compaq Tru64 UNIX, SCO UnixWare, FreeBSD, and NetBSD are actually a combination of features from both these lineages.

There have been attempts to merge or submerge the various different versions of UNIX, but pretty much through and through both BSD and System V have

continues

UNIX in Retrovision *(Continued)*

survived to the end. Most commercial UNIX from large vendors is still based on the System V model, although there have been so many changes, everyone has given up the pretense that they are compatible. Development now continues along the lines of each of these products through their respective vendors and developer communities, although there continue to be private individuals and groups working on the next best UNIX.

The official UNIX standard is now in the hands of the Open Group (www .opengroup.org), an independent nonprofit organization. It was sold by AT&T to Novell in the early 1990s, then by Novell to SCO, and then was handed over to the group. SCO's UnixWare (formerly Novell's and AT&T's) is closest in specification to the official UNIX 98 standard, but then again, the standard is mostly a list of supported APIs and command tools. You want to know something really bizarre? By the definition and product testing of the Open Group, a number of other operating system platforms can also legally be called UNIX, including the IBM OS/390 running on mainframes (the same ones UNIX fought against decades ago) and another product called Interix from Softway Systems that—get this—actually runs on top of Windows NT!

In any case, independent development of UNIXlike platforms never ceases. One famous example today is Linux. Back in 1991, a Finnish developer decided to put his free time into making a completely new version of UNIX, which borrowed the ideas but not the code and intellectual property of UNIX. Soon, Linus Torsvald and his friends combined their efforts with others across the Internet to build on this version, called Linux. It was picked up by enthusiasts everywhere, and today there are an estimated 7 million Linux users. A number of companies offer different distributions of Linux for sale for the packaging, not the actual OS itself.

In recent years, Linux has become the best-selling OS from the UNIX-like group of operating systems, and continues to be so because of its model of open source contribution in which anyone is allowed to see, modify, and release versions of the operating system without any need for a license fee. The fact that it has a free license makes it very appealing to individuals and companies alike. Development of Linux is still controlled by Linus and his core developers, but most releases come packaged from organizations such as Red Hat, Debian, Caldera, SuSE, and TurboLinux.

the operating system. Wrapped around this are other layers, which build up the applications and tools, and covered at the very outside is the *shell*, the environment that the users interact with.

Although the original OS model was a monolithic design in which all kernel operations were combined together into the same executive, today there are microkernel versions of the operating system as well, separating each component, such as memory management, file systems, input/output (I/O) processing, and so forth, into separately loadable kernel components. The System V and BSD device driver models differ quite radically. BSD devices are typically monolithic, whereas STREAMS drivers in System V allow drivers to layer themselves over each other to facilitate extensibility.

The kernel/user space separation allowed developers to cleanly implement user applications without having to worry that changes to the system components would have adverse affects on their code. This was accomplished by providing a standard set of system libraries for programmers to develop and allowing other applications to add other libraries on top of these. The actual contents of the libraries vary to some degree from one version of UNIX to another, rendering some applications incompatible between different UNIX platforms.

Processes and Threads

A *process* in UNIX is a specific instance that an application program runs in. This includes all the memory required to run the program, any devices that it owns or uses, and control or execution information for the program. The process is essentially the most basic entity that can be scheduled to run in the operating system. All processes share execution time on the central processing unit (CPU), hence the old description of UNIX as a *time-sharing* system. In a multiprocessor system, several processes may be running at the same time, but only one per CPU.

All processes are children of the first process, known as *init*, except for the *swapper* and *pagedaemon* processes for memory management. When the system is booted it creates the data structures associated with the series of terminal devices and network devices needed for users to log in. When a user logs in, the init process creates or *spawns* a new child process that is assigned to the user, using the *fork* system call. Every process has a *process identifier* (PID) by which the kernel and all applications can refer to it. When a new child is created, it is assigned a new PID, as well as a pointer to its parent process, known as the *parent process identifier* (PPID). This first process after login is normally the user's command-line interface or *shell*, and the launching point for other applications.

A process can be put on ice temporarily, and go into the *stopped* or *suspended* state. This is usually done either by the program that is running within or by direct control of the parent process. At this point the process is sitting idle, not executing in memory or performing any tasks. The process can later be unsuspended when it receives the continue signal from another process. A process can also be put to *sleep*, to wait for a certain amount of time to go by. During this state, the process is actively waiting for a timer to go off, and not terminated.

When a process terminates or is killed, it first goes into a zombie state, waiting for any devices associated with it to close properly and do their housecleaning. The process information is then destroyed and removed from the system. This does not destroy the application that was running in the process just the specific instance that was running within the process. Once terminated, the process no longer exists on the system.

Every process contains a certain set of data structures: the address space, the control information, the security information, the hardware context, and process environment variables. The *address space* of a process is subdivided into several parts to hold the executable code of the program, the program stack that describes the flow of the application, and the data heap that stores the variables of the program. The *control information* contains important data structures that point to all the other data structures. The *security information* indicates who owns the process and what permissions they are allowed. The *hardware context* is a set of hardware-related registers and pointers that indicate at which point the application is running. Finally, the *environment variables* contain information inherited from the parent process.

Processes are scheduled for execution in a system known as *preemptive round robin*. Each process is allowed a certain amount of time, called a *quantum*, that it can execute in, and when it is done, the system puts the current process to sleep and moves to the next one.

Processes also have a priority value indicating which ones should be run first. This is actually a pair of values known as the *base priority* and the *current* or *scheduled priority*. The base priority defines the process's overall ranking on the system and the current priority indicates what it is set to at the current time. Those with the same base priority are scheduled to execute one after the other, then followed by those with a lower priority. UNIX uses lower numerical values to indicate higher priorities, so those with a value of 1 will take precedence over all others. Since this could lead to some processes running all the time while others wait forever, the current priority value is used as a breaker. A process that has been waiting for a long time to run is temporarily bumped up in priority so that it can execute the next chance it gets. Once it is done, it can go hide with the others under the stairs, waiting at the low base priority. This cycles all the processes through over time. Since each process typically runs within 100 milliseconds or so on the processor, all the processes almost appear to run in real time to us comparatively slow humans, when, in fact, they don't.

All processes may respond to a common set of predefined signals that can be sent by the system or other processes. These signals are handled either by the parent of the process or by the process itself. Common signals include interrupt process, quit process, suspend process, send a hardware error, indicate an I/O control message, indicate a memory access error, indicate that a timer has gone off, and so forth. A listing of the common signals, their default behavior, and what they do is provided in Table 1.1.

All signals initiate some action on the behalf of the process, and almost all can be caught or *trapped* by a piece of code in the program known as the *signal handler*. This handler then executes some other piece of code in response to the signal. A default signal handler that is part of the user's session will cause an action if the application itself does not trap it first.

Some UNIX systems also support *threads* within a process, to define an even smaller unit of execution that contains code but shares most of its memory with other threads that are part of the process. By designing an operating system with support for threads in the kernel, you make it ready to run in multiprocessor machines, since threads can often run separately at the same time on separate CPUs.

Kernel-mode threads are similar in concept but do not run in the context of any user process. They are normally used by the kernel to handle fast asynchronous I/O operations such as memory paging and communicating with file systems. They can also be used to develop kernel-mode applications that can run even faster than normal user-mode applications, but also pose a threat to the stability of the system if not done right.

Memory Management in UNIX

UNIX implements a virtual memory management system that creates a total memory space of 4GB per process for 32-bit machines and signifi-

Table 1.1   All the Process Signals

SIGNAL NAME	DEFAULT ACTION	DESCRIPTION
SIGABRT	Create core image.	Abort function call (formerly SIGIOT).
SIGALRM	Terminate process.	Real-time timer expired.
SIGBUS	Create core image.	Bus error.
SIGCHLD	Discard signal.	Child status has changed.
SIGCONT	Discard signal.	Continue after stop.
SIGEMT	Create core image.	Emulate instruction executed.
SIGFPE	Create core image.	Floating-point exception.
SIGHUP	Terminate process.	Terminal line hangup.
SIGILL	Create core image.	Illegal instruction.
SIGINFO	Discard signal.	Status request from keyboard.
SIGINT	Terminate process.	Interrupt program.
SIGIO	Discard signal.	Asynchronous I/O event.
SIGIOT	Stop process.	I/O trap event.
SIGKILL	Terminate process.	Kill program.
SIGPIPE	Terminate process.	Write on a pipe with no reader.
SIGPOLL	Stop process.	Pollable event.
SIGPROF	Terminate process.	Profiling timer alarm.
SIGPWR	Terminate process.	Power failure.
SIGQUIT	Create core image.	Quit program.
SIGSEGV	Create core image.	Segmentation violation.
SIGSTOP	Stop process.	Stop (cannot be caught or ignored).
SIGSYS	Create core image.	Nonexistent system call invoked.
SIGTERM	Terminate process.	Software termination signal.
SIGTRAP	Create core image.	Trace trap.
SIGTSTP	Stop process.	Stop signal generated from keyboard.
SIGTTIN	Stop process.	Background read attempted from control terminal.
SIGTTOU	Stop process.	Background write attempted to control terminal.
SIGURG	Discard signal.	Urgent condition present on socket.
SIGUSR1	Terminate process.	User-defined signal 1.
SIGUSR2	Terminate process.	User-defined signal 2.
SIGVTALRM	Terminate process.	Virtual time alarm.

Table 1.1 *(Continued)*

SIGNAL NAME	DEFAULT ACTION	DESCRIPTION
SIGWINCH	Discard signal.	Window size change.
SIGXCPU	Terminate process.	CPU time limit exceeded.
SIGXFSZ	Terminate process.	File size limit exceeded.

cantly more (it varies) for 64-bit machines. This is accomplished by clever use of physical memory, and by storing most of it onto hard drives.

Virtual memory allows all the processes on the machine to run without interfering with one another in memory, allows multiple programs to be kept in memory, and, most important, relieves programmers of constantly having to work on managing the memory use of their applications. At the same time, virtual memory can support much more memory space that programmers can use than what is actually available in physical hardware. After all, there was a time not too long ago (around 1995) when 4GB of physical memory on a machine was worshipped, available only in the largest servers on the market. Even today, when it's not uncommon to come across small personal computer (PC) departmental servers with 4GB of physical random-access memory (RAM), virtual memory still plays an important part.

Virtual memory management came to UNIX in the late 1970s after the first public release of Version 6. It really needed to wait for computers that could actually support virtual memory, such as the PDP-11 series.

The original method of virtual memory management in UNIX was to *swap* entire programs in and out of memory onto a hard-drive-based *swap space*. This was either a file or a special file system where a copy of the program in memory was stored. Later, with the arrival of the very popular Digital VAX computer series, came the concept of *paged* memory. In this system, all memory is stored in fixed units called *pages*, which are usually a few kilobytes big. Every process is allocated a certain number of pages in virtual memory into which it loads its programs. When the process is set to run by the operating system, these pages move from virtual memory into matching *page frames* or *physical pages* within the physical RAM itself. By working with pages, it is possible to work in much smaller fixed units in a much faster fashion.

Paged virtual memory has been around ever since. Although there are complex algorithms that decide which pages to leave in physical memory and how to replace them, the concept remains the same. The older concept of a swap space still exists, but these now hold pages of memory instead of whole programs. In some UNIX systems, there can even be multiple swap spaces on different drives to speed the whole virtual memory system by having them work in parallel across the drives.

There is also a concept of *segments* in UNIX memory management. Each processes address space is divided into several segments, each of which consists of a contiguous area of memory that can be loaded into physical memory. The system can load the separate code and data pages for an application into different segments. Since code pages are very likely to be in consecutive blocks of memory, this works fairly well. By combining the paging and segmentation system, it becomes possible to manage memory more easily for both the operating system and the applications.

UNIX File Systems

UNIX file systems have been around for a long time without any significant change, indicating that they were mostly done right the first or second time around. The most widely used one today is the Berkeley Fast File System (FFS), now just called the UNIX file system (ufs). Other new file system types emerged in the 1990s to cover some of the shortcomings not anticipated in the earlier ones. They recover much better and implement concepts such as software-based redundant arrays of independent drives (RAIDs). Even more file systems exist in the distributed arena, intended to merge the file systems of multiple computers so that the combined storage can be used by all. This section focuses mostly on how the basic UNIX file system stores and accesses data, as well as some of the common file system constructs across the UNIX versions.

Files and Directories in UNIX

In UNIX today, filenames can usually be up to 255 characters in length, although this still varies from one UNIX version to another. Any 7-bit ASCII characters are allowed, including all characters on the keyboard, except for the forward slash (/). UNIX files can have file extensions to indicate their document type, but this is simply included as part of the name, and is not a separate entity as in MS-DOS. Thus, you can have many extensions successively following each other in the filename (e.g., theword.doc.tar.gz). The file system leaves this to the application to sort out. Filenames are case sensitive, so two names like *Smith.doc* and *smith.doc* are considered two distinct files. The names of files need to be distinct only when they are in the same directory.

There is an added distinction for files that begin with a period character. A single period character is always used to indicate the current directory. Thus the system, users, and applications can always see a listing called "." in their current directory. In addition, two periods (..) are used to indicate the parent directory. Finally, all files that begin with a period followed by any other series of characters (e.g., .cshrc, .profile, or .xinitrc) are referred to as *hidden* files, since they show up in a directory listing only when you give a special flag. These hidden files are usually configuration and data files for other applications that are needed per user but simply clutter up their screens, and so are put away so that they don't bother users. Other than this, there is no difference in the file system structure of these files compared to others.

The human view of the UNIX file system is that it is laid out like a tree blown over by a tornado, with the roots on top and the branches and leaves below. At the very top is the *root* of the file system, always designated by the single character / (forward slash). Each subsequent directory below this has its own name, which follows the same naming scheme as regular files, described earlier. Every file can be referred to by its *pathname*, that is, the list of directories starting at the root, down through the subdirectories, and, finally, to the filename itself. For example, */usr/local/games/mahjongg* indicates that the file called *mahjongg* is stored in the *games* directory under the subdirectory labeled *local*, under *usr*, and the root directory. To distinguish that it is traversing directories, we use the forward slash as indication.

Every file can also be referred to by a *relative pathname* based on the concept of the *current working directory* of the user. When users log in, they are placed in an area of the operating system that is their home directory. From this location they can move about to other directories that they are allowed into by using the **cd** or **pushd** command. Each time they move, their current working directory is updated to indicate their new location.

From any directory you can refer to files at other locations using their relative pathnames. For example, if you are in your own home directory, called */usr/home/boogeyman*, and you want to access a file in another location, such as */usr/home/timmy/brains.txt*, you could type in the full path name to get there, or you could abbreviate it. Since both *boogeyman* and *timmy* are subdirectories under */usr/home*, from the boogeyman location you can refer to the parent directory and then the timmy subdirectory and file as *../timmy/brains.txt*. You can use this combination parent directory name ".." and subdirectory name to refer to every other location in the file system.

Every file contained in a directory is said to have a *hard link* from that directory. This means that in the file system structure, there is an entry under that directory that points to the location of the file on the disk. A single file can have hard links from any number of directories. When each link is removed, that file can no longer be accessed from that directory, until all the links are gone, and that file is essentially considered deleted. UNIX also allows you to create *soft* or *symbolic links* from one location to another. In a soft link, only the name of the other file is stored and not all its file information. This makes it convenient to access the file from another directory, rather than having to refer to its full or relative pathname every time. Since it is referred to by name only, the file in its actual location can be removed and replaced with another and the link will remain. If the file is removed, the link will continue to point to it, but when users try to read or write to that file, they will get an error saying that it does not exist. A file or directory can have any number of soft links, but only the hard links matter when it comes to accessibility. If all the hard links for the file are removed, the file is considered deleted, and there is no way to get it back. If all the soft links for the file are removed, it has no effect on the original file itself.

Every file has a certain set of attributes that go along with the raw data contents. These attributes include the file type, the number of hard links, the file size in bytes, the device on which it is located, the *inode* number, three different time stamps, the user and group identifiers, and the permissions flags. UNIX supports a number of different file types that designate how the file is accessed and used. This is independent of the actual contents of the file itself. These types include regular files, directories, symbolic links, device driver files, and queue files. Within the code, these files are accessed differently and have different properties. The inode number describes where the file is located on a hard drive according to the file system structure. The time stamps record the last time it was accessed, the last time it was modified, and the last time its attributes and time stamps were changed. The user ID, group ID, and permissions flags are explained in the upcoming section on security.

Special Files on UNIX File Systems

There are several types of files that are not used to contain directories, data file contents, or symbolic links. These special files are used as interfaces to device drivers or queues. They look and behave like files but are implemented differently internally.

Hardware I/O devices in UNIX are mapped to file identities to create a logical view of each device that programs can manipulate like files. Each device is identified by the kernel with a pair of numbers, the *major device number* and the *minor device number*. The major device number identifies one class of devices by the driver that supports it. For example, pseudoterminal devices in Linux map to the major device number 2, and real terminals to the number 3. This number is used as an index to a table of all device drivers.

The minor device number identifies a specific instance of the device as a logical entity. This means that two physical terminals that both use the same type of device driver (e.g., major devnum 3) would need two separate minor devnums, say 1 and 2. Thus, once the driver is located with the major devnum, the program can use the minor devnum to pick out exactly which instance of the device it needs.

One last distinction between these logical device driver files is that there are two main types: the *character device file* and the *block device file*. They differ based upon how you access individual data items from them. A character device file allows you to write or read one character at a time from the device. This is common in serial interfaces and terminal devices. The block device reads and writes whole blocks of data at a time, as in hard drives and network interfaces.

Pipes, or first-in, first-out (FIFO) queues, are special files used to communicate between processes. Essentially, the queue acts as a file-based buffer that one or more programs can write to, while others can read off of the queue and then process the data accordingly. File-system-based FIFOs are not used as much since the adoption of the *sockets*-based system for interprocess and intersystem communications. In fact, in BSD systems today, the FIFO file is just a file system interface on top of a sockets interface.

Structure of UNIX File Systems

The method of supporting disk systems does vary across UNIX versions in specific areas, but the general concept is similar in all of them. The popular UNIX file systems in use today include *ufs* (the Berkeley Fast File System or UNIX file system), *s5fs* (the System V file system), *vxfs* (the VERITAS log file system), *advfs* (the Digital UNIX file system), and *ext2fs* (the basic Linux file system). Most UNIX systems now use the ufs file system, although the specialized ones, such as advfs and vxfs, are more commonly found in high-end systems, and the open-source ext2fs in versions of Linux. A comparison of the different features of each is listed in Table 1.2.

Each UNIX file system is mounted under a different location in the over-all system file tree. Any partition can be mounted under any directory,

Table 1.2 Comparison of Various UNIX File Systems

FEATURE	UFS	S5FS	ADVFS	VXFS	EXT2FS
Maximum storage capacity	Terabytes	16GB	Terabytes	Terabytes	Terabytes
Minimum disk size	320KB	320KB	1MB	1MB	760KB
Volume-level compression	No	No	No	No	No
File- or directory-level compression	Manual	Manual	Manual	Manual	Manual
Per-user quotas	Yes	Yes	Yes	Yes	Yes
Automatic file system encryption	No	No	No	No	No
Multiple-disk-spanning volumes	No	No	Yes	Yes	No
Disk mirroring	No	No	Yes	Yes	No
Disk striping	No	No	Yes	Yes	No
Fault -tolerance	No	No	No	Yes	No
Access permissions	Yes	Yes	Yes	Yes	Yes
Access control lists	No	No	No		No
Transaction-based disk operations	No	No	No	Yes	No
Distributed file system features	Yes, with vfs	No	Yes, with vfs	Yes, with vfs	Yes, with vfs
Mounting/unmounting volumes without rebooting	Yes	Yes	Yes	Yes	Yes

with the exception of the root directory. These *mount points* that the file systems go under replace the contents of that directory with the file system's own top-level contents. In essence, what you have is a tree of file systems, each of which could theoretically be its own subroot.

Every UNIX drive is viewed as a set of *partitions*, or physical locations that can each be a separate file system volume. The sizes of these partitions vary, but in most cases, the smallest is the minimum disk size supported by a particular file system and the maximum is the size of the entire disk itself. Each partition is looked at as a sequence of *blocks* that can be 512, 1024, 2048, 4096, or 8192 bytes long. Each block is the smallest possible unit of storage for the file system, and hence also the smallest possible *real file size*. The difference between the real file size and the amount indicated by the file system is that each file constitutes a sequence of blocks, and when a file is smaller than the block size of the file system, then a whole block is still allocated but only part of it is actually used. The rest of that block is empty for all purposes and available for later use if the file is added to, or simply wasted if not. Thus, with a larger block size, storing lots of files that are smaller than the block size will result in lots of wasted space on the disk. On the other hand, using larger block sizes makes it easier to retrieve large files, since fewer blocks will be used to represent the whole file.

The block is simply an abstract notion. On the disk itself, this is translated to a certain disk cylinder, track, and sector, where the information is stored. The disk itself may store data in sizes other than the logical block size. Most disks in the United States and Europe have a hardware block size of 512 bytes, while those in parts of Asia have 1024. Mapping a logical disk to a multiple of the hardware block size makes for the least amount of wastage.

Every partition contains at least four distinct areas. The first is the *boot area*, and it contains information on how to boot the system from a file stored somewhere on that disk. This, of course, is used only when that drive contains a bootable system. It is also referred to as the *master boot record* on DOS and Windows machines. The second area is called the *superblock*, and it contains information on where all the free blocks are, how many blocks there are in total, and now many files there are. There are now usually two superblocks on UNIX file systems so as to keep redundant copies of this very important information. The third area contains the *index nodes* or *inodes*, which each point to a different file.

Each inode in UNIX is typically 64 bytes long and contains metadata about the file itself (its owner, permissions, and all other attributes of the file) and an array of addresses to the data blocks that contain the file itself. The last area of the partition is the *set of blocks* where the actual data for each file is stored.

Each UNIX file is considered a chain of blocks. They don't have to be in sequence, but the inode for that file has to know where they are located. The original inode of the System V file system has 39 bytes that point to these data blocks. Each data block is addressed by a 3-byte number, and thus this block array points to only 13 different data blocks.

If those were all the pointers to the data blocks, it would certainly limit the size of files down to 13 times the block size, or 6.5- to 104KB for 512- to 8192-byte blocks. Instead, the design uses the last three blocks to point to other arrays of blocks. Block address 10 points to another 256 block addresses. Block 11 points to another 256 blocks, each of which, in turn, points to 256 blocks (giving 65,536 blocks). Finally, block 13 points to 256 blocks of 256 blocks of 256 blocks (about 16 million). This single, double, and triple indirection to more blocks allows the file to grow to huge sizes. At the same time, very small files can still be efficiently stored in a handful of blocks. Each level of indirection also makes it slower to access all the data of a file, but the performance hit is minimal compared to the amount of storage it supports.

The ufs file system supports the larger block sizes of up to 8192 bytes, but to avoid wasted space, it also allows these blocks to be broken into *fragments* as small as 512 bytes. This fragmented information is stored in the inode just as is the block address information. Ufs also bypasses the limitations of s5fs that limit filenames to only 14 characters in length, by allowing a variable name length for each filename, up to 255 characters.

Organization of the UNIX File System Environment

As I said, the UNIX file systems are laid out like an upside-down tree with the root at the very top. Below this are the top-level directories where important system files are stored. In almost all UNIX systems these include the directories called *bin*, *dev*, *etc*, *lib*, *tmp*, and *usr*. The usr directory also has its own subdirectories which play an important role: /usr/bin, /usr/sbin, /usr/lib, /usr/libdata, /usr/libexec, /usr/etc,

/usr/include, /usr/local, /usr/share, and so forth. In many modern versions of UNIX there are also several other top-level directories such as *home, opt, proc, sbin,* and *var.* There used to be strict separations for what is contained in each of these directories, but in most cases today, they overlap to some degree (see Table 1.3).

The /bin, /sbin, /usr/bin, and /usr/sbin Directories

These directories contain most, if not all, of the system and user applications. The sbin directories are reserved for applications that pertain to

Table 1.3   Top-Level Directories in UNIX and Their Functions

DIRECTORY	DESCRIPTION
bin	This is the main directory where binary executable files are kept. Most, if not all, of these files belong to the system.
sbin	The most important system files that start up, shut down, and control important devices are now stored in this separate directory.
dev	This is the device directory, where all block and character devices representing interfaces to software and true hardware devices are stored.
etc	This contains most of the data files for the configuration of the system and system applications. Most are stored in plain-text files that are visible mostly to system administrators.
lib	This contains the standard system library files that all applications use.
tmp	This directory stores temporary files that are created and then removed by system applications and users.
opt	In Solaris and other System V-derived UNIX, this is where packaged applications are normally installed.
var	This is an alternative area for storing less-than-temporary files used by system applications.
proc	This is a special nondisk file system that maps information about each and every process running on the machine in a form accessible as files. Thus, you can read the memory usage, process information, and execution status of each process as if it was a file.
home	Many UNIX systems now store their user accounts under the /home directory rather than the /usr directory as before.
usr	This contains all user-installed applications, libraries, configuration files, programming header files, and share data. In fact, most of the system now actually resides in /usr.

the run of the system. These can be seen by the user, but many of the important programs have built-in checks to ensure that only privileged users are allowed to access them. There are simply multitudes of programs in these directories, and they vary significantly between UNIX versions, so I won't try to name them individually.

The /usr directory at one time was set for user accounts and applications, but now pretty much maps the rest of the system itself, containing application programs and scripts, application libraries, documentation, program header files, source files, and even temporary files, all stored under subdirectories. User-installed applications now normally go under the /usr/local subdirectory.

The /etc Directory

Most of the important system configuration files are stored in /etc, but with the variations across UNIX, the actual important files differ. Several common files and directories are evident in most systems, however, and are shown in Table 1.4.

The rc.d subdirectory needs particular attention. This is where the scripts executed during a transition from one system init state to another are kept. In BSD UNIX systems this is usually not evident, or the scripts are combined into one or two files stored directly in /etc, called *rc*, *rc.local*, or *rc.sysinit*. In System V and Linux systems, each system state has a different subdirectory under rc.d, called *rc0.d*, *rc1.d*, all the way to *rc6.d*, containing the various scripts. These scripts have a specific format. The first character is either *S*, to indicate that a subsystem is about to be started, or *K*, to indicate that the subsystem is to be killed. This is then followed by two numbers, the first indicating the first-level priority to execute the script, and the second, a second-level priority. Finally, this is followed by the name of a subsystem or server application process. Within the script is information on how to start or kill that subsystem or server application process. Theoretically, this gives only 100 different combinations each of start and kill scripts, but there has almost never been a case when more have been needed. All of these scripts are written in the Bourne shell to maintain the highest level of compatibility across all the init states.

The /dev Directory

This is the logical device drivers directory. It contains all drivers that map to hardware devices, and may have more than one logical mapping

Table 1.4 Important Common Files in the /etc Directory

FILENAME	DESCRIPTION
passwd	The user password and information file, with each user entry shown in a colon-separated list.
group	The group file, showing all user account memberships in the various groups defined for the system.
fstab	The list of disk partitions and file systems, and where they should normally be mounted.
mtab	The list of file systems and how they are currently mounted.
exports	The list of files and directories exported to Network File System clients.
services	The list of all system network application services and which ports and protocols they are assigned to.
protocols	The list of Internet protocols supported by the system.
rpc	The list of remote procedure calls supported by the system.
hosts	The static list of network hostnames and addresses for resolving names.
hosts.allow, hosts.deny	The list of hosts to allow or deny access to the system.
hosts.equiv	The list of hosts that allow remote logins into the system.
resolv.conf	The list of domain name servers that the system should use to try to resolve hostnames not in the *hosts* file.
inetd.conf	The configuration file for the inet daemon, for launching server applications.
motd	The Message of the Day file displayed to users when they login to the shell.
shells	The list of valid shells that users are allowed.
rc	The resource configuration file that is executed at system startup.
rc.d	The directory resource configuration files for different system init levels (single user, multiuser, multiuser with network, etc.).
inittab	The list of processes that must be created by the *init* process when the system boots.
profile	The systemwide default *.profile* configuration file for *sh, bash,* and *ksh* assigned to user accounts.
bashrc	The systemwide default *.bashrc* configuration file for bash shell users.
cshrc	The systemwide default *.cshrc* configuration file for C-shell users.

for the same hardware device. Multiple instances of a device keep separate unit numbers (or alphanumeric sequences) for each file following their actual device abbreviation. For example, two common groups refer to physical terminals (ttys) and virtual or network terminals (ptys), and each configured terminal has an associated terminal number, such as tty01 or ptyx1. When users log in they are assigned one of these terminal devices so that they can communicate with applications trying to get input from or send output to them. Each of these devices is a special device file with its associated major and minor device numbers.

UNIX Network File Systems

Several different network file-sharing and access systems are available for UNIX machines. Of these the Network File System (NFS), the Andrew File System (AFS), and the Distributed File System (DFS) are the most common. NFS and DFS are mostly intended for local area networks (LANs), whereas AFS was specifically designed for the wide-area network (WAN) environment. A network file system is a much easier way of working with files than using a file transfer system such as FTP. The files seem to be the same as any other files on the local disk drives, when in reality they are actually stored on a server elsewhere. Thus, they can be manipulated by application programs and users like any other local disk-drive-based file.

The Network File System, the conceptual granddaddy of most file-sharing systems between machines, emerged from Sun Microsystems back in 1985. For the first time, it was possible to access a file system on another machine as if it were running directly on your own. It was slower, having to run over an Ethernet link rather than the internal disk drives of the computer, but it worked, and worked well enough to still be around today. It allowed computers to share disk space at a time when it was still very costly, and mostly for server computers. NFS is now supported in nearly all UNIX systems, as well as Windows, Macintosh, Open-VMS, and a number of other operating systems.

NFS works between a *client* computer that accesses the file system and a *server* computer that shares it out. It communicates between the two using another creation of Sun Microsystems, the *Remote Procedure Call* (RPC) mechanism. This programming mechanism allows applications to execute code on other machines across a network, as if they were part of the same local application.

NFS is a *stateless* protocol, meaning that the client and the server do not maintain a live connection at all times. The NFS client does not really *open* a file for reading and writing. Rather, it only takes pieces at a time when it needs them. When a client needs to read a file or a portion of the file, it sends the requested filename and the number of bytes to read. The server responds by sending only the requested data, rather than the whole file. This allows the client to read the file a portion at a time, making it more interactive. Writing to files on NFS-mounted volumes can be implemented in two ways. In the first method, the clients do not care and simply send updates to the server. The last client to send the update will put its info into the file. The second, safer method requires a file-locking mechanism, so that when one client has the document open, other clients are locked out until the changes are complete.

The NFS server exports a directory or file system to a defined list of clients for read-only or read-write access. This is usually entered into a file called */etc/exports*, */etc/nfsexports*, or */etc/dfs/sharetab* manually or by using a command such as **share** or **share_nfs**. For example:

```
/home/rawn  -rw=client1:client2:server2
/home       -ro all
/u2         -maproot=root server2
```

The actual formats for this file vary according to the UNIX version, so consult your own man pages for correct information.

The NFS client then mounts this exported "file system" onto a directory or drive location of its own, using the command **mount, nfsmount,** or **mount_nfs** as the system administrator account. For example:

```
# mount_nfs -o rw,timeout=600,retrans=7 server1:/home/rawn
  /home/rawn/server1
```

The preceding command mounts the exported file system */home/rawn* from server1 onto the current machine placed under the directory /home/rawn/server1. Once mounted, all the files under the other directory appear in directory listings on the client machine.

NFS is implemented with the help of the Virtual File System (vfs), which maintains a separate mapping on top of a real file system such as ufs. The mapping defines a uniform network view of the file system with defined sizes for read and write operations. It basically separates the specifics of the real underlying operating system with something that all other network clients can agree on.

Networking in UNIX

Networking has been a part of UNIX since the mid-1970s, and in fact the first implementation of the Transmission Control Protocol/Internet Protocol (TCP/IP) family of protocols was on UNIX machines. Thus, the Internet has grown up around UNIX servers, and the platform still proves to be the mainstay of small and large Internet businesses alike.

In fact, TCP/IP was so ingrained into UNIX that until the arrival of the AT&T STREAMS driver model, it was fairly difficult to add other protocols. STREAMS and most device driver systems in UNIX now allow layering of all protocols. This allows other non-IP-based protocols to run alongside the system. For programmers, the creation of the Berkeley *sockets* model has resulted in one of the best and most well-known libraries for networking.

A more detailed discussion of the TCP/IP protocol family is available in Chapter 4.

UNIX TCP/IP Applications

There are a number of common TCP/IP user applications on UNIX, including **telnet**, **ftp**, **rlogin**, **rsh**, **rcp**, **rexec**, **ping**, and **traceroute**. Most sysadmins are familiar with Telnet, used to connect to remote TCP/IP machines, and the File Transfer Protocol (FTP), used to transfer files from one TCP/IP machine to another.

The Remote Login (rlogin) tool is similar to Telnet but uses a different protocol for connecting to systems and supports an additional authentication system. There are a family of these applications including **rlogin**, **rcp**, **rexec**, and **rsh**. These are commonly found only on UNIX machines. With these applications it is possible to designate trusted hosts that are freely allowed to connect to the UNIX machine and execute commands on behalf of the user.

There are two ways to implement this trust relationship. First is a single file called */etc/hosts.equiv* that contains entries of the trusted hosts with a plus sign (+) before them. The second method involves users creating *.rhosts* files in their home directories that indicate which hosts they trust to execute commands as their local accounts. Both systems can bypass password checking, and simply verify that the account name and the hostname match those on the UNIX system.

This entire trust system is fairly dangerous because of *IP hostname spoofing*. Crackers set up a machine with the exact same name as that indicated in your .rhosts or /etc/hosts.equiv file and then attempt to execute remote commands on your server based upon the trust relationship. Even if you are not connected to the Internet, this isn't a very safe environment to maintain. It's convenient, but unsafe.

The commands **rsh** and **rexec** use this same system to execute single line commands on a remote host. The only difference between the two is that **rsh** invokes a full shell session with the user's personal configuration, environment variables, aliases, and so forth, while **rexec** only executes the command line as is. The command **rcp** is a remote copy utility that works very much like the standard UNIX **cp** command except that each filename is normally preceded by *username@hostname*: before the filename or file path, where *username* and *hostname* match the host you are copying to or from.

The **ping** and **traceroute** programs are used to check the status of network hosts and routes. The **ping** command sends a message to a designated remote host using the Internet Control Message Protocol (ICMP) and determines if the host is reachable. Another way to use ping (**ping -v <hostname>**) sends continuous 64-byte packets to the remote host and calculates the latency (speed) of the network path to that host. Some ping packets may be lost on the way, due to the unpredictable nature of IP packet delivery. So, when you can, use the verbose ping mode; it will summarize the statistics, indicating the average ping time and the percentage packet loss to that remote host.

The **traceroute** command sends User Datagram Protocol (UDP) packets to each machine along the network path to the remote host. This will show all the network routers, gateways, and hosts—simply called *hops*—that the packets have to travel through, along with three sets of latency responses from each hop. It's a nice way to determine which networks your packets are traveling through and is especially handy for debugging, if you cannot connect to the remote end for some reason.

Routing in UNIX

Routing protocols began on UNIX servers, and it is no secret that some of the best routing hardware out there uses a modified version of UNIX as its central operating system. It is easy to configure UNIX machines as firewalls, gateways, or proxy servers using freely available packages.

Static routing is included with every UNIX system. To look up entries in the system routing table, you can use the **netstat -r** command, which lists all incoming and outgoing routes from the machine. At the very least, with just one network interface card, the table contains three or four default entries to refer to the local machine and its default outgoing route. For example:

```
Destination     Gateway       Genmask          Flags  irtt  Iface
192.168.20.22   *             255.255.255.255  UH     0     eth0
192.168.20.0    *             255.255.255.224  U      0     eth0
127.0.0.0       *             255.0.0.0        U      0     lo
default         192.168.20.1  0.0.0.0          UG     0     eth0
```

This shows, first, a route for the machine to contact itself through the Ethernet interface (eth0); next, a route to other machines within its LAN; third, an internal or *loopback* address to itself without going over the Ethernet; and fourth, the default outgoing route to all other machines not within the same LAN. The netmask in the second item would read 255.255.255.0 if this was a Class C address block of 255 addresses. Instead, this is a /28 classless interdomain routing (CIDR) block with only 32 addresses, and thus the alternate netmask is 255.255.255.224, indicating that only the addresses from 192.168.20.0 through 192.168.20.31 are valid for this address.

Every UNIX system includes the **route** command to set up static routes outgoing from the machine. The route command usually follows a similar format across versions, but there may be additional options or variations on the syntax required on your particular UNIX version. To add a new route to another network, you need the network ID of the destination network and the host IP address of the gateway between your UNIX machine and the other network. For example:

```
# route add -net <destination network> <gateway host>
# route add -net 192.168.30.0 192.168.20.253
```

To delete a route, it is usually the same command with the command *del* instead of *add*, and the gateway address is optional. I used IP addresses instead of hostnames here, but it works just the same.

Remote Access in UNIX

Remote access in UNIX systems shows a good deal of variance across the versions. This is primarily because terminal access and management systems are so different. Every remote access point is associated with a terminal or pseudoterminal device.

The standard remote connection protocol used on most UNIX systems is the Point-to-Point Protocol (PPP). Most UNIX systems can be set up as PPP clients or servers. As a client, the system uses a remote dial-up application to connect to the PPP server at the other end, and then passes the remote user account and password. The dial-up application varies from platform to platform, but common ones include Kermit, Chat, and Minicom.

The system then sets up the default route to go over the PPP interface (typically called *ppp0*) so that all traffic is sent out through the other end. Once the connection is established, the UNIX client is ready to send traffic for any local user.

A UNIX machine can be set up as a PPP server either by having modem ports directly connected to its serial interface or by attaching to a *terminal server system*. The directly attached modem system requires that each physical modem serial port be configured as a logical *tty* port on the UNIX server. Thus, when users connect to the modem, they are put right at the login screen for the UNIX machine.

The second approach, with the terminal server, allows the UNIX server to connect to modems over a LAN interface. The terminal server either contains all the modems within itself, or are attached to them through cables. The terminal server acts as a proxy for the UNIX machine and performs login authentication by passing information back and forth between the client and login server sides. To do this, there is a standard protocol known as Remote Access Dial-in User Service (RADIUS), that both the terminal server and the UNIX machine use to exchange information. This protocol allows the UNIX machines to be placed anywhere else on the network, even in a separate LAN or WAN from the terminal server, to provide the authentication. The benefit of this is that you can set up remote access servers in different locations or cities and have them all communicate with a single UNIX server at the headquarters. It makes it easier than managing separate user accounts at each location.

For each incoming modem connection to the UNIX server, you have to define the logical device. This means defining the properties of a terminal device and/or its network access properties. Direct modem connections are simply seen as serial port interfaces on the machine. On many UNIX servers, you need to define the port speeds and serial connection attributes in the file called */etc/gettytabs* or */etc/ttydefs*. This can be a very cryptic file with many two-letter codes, or special abbreviations for each of the attributes. It is particular to the UNIX variant you use, so you should look up the man pages for explanations.

UNIX Security Systems

UNIX has a long history of both security breaches and strengths. The prime reason for the breaches is that UNIX is so widespread, and many UNIX system owners simply do not put any effort into maintaining security. Every few weeks or so a new patch to different versions of the operating system comes out when yet another security hole is found.

The good thing is that there are many fewer ways to actually bring down or crash the operating system. Most of the security features for UNIX were developed over its 30-year life span, and this continues to be the spirit. It is still used in some of the most secure systems in the world, which is always a good sign.

UNIX security is built on the concept of users, groups, and file permissions. Every user and group has a simple integer ID value that is compared to check on the user's right to access the data. This information is stored in the *passwd* and *group* files, along with other account information.

The only really privileged account supported in UNIX is the *root* or superuser account (user account ID 0). This account has total access to all areas of the system. Other accounts can be given similar privileges if they are also included in the superuser group ID 0. However, some applications specifically check that the account ID is for the root rather than the group ID. Thus, to perform any system administrator command, the user has to have access to the root account. This can be achieved with other sysadmin tools such as **slide** and **su** that change the user ID into the root ID. The user accounts have to be configured to be allowed into the group that can execute this application, or they have to have the root password at hand. In either case, this still goes through the root account ID.

Each user's login session runs in a different area of memory from others, and the only ways a user can access another user process's memory are either by being root or through the shared memory system. Otherwise, there is no chance that one user's memory will overrun another's, a problem in Windows and Macintosh systems that still have some memory areas that allow one process to interfere with another.

Since most objects are treated as files, the access is compared to a set of file permission bits. Each file has an owner and a group membership. Looking at the following directory entry, you can see these permission bits listed in the very first column.

```
-rwxrw-r-- 1 rawn staff 27136 Jul 12 12:16 webcache2.doc
```

They come in three sets of three letters designating a particular bit: r designating the ability to read, w designating write, and x designating execute permissions. The very first bit in the entry, shown simply as a hyphen, indicates the file type-in this case, a normal file. Other file types include directories (d), symbolic links to other files (l), character device drivers (c), and block device drivers (b).

The first set of 3 bits after the initial bit constitutes the owner permissions. The owner of this file, in this case *rawn*, can read, write, and execute this file at will. The owner can also naturally change the ownership or the permissions of this file. Executing the file does not always do something; it depends on whether the file itself is a script or a program, or simply contains raw data. The second set of bits refers to the permissions for the group (in this case, *staff*), and the final 3 bits indicate the permissions that everyone else (the *World*) on the system has to that file.

One other triplet of bits, not shown here, constitutes the mode bits. Two of these allow other users to impersonate the owner or the group that the file belongs to, called the *set user ID* (*SetUID*) and *set group ID* (*SetGID*) bits. These come in handy for executable programs mostly. Each process has its normal user and group IDs assigned to its account. In addition, it also has an *effective user* or *group ID* that indicates its current disposition. By setting an executable program file to be SetUID, and setting the World read and execute permissions, anyone else can execute the file as if they were the owner themselves. This comes in handy when an application needs to perform a particular action as the root user but is not to be given full access by being given the root account. Any SetUID application owned by root has to be handled with extreme caution by sysadmins, since it might possibly be a Trojan-horse program trying to break into the system.

The same scenario works for the SetGID bit, but it also serves a second purpose in some UNIX versions. If the SetGID bit is on but the file is not set to be executable, then that file is marked as having *mandatory file locking*. In other words, when one user is accessing that file, no others can write to it and change the data. This comes in handy in database systems.

The last bit from this triplet is called the *sticky* bit and works differently for directories and files. For directories, it indicates that the process that has access to a file in that directory has to match to the same user ID. This allows the process to remove or modify that file in the directory. Such directories usually are set World writable so that anyone can create files in them. One such use of the sticky bit can be seen in the /tmp directory.

For executable files, the sticky bit designates that the program, once loaded into swap memory, should be left there even after the user exits. This makes it faster the next time around, since the program is already sitting in memory and does not have to be loaded again.

Unfortunately, basic UNIX systems do not come with an access control list (ACL) system identifying exactly which other users are allowed access. They rely more on the limited functionality of groups instead. More advanced Secure UNIX systems are available from a handful of vendors. These systems are mostly built according to criteria defined by the U.S. Department of Defense. Such systems have different ratings, ranging from A1 (for top-security systems) to D (average systems). Most UNIX systems can be certified to be rated C2, which has higher than normal security features, such as access control lists, completely erasing and rewriting over deleted files, completely erasing memory pages no longer used by processes, and so on. A very select group of UNIX products from IBM, Compaq/Digital, Sun, and SGI have received the B2 standing, an even higher rating, that involves both system and physical security.

UNIX User Interfaces

UNIX systems come with a variety of user interfaces, both graphical and textual. Unlike the Microsoft Windows graphical environment, UNIX user interfaces are user-mode applications and do not run within the kernel environment. They do communicate with drivers for input and output devices such as the graphics adapter, keyboard, and mouse, but these are accessed through standard library calls. Each user interface also runs within the context of a user's login session and is not tied down to a single system account. Even graphical applications run within one user's environment, within the user mode.

All this allows UNIX user interfaces to operate independently of the kernel and other users. Thus, if one user's interface crashes for some reason, it does not lock out the kernel or any other user, allowing the system to run without interruption.

The Shell Environment

The traditional interface to UNIX is the command-line interface known as the *shell*. Once users are logged in they are presented with a command line to execute any UNIX command. All UNIX commands in this respect can be started from the command line, and many execute as text-only applications.

The original command-line interface, called the *Bourne shell* (after its creator), or simply *sh*, still exists and is the lowest common denominator for shells in all UNIX systems. This was later superceded by the *C-shell* (*csh*), which offers more command structures to create better shell scripts. The *KornShell* commercial software was released by AT&T as another improvement over *sh* and is also available in a free software form, known as the *Bourne Again Shell*, or *bash*. Each of these shells provides basic programming language constructs that allow a sysadmin to quickly write a script to perform complex tasks with the help of simpler UNIX command-line tools. The syntax actually differs for each, but the context is the same.

Shell Script Programming

Creating a scripting language as part of the shell is one of the great things that the originators did with UNIX. What's more, the scripting languages are capable of performing any task of the system, some without having to write any real programming-language code whatsoever. The difference between a *script language* and a *programming language* is that scripts are usually interpreted and do not require compilation for a given platform. This means that they are more portable between hardware platforms, being able to run on any of them that have the same script environment. On the downside, they normally perform slower than compiled code.

Most UNIX shells have scripting language constructs, even the ancient and limited Bourne shell. The C-shell, KornShell, and Bash all have language constructs very similar to those in full programming languages like C. This includes constructs such as the **if..then..else**, **while**, **do..until**, **switch**, and—unfortunately—also the **goto** statements. They provide means of control to run blocks of code to perform actions. They also support procedures and functions, and abstract data types such as arrays, lists, stacks, and even pointers. They don't go the full road to object-oriented scripting, but there are other non-shell-based scripting languages, such as Perl, Python, and TCL, that can be called from shell scripts to do so.

As part of the shell, *environment variables* provide a way to store information that can be reused by other applications, or shell scripts for use during the user's login session. These variables are normally nontyped, or simply strings of characters that have to be interpreted elsewhere. For example, the MAIL environment variable contains the filename location of a user's mail folder, and LOGNAME is the user account name that the user logged in as. These variables are also used as part of the language constructs to create scripts.

There are three standard file descriptors associated with every process: *stdin*, *stdout*, and *stderr*. These define the standard input, output, and error-output file streams, and allow users to combine several command-line tools together. Stdin is basically the input stream into a command-line tool, so anything that you have to type into a text application goes in through this file stream. Stdout is just the opposite; all output from the application comes out through this file stream. Stderr is similar to stdout, but is a special file stream to send only the error output of a file to.

You can also redirect stdin, stdout, and stderr into other files so that you have a record of what occurred. These are often presented in slightly different forms depending upon the shell, but in most cases they use the less-than (<) and greater-than (>) signs for stdin and stdout respectively. Stderr is sometimes represented as the combination of characters $> in the C-shell and Bash.

It is also possible to tie the output of one command-line tool to another using what is called a *pipe*. Normally represented by the vertical bar character (|), it takes the stdout of one application and sends it into the stdin of another application while executing the second application, as well. This makes it possible to perform complex tasks by tying together several simpler command-line tools, and simplifies tool building, as well. For example, by taking the output of the command **uptime**, and piping it into the stream editor **sed**, you present the current load on the system. You don't even have to rewrite the code for the system **uptime** command to reprint the information this way.

```
% uptime | sed -e 's/^.*, 1/L/'f
Load averages: 0.24, 0.36, 0.31
```

It seems like an obvious addition now, but piping together several commands was a revolutionary way of building and using applications. It is part of what makes some shell environments so powerful as system scripting tools.

The X Windows System

In the later 1980s, a group at the Massachusetts Institute of Technology (MIT) known as Project Athena began working on a graphical user interface (GUI) that came to be known as the X System. This GUI system creates a network representation of a display and input and output devices, and allows a client application to be run from anywhere on the network. The preference is for LANs in particular, but X Windows can work over WANs as well, albeit slower.

It was the first system that allowed UNIX users to run cheaper workstations with less memory and processing power, while the actual computation of the application was run on a more powerful, expensive UNIX server system over the network. The workstations then cost only about $20,000, but they didn't have enough processing power to run the full application in their limited 2- to 8MB RAM, and some didn't even have hard drives. The servers, on the other hand, reached hefty prices of $50,000 to $500,000, boasted 64MB and more RAM, and could store almost a gigabyte on hard drives. Amusing in retrospect, huh?

Today we don't have such limitations on our desktop hardware anymore, but there is still the notion that managing 1 server is much simpler than managing 100 workstations, and thus X Windows still plays an important role in UNIX computing.

The three sides of the X Window equation are the *X server*, the *Window Manager*, and the *X client* application. The X server handles the input and output device communications and the display of application windows. The Window Manager provides a means to manage the various application windows more easily, allowing the user to move them around the screen, iconize them, or resize them. The X client application does the actual processing of the application itself.

The funny thing is that this is all backward from the normal point of view of client/server networking (see Figure 1.2). The X server is normally run on the desktop machine, whether it is a UNIX workstation, a PC desktop, or an X terminal. It is called *X server* since it accepts incoming connections from other machines and does the hard work of graphical display processing. The X client application, on the other hand, is normally stored on a network server system that has the heavy computing machinery to do the application processing. The Window Manager is even more fickle and can be run from either the desktop machine, the network server, or even a completely different machine.

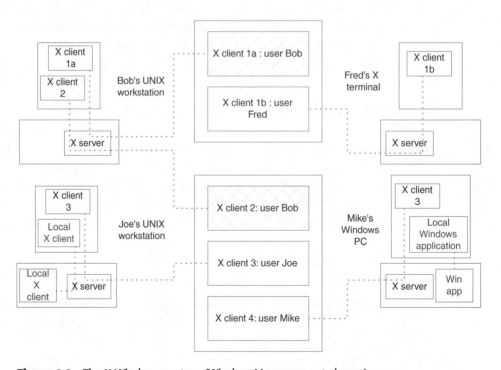

Figure 1.2   The X Windows system (Window Managers not shown).

In Figure 1.2, we can see several desktop machines of different types accessing applications over the network from two servers. Two of the machines are UNIX workstations, one of them an X terminal and the other a Windows PC running X Windows software. An X terminal is a specialized desktop machine that runs X Windows and nothing else. It can only run X client applications from a network server, but does it very fast. Each user logs onto a network server and then launches an X client application to be displayed on the X server desktop. It shows the various combinations in which applications can be run through X Windows. User Bob is running two different X client applications, one from each server. Joe, on the other hand, is running one X client application from his own workstation and another from the second network server. Mike's Windows PC is running an X client application from the second network server, as well as a local Windows application directly on his machine.

X client applications are written specifically for the graphical environment of X, just as Windows applications are written for the Win32 graphical environment. At the very basic level, X Windows provides the application libraries that draw the images, position them, move them around, and define how they interact with each other through cut-and-paste. On top of this, another set of application libraries draws the graphical objects—known as widgets—such as scrollbars, icons, menus, dialog boxes, and so forth. The Window Manager presents a defined style as to how these widgets are presented and how they communicate with one another.

Window Managers bring variety to the X Windows system. There are two dozen or more different Window Managers out there including Common Desktop Environment (CDE), Motif (mwm), OpenWindows (olwm), Tom's Window Manager, Free Window Manager (fwm), GNOME (gnome), K Desktop Environment (kde), and so forth. There is a subcategory called *virtual window managers* that extends the standard system to include multiple virtual desktops that map onto the same physical screen. Usually a small box shows a map of the various virtual desktops and the windows within them, and you switch between desktops by either scrolling past one side of your screen or clicking within the virtual desktop box. This gives you more screen real estate to place windows side by side without cluttering your view. Users of Microsoft Windows and Macintosh can't understand how you can have different Window Managers and still be able to use them properly, but the fact is that many UNIX users do. They configure their Window Managers to their liking and most often stick to them even across machines. The variety simply gives them choice.

The X Windows code has been surprisingly stable, at least for the protocol. The most current version of the protocol is X11 Release 6.3 (X11R6.3). Almost all the versions from X11 Release 3 through 6.3 can still work together. The newer versions build on the features of the earlier ones, which allows this compatibility. Although there are a number of different X servers out there, almost all still adhere to the same X11 protocol, making them compatible with each other despite the differences in OS platforms and hardware capabilities.

Launching the X Windows environment usually involves running the program **xstart** or **startx**, which then goes on to load the environment based upon the system properties. X server products these days are optimized for specific graphics adapters, thus requiring the sysadmin to install and configure the system properly before the users can run the environment. It is also possible to always leave a UNIX workstation in X Windows, by setting up the X Display Manager (XDM). This installs a login window for users to get onto the UNIX workstation and then switches over to their desktop environment. When they log out it goes back to the login window. With XDM, users may never see a shell environment running on the desktop if they use only the graphical applications.

There are many common applications that either come with X by default or are available from the Internet. Since these applications have to be written to use X Windows, they run differently than command-line tools even when they share similar functions. For example, every UNIX server with X installed has the **xterm** application, which pops up a shell environment within an X window. This does actually run a shell on the UNIX server, but it also has other properties, such as a scrollbar, fonts, colors, and so forth. Other common applications include **xclock**, **xlockscreen** or **xscreensaver**, **xcalc** (calculator), **xwd** (a screen dump utility), **xfm** or **xfilemanager**, **xpaint** (a drawing/painting program), **xbiff** (a mail-received notifier), **xload** (a system load meter), and so forth. There are a number of classic applications that have been available for free for quite some time, including **xemacs** (a powerful text editor), **xv** (a graphics file display/editor/convertor), **xmh** (a mail reader), and **xrn** (a Usenet newsreader).

The downside of X Windows is that it has limited security. First, users have to be able to log into the network server and have access to run the

X client application, and have it displayed on their X server. The X client, normally running on a UNIX server, looks for an associated environment variable named **DISPLAY,** which specifies the IP hostname of the machine and screen—desktop X servers can support multiple monitors and screens—that the application should be displayed on. Alternatively, users can launch the client application and specify the display name as an option to the launch command. On their desktop X server, they have to specify that it will accept connections from the network server that hosts the X client application. This is done using the **xhost** command. For example, **xhost +server1.straypackets.com** allows any connections from the indicated server, whereas **xhost -server3.straypackets .com** disallows any connections from the indicated server. Many users also execute the remote shell command **rsh**, to start up their X client applications without having to log in to the server. This relies on the server trusting the user's desktop machine rather than performing an authentication each time. This is also one of the first places that crackers look for to break into computers.

Normally, there is no encryption of the information on the X11 wire protocol. There is some security in the fact that the wire protocol itself contains only updates to the screen and graphical information, which makes it hard to get the full picture of the environment unless you try to capture all the network packets from the very beginning of the connection. It is possible to use network-level encryption such as Virtual Private Networking or the IP Security protocol to establish this wire-protocol-level security, however.

Summary

The UNIX operating system was the breaking ground for many of the innovations seen in other operating systems today. In fact, what we call UNIX today is an amalgamation of many different research and development efforts. It provides a firm multiuser kernel-based platform from which all system services and user applications can run. This concept, where everything is built above the core elements that maintain the operational status of the machine, is what makes it one of the most resilient operating systems around.

There are many variations on the UNIX platform depending on which vendor you go to, including one popular system, Linux, which looks and acts like UNIX but is not derived from any of the original code. The source of development and support for these various UNIX systems comes from their respective vendors. Although concepts and even tools look similar, there are changes that can make trouble for even seasoned system administrators.

As we look at the UNIX system, it continues to undergo change. The biggest recent change has been the switch from 32-bit to 64-bit UNIX systems from vendors Sun, IBM, IRIX, and HP. This is primarily a technical and implementation difference, rather than a functional difference, which is why I don't really mention it. On another front, the ufs file system has served well for most purposes, although it is now being replaced by several other *journaled* file systems. Similarly, NFS continues to reign supreme, although it, too, is being replaced by more advanced distributed file systems. The kernel has transformed from the once-monolithic model to microkernels and multithreaded kernels. The shell and X Windows environments continue to be the core interfaces for UNIX systems, the shell providing a text and command-line-based environment, and X Windows providing a networked graphics system.

The differences between UNIX and Windows are apparent when you start looking at each of these pieces separately. Although Microsoft has been more open to using standardized protocols for network services, its motto of *Embrace and Extend* causes lots of compatibility problems with existing services running on UNIX. Look to the next six chapters to see what I mean.

The Windows 2000 Operating System

The Windows NT operating system began as a push toward an advanced operating system for the business environment that was more robust, reliable, and powerful than the then-existing Windows 3.x systems. With NT, Microsoft implemented some of the leading ideas for operating systems: a microkernel, a security monitor, a modern file system, multiple application environments, a structured network protocol system, and a better device driver model. Windows 2000 brings the next generation of the NT system to everyone, removing all the dependencies on 16-bit code that Windows 3.x, 95, and 98 had and replacing the entire software model with the Win32 system.

The focus of this chapter is on introducing the basic design of the Windows 2000 operating system. We start with a comparison of this new version with its predecessors, then take a look at the OS kernel and executive components, and finally move on toward the important features of the OS environment that are relevant to the sysadmin.

Windows 2000 Operating System Overview

As just mentioned, Windows 2000 (Win 2000) is actually the latest version of the 32-bit Microsoft Windows NT operating system, named 5.0. The line of desktop operating systems from the 16-bit DOS heritage, Windows 3.x, 95, and 98, ends at the last version. Although their user interface appears similar, and there still is backward compatibility with the older operating systems, Win 2000 systems are based on a different OS design and implementation.

The product was originally designed to support robust and efficient high-end business desktops and server systems as well as personal home computer systems. However, Microsoft has changed its mind about shifting their consumer-oriented Windows platform to the NT platform and thus, the Personal edition of Win 2000 has been dropped. There are still several editions, focused on different computer types: the *Professional* edition for business desktop systems, and the *Server* edition for small workgroup servers, the *Advanced Server* edition for departmental servers, and the *Datacenter* edition for large enterprise servers. We will discuss only the Professional, Server, and Advanced Server editions here.

The core architecture remains the same across each of these variants. Some components may be more useful in a laptop (e.g., the Power Manager) than in a desktop unit, but all editions still contain the same components. The basic structure is divided into user-mode and kernel-mode components, as in UNIX systems. However, Win 2000 is based on a micro-kernel design that allows the core system operations of device driver management, memory access, and process scheduling to be kept separate from the application-level APIs. This allows the creation of environmental subsystems that emulate a particular style of user and application environments. This has allowed Microsoft to build in application-level compatibility with Windows, POSIX, and OS/2.

Changes since NT 4.0

Win 2000 is basically the next generation of the NT 4.0 operating system and thus retains many of its features and structures. Microsoft renamed Windows version NT 5.0 as *Windows 2000* for marketing reasons. The company wanted to move away from using the *NT* moniker, which was an acronym for *new technology*, and it wanted to promote the use of the Windows name brand to fall in line with its consumer desktop naming scheme. The Windows 95 heritage will continue past Windows 98 to another coming generation product. Win 2000 code comes primarily from the NT lineage. The initial plan to combine the consumer (Win 95 and 98) and business (NT) operating systems into a single platform in

Win 2000 has been delayed. There will still be a separate consumer OS based on the Win 9x lineage to be released in the near future. Eventually this consumer line will also be merged into the NT based Windows 2000 line.

Still, there has been considerable modification to many of the components—in particular, the driver model, the directory and user system, and the security system. On the general system side, Win 2000 adds the following features:

- The *NTFS 5.0 file system adds a number of new features* such as encrypted files and directories, per-user quotas, support for distributed file systems, layering other file systems on top of NTFS, and support for huge files tens or hundreds of gigabytes long.

- *Active Directory replaces the older domain/workgroup model* and allows you to integrate your entire enterprise under a single directory service. It has proprietary interfaces (Active Directory Service Interface version 2) as well as standard interfaces (Lightweight Directory Access Protocol version 3) allowing it to interact with other directory service systems.

- The *Windows NT Terminal Server Edition system for multiuser server-based application processing has now been integrated into the Server kernel.*

- *The Advanced Server and Datacenter versions of Win 2000 now support much larger physical memory models* than 4GB of RAM. Intel- and Alpha-based Server systems can now use *64GB* of RAM. This allows memory-intensive applications like database management systems (DBMSs) to load large databases directly into memory to increase performance.

- *Windows Clustering service is now built into the Advanced Server and Datacenter versions* allowing multiple servers to be clustered together to provide faster, more resilient computing services.

- *The Server versions now also include support for system services* such as Web transactions, message queuing, distributed file systems, and distributed remote access services.

- *Microsoft's latest version of the Component Object Model, COM+, is now part of the system.* It is now integrated with the Microsoft Transaction Services and supports in-memory databases, queuing objects, and dynamic load balancing across multiple machines.

For system administration and management, we now have the following features:

- The *Microsoft Management Console* (MMC) integrates almost every system administration tool into a single application. The old tools in NT 4.0 are still available separately, but the new MMC system integrates them into a central management system not only for one machine but an entire network.

- *Windows Management Instrumentation* (WMI), based on the Web-Based Enterprise Management (WBEM) standard, provides a uniform administrative interface to Windows and non-Windows devices on a network that is integrated with other management services. It provides a system conceptually similar to the Simple Network Management Protocol (SNMP) but with greater control for Windows systems.

- *Zero-Administration Windows* (ZAW) is now a standard component of the system. The *Intellimirror* system allows servers to maintain copies of entire disk trees of clients on the network. This allows for a more secure server-based system and moves away from reliance on the local desktop.

- The *Windows Scripting Host*, a new API for creating scripts in several programming languages, including Visual Basic, Jscript, and Perl, can help administrators develop command-line tools for management.

- *Service Pack Slipstreaming* now does not require service packs to be reinstalled after new system components are installed. Previously, when some system components such as remote access services were installed, the service pack had to be reinstalled, as well.

- New *group policies* replace the older user-policies method of defining specific settings for the user's interface and access to the system.

- *Windows Installer Service* is now improved to reduce or eliminate the conflicts between the dynamically linked libraries of different applications, allow partial installations to be repaired, and provide a new installation package format.

- There now is *remote OS installation,* as well as an enhanced unattended installation process.

- *The system now does not need to be rebooted* after configuring devices, installing or modifying network protocols, adding disk space to an NTFS 5 volume, changing the mouse attributes, changing the video display attributes, and installing applications such as Exchange 5.0, SQL Server 7.0, NetWare File, and Print Services.

The improvements to the network applications, communications, services, and security architecture include the following:

- The *Distributed File System* (DFS) service, which ties volumes together in a tree hierarchy rather than in individual drives, is now available.

- The new *Internet Printer Protocol* allows users to print over the network by simply specifying a URL for a printer name.

- *Kerberos-based Private-Key security authentication* replaces the older Microsoft login authentication systems. Users each have an associated key used to access network services.

- *Network Load Balancing* services allow multiple servers to balance the performance of IP-based application services such as for Proxy, Web, and FTP servers.

- *Dynamic Domain Name Service* (DDNS) is now a service on all Server versions. Microsoft is trying to move away from a dependence on the older Windows Internet Naming System (WINS), a NetBIOS-based service. DDNS is an important part of the Active Directory system for hostname lookup.

- The Internet *Resource Reservation Setup Protocol* (RSVP) is now a standard component providing guaranteed quality of service (QoS) for network communications.

- *TCP/IP packet security* is now standard with the implementation of the Secure IP (IPSec) protocol for encrypting transport-layer (TCP and User Datagram Protocol [UDP]) packets.

- Multiprotocol routing using the *Routing and Remote Access Services* (RRAS) system (once codenamed Steelhead).

- The system can act as *a network address translator* to convert internal IP addresses to external ones, keeping a separate private network.

- *Asynchronous transfer mode (ATM)* network interface cards and protocols are now supported with native device drivers.

- *Internet Explorer 5.0* has been integrated into the desktop Explorer shell.

Microsoft has increased the type and diversity of device driver and hardware support, in particular to support popular emerging device types and plug-and-play driver systems. The enhancements to device support include the following:

- The older Compact Disc File System (CDFS) has been replaced with the ISO-standard Universal Disk Format (UDF) for CDs and digital video discs (DVDs).

- The old NT driver system has been unified with the *Windows Driver Model* (WDM) in Windows 95 and 98 to create a single set of drivers for all platforms. Older NT drivers will still work, albeit with changes to their configuration files.

- WDM can now support *multiple monitors and graphics cards* as one seamless desktop, finally catching up with other vendors.

- WDM also brings *Plug-and-Play* services found in Windows 95 and 98 for controller cards and devices to Windows 2000.

- Drivers can now *be signed and verified*. This allows administrators to tell the difference between authorized versions of drivers from a vendor when they have passed Microsoft's Windows Hardware Quality Labs tests. It improves the reliability and security of the driver.

- The graphics and device support system has been *updated to support the latest DirectX*, the software API for direct access to the hardware features of 2D/3D cards, game controllers, sound boards, and so forth.

- The *Intel Intelligent I/O system* has now been incorporated into the OS. This reduces the I/O processing load on the workstation and server system by allowing a secondary I/O processor to handle some of the load from cards and peripherals.

- There is a new power management system, the *Advanced Configuration and Power Interface*, which integrates with WDM to distribute power to devices more efficiently, especially for laptop systems.

- *New device types* supported include Fibre-Channel devices and drives, Smartcard readers, multidisc compact-disc read-only memory (CD-ROM), tape, and optical disc changers.

Differences between Professional and Server Editions

There are four business versions of Win 2000. The first is a desktop or client product to replace NT 4.0 Workstation, known as *Windows 2000*

Professional. The rest are three different versions for server environments: *Windows 2000 Server, Windows 2000 Advanced Server*, and *Windows 2000 Datacenter*. The primary differentiating points between the products are shown in Table 2.1. Although it is designed for multiple users, Windows 2000 Professional is intended to be used only as a desktop client system and has limitations that prevent it from being used as a server. It is also the only version that is designed to support laptops, provide docking stations, infrared connectors, and features for disconnected operation and saving battery life.

System Architecture

The Windows NT and 2000 operating system architecture draws its heritage from Digital (now Compaq) OpenVMS and Carnegie-Mellon University Mach OS. The original architect, Dave Cutler, came from the OpenVMS OS design team and together with other members of the team

Table 2.1   Features of the Windows 2000 Operating System Family

FEATURE	WIN 2000 PROFESSIONAL	WIN 2000 SERVER	ADVANCED WIN 2000 SERVER	WIN 2000 DATACENTER
Maximum number of CPUs	2	4	8	32
Maximum memory	4GB	4GB	64GB	64GB
Number of net connections	10 simultaneous	Unlimited	Unlimited	Unlimited
Active Directory (AD) services	AD Client only	AD Server	AD Server	AD Server
Security	Kerberos Client	Kerberos Authentication Server, Certificate Server	Kerberos Authentication Server, Certificate Server	Kerberos Authentication Server, Certificate Server
Other features	Docking station support, infrared connector support, Intellimirror client, Terminal Server client	Terminal Server, Intellimirror	Cluster Server, Windows Load Balancing System, Terminal Server, Intellimirror	Cluster Server, Windows Load Balancing System, Terminal Server, Intellimirror

created a new construct that imported ideas from those other OSs. The process, memory management, native file system, remote procedure calls, and security models are similar to those of OpenVMS; the micro-kernel and executive are based on ideas in Mach; and the application interface, of course, comes from Windows. Other new ideas, such as object-oriented features, were introduced over time.

The Win 2000 architecture has a kernel and a user space just like in UNIX systems (see Figure 2.1), but that is where most of the similarity ends. Win 2000 separates the components of the OS into specific functions for handling various kernel services. The user environmental systems and libraries are kept as strictly separate components from systems services. This has allowed the system to emulate UNIX (in the IEEE POSIX inter-face) and OS/2 environments to some degree.

Windows 2000 Kernel-Mode Components

The kernel space consists of the following components:

- The *Hardware Abstraction Layer* (HAL) creates a software interface to the basic input/output system (BIOS) and to hardware system architecture that is accessed by the microkernel, the drivers, and the Executive.

- The *Microkernel* schedules threads and processes and synchronizes communications between them, as they are run on single and multi-processor systems.

- The *Windows Driver Model* (WDM) *device drivers* control all hard-ware devices and allow the software system to communicate and exchange data with these devices.

- The *Executive* consists of system services for handling I/O, the file systems, process and thread creation and management, power man-agement, interprocess communication, security, system cache man-agement, and virtual memory management.

- The *Win32 graphics system* handles all graphical user interfacing, window controls, screen drawing, and user I/O. It is part of the kernel space primarily to improve performance by eliminating the overhead of intermediary layers.

- Any number of *system threads* may also exist here as created by sys-tem processes or privileged user applications.

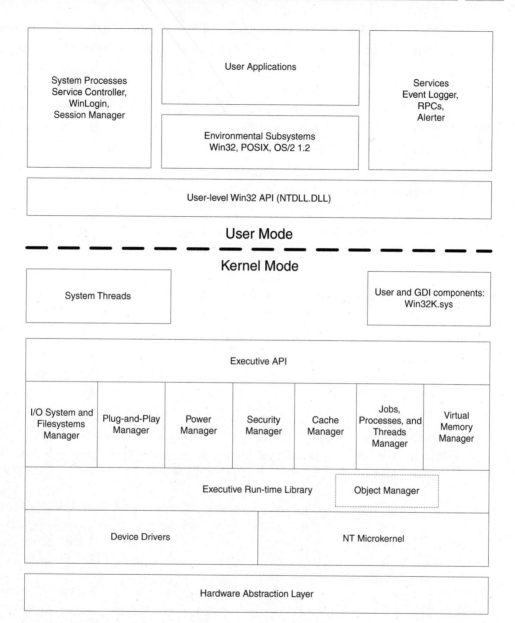

Figure 2.1   The Windows 2000 operating system architecture.

There are intermediary layers between the Microkernel (the Executive Run-Time Library) and on top of the Executive (Executive API) to create a more object-layered communication system between the different components. In addition, the Executive consists of several separate functions, as in the following:

- The *Virtual Memory Manager* implements the virtual memory system and the address spaces of all threads and processes of execution.

- The *Process and Thread Manager* creates and destroys processes and threads as required by applications. Actual threads are created, scheduled, and executed by the Microkernel but the Executive maintains object data structures for each item such that they may be referenced by other objects on the system.

- The *Cache Manager* optimizes file system I/O by using memory-mapped files (i.e., loading the contents of the file straight into memory) for quicker access.

- The *Security Reference Monitor* handles all security checks and auditing of data structures and objects.

- The *Power Manager*, a new addition in Win 2000, actively monitors power usage by the hardware system and routes power accordingly. It can power-up and shut down devices dynamically to conserve power.

- The *Plug-and-Play* (PnP) *Manager*, another addition, allows automatic recognition of hardware cards and devices on initial boot or in hot-swapping situations (swapping devices while the system is running and power is on).

- The *I/O System* provides device-independent I/O services and access to all I/O devices at the system layer. This component also translates file system calls into disk device accesses.

The Executive maintains kernel-mode access to these services. There are often user-mode counterparts within the environmental subsystems (which we will discuss shortly) that communicate with these Executive components. All of these Executive components, in turn, use several other common support functions and components:

- The *Object Manager* is responsible for creating, accessing, and destroying any executive-level objects.

- The *Local Procedure Call* (LPC) System handles message passing between separate processes on the same computer.

- The *Executive Support Routines* handle system memory allocation and special synchronization objects.

- The *Executive Run-Time Library* provides simple functions for arithmetic operations, string processing, and data type conversion.

Windows 2000 User-Mode Components

The user space consists of the following components:

- Various *system support processes*, including the Session Manager process, the WinLogon process, and the Services Controller process, help keep the user and system environments running and available at all times.

- *System services* such as the Event Logger, the Remote Procedure Call, the Distributed File System (DFS) monitor, and so forth are launched by the Services Controller process and run in the background to maintain the services environment for applications.

- The *environment subsystems*, the Win32 and the POSIX subsystems, provide a native software API environment for applications. These subsystems allow different API systems to exist and run on the same kernel and provide different shared libraries for applications to link to. Each subsystem consists of an active subsystem process (e.g., PSXSS.EXE) and an API library (e.g., PSXDLL.DLL).

- *User applications* run on top of an environment subsystem by loading API libraries and execute as processes and threads in this space.

- *NTDLL.DLL* is used by user-mode processes and the environmental subsystems to access the kernel. It provides API services that call similar functions at the kernel executive-level API. All user and system applications access the system to this common API.

Kernel and Executive

The Microkernel (simply called the Kernel, for short) provides the scheduling of processes and threads, and the Executive provides kernel-mode system services. When compared to the design of NT 4.0, the microkernel has been tweaked to work better in systems with four or more processors. There have also been some changes to the I/O, file system, and memory management components of the executive, as well as the introduction of two new components for power management and plug-and-play device management.

On the file system, the Kernel and Executive are combined into a single file image. There are two versions of the OS Kernel and Executive image, one optimized for single-processor systems, known as NTOSKRNL.EXE, and the other for symmetrically multiprocessing machines, known as NTKRNLMP.EXE. The SMP version will run on uniprocessor machines as well but has additional overhead that is not needed in such systems. There are yet other executables for the Advanced Server and Datacenter versions of Windows 2000 Server. The differences in these models support larger physical memory and a larger memory cache for the file systems (up to 960MB of disk-based files can be cached in memory).

When you first begin the installation of Win 2000, the system automatically pops in the SMP version first even if you don't have such a machine. The installation program will reconfigure the system with the uniprocessor executable toward the end of the installation session. However, after installation, the executable file (whether it's a uniprocessor or SMP version) is renamed NTOSKRNL.EXE in the \Winnt\System32 directory.

Environmental Subsystems

There are three environmental subsystems in the Win 2000 platforms. In the original Mach microkernel operating system, the idea was to build operating system "personalities" on top of the microkernel such that it would be able to run various types of UNIX applications as well as other OS personalities such as MacOS or Windows. In Win 2000, these personalities have been implemented as environmental subsystems. There is one for POSIX.1 (the standardized IEEE UNIX interface developed in 1990), one for OS/2 version 1.2, and, of course, one for Win32 (32-bit Windows).

Each subsystem allows programmers to write applications that will compile on that system and on other systems that conform to it. The reality is that the POSIX.1 subsystem is far outdated (there's a third-party replacement for this that is up to date and works significantly better), and OS/2 version 1.2 had very few applications. Essentially, both these subsystems are not very useful anymore for software development. Thus, the remaining application environment that is of practical use is Win32.

Since NT 4.0, the Win32 subsystem has taken over the majority of the user and environment APIs. In fact, any graphics calls to the other environmental subsystems will go through the Win32 subsystem. It is made up of several major components:

- The *client/server runtime subsystem* (CSRSS.EXE) that supports the virtual DOS machines and console windows, and is responsible for creating jobs, processes, and threads.

- The *kernel-mode graphics system* (WIN32K.SYS) that implements the window manager; I/O support for keyboard, mouse, and similar devices; and the Graphical Device Interface library for any graphical operations in software.

- The *subsystem shared libraries* (USER32.DLL, ADVAPI32.DLL, GDI32.DLL, and KERNEL32.DLL) that execute kernel-mode system calls to the kernel and WIN32K.SYS.

- The hardware-dependent graphics, printer, and video device drivers.

Jobs, Processes, Threads, and Sessions

Win 2000 has a preemptively multitasked environment that supports threads, processes, and jobs as units of execution. A *thread* is the smallest unit of execution that is aware of the system state at the moment it is created and has a memory heap for its use. A *process* consists of one or more threads, can use portions of virtual memory for its system resources, and has a security identity. A *job* is a secure named collection of processes created by a user when starting an application. Jobs allow the user or system administrator to define limits on the memory usage, CPU time, process priority, and maximum number of processes allowed.

In UNIX systems, threads and processes have existed for awhile. However, the UNIX process is somewhat different from that in Windows. When a UNIX process is created, it inherits the environment of the parent process that created it. The parent process can create a number of child processes and treat them as a group. When you kill a UNIX parent process, you can automatically kill the child processes, as well. Every process is a child of another, starting with process 1, the *init* process. Win 2000 processes do not have a parenting scheme and are independent of each other. The job object defines a relationship between groups of processes and is a new concept introduced in Win 2000. Jobs, however, go beyond the UNIX process hierarchy system and can exactly specify limitations on a process or group of processes as to how much of the system and system resources they can use.

The multiuser Terminal Server Edition now incorporated into Win 2000 introduces the session object. Each separate Windows Terminal login is treated as a session; it has its own jobs and processes, its own user environment, and its own copy of several system processes. Each session has its own copy of the graphics system Win32K.sys within the kernel. Session objects exist only when multiuser terminal services are enabled.

All threads, processes, jobs, and sessions are considered objects, in particular execution objects, and like all objects, they have a reference or *handle* to them. Processes have process identifiers (PIDs) as well as a quick method of referencing them. The kernel and executive interact with these objects by their handles. This basic structure lends to the object-orientation of the Win 2000 operating system.

System Processes

There are a number of processes that are created by the system to keep the system and user environment operational. System processes are launched by the executive while it is booting to create the user and application environments. These processes include the Idle process, the System process, the Session Manager process, the Win32 subsystem process, the WinLogon process, the Local Security Authentication process, and the Service Controller process.

The Idle process (PID 0) is always on the system. It's not an application, only a reflection of the kernel state. There is usually one Idle process per CPU. The System process is responsible for launching kernel-mode system threads, such as to handle the swap file and device driver interaction. In NT 4.0 this had a PID of 2 or 4 (depending upon the number of CPUs), but in Win 2000, this always starts at 8. In the Datacenter model, this may start at PID 8 or 16.

The Session Manager is the first user-mode process created at start time and is responsible for initializing the system and creating other user-mode processes. It creates local procedure call ports for client requests, creates the system variables and additional paging files, defines MS-DOS devices (COM1, LPT1, etc.), opens system dynamic link libraries (DLLs), loads the kernel-mode graphics portion of Win32 (Win32k.sys), starts the subsystem processes, creates the WinLogon process, and creates local procedure call ports for debugging. After this initialization step, it sits idly on the machine unless the Win32 subsystem crashes; it will then generate the Blue Screen of Death (the fatal system-crash screen).

The Win32 subsystem process is crucial to the system environment. It is called *CSRSS.EXE* for *client/server runtime subsystem*. As described earlier in the *Environmental Subsystems* section, Win32 handles I/O for all the subsystems.

The WinLogon process handles interactive user sessions. It is activated when the user executes the *secure attention sequence* (the Control-Alt-Delete buttons, by default) to bring up the login/logout window. It checks the user account and password with the security process and runs a temporary process called *userinit.exe* that creates the user environment and shell. When a user is already logged in and presses the secure attention sequence, WinLogon pops a dialog window allowing the user to lock the desktop, change his or her password, log out, or bring up the task manager. If they have security privileges, they may also be allowed to shut down the system.

With the multiuser kernel addition, there may be multiple copies of the Win32 and WinLogon processes, created by the Session Manager, sitting idly on the machine for each potential network Windows Terminal connection. The Session Manager handles individual session crashes independently unless a fatal system crash occurs that locks up the entire machine.

The Local Security Authentication process handles the task of authenticating the user account information sent by WinLogon. In Win 2000, it also handles the Kerberos network authentication system for user logins.

The Services Controller process is in charge of launching user-mode system services and server applications. It works much like the UNIX init daemon for starting system services and server applications.

One last process is really a system service known as the *Services Host* (svchost.exe). This process does some of the work the UNIX inetd process does, in that it listens for requests from the system or the network for a network service and launches the server application appropriately. Table 2.2 shows an example list of processes running on a Win 2000 Server, including system, service, and user processes.

System Services

System services are the equivalent of the UNIX daemons for system-level services. All intercomputer access to systemwide services on the local machine go through the system services. In addition, many local applications also access these system services to exchange data and

Table 2.2   Examples of System Processes and Services

PID	EXECUTABLE	TYPE	DESCRIPTION
0	System process	System	System idle process
8	System	System	Kernel-mode system threads
132	smss.exe	System	Session Manager
164	csrss.exe	System	First Win32 subsystem
188	winlogon.exe	System	First WinLogon process
216	services.exe	System	System services controller
228	lsass.exe	System	Local Security Authentication
380	rpcss.exe	Service	Remote procedure calls
416	spoolsv.exe	Service	Spooler service
448	msdtc.exe	Service	Distributed Transaction Coordinator
572	svchost.exe	Service	Service Host-COM+ Events
580	tcpsvcs.exe	Service	MS DHCP Server, MS TCP/IP print service (LPD), other TCP/IP services (daytime, chargen)
612	llssrv.exe	Service	License logging services
636	sfmprint.exe	Service	Print services for Macintosh
660	ntmssvc.exe	Service	Removable Storage Management services
699	lmrepl.exe	Service	Active Directory replication services
771	ntfrs.exe	Service	File replication services
796	svchost.exe	Service	Service Host-Remote access connection manager
828	rsvp.exe	Service	Admission control service (RSVP) for TCP/IP
848	cisvc.exe	Service	Indexing service
852	scesrv.exe	Service	Security Configuration server
883	ismserv.exe	Service	Intersite Messaging services
936	snmp.exe	Service	Simple Network Management Protocol agent
938	snmptrap.exe	Service	SNMP Trap monitor
970	smlogsvc.exe	Service	System Monitor Log service
981	mstask.exe	Service	MS Task scheduler

access shared resources. These service applications automatically manage incoming requests or the behavior of other applications running on the system.

System services are launched by the services controller when the system first boots. Some services are automatically started, while others have to

Table 2.2   (*Continued*)

PID	EXECUTABLE	TYPE	DESCRIPTION
1016	termsrv.exe	Service	Terminal Server
1064	wins.exe	Service	Windows Internet Naming System server
1067	tftpd.exe	Service	Trivial FTP server
1077	ups.exe	Service	Uninterruptible Power Supply manager
1092	dfssvc.exe	Service	Distributed File Services
1108	scardsvr.exe	Service	SmartCard resource manager
1120	dns.exe	Service	Domain Name Service
1122	faxsvc.exe	Service	FAX services
1148	inetinfo.exe	Service	Internet Information Server, Web, Mail, FTP Server
1177	locator.exe	Service	RPC network locator service
1189	netdde.exe	Service	Network Dynamic Data Exchange protocol services
1200	sfmsvc.exe	Service	File services for Macintosh
1233	msiexec.exe	Service	MS Network Installation server
1348	ttermpro.exe	User	Tera Term application
1492	explorer.exe	User	Program Manager
1524	systray.exe	User	Desktop system tray
1576	cmd.exe	User	Command shell
1592	svchost.exe	Service	Service Host-Telephony API
1595	cimom.exe	Service	Windows Management services
1612	csrss.exe	System	Second Win32 subsystem
1672	winlogon.exe	System	Second Winlogon
1684	csrss.exe	System	Third Win32 subsystem
1712	winlogon.exe	System	Third Winlogon
1744	iexplore.exe	User	Microsoft Internet Explorer
2164	ntvdm.exe	User	Virtual DOS Machine
2201	wowexec.exe	User	Windows on Windows service

be manually launched by running an application or through the management tool. Still other services may be disabled to prevent access to a type of service. This allows service applications to be taken offline for maintenance or security purposes. Applications may also add more services to the system when they are installed.

In earlier NT versions, you could get to the services through the Services control panel. This has since been replaced with the Services Manager. The Microsoft Management Console provides a description of all services and what they are used for. You can also use the *net* command-line tool in a command window to start, pause, continue, or stop any of these services.

Windows Driver Model

The *Windows Driver Model* (WDM) replaces the NT driver model in previous versions. WDM was originally developed on Windows 95 to create plug-and-play and power management services, two hardware service features NT sorely lacked. WDM drivers will work under Win 95, 98, and 2000 with one corollary: Although the driver itself is the same, it has to be recompiled for the specific operating system type. This means that you cannot simply take a driver installed on a Win 98 machine and install it on a Win 2000 system; you have to have the proper Win 2000 version. The benefit is mostly to device driver developers rather than system administrators. PnP WDM drivers are particularly useful for hardware devices that can be temporarily disconnected or are removable from the system, such as devices for the universal serial bus (USB), PC (PCMCIA) Cards, and even peripheral computer interconnection (PCI) cards.

Plug-and-play drivers automatically configure themselves to the platform during installation. Upon installation, the driver will check the current hardware resource allocation and send a request for allocation; create a control interface to the PnP manager; install the appropriate driver files; interact with the power manager to register any power requirements; and register for device notification events.

The components of WDM and the PnP system, as shown in Figure 2.2, are described in the following, starting at the bottom:

- The lowest level has WDM bus drivers (for USB, PCI, PC Card, ACPI, SCSI, and P1394) and WDM device drivers, which service a specific type of bus controller, adapter, bridge, or any device that has multiple child devices. For example, a multiport Ethernet card with four network interfaces would need a bus driver if each of the interfaces is to work independently.

- In parallel with the bus drivers are other drivers that are directly on the system, such as the BIOS, system clock, and so forth, and are independent of the buses. These devices do not need PnP support since they are always connected.

■ Also in parallel are older NT 4.0 device drivers. These devices will run in Win 2000 but are not dynamic as with PnP devices and are loaded at boot time. The older drivers can also hook onto the bus drivers if needed.

■ In the PnP system, there are higher-level *function* and *filter* drivers that perform additional services before they interact with the raw device. A function driver is a control interface for devices that perform multiple device functions. For example, a voice modem can not only perform modem dial-up services but also act as a telephone. A filter driver sorts or prioritizes I/O requests for the driver as programmed by the hardware manufacturer. There can be one or more filter drivers to perform multiple levels of sorting.

Drivers are a common source of system troubles. Although the best idea is to install only devices and drivers that are certified or on the official hardware compatibility list from Microsoft, the list lags product developments in the industry by months. In the past, drivers for NT usually lagged behind those that were available for Win 95/98. With WDM, this should be less problematic, and there should be fewer inconsistencies between the driver models.

In Win 2000, all drivers are installed either during installation or at boot time. The bus drivers are installed during the system installation process, as well as support for drives (floppy, IDE, CD-ROM, etc.), keyboards, mice, and audio and video drivers.

If a new device is added to a bus that allows disconnected operation, it will communicate with the system to request that a PnP driver be installed. The system will first check the driver database, then any OS cab (installation) files on disk. If the necessary driver is not available, the system will display a list of similar drivers available from the vendor and query you to select one from the list or search elsewhere for a driver. You can also select the Add New Hardware wizard from the control panels to search for a device that has just been plugged in.

Devices that are not recognized or are not behaving properly on the system are listed as *unknown* devices. This is normally the result of misconfigured, conflicting, or failing devices. The Device Manager tab of the System control panel lists all the devices by type or name. If any items

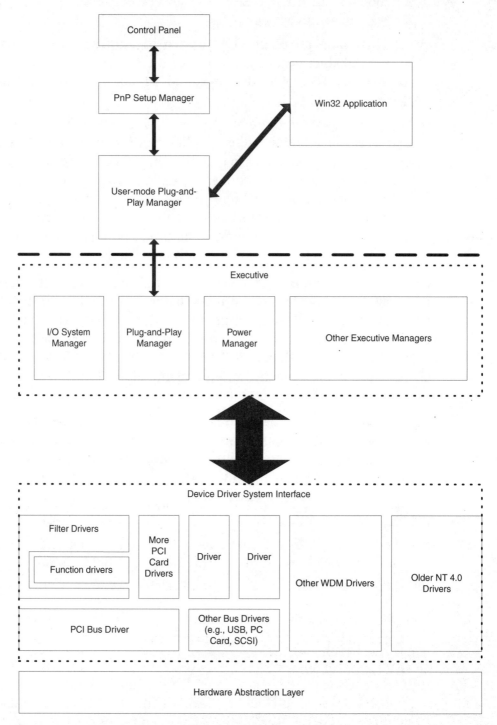

Figure 2.2 Windows Driver Model and Plug-and-Play architecture.

appear under the *unknown* category (the bold yellow question-mark icon), there is a problem with one of the hardware devices. Clicking on the Properties of the item will show if there is an interrupt request (IRQ), I/O address, direct memory access (DMA) port, or other type of conflict with the other devices on the system. An exclamation-point icon on top of the device indicates that a device is improperly installed or its driver is not responding. It is normally safer to remove the device, then reboot the machine, and let it search for the device and its drivers again.

If a device has other configuration settings, there will normally be a control panel for it. For example, all modems, mice, and audio and display devices have separate control panels to configure speed, volume, color, resolution, and other related settings.

Registry

The System Registry is where all information on system configuration and installed software is stored. It is a central repository of information on the operating system version and configuration, installed user applications, installed and active services, active and inactive hardware, device options and configuration, network configuration, and user-profile information.

The closest approximation to it on UNIX systems would be the /proc file system. Unlike /proc, which contains variables and configuration information about the system, the registry does not give you all the live information about the state of the machine, thus limiting some of the possibilities of using it for performance analysis. Some of this information is stored internally in system variables that cannot easily be accessed by the administrator and require you to rely on management tools. The registry does contain some entries on which system performance variables are to be monitored, but you need the Performance Monitor application to accurately measure the value of these variables.

The registry is supposed to be accessed and used by applications and not users or administrators. In most cases you should change the system configuration only through the control panels and the management tools.

You can directly modify the registry itself, but this should be done with extreme precaution. Changes to the registry by hand can have consequences to applications in ways you may not foresee. There is the potential of seriously destabilizing the system.

For system administration purposes, most configurable features are accessible through the management console explored in the next section. Only the really advanced should try to edit the registry directly. Throughout this book we point out items within the registry that pertain to the topic being discussed. You can run the registry editor and look through its hierarchy, but do not modify any of the items or create new ones unless explicitly told. With this in mind, you can launch the registry editor from \Winnt\regedt32.exe (see Figure 2.3). There is another editor, called \Winnt\regedit.exe, which is a backward-compatible 16-bit application but does not provide the all the functions of Regedt32.

The registry is a database of *keys* and *value entries*. In Regedit32, the keys appear as folders, some with other subfolders (or subkeys) inside them. A single key can have different value data, as shown in Table 2.3. Each of these value entries has a name and the associated type of value. There is always at least one entry called *(Default)*, with an actual value of REG_NONE, that may or may not be used by that key.

Registry information is organized in top-level keys, or *hives*, as they are called. There are six top-level keys or Registry Root Hives, as described in the following:

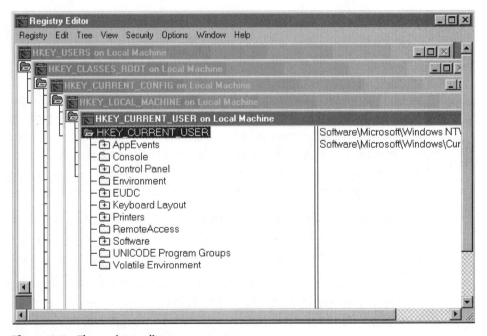

Figure 2.3 The registry editor.

Table 2.3 Registry Entry Value Data Types

VALUE DATA TYPE	DESCRIPTION
REG_BINARY	Raw binary data in hexadecimal format.
REG_DWORD	A 32-bit value in binary, hexadecimal, or decimal format.
REG_DWORD_BIG_ENDIAN	A 32-bit value in binary, hexadecimal, or decimal format stored in an alternative data format (big-endian values).
REG_EXPAND_SZ	An expandable string data value used often in system environment variables.
REG_MULTI_SZ	An array of strings.
REG_SZ	A string that is normally a description of the key.
REG_LINK	A Unicode symbolic link to other registry keys.
REG_NONE	A null value.

- *HKEY_CLASSES_ROOT* contains all associations of file extensions to applications and registered OLE/ActiveX application information.

- *HKEY_CURRENT_USER* contains the profile of the user currently directly logged on to the console and settings for the desktop.

- *HKEY_USERS* contains profile information of all users logged into the machine.

- *HKEY_LOCAL_MACHINE* is a definition of the hardware, operating system version, and all installed system services.

- *HKEY_CURRENT_CONFIG* is the set of data on the startup configuration of the system and the current hardware profile in use.

- *HKEY_DYN_DATA* allows for temporary system variables for communicating between the registry and Win32 applications, ActiveX/OLE components, and device drivers.

These hive keys are hardcoded into the operating system. You cannot create new top-level keys or delete or rename these keys. Some of these hives are actually stored within the hierarchy of the others and are really just shortcuts at the top level into the structure of the other hives (see Table 2.4).

The registry itself is stored in multiple files for faster access to some of the more important information. These files are all stored under \Winnt\System32\Config with emergency backup copies in \Winnt\Repair. They are not really separated by hives, but rather by key areas that are

Table 2.4 Hives That Are Actually Shortcuts to Other Keys

ROOT KEY/HIVE	ACTUAL PATH
HKEY_CLASSES_ROOT	/HKEY_LOCAL_MACHINE\SOFTWARE\Classes
HKEY_CURRENT_CONFIG	HKEY_LOCAL_MACHINE\SYSTEM\CurrentControlSet\Hardware Profiles\Current
HKEY_CURRENT_USER	HKEY_USERS\ (username)

most frequently accessed, such as the user login information, the current user and environment, the system configuration, and so forth, as shown in Table 2.5. Except for NTUser.DAT, none of these files have any file extensions at all; the underscore symbol in the table is just used to indicate that.

If any of the files for the registry are corrupted, you may have a serious problem on your hands. Although repair information is stored under \WinNT\Repair, you should always make offline backups of the system registry using the Emergency Repair Disk tool. This saves this information to a floppy disk in case of emergency system recovery. To create a new repair disk, run the tool as **rdisk**.

Table 2.5 Important Registry Files

FILENAME	ROOT KEY	DESCRIPTION
SAM._	HKEY_LOCAL_MACHINE\SAM	Security Authentication Manager configuration and the user account database.
Security._	HKEY_LOCAL_MACHINE\SECURITY	User and group permissions; user access rights.
System._	HKEY_LOCAL_MACHINE\SYSTEM	Profile of the operating system and Executive configuration.
NTUser.DAT	HKEY_CURRENT_USER	Information on current user logged on to console, including keyboard layout, network drive mappings, and desktop settings.
Default._	HKEY_USERS\DEFAULT	Default user profile information.
Software._	HKEY_LOCAL_MACHINE\SOFTWARE	Registry information for all installed applications.

Once you have created a repair disk, you should update it periodically by running the tool (with **rdisk /s**) to save changes to the registry that occur each time a new application is installed, system configuration is changed, or a user profile is updated.

System Controls

There are several levels of controlling, configuring, and managing Win 2000 systems. The most immediate are the control panels, which are accessible through the desktop. These display and modify the current configuration of the hardware, operating system, user environment, and application system. The Task Manager, another user-level tool, allows users to end any processes or applications that have stopped responding.

At the administrator level, there are other tools to manage one or a network of Win 2000 systems. The Microsoft Management Console, newly introduced in Win 2000, contains most of the administrative functions of the system. These functions were, at one time, separate applications, requiring administrators to remember numerous names and the uses of each. With the new console, most of these functions are now under a single structure.

We say *most*, for now, since not all of these applications have made it into the console. Microsoft promises that eventually everything will be, and no other tools will be required. One important separate administrator tool is the Event Log, which keeps an audit of all system events and actions. It works very similarly to the UNIX *syslog* monitor. One other very important administrator control is the Active Directory Manager, for configuring and managing the new enterprise directory services introduced in Win 2000. We discuss Active Directory and the management system in a later chapter.

Control Panels

The control panels give access to system configuration information. Some items here can only be accessed and changed by a privileged account, but most desktop users have some access to the control panel, if only to change their user environmental settings. If needed, the administrator can configure the users' desktop so that they have no access at all to the control panels. They are normally accessible through the Start-button menu or through the Windows Explorer file system browser.

The Control Panels folder contains these items. This folder is not a real directory but an application interface to the system configuration. By default, a number of control panels are always available, as shown in Table 2.6.

Other control panels may appear when you add Microsoft or third-party software applications to the system (see Table 2.7).

Task Manager

The task manager is a desktop user-level function that displays running applications and processes and allows users to cancel any of their running processes. It can be brought up by doing the *secure attention sequence* (Control-Alt-Delete) and selecting Task Manager. It is a quick way to directly end a hung application as well as to check the system performance level and see what other processes are running.

There are three tabs, *Applications*, *Processes*, and *Performance*, that present each of the features. The Applications view will show what applications the current user is running. It does not show system applications or those of other users. The Processes view (see Figure 2.4) shows the active state of all processes by executable name, process identifier, CPU usage, total CPU time used, and memory usage. If you click on View, Select Columns, you can bring up a list of other system data structures and events to display. An account with proper privileges will be able to end running processes from this view. The Performance view shows continually updated CPU- and memory-usage graphs. It will also display other system performance information to give a quick view of current machine performance status.

From an administrative point of view, the task manager is handy for killing any hung applications. The active processes list may also prove useful to view what executables are running or to quickly kill another process on the system. The performance window gives a quick glance at current performance status, but there are other tools (MMC and the Performance Monitor) that are much more detailed and helpful.

Microsoft Management Console

In Win 2000 most of the administrative tools from NT 4.0 have been combined into one application called the Microsoft Management Console (MMC; see Figure 2.5). Individual functions such as disk management,

Table 2.6 Standard Control Panels in Windows 2000

CONTROL PANEL	FUNCTION
Accessibility Options	Changes ease-of-use and accessibility options.
Add/Remove Programs	Installs and uninstalls applications to the system.
Add/Remove Hardware	Installs and configures any new hardware devices.
Administrative Tools	Quick access to all administrative tools.
Date/Time	Changes date, time, and time-zone settings.
Display	Changes settings for monitors and graphics cards.
Fax	Changes settings for installed fax system and hardware.
Folder Options	Changes folder viewing options.
Fonts	Installs or views all fonts on system.
Game Controllers	Configures attached game controllers.
Internet Options	Configures Internet application services running on the system.
Keyboard	Configures keyboard preferences.
Licensing	Installs and uninstalls application licenses.
Mail and Fax	Configures information regarding e-mail addresses and fax routing.
Message Queuing	Configures the Message Queuing service databases.
Mouse	Configures the mouse options.
Network and Dial-up Connections	Installs and configures network hardware, protocols, and services.
Open Database Connectivity	Configures ODBC database and file access.
Phone and Modems	Installs and configures modems attached to the system and the telephony system.
Power Options	Configures advanced power management system.
Printers	Installs and configures local and network printers.
Regional Options	Configures regional settings for languages, character formats, currencies, times, and date display.
Scanners and Cameras	Installs and configures scanners, cameras, and devices supporting the TWAIN driver format.
Scheduled Tasks	Manages tasks scheduled for the system.
Sound and Multimedia	Configures system sound options and multimedia devices.
System	Displays system information and settings.

Table 2.7 Other Control Panels for Application-Related Services

CONTROL PANEL	FUNCTION
Gateway Services for NetWare	Configures MS Windows to NetWare application and protocol gateway services.
NT Services for UNIX	Configures MS Windows to UNIX file sharing and access gateway services.
Microsoft DTC	Configures MS Distributed Transaction Client and gateway for transaction or services.
Quicktime 32	Configures the Apple Quicktime media system.
SQL Server Client Configuration	Configures MS SQL Server client access and network libraries.

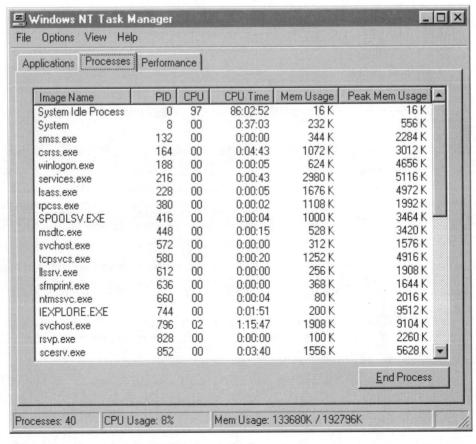

Figure 2.4 The task manager (Processes view).

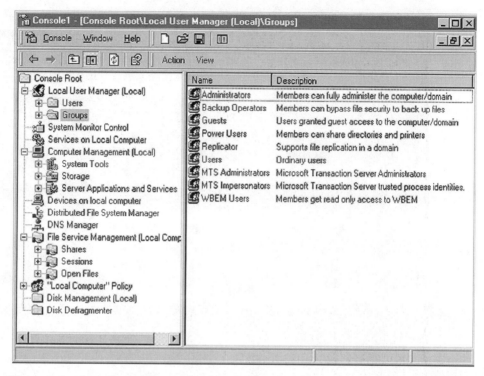

Figure 2.5 The Microsoft Management Console.

user management, system monitoring, and so forth have become modules called *snap-ins* (see Table 2.8) that are loaded into the Explorer-like MMC system.

The MMC system allows you to have separate console views, each with its own set of snap-ins. Although you can load all snap-ins into one console view, it is better to keep some in separate views. Each snap-in is an application and will use up memory when loaded. To save on system memory usage and processing, you may want to keep separate console views for the system monitor control, all the disk and file services management components, DNS and network services, local services management, and the users, groups, and policies. Chapter 17 details the use of the MMC.

Event Viewer

The Event Viewer (see Figure 2.6) allows you to examine all system events that occur from boot time, similarly to the UNIX *syslog* daemon.

Table 2.8 Standalone Snap-ins for MMC

SNAP-IN	DESCRIPTION
Computer Management	Wide-ranging system toolset including most other snap-ins.
Local User Manager	User and group account management.
System Monitor Control	System activity and performance monitor.
Services on Local Computer	System services management.
Devices on Local Computer	Hardware device management.
Distributed File System Manager	Distributed File System management.
DNS Manager	Domain Name System management.
File Service Management	File sharing and usage management.
"Local Computer" Policy	System, application, and user policy management.
Disk Management	Disk partitioning and volume management.
Disk Defragmenter	Disk defragmentation tools.

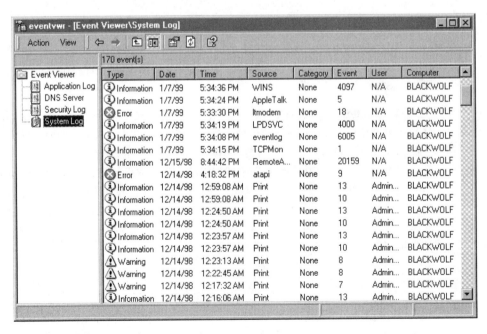

Figure 2.6 The event viewer.

Table 2.9 Types of Events

EVENT TYPE	DESCRIPTION
Error	Indicates a loss of data or the failure of a system service or component.
Warning	Indicates a situation that is not immediately problematic but might affect the system in the future.
Information	Indicates successful operation of an application, driver, or service.
Success audit	Indicates successful access to a file or object that is being audited.
Failure audit	Indicates failure to access a file or object that is being audited.

The original event-viewer application in NT 4 has been replaced with an MMC snap-in that looks nearly identical but also supports the multiple log-files system. The event-logging system is handled by a system service called *EventLog*, part of the System Service Controller executable.

Events are critical and noncritical occurrences to the operating system, system services, or any applications, as shown in Table 2.9. By default, there are three types of log files for these events: the *Application, Security*, and *System* logs. On Win 2000 Servers, you may also have logs for the Active Directory Server and the DNS Server, and a File Replication Service log for the Distributed File System. These logs are each stored in the \Winnt\System32\Config directory as AppEvent.evt, SecEvent.evt, SysEvent.evt, and DnsEvent.evt, respectively.

You can create a new log-file view based on one of the system log files and set a filter to capture information by specific services and devices, computers, users, and event types between specific times. By default, log files are 512KB in length and can be increased in 64KB increments. The default limit is set to record for 7 days, although this can be extended or left unlimited (a potential source of error events when it fills up your disk).

Summary

The Win 2000 architecture introduces a whole new set of core components as well as revises the look and function of many existing ones. The core design based upon the microkernel of NT still exists but new services that were once separate products such as Terminal Server, are now included as standard in Win 2000 server editions. Thus you should consider Win 2000 separately from that of NT. The differences are almost as significant between that of System V and BSD UNIX.

When compared against UNIX platforms, Win 2000 has many conceptually similar ideas but differs radically in the implementation. The design of Win 2000 is more compartmentalized and leans towards newer operating systems concepts. This greatly increases the complexity and the size of the operating system. Those who design and work with the internals of operating systems can appreciate this design, but they will also argue that it will make the system slower.

Be that as it may, Win 2000 actually seems to run faster in some cases when compared to earlier NT systems given that it has sufficient memory. To improve the performance of the system, more important system data is stored in memory, making it faster to access.

One of the most significant changes for system administrators is the new Microsoft Management Console. This finally unites the diverse configuration and management programs in NT under one umbrella and accomplishes this without significantly changing the actual function of those programs. Thus software developers will find it easy to incorporate other management applications under this framework. It provides consistency and ease of use that benefits the system administrator and thereby the user as well.

3

Windows 2000 File Systems

W indows 2000 provides support for several file systems, from the latest NTFS 5.0 to the classic FAT-16. The latest native file system, NTFS 5.0, brings long-awaited features and exciting new possibilities while maintaining backward compatibility with older file systems. These additional features take it beyond those available in most UNIX file systems.

Win 2000 supports several types of hard-disk-based file systems: the 16-bit file allocation table (FAT-16), the 32-bit file allocation table (FAT-32), and the NT File System (NTFS). In addition, other removable media file systems it supports include the international standard ISO 9660 CD File System (CDFS), and the Universal Disk Format (UDF) for CDs and DVDs, according to the ISO 13346 standard.

This chapter takes a look at the differences between these file systems, primarily the hard-disk-based ones. This is followed with some technical details of the most important one, NTFS version 5 and how it is managed in a Win 2000 system.

Supported File System Types

As just mentioned, Win 2000 supports three types of disk file systems: FAT-16, FAT-32, and NTFS. In the early NT 3.1 and 3.51 releases, there was also support for IBM OS/2's *High-Performance File System* (HPFS), but this was dropped in version 4.0 when Microsoft figured it wasn't particularly needed anymore. All three file systems can run on servers, but the FAT file systems are simply too thin on enterprise features when compared to NTFS. In Win 2000, NTFS has been enhanced to include features in much demand by users. NTFS Version 4.0 is the system available on NT 4.0 systems. Win 2000 can still use NTFS 4.0 disks, but you cannot install the additional features that 5.0 has without upgrading it.

In particular, version 5.0 of NTFS brings features such as per-volume user quotas, a single-tree distributed file system, native property sets for files, a volume-wide file changes log, encrypting file system services, and sparse files. Table 3.1 explains the differences between these file systems and overviews some of the features available in the latest version. We explain these features in the rest of the chapter.

FAT-16 and FAT-32

FAT-16 (also just plainly called FAT) and FAT-32 are included for compatibility with disk systems from Windows 3.x, 95, and 98. FAT-16 is the same file system used in early versions of DOS, with its filename limits, lack of support for large drives, lack of security, and drive-format dependencies. It was first developed for 760KB floppy disks and then taken over to the first 1- to 10MB PC hard drives. As disk sizes grew, FAT saw minor extensions to the cluster size to support the larger drive capacities.

The *cluster* is a fixed-size area on the disk that contains data. Depending on the overall capacity of the disk, the cluster size changes. The total number of all clusters remains the same for a given file system type. Each cluster in FAT-16 is identified with a 16-bit number address; thus, FAT-16 allows a total of 2^{16} or 65,536 clusters. Since a cluster is the smallest unit that a file can be, this, in turn, limits the total number of files on a FAT-16 to 65,536. This number remains fixed, but as the disk capacity gets larger the actual disk space available for each cluster rises. For example, a 512MB disk has a cluster size of 8KB. On such a disk, the smallest unit of allocation for a file is 8KB even if the file contains only 500 bytes of information. The minimum size for clusters on any modern disk is 512 bytes, since this is what most drive hardware can access with a single read operation; on some international models, the minimum cluster size can be 1024 bytes or 1KB. FAT-32 and NTFS have different numbers of total clusters and cluster sizes, as we will soon see.

Table 3.1 Comparison of Various Windows 2000-Supported File Systems

FEATURE	FAT-16	FAT-32	NTFS 4	NTFS 5
Maximum storage capacity	2GB	64GB	1.84×10^{10} GB	1.84×10^{10} GB
Minimum disk size	1MB	1MB	8MB	7MB
Volume-level compression	No	Yes	Yes	Yes
File- or directory-level compression	No	No	Yes	Yes
Per-user quotas	No	No	Third-party	Yes
Encryption	No	No	Third-party	Yes
Multiple-disk-spanning volumes	No	No	Yes	Yes
Disk mirroring	No	No	Yes	Yes
Disk striping	No	No	Yes	Yes
Fault tolerance	No	No	Yes	Yes
Access permissions	No	No	Yes	Yes
Access control lists	No	No	Yes	Yes
Transaction-based disk operations	No	No	Yes	Yes
Distributed file system features	No	No	No	Yes
Usable by Win 3.x	Yes	No	No	No
Usable by Win 95	Yes	Yes, in Service Release 2	No	No
Usable by NT 4.0	Yes	Third-party	Yes	No
Usable by Win 2000	Yes	Yes	Yes	Yes
Mounting/unmounting volumes without rebooting	No	No	No	Yes, with dynamic disks support enabled

All files and directories on a FAT-16 volume are readable and writable unless designated with a different attribute. The file system can designate files as *hidden* (they do not show up on a basic directory command), *read-only* (you cannot write to them), *archive*, or *system-related*. The last two were used in earlier versions of DOS and do not have much significance now. FAT-16 still survives today, in systems as recent as Windows 95 and some NT 4.0 systems.

FAT-32 was introduced in the second service release of Windows 95 in 1997, when Microsoft acknowledged that the huge clusters made for extra fat used up by the system to support the larger disks. To trim away some of this needlessly wasted space, they created FAT-32, with the address size for a cluster increased from 16 to 32 bits. Thus, FAT-32 allows 2^{32} or approximately 4 billion files on a single disk. FAT-32 was designed with 1GB drives as the minimal model available. All drives 1GB or smaller have a cluster of 512 bytes. Compare this with the 16KB cluster size for FAT-16 disk volumes (see Table 3.2) and you can see how the new file system is far more efficient.

Furthermore, it removes the restriction that the critical file system data structures be allocated at the very first few clusters of the disk. This allows the root directory to be located on any part of the drive and allows multiple copies of the root directory clusters, thus creating a more reliable environment. You won't lose the entire drive contents if the first few clusters are overwritten accidentally or go bad.

However, the default file system for Windows 98, FAT-32, like FAT-16, has no level of ownership or user identity and no support for access control lists, making it inappropriate for enterprise use. FAT-32 was intended as an update to the older version without adding the complexities of NTFS. A system with device drivers for FAT-16 cannot read a FAT-32 disk, although, vice versa, it works. NT 4.0 and earlier versions had drivers for FAT-16 and can read and write to disks of this format. However, they do not support FAT-32 out of the box. If you really need access

Table 3.2 Cluster Size versus Partition Size in FAT-16 and NTFS

CLUSTER SIZE	SECTORS PER CLUSTER	FAT-16 PARTITION SIZE	FAT-32 PARTITION SIZE	NTFS PARTITION SIZE
512 bytes	1	<32MB	<1GB	<512MB
1KB	2	<64MB	<2GB	<1GB
2KB	4	<128MB	<4GB	<2GB
4KB	8	<256MB	<8GB	<4GB
8KB	16	<512MB	<16GB	<8GB
16KB	32	<1GB	<32GB	<16GB
32KB	64	<2GB	<64GB	<32GB
64KB	128	Unsupported	>64GB	>32GB

to FAT-32, Microsoft provides a read-only driver for FAT-32 that you can install on NT 4.0. Since this is read-only, you cannot write to FAT-32 volumes using this driver. A company called *Winternals Software* (www.winternals.com) sells a full FAT-32 driver for NT 4.0 for $39; it allows you to read, write, or create FAT-32 volumes.

NTFS

NTFS first appeared with NT 3.1, as a replacement for the aging FAT-16 and to introduce advanced file system features to the operating system. In comparison to the features of the standard UNIX file system (ufs) and the BSD file system (bsdfs) available on many UNIX platforms, NTFS is far more advanced. It implements user and group permissions but also provides *access control lists* to directly specify per-user permissions to a file. It implements log-based file system services like those of the VERI-TAS File System, to maintain file system consistency in the event of a system crash.

In UNIX, the file concept is used as the basis of many different system devices (text files, executable programs, directories, symbolic links, device objects, named sockets, and named pipes). NT, on the other hand, views files and directories as objects of similar types. Each file object has a set of permissions and attributes.

NTFS has remained mostly the same between 3.1 and 4.0 until this latest version of Windows and the introduction of NTFS 5.0. A Win 2000 system is still able to use pre-5.0 version NTFS volumes, but any new file systems created are only of the 5.0 variety. Furthermore, although you can have NTFS 4.0 disks on a Win 2000 system, you cannot use the new features introduced in 5.0 with the 4.0 disks and must convert the drives, if you wish to.

Like many modern file systems, NTFS has an on-disk structure and a logical volume structure. The on-disk structure describes how data is written to different parts of a disk drive or across multiple drives. The logical volume structure defines how the users, applications, and system services interact with the on-disk structure. An NTFS volume may be a partition on a drive, an entire drive, or a set of drives. Although the on-disk structure varies according to these scenarios, the logical structure remains the same, thus allowing user applications to access files and directories in the same manner despite the configuration.

NTFS Volume Structure

NTFS volumes are defined with *metadata* that defines file system activity, status, attributes, and user information. In particular, NTFS volumes have 11 metadata files describing the rest of the volume, as shown in Table 3.3.

The *master file table* (MFT) defines the relationship between the logical disk structure and the on-disk structure. The MFT is a set of records describing the characteristics of each file and directory. It is normally the very first file on the NTFS file system, with a backup copy ($MFT-MIRR) somewhere toward the middle of the file system. All file access begins by searching the MFT record corresponding to the file. The MFT itself is a file and can be broken up into multiple clusters spread across the drive (a process called *fragmentation*) if the contents of the volume

Table 3.3 NTFS Metadata Files

NAME	MFT RECORD #	DESCRIPTION
$MFT	0	Master file table record.
$MFTMIRR	1	Copy of the first 16 records of $MFT elsewhere on disk.
$LOGFILE	2	Transactional file system log file.
$VOLUME	3	Volume serial number, creation time stamp, and dirty flag.
$ATTRDEF	4	Volume attribute definitions.
..	5	Root directory of volume.
$BITMAP	6	Drive's cluster usage bitmap.
$BOOT	7	Boot record on the disk.
$BADCLUS	8	List of bad clusters on the disk.
$QUOTA	9	User quotas per volume (used only in NTFS 5.0).
$UPCASE	10	Maps lowercase characters to uppercase ones.
N/A	11	Undefined.
N/A	12	Undefined.
N/A	13	Undefined.
N/A	14	Undefined.
N/A	15	Undefined.
—	16	User files and directories start from this number.

change very often. Fragmentation of the MFT makes for inefficient file access and requires defragmentation (reconsolidation of the separate pieces into a single continuous series of clusters). Fragmentation can occur to any large file and is fairly common to most modern file systems.

The *$LOGFILE* metadata file is used by NTFS to keep transaction logs of open files, disk writes, and all attribute changes to the file system. If the OS or the disk system should crash at any point, this allows the OS to reload the file system back to the state just before the crash. Many older file systems without transactional logging capabilities lose volume consistency and can lose links to files that were open or in the process of being written to during a system crash. The transactional system was based on the VERITAS file system technology, which provides similar file systems for UNIX machines.

$VOLUME and *$ATTRDEF* contain standard volume information, timestamps, and attributes. The dirty flag in $VOLUME indicates that a volume has been changed since the last disk operation recorded by the transactional system. The "." is a record indicating the root directory of the entire disk, what UNIX administrators would recognize as "/". NTFS also maintains a bitmap record, *$BITMAP*, describing clusters in and not in use on the disk; a *$BOOT* record for the drive; and a list of clusters that cannot be used anymore by the file system due to imperfections or nonfixable errors on the disk media (*$BADCLUS*). The *$UPCASE* record maintains a character mapping between lowercase and uppercase to make it easier for users to type in filenames.

The *$QUOTA* record, until NTFS 5.0, has been mostly unused. In 5.0, it points to a directory called *$EXTEND*, which keeps a list of quota assignments per user for the entire volume. The quota system works as in UNIX, with a value indicating the maximum disk space that a user can allocate for files and directories.

NOTE

Each of these metadata records actually exists as hidden files on an NTFS volume in the root directory. You can see a directory listing of each of these files as in the following example:

```
F:\<\>> dir /ah &MFT
Volume in drive F is NT50b2
Volume Serial Number is C061-7695
Directory of F:\
```

```
11/30/98 09:06a                    13,111,296 &MFT
              1 File(s)            13,111,296 bytes
              0 Dir(s)      3,555,491,800 bytes free
```

This can help you figure out how disk space is being allocated. You should never try to edit or change any of these files directly unless you have no fear of losing your entire volume.

Files and Directories

Every file and directory has a set of attributes and a set of permissions. The attributes include information on the filename, the volume, file creation and modification times, property sheets, and the data contents of the file (see Table 3.4 for a full list). These describe the contents and behavior of the file.

Security information for a file can also be accessed through the attributes but is directly represented by access rights or permission flags and

Table 3.4 NTFS File and Directory Attributes

ATTRIBUTE	DESCRIPTION
$FILE_NAME	Full filename.
$DATA	Pointer to data contents of file.
$VOLUME_VERSION	NTFS volume version number (3.1, 3.5, 4.0, 5.0).
$VOLUME_NAME	NTFS disk volume name.
$VOLUME_INFORMATION	NTFS version, volume modification, and dirty flag.
$STANDARD_INFORMATION	Time stamps and flags for hidden, system, read-only, and archive bits.
$SECURITY_DESCRIPTOR	Pointer to file security information. In NTFS 5.0, all security descriptors are stored in one file, and this is just an index to a record within the file.
$INDEX_ROOT, $INDEX_ALLOCATION	Filename allocation for directories.
$BITMAP	Filename mapping for large directories.
$ATTRIBUTE_LIST	List of other attributes as located in the MFT. Used rarely when a file has more than one MFT record.
$SYMBOLIC_LINK	Used in NT 5.0 for symbolic filename links.
$EA, $EA_INFORMATION	OS/2 compatibility extended attributes. Unused in NTFS 5.0.

access control lists (ACLs). Unlike the UNIX triples of triples (Read, Write, Execute for the Owner, the Group, and the World), the NTFS file has six access rights: *Read, Write, Execute, Delete, Take Ownership,* and *Change Permission* (see Table 3.5). The first four are pretty obvious; the Take Ownership flag indicates that the owner can change the ownership of this file to another user, essentially relinquishing ownership, and the Change Permissions flag indicates that the user is allowed to modify these six access rights.

Group and world permissions are assigned by ACLs. An ACL is essentially a second set of access rights for a file as pertaining to another user or another group. The world group in UNIX is known as *Everyone* and is usually represented as a group.

The ACL for a file consists of individual access control entries (ACEs). An ACE may be one of three types: *allowed, denied,* or *system audit.* An access allowed ACE indicates that the identified user or group is allowed access to the file according to an associated set of permission flags. The access denied ACE, as you can guess, means the user or group is denied any access to the file and there is no need for permission flags. The system audit ACE indicates that access and attempted access activity for this file is to be logged. There is a long list of different items that can be audited, as shown later in the *File Properties and Security* section.

The permission flags for a directory work differently. If you have *Read* access to a directory, you can get a detailed listing of all files, including their access rights. If you have *Write* access to a directory, you can edit files in it. You need Read and Execute permissions to view the attributes

Table 3.5 File Object Permissions

PERMISSION	NAME	DESCRIPTION
R	Read	Object is readable.
W	Write	Object is writeable; the user can change file attributes.
X	Execute	Object is executable.
D	Delete	Object is deleteable.
O	Take Ownership	Owner of the object can change ownership to another user.
P	Change Permissions	Owner of the object can change the permissions/attributes of the object.

of a file. You need Write and Execute permissions in the directory to create a new file. An Execute permission by itself does not do the same thing as in UNIX, which is that it allows you to change your current working directory into that one.

In NTFS, access rights for files and directories are automatically inherited from the parent directory. This saves time on file creation. The permissions can be changed after the directory is created, if the Change Permissions right is given.

NTFS files have an interesting capability known as *multiple data streams*. A *stream* is a set of data belonging to the file. When you create a file and add information to it, you use the default *unnamed stream*, and all regular information goes into it. In addition, it is possible to create other streams on a file that already has data content. When you create an additional stream, you assign it a name, making it a *named stream*. When you look at the regular data content, you won't see these other streams unless you try to access those streams directly. A practical use of streams in files and directories is to emulate the Macintosh file system, where every file is made of a data fork, containing the actual data of the file, a resource fork, containing resource information such as associated images, a link to the application that created it, and other nondata information about the file.

With NTFS 5.0, every file now has a native property sheet for administration information. This sheet contains information on who created the

Creating Named Streams and Security Issues

You can create a named stream as easily as this:

```
C:\>edit newtext.doc:mystream
```

The file newtext.doc may not exist before this. In fact, once the named stream is created, the file will still show up as being 0 bytes long. The directory command only looks at the default unnamed stream of a file. This makes for an interesting way to hide information within a document. You can create a harmless-looking document and then create an additional stream with other information. Thank goodness that these streams are not executable by default, or they would be a serious security loophole. Still, abusing unnamed streams can confuse sysadmins when a seemingly tiny 10KB file in a directory appears to be taking up 1GB by itself.

file, information on their affiliation or department, possibly a word count of the document, what type of image it might be, and so forth. Property sheets are a basic way of finding out commonly requested information about a file without having to open the whole file and process it. They are viewable by the user through *File, Properties* and stored as a named stream in the file.

Filenames

In supporting several generations of Windows files, the various file systems had to maintain backward compatibility, especially with filenames. Pre-6.x-version MS-DOS systems were limited to a convention commonly known as *8.3 filenames*, where the first 8 characters are an assigned name and the last 3 characters are a file extension, describing the format of the file. 8.3 exists in FAT-16 and FAT-32 systems.

Windows 95, 98, 2000, and NT can support filenames of up to 255 characters on FAT-16 and FAT-32 volumes. However, on both systems, they

Table 3.6 Allowable Characters in Filenames

CHARACTERS	DOS	WIN32	POSIX
a-z, A-Z	Yes, but non-case sensitive.	Yes, but non-case sensitive.	Yes.
0-9	Yes.	Yes.	Yes.
+ − _ = [ ] { } ~ ' ' ! @ # $ % ^ & * ( )	Yes.	Yes.	Yes, but only when quoted.
" / < > \		No.	No.	Yes, but only when quoted.
.	Only before file extensions.	Only before file extensions.	Yes.
;	No.	Yes, but not recorded.	Yes, but only when quoted.
?	No.	No.	Yes, but only when quoted.
Space	No.	Yes, after first character.	Yes, after first character.
Foreign language Unicode characters	No.	Yes.	No.

are actually stored in the traditional 8.3-length filenames. The operating system associates a mapping of the long filename to the short format for each file and directory. Usually the mapping truncates the name at 6 characters (not counting the extension), and attaches a tilde (~) and a number. For example, a file called *Cheesy Poofs.doc* would be stored as *cheesy~1.doc*. Another file called *Cheesy Comedies.doc* in the same directory would be stored as *cheesy~2.doc*. Unfortunately, these systems do not support case-sensitive filenames on FAT volumes. Table 3.6 shows the filename particulars of each file system.

NT also supports Unicode, an international standard for character sets. This allows the filenames to be in any character format supported by Unicode, which is pretty much most of the major and many minor languages of the world.

One final requirement is filename support in the POSIX subsystem. Since POSIX is based on UNIX-style filenames, the files can have any number of trailing periods or spaces, which is not allowed in Win32 or DOS. Furthermore, POSIX filenames are case sensitive, just as in UNIX—meaning that two files with the same name but with characters of different case will be recognized as separate files. Files named using the POSIX system as such cannot be accessed by the Win32 or DOS systems.

Examples of Filenames

Several DOS filename possibilities:

```
"MYWORDFL.DOC", "EIGHTLMT.TXT", "CHEESY~1.DOC"
```

Several Win32 filename possibilities:

```
"SureIsALongFileName", "This.is.a.Win32.file.with.multiple.dots.doc",
"Or you can separate them by spaces",
"Φρεδ A Cool UNICODE Name.IXNAY"
```

Several POSIX filename possibilities:

```
"This is UNIX compatible+"
"DifferentCaseMeansDifferentFile"
"differentCasemeansDifferentfile"
"Spaces trailing      "
```

Advanced File System Features

The advanced features of the NTFS file system include *volume, mirror, stripe,* and *parity* sets, a log-based file system, an encrypting file system, per-user quotas, a user-extensible file system, reparse points, and automatically compressing sparse files.

A volume set is a merging of several disk partitions on one or more drives into a single unit with one file system. This allows the sysadmin to consolidate extra space on drives into a usable volume. Two partitions of 500MB would create a 1GB volume set. The set appears with a single drive letter and for all intents and purposes is one logical disk. If any of the partitions were to be corrupted, even if the volume set spanned several disks, the entire volume set would be corrupted.

A mirror set takes a pair of disks and keeps identical copies of all data on both disks. Mirroring is also commonly known as *redundant array of independent disks* (RAID) *level 1*. The file system appears as one logical volume but maintains separate copies of all files and directories on each. If one disk were to fail, the other would still be immediately accessible.

A stripe set uses multiple disks and records pieces of files and directories across all the disks. This is commonly known as *RAID 0*. Each read and write operation is then spread across multiple disks, speeding the process. Basically, disk access is magnitudinally slower than main memory access and CPU processing. This speeds it up by spreading the operations across multiple disks, which can each do part of the processing in parallel.

Parity is the concept of using extra bits or bytes as values with a little bit of mathemagic to check against so that the original byte can be guaranteed accurate. Such parity bits use up space on the disk but guarantee that the data read is correct. This ensures against physical disk corruption. NTFS supports *stripe sets with parity* to create an error-correcting volume that is optimized via striping over several volumes. This is the equivalent of *RAID 5*.

NTFS implements the log-based file system available in VERITAS. Each transaction to the on-disk structure of a volume is specifically recorded in a log. In the event of system failure, the system runs back the log to last-known-safe status and issues the disk operations until the system is consistent once again.

NTFS 5.0 introduces auto-encrypted file system services. This service is provided by the new CryptoAPI and security authentication system. Essentially, every user has a unique identification key. When any files or directories are created and assigned this level of security, their contents are automatically encrypted. When a user attempts to read the file again, the system will check if the file recognizes the key and can be decrypted with it. With directories that are encrypted, users are unable to list the directory or create or change any files within unless they have the proper key.

Per-user quotas are common on UNIX systems but have only been introduced into NTFS in version 5.0. The concept is very similar. Every user has a set limit of total disk space that they can use up on a particular volume. Each volume maintains a tally of disk space usage by that user within its volume structure. When the maximum limit is reached, the user cannot create any more files or add to existing files.

A new system with NTFS 5.0, known as the *Installable File System* (IFS), allows developers to create their own modifications to the NTFS system. For example, an IFS might automatically create a searchable index of each file and add that information to a central database. IFS allows you overlay other file system types on top of NTFS as long as there is a way to represent the information in a manner that can be handled by it.

Reparse points have been added to directories and volumes. These are software-level interfaces that reparse or translate the directory path to an alternative path when accessed. Think of them as similar mount points of remote volumes on UNIX systems. Since a volume can be mounted to any location of the directory tree, the file system has to know how to build a proper path from the root directory down to a file within that directory. If the volume were to be mounted at a different location the next time, a new path would need to be calculated. Reparse points are what made the *Distributed File System* (DFS) much simpler to implement in Win 2000.

To support huge files for databases, for example, you can now create a file of very large size (e.g., several gigabytes), and not actually allocate all that disk space at creation time. This concept of huge but *sparse* files keeps a compressed version on disk, with all the empty sections of the file unallocated until they are used. Sparse files help in quickly reading the contents of the file as well as saving disk space.

File System Administration

File system administration on Win 2000 involves the creation of partitions and volumes through a common sysadmin tool, and the editing of file properties and security settings on a per-file basis through the Explorer.

Just for starters, disk systems in the Windows world come in certain packages. Although the physical disk unit may be identical to the one you use in a UNIX system, the roles they play are slightly different. Unlike a UNIX drive, with its multiple partitions of equal status, NT and Win 2000 still have some throwbacks to the DOS disk-partitioning days.

Basically, disks for the PC architecture have only two real partitions, the *primary* partition and the *extended* partition. In Win 2000, each partition can be of any size, except in FAT-16 file systems, which are normally limited to 2GB disks; you can create a FAT-16 file system larger than 2GB but it will not be backward compatible with Windows 3.x or 95 Release 1. The primary partition may use part of the disk, or the entire disk, if no other partitions are necessary. The extended partition can be split up into one or more *logical drives*. Each logical drive acts as additional logical partitions on the same drive. When you use the *fdisk* partitioning tool in DOS or command-line mode, you can create primary partitions, extended partitions, and logical drives. In Win 2000, where there is no more DOS system, you can use a significantly better graphical tool for creating partitions, as we will see shortly.

At the Windows system level, all this partition stuff is transparent. Each partition and logical drive looks the same as another. The only difference is that the logical drives are always assigned drive letters in sequence after the primary partition. This means that your boot sector will be on the primary partition.

When you format the partition and create file systems, each one is assigned a letter, starting from the letter *C* (letters *A* and *B* are usually reserved for floppy drives). You can have up to 23 different logical file systems on your system. You can certainly have more drives, but you have to create multidisk file systems (something you can only do with NTFS) to support more drives. You are still limited to 23 mounted file systems.

Win 2000 now allows a standard method to mount and unmount nonremovable drives while the system is running (i.e., without rebooting).

This feature is very valuable for hot-pluggable drives, which can be removed while there is active power to the system and the OS is running. Win 2000 does this with the use of dynamic disks, created with the disk management tools.

Disk Management MMC Snap-in

The majority of disk administration tasks are performed through a single application known as *Disk Administrator* in NT 4.0 and the *Disk Management Snap-in* in Win 2000. The snap-in is basically the Disk Administrator tool redone as a snap-in for MMC that supports the new facilities in NTFS 5.0. When you first start up the tool, it scans all drives connected to the system, collates the necessary information, and stores it as part of the system registry.

Win 2000 creates a distinction between *basic* and *dynamic* disks. A basic disk is one that has primary partitions, extended partitions, and logical drives; the format is accessible through the MS-DOS *fdisk* command tool. A dynamic disk is created by the disk management tool, does not use extended partitions or logical drives, and cannot be administered in DOS. Both can have any of the file system types installed, but the system allows you to change the on-disk or volume structure of a dynamic disk without having to reboot the computer. If you have a blank disk drive that has not been partitioned and formatted, and you use the disk management tool, you will by default create a dynamic disk.

For example, Figure 3.1 shows a multidisk environment in the Disk Management console. The console is split into a text view of individual partitioned volumes and a graphical representation of the drives, their partitions, and the file systems. There are four drives showing here: two removable (a ZIP disk and a CD-ROM), and two fixed (6- and 10GB IDE drives). Both removable drives have no media and appear as empty. Disk 1 has two partitions (one primary and one logical drive) and some free space. Disk 2 is a single 6GB FAT-32 volume. The color coding indicates the different file partition types (not file system types). The text window shows basic information such as file system type, volume health/corruption status, capacity in raw space and as a percentage of the whole, whether fault-tolerance is enabled, and the amount of system overhead required for the file system. The overhead entry is particular to the advanced file system types and is used up, for example, by parity information in a RAID 5 system.

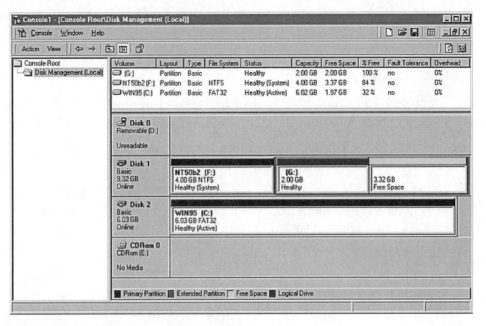

Figure 3.1 The Disk Management console.

Creating Disk Volumes

With the Disk Management console you can partition disks and create FAT-16, FAT-32, and NTFS 5.0 volumes on any type of recognized hard disk. All floppy disks are still limited to FAT-16 since the other two file systems add too much overhead to the disk.

- *Creating partitions and simple FAT, FAT-32, and NTFS volumes.* In the Disk Management console, right-click on an area of free space and select *Create Partition*. The wizard will take you through the steps to specify the partition type, the amount of disk space to use for the partition, the drive letter assignment, and the file system format for the drive. The file system can be FAT, FAT-32, or NTFS (5.0 only), and you can specify a cluster size between 512 bytes and 64KB for standard disks that support 512 byte sectors and up to 256KB for non-standard disks with 1KB or larger sectors. One last significant option allows you to enable automatic compression on files and folders.

- *Creating dynamic volumes for spanning, mirroring, striping, or RAID 5.* In the Disk Management console, select two or more unpartitioned areas and click on the Create Volume option. Follow this wizard to create the various types of disk volumes. Keep in mind that mirrored volumes require an even number of partitions or drives, while all the others can use two or more.

Converting to NTFS 5.0

If you have older NT disks, you should upgrade to NTFS 5.0 to take advantage of, at minimum, the quota system. You should use the following command:

```
C:\> chkntfs /e <old NTFS disk>
```

This is a one-way step. The next time you reboot the disk, the system will check the drive and upgrade it to 5.0. If you have a dual-boot NT 4.0 and Win 2000 system for some reason, the NT 4.0 system will not be able to read that disk anymore.

You can also convert an existing FAT-16 or FAT-32 volume into an NTFS 5.0 volume with the *convert* command-line tool. Essentially, this tool copies portions of the FAT file system to memory, overlays an NTFS structure, and then copies back the file data. The files are all set to default ownership by the administrator account. The utility will keep the data on that FAT volume intact and accessible after conversion to NTFS. As with any disk operation with high risk to the data, you should always back up the volume first. For example:

```
C:\> convert <FAT disk> /fs:ntfs /v
```

This is one-way only. You cannot convert NTFS volumes into FAT volumes. In fact, there is no standard way to convert an NTFS to a FAT system at all while still keeping the data.

File Properties and Security

The properties of any accessible file are viewable through the Explorer browser. Figures 3.2 through 3.6 show the significant areas of file properties, especially security and auditing.

Figure 3.2 shows the file properties dialog window, including the filename; the application type; a text description; the size of the file; the actual disk space used; when the file was created, last modified, and last accessed; and whether the file is designated as read-only or is hidden. A hidden file is simply not shown by default in the Explorer browser or through a directory command. Other than that, it is just the same as any other file. The advanced properties button brings up the dialog window shown in Figure 3.3, which allows the sysadmin to indicate other options. The Archiving flag indicates that the directory can be backed up. The Fast Indexing flag uses the new indexing features of NTFS to create quick-searchable files. The Compression and Encryption flags are self-explanatory.

The Security tab in the file properties dialog (see Figure 3.4) shows who has access to the file. Users and groups are represented in the top window by either their name or their unique security identifier. The advanced properties button will bring up another dialog showing full ownership, security access rights, and auditing details.

The Auditing tab of the file security dialog (Figure 3.5) shows a list of computers and users for which access to this file is enabled. Each audit

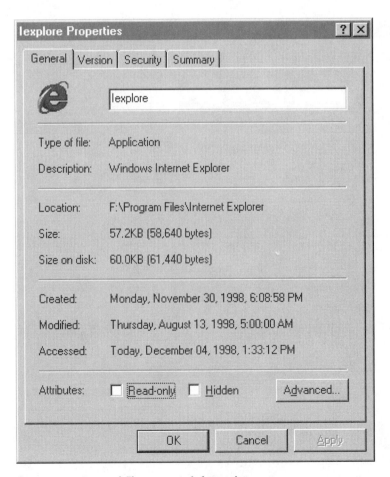

Figure 3.2 General file property information.

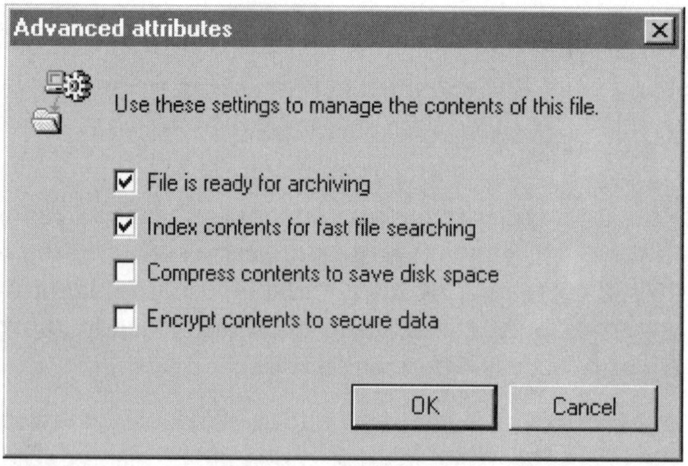

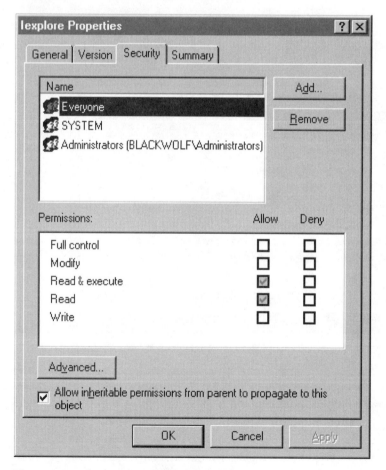

Figure 3.3 Advanced file property information.

Figure 3.4 File security information.

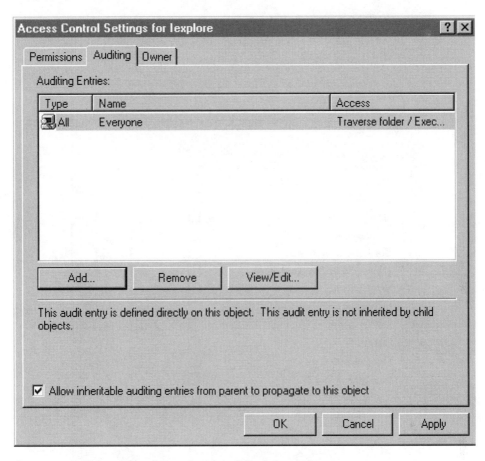

Figure 3.5 File security advanced and auditing information.

entry has a detailed list of options, shown in Figure 3.6, that can be logged to the system for every successful or failed attempt to access this file.

System Files, Folders, and Directories

System directories and folders are similar for the most part, with the difference being that a system directory is a direct representation of an on-disk directory containing files and other directories and can normally be specified with a full path starting at the root directory. A folder, on the other hand, may be a directory as just described, or it may be a specialized application or a representation of multiple system services and configuration options. For example, *Winnt* is a directory, whereas *Control Panels* is a folder. There is no direct representation of the control panels as an independent set of files in a single directory. It is a mix of informa-

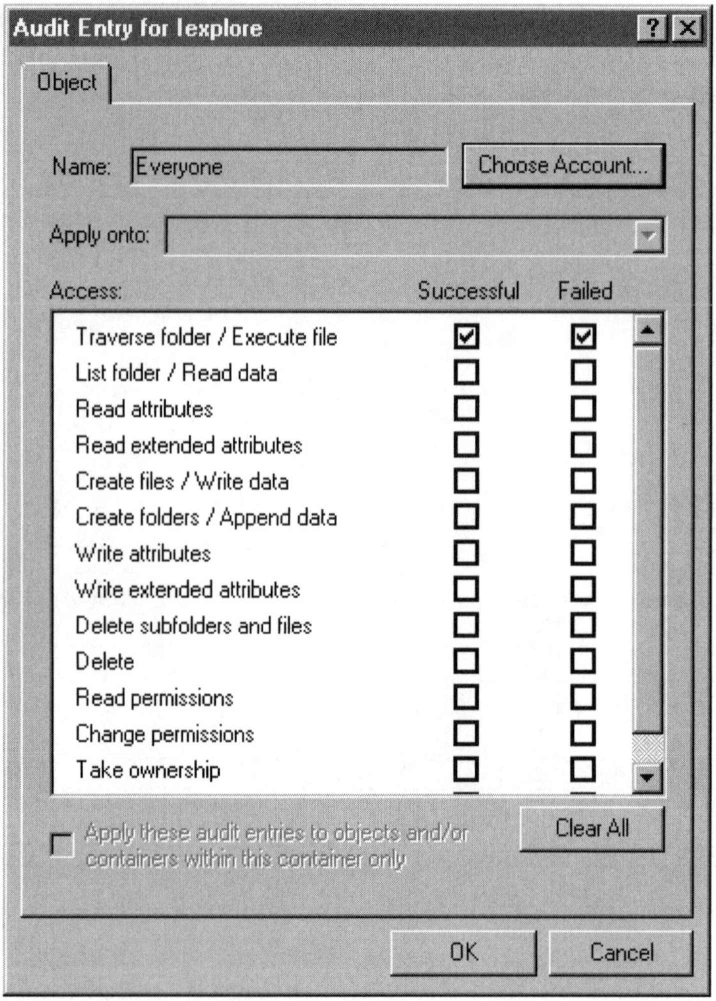

Figure 3.6   File security auditing details.

tion from several sources. On the other hand, some folders do have a directory counterpart (e.g., the Scheduled Tasks folder). In Windows terminology, the word *folder* is often used interchangeably with the word *directory*.

System Directories and Folders

Directory structure for Win 2000 uses the NT model rather than the Windows 95/98 system, although there is only a slight difference between the two. To begin, user account directories and files are stored under a new folder called *Documents and Settings* (listed in Table 3.7).

Table 3.7 Description of User Files in \Documents and Settings

FOLDER	DESCRIPTION
All Users\Desktop	Per-user desktop folder.
All Users\Favorites	Per-user favorites folder.
All Users\Documents	Per-user Start menu folder.
All Users\Send To	Per-user shortcuts to applications and devices.
Administrator	Contains the same subfolders as above but in a separate directory location specifically for the Administrator account.

All new system services and driver information should now be stored under the \Winnt\System32 folder (see Table 3.8). Almost all system configuration, data, and executable files are stored under the \Winnt directory (see Table 3.9). We say *should* since not every application vendor follows this rule, often with their own drivers located elsewhere.

The *Program Files* directory is directly under the root directory of the boot drive and is a common area for all applications. Although you can install most applications in any directory you wish, they are best kept under this hierarchy. The InstallShield system for applications has been a common part of Windows since Win 95. It creates an appropriate directory, installs the product, registers the product in the registry, and creates an installation log. When registered, applications show up in the Add/Remove Software control panel. They can be uninstalled either directly from the application directory or through this control panel.

The *Repair* directory contains emergency copies of system registry, security, and boot files. Since the system is particularly susceptible to failure if certain files are damaged, it keeps a secondary copy of the important ones needed to bring it back into a stable mode. These include the following:

Autoexec.nt and **Config.nt.** Both are used to initialize the virtual DOS machine system.

Default._. This is a registry hive containing \HKEY_USERS\DEFAULT.

NTUser.DA_. This is a compressed version of \Winnt\Profiles\Default-User\Ntuser.dat.

SAM._, Security._, Software._, and **System._.** These are each hives of the registry under \HKEY_LOCAL_MACHINE in compressed formats.

Setup.log. This is a log of the installed system and application files.

Table 3.8 Description of System Folders in \Winnt\System32

FOLDER	DESCRIPTION
Cache	Cached system data files.
CatRoot	Security catalog files.
Config	System registry hives.
clients	Configuration details for various Windows clients to support Terminal Server.
Com	Configuration files for the COM+ service.
dhcp	Dynamic Host Configuration Protocol data files.
dllcache	Cache directory for specific dynamically linked libraries.
dns	Applications and configuration files for Domain Name System.
drivers	All standard device drivers.
export	System files that are exported to clients as necessary.
ias	Configuration database for Internet Authentication Server.
inetserv	Internet and IIS application and configuration files.
LogFiles	System log files.
msmq	Configuration files for Microsoft Message Queuing.
Mts	Configuration files for Microsoft Transaction System.
Netmon	Common tools for domain administration.
ras	Remote Access Service configuration.
RemInst	Applications and configuration for remote installing Windows.
RemoteStorage	Configuration files for remote storage and distributed file services.
Rep1	For file replication services.
Setup	Configuration files for many system services.
ShellExt	Libraries and configuration for extensions to the GUI shell.
Spool	Spool directories for print services.
viewers	Libraries for application-specific viewers.
wbem	Applications and configuration for Web-based Enterprise Management service.
wins	Applications and configuration for Windows Internet Naming System.

You can make offline backups of these files using the emergency repair disk utility (see Registry in Chapter 2).

The desktop view in Explorer will show several special folders: the *Recycle Bin*, the *Printers*, the *Control Panels*, the *Scheduled Tasks* list, the *Network Connections*, and the *Network Neighborhood* folder. These

Table 3.9 Description of System Folders in \Winnt

FOLDER	DESCRIPTION
Application Compatibility Scripts	Scripts for compatibility with older NT software under Terminal Server.
Config	Hardware configuration definitions.
Cursors	Definition files for different cursors.
Downloaded Program Files	Any files downloaded with Internet Explorer are temporarily stored here.
Driver Cache	Used to keep a database of all drivers.
Fonts	Fonts folder.
Help	System and application help files.
inf	System and application configuration files.
java	Java Virtual Machine and classes.
Media	Standard audio and video files for system.
NTDS	Used by ActiveDirectory Server to contain its database.
ntfrs	Used by File Replication Service in Intellimirror to keep configurations and synchronization info.
Offline Web Pages	Used by Internet Explorer to keep Web pages cached for offline use.
Registration	Used to store some system and application registration files.
Repair	Duplicate files to help repair damaged system files.
Security	Security system configuration files.
Speech	Text-to-speech system configuration files.
System	Folder for backward compatibility with older device drivers, applications, and libraries.
System32	Device drivers, system cache, log files, and spool folders.
Tasks	Scheduled tasks set by sysadmins.
Temp	Temporarily created files, temporary folders for installation packages, copies of open documents, unarchived files, and downloads.
Web	A general folder to store system Web files.

provide control and configuration access to the system and devices. They do not necessarily conform to any specific directory in the disk hierarchy and are instead maintained in a specific portion of the system registry.

The Recycle Bin folder is where files to be deleted are placed. By default, all files are not immediately removed, just placed in this folder. You have to explicitly empty the bin by opening the folder and selecting the command. Alternatively, when the folder grows to its maximum limit, it will start removing some of the oldest contents. The deleted files size limit is normally set at 10 percent of the maximum storage capacity of the drive. Each drive can have its own set limit if you change this default setting. Within the folder, each file has an origin folder from which it was deleted, a time stamp on when it was deleted, the file type, and its size. All recycle bins, however, appear to be linked, and when you open the folder you will see deleted files from any drive. In reality, the Recycle Bin application keeps separate tabs on deleted files from each drive and accounts for their disk-space usage on a per-drive basis. There is an option to immediately remove any files dropped into the bin, but on server machines you should not use this option just as a safekeeping measure.

The Printers folder shows all configured printers and a task to create a new printer specification. When you click on an existing printer definition, it will show the current queue for that printer. To change the configuration of the printer, in the printer queue, select *Printer*, *Properties* or right-click on the icon and select *Properties*. As the administrator, deleting any icon from this folder deletes the printer definition for all users.

The Control Panels folder displays all the control-panel items discussed in Chapter 2. The Scheduled Tasks list is a link to the Tasks folder in the Windows directory. The Network Connections folder is a list of other network connections through a dial-up modem or through a direct serial connection to another computer. The Network Neighborhood is a list of other computers connected through a network-interface card, such as an Ethernet card.

System Files

System files for Win 2000 are kept in several locations. The majority of the configuration files, system applications, device drivers, and security data are stored under the \Winnt directory hierarchy. There are some files that go into the root directory of the boot drive: Boot.ini, Ntdetect, Ntldr, Io.sys, MSDOS.sys, and Pagefile.sys. The Boot information file (Boot.ini) is a plain-text file describing which drive and folder the system should boot from. NTDetect and NTldr (NT Loader) are used to bootstrap the operating system by checking the hardware configuration profile and loading the NT Executive. The Executive checks Io.sys for user I/O device information. MSDOS.sys exists simply to maintain backward compatibility and is mostly unused. Finally, the System Page file is stored as one large file as Pagefile.sys in the root directory for quick access.

With the integrated Web browser and desktop file system Explorer, there are some additional files which may from time to time appear in folders. These exist primarily to provide special properties to a folder or directory or to give a Weblike interface to the folder. The *folder.htt* is an HTML file describing the style and layout of the folder. Explorer sometimes has special buttons and commands associated with a folder that are defined in JScript (Microsoft's version of Javascript). Another file, called *desktop.ini*, describes special options and associations for that folder as specified within the system registry. For example, the folder might be associated with a special bitmap icon or an application.

The system is very particular about any files under the \Winnt directory. Moving or renaming any files in these directories can give the system a quick heart attack. Even innocuous-looking files that are 0 bytes long often serve a purpose. There are some data files you could probably do without in this area, but you have to know the difference between system files and nonsystem files. You should avoid touching the contents of these directories unless you are absolutely sure that you know what you're doing—and even then, ask your conscience.

You can tell many system files by their three-character file extensions (see Table 3.10). Microsoft user and system applications are often made up of many separate files and shared libraries, which can be strewn across the file system. It's gotten better in recent years, with an attempt to keep as much system information as possible in the \Winnt and \Winnt\System32 directories. To maintain backward compatibility, Microsoft and many application vendors still use these conventions for naming files. It's important you do not move or delete the files listed in Table 3.10—doing so may cause system instability and unpredictable behavior. Other files, listed in Table 3.11, are usually just data files that can be moved around as necessary.

Finally, there are some files that are maintained for backward compatibility with older applications. In the Windows 3.x days, the system did not use a registry at all. Instead, it used plain-text files to define the same

Table 3.10 Common Filename Extensions That Should Be Deleted, Renamed, or Moved Only with Caution

EXTENSION	FULL NAME	DESCRIPTION
386	Virtual Device Driver	32-bit device driver file.
ani	Animated Cursor Information	Animated cursor bitmap or information file.
bat	Batch	DOS script file.
com	Command	System executable file.
cpl	Control Panel	Control Panel extension file.
cur	Cursor Information	Cursor bitmap or information file.
dat	Data	Application data file (usually binary).
dll	Dynamically Linked Library	Application or system library loaded when the application is run.
drv	Driver	Standard device driver file.
exe	Executable	Binary executable file.
fon	Font	Older non-TrueType bitmap font file.
grp	Group	Group file of a set of applications in a window or in the Program Manager (Win 3.x).
icm	International Color Code module	Color description file for screens.
ico	Icon	Icon bitmap to be used by an application.
idf	MIDI Instrument Definition	Definition file for electronic musical instrument devices.
inf	Installation or Setup Information	Data file for application installation/setup.
ini	Initialization	File containing initialization parameters for an application or the system.
key	Registration key file	Application registration key to be stored in system registry.
log	Log file	Text-based log file for an application or the system.
ocx	OLE Control Extension	ActiveX (formerly called OLE) executable.
pif	Program Information File	System executable or application executable definition file.

Table 3.10 *(Continued)*

EXTENSION	FULL NAME	DESCRIPTION
reg	Registry	System Registry data file.
sys	System	System data file (either text or binary).
ttf	TrueType Font	Font information file.
vbx	Visual Basic Extension	Visual Basic executable file.
vxd	Virtual Device Driver	32-bit device driver file.

kind of information. Even some applications for NT 3.51 (which had a registry) still used these files. These files include the following:

Win.ini. Contains file associations, printer configurations, and systemwide variables.

System.ini. Contains system device driver information.

Control.ini. Contains desktop profile and control-panel information.

Protocol.ini. Contains network-protocol-specific configuration.

Lanman.ini. Contains NetBIOS service configuration.

Table 3.11 Common Filename Extensions That Can Usually Be Deleted, Renamed, or Moved Safely

EXTENSION	FULL NAME	DESCRIPTION
avi	Audio/Video Information	Microsoft's video file format.
cab	Cabinet	Microsoft Cabinet archive (similar to tar) of other files and directories.
doc	Microsoft Word Document	Microsoft Word document (may be any version of Word and not 100% compatible through all versions).
hlp	Help	File with usage or help instructions (like man pages).
htm	HTML	Web document.
lnk	Shortcut Link	File alias or soft link to another file or application.
scr	Screen Saver	Screen saver description and executable.
tmp	Temporary file	Temporary files created by applications.
txt	Plain text	Plain-text file.
wav	Wave Audio	Microsoft's audio file format.
zip	ZIP	ZIP archive file.

These still exist, although they are used very little. Since they are simple text files they can be read and modified directly by the system administrator. Sometimes configuring a device requires adding driver configuration information by hand, and any small errors to these files can cause the system to boot improperly. Most of these functions have been taken over by the registry now.

Summary

The Windows 2000 file system differs in structure and layout from NT 4.0 in many ways. The improvements to the design of the file system are to create a more secure and higher performing system needed for enterprise use. The storage locations of many system files have been renamed and moved about. Furthermore, new files have been added that contain new or additional content to support the new features.

The important new feature of dynamic disk partitions now allow NT file systems to be more easily manipulated by the system administrator while the system is running. Thus new volumes can be added, repartitioned, or removed without having to shut down the system from the users. This is another feature important to busy servers that need to run 24 by 7.

The NT file system differs entirely from that of UNIX. There is very little in common between the two. The file attributes are much more complex, and this does add overhead when accessing and manipulating the files. However, this also enhances the flexibility and manageability of files. The layered file system of NTFS allows other file systems to be built on top of it or into its structure. NTFS was designed with RAID systems in mind. Since these have become such a common part of enterprise server systems, the built-in RAID properties of NTFS make it easier to implement.

UNIX has always been hobbled in some part by the inflexibility of its file systems. To add new features or file system services, often a separate component has to be built and run in parallel to the existing file system. Another option is to build an entirely different file system, but this leaves you in a complex when it comes to compatibility issues.

Unlike UNIX, NTFS does not follow the metaphor of describing devices and other system objects as files. The file system is not overloaded with tasks it is not designed for, though it does make it more complex for the software developer to write code to access these devices.

Win 2000 file sharing continues to work with the Microsoft standard protocol that we will describe in more detail later: the Common Internet File System (CIFS). To this Win 2000 also adds DFS which brings the UNIX-like feature of combining many disks from different systems under one hierarchical structure. Such network sharing is covered in more detail in coming chapters.

Windows 2000 Networking

Windows 2000 is moving towards TCP/IP as its primary network protocol. It now formally supports the IP Security protocol as well as Dynamic Domain Name Service. However, it does not abandon its roots in NetBIOS, and neither does it leave behind support for other protocols such as Internet Packet Exchange (IPX), AppleTalk, and System Network Architecture (SNA). The networking architecture under Win 2000 also supports Layer 2 tunneling protocols to help create virtual private networks.

This chapter goes over some of the basics of networking simply because a lot of sysadmins are not familiar with the new network technologies that are implemented in Win 2000. These are fundamental changes to the way networking services are used, so to get it straight we will just run through the whole thing. This is followed by details of the service protocols that are specific to the Windows environment.

Windows Networking Concepts

Before we examine the architecture of the Windows networking system, there are a number of concepts and terms used in networking technology that you should review first. This is just a quick overview of general networking concepts and can apply to any number of different network protocol families, such as TCP/IP or IPX.

Packets, Datagrams, Connections, Circuits, and Sessions

Whenever you send data over the network you are temporarily using up a portion of the available bandwidth. To deliver application data between networks or deliver information over a network, computers have to agree on a common language or *protocol* on how they will establish communications between each other. There are common groups of protocols, which are organized into *protocol families*. Once the protocol is agreed upon, the two computers have to agree on how to deliver the actual data.

Each computer represents a communication *node*. Each node can identify other nodes on the network based on their network *addresses*. An address consists of two portions: the *network identifier* and the *node identifier*. The network ID indicates which network the node is a part of, and the node ID defines the unique address within that network for that node. These two terms are also sometimes referred to as the *network address* and the *node address*.

Every network in existence has a limit on how much data it can carry, known as its network *throughput* or its *bandwidth*. All the computers in a network share this bandwidth with each other. It is possible to evenly divide the network between all the computers and set up a permanent connection from one computer to every other one. However, this becomes incredibly inefficient even after only a handful of computers. A better way is to set up a temporary connection between one computer and the next for the duration of the data delivery.

Network applications within each node define communications *end-points* to communicate with other network applications. End-points are also often called *sockets*, or *ports*. In connection-oriented network communications, two applications initially negotiate and establish an agreement that they intend to communicate before a *connection* is established between them. In connectionless network communications, network applications can send information to other network applications without having to negotiate beforehand.

A *network path* defines the source and destination nodes and a list of intermediate network nodes that the data has to traverse to get from one application endpoint to the other. Each network node that the data traverses is also called a *hop*. When you consider a network path only in the context of the addresses and the intermediate nodes that it has to traverse, this is called a *network route*. A path also includes endpoint information.

You can send data either in pieces between two computers or in a continuous stream until all the data is delivered. A continuous stream is more likely to complete faster than little pieces, but for the duration of the stream's existence, that portion of the network bandwidth is not available for other computers. By breaking up the data into little pieces, and sending out a little at a time, you can more evenly share the bandwidth with other computers. The stream mechanism involves using a circuit and the individual pieces mechanism involves using packets. Conceptually, they are complementary.

A *packet* contains a finite amount of data. Each packet has a *header* and a *payload*. The header contains information about where the packet comes from, where it is going to, what kind of information it is carrying, and sometimes even instructions on how to handle this information. The payload is the actual data from an application that needs to be transmitted to another computer. The endpoints have to agree on how the packets are broken up and reassembled to maintain the consistency of the data between the source and destination endpoints.

A *circuit*, on the other hand, has a continuous stream of application data traveling from the source to the destination. Before the data delivery begins on a circuit, the two computers agree on what kind of information is being sent, how to handle it, and what to do with it when it arrives. Since there is a dedicated connection along the path between the source and destination nodes, the circuit does not need to pass too much information about the connection or even address information of the nodes. After the data is delivered, the circuit can sit around idly waiting for new data to transmit or be taken down to free up the bandwidth along the network path.

If you think about it, you can create a circuit out of packets as well, by simply sending the packets in sequence, one immediately after another. However, unless you deliver all the packets in a reliable, periodic fashion, packet networks do not necessarily guarantee that the packets will arrive in proper sequence. The good thing about a packet network is that if there is a temporary failure in part of the network and a number of packets are lost, you still have the other information and simply have to retransmit the missing portions. On a circuit network, once there is a failure in the network, you have to retransmit everything since the failure.

Another good thing about packet networks is that you can send the packets in parallel through several different paths or routes between the source and the destination endpoint. As long as the packets are sequenced, they can be reassembled to create the original data. If data on a circuit is to travel through separate routes, it must be broken up into several portions, in which case the circuit simply becomes an alternative form of the packet network.

Two network applications can communicate to each other in a *session*. A single session may involve one or more connections, either at the same time or at different times, until the two applications are done communicating. In packet-based networks, a session is an abstraction that implements circuits between endpoints over a packet mechanism.

Unicasting, Broadcasting, and Multicasting

In packet networks, there are three ways of communicating with other nodes. *Unicasting* is the process of communicating directly between the source computer and the destination computer. Unicast information is intended to be delivered only to the destination computer.

Broadcasting is the opposite of unicasting, in that it is a message sent to all the nodes on the same network. A broadcast message is usually sent when the node is trying to communicate with all others or wants to ask all the other nodes for a particular service. Nodes receiving a broadcast message can either ignore it or act upon the information. A client might use this, for example, as a means of discovering all the servers on the network; the client sends a broadcast message asking for servers to respond, and they do likewise. You cannot control who to send a broadcast message; it is sent to every node on the network.

Multicasting is similar to unicasting, but it supports communicating with more than one computer at the same time. This allows a small group of computers on a network to communicate with each other without having to broadcast this information to all the other nodes. Multicasting features greater security in where the information is directed, as well as tighter communications between applications within the group.

Circuit networks are normally either unicast or multicast. When a circuit is directly established between two nodes, you have a classic unicast system. Circuit networks often use a *hub* for multicast communications.

Windows 2000 Networking | 107

This may be a circuit switch or even a node. The hub acts as the central exchange for data between each of the nodes in the multicast group. Each node establishes a unicast connection to the hub directly. Hence, the multicast system is built on the model of several unicast sessions all connected into a central hub.

Communication Protocols

Protocols are how computers and applications communicate with each other. A network interface card (NIC) interacts with another NIC through a signaling mechanism, such as Ethernet. A NIC communicates with the OS kernel through a device driver interface. The kernel communicates with various network protocols through protocol stacks. And network protocol stacks communicate with user applications through presentation protocols.

Since they can communicate on several different levels, there are, appropriately, several levels of communications protocols. The typical model used to identify the type of the protocol is known as the *ISO protocol layer* system. You have probably seen this many times before, but it is presented in Figure 4.1. The ISO protocol layers are shown on the left,

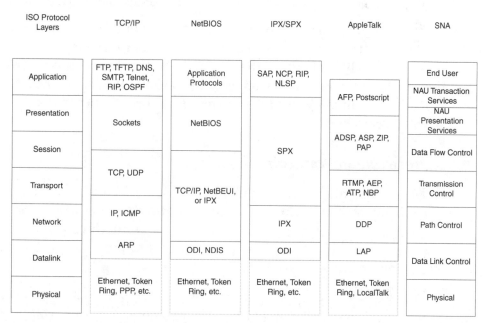

Figure 4.1 ISO protocol layers and other protocol families.

and compared against them are several popular network protocol families used with NT. Each protocol family is implemented in a *stack* on which application software is built.

Network Protocols

Network protocols provide the communications delivery mechanism between computers. The protocol systems on each machine have to be compatible for them to be able to communicate. If you look at the ISO protocol layers on the left-hand side of Figure 4.1, you will see a *Network layer*, a *Transport layer*, and a *Session layer*. Together these provide the mechanisms for establishing communications between machines and managing the delivery of data between them. They convert the data from applications into cells or packets appropriate for network delivery and manage how these packets are sent and received through the various network interfaces.

Network protocols are usually implemented as a privileged part of the operating system since they directly interact with network hardware devices. The OS normally handles the tasks of creating communications endpoints and managing network protocol activity. User applications interact through an intermediary *Presentation layer*. The *Windows Networking Architecture* section discusses specific network protocols.

Network protocols are used for direct communications between nodes, however, they can also be used to deliver other foreign protocols within themselves by embedding them as data. This system allows you to create virtual networks on top of existing real networks. In fact, this is a method commonly used to create virtual private networks, which we will discuss later.

Presentation Protocols

The Presentation layer implements communications endpoints that applications can use. Often called *interprocess communication* (IPC) mechanisms, they implement different data structures and concepts in computer science that allow programmers to build network communications software.

In the UNIX world, this is most commonly implemented in *sockets* (or *Berkeley sockets*, if you prefer). Using a socket, an application simply plugs into a direct communication channel with another application on a remote machine. In UNIX it sends data through the socket almost as if it were another file. The OS then handles the issues of taking the data pumped into the socket, creating memory buffers, establishing a network protocol session, sending the data, and so forth. Windows implements a number of different IPC mechanisms, including sockets, which the *Windows Network Architecture* section examines.

Application Protocols

Applications protocols are specialized to the needs of a particular application. These protocols are built either on approved standards, such as the Domain Name System (DNS) or Dynamic Host Configuration Protocol (DHCP), or they can be proprietary, such as Microsoft Windows Internet Name Service (WINS).

An application protocol uses IPC mechanisms to support a client/server application between two or more machines. The format and use of these protocols vary widely with the type of application in use. For example, the Telnet protocol establishes a terminal session on a remote server and defines how the text screen appears and how special keystrokes are to be interpreted. The FTP protocol defines how data is ordered either in ASCII or binary format for delivery between two platforms that might have different byte-ordering styles.

Application protocols can vaguely be categorized into *user application protocols* and *system application protocols*. User application protocols enable end-user applications to communicate across a network. They do not require special security requirements or management by the administrator. A system application protocol needs to be secure and managed only by an authorized system administrator since it affects the communications between two or more operating systems.

The differentiating factor between these two types of protocols is in how their services are advertised. Client applications on one machine look for an appropriate server application on another machine through advertised endpoints or ports. Each port is unique and identified either with a name or a number. The server application sits on a specific port waiting for an incoming request from a client. When the server receives a request on the advertised port, it either services the client completely, if the communication is very brief, or tells it to use a different port, if the client and server are to communicate for some time. In either case, the server needs to keep the port open so that other clients can contact it if necessary.

These advertised ports are a limited resource; there can be thousands of them, but when a port is used by one server application, it can't be allocated to another, which is a limiting factor. Most network systems have common applications that are available in every implementation. On UNIX these include applications such as Telnet, FTP, and so forth. Each of these applications uses a common set of standardized *well-known ports*. This way, a Telnet client will always be able to connect to a Telnet server using the default well-known port (port number 23).

It is quite possible to set up secondary Telnet servers on other ports rather than port 23, but the client application has to know in advance that the server is on a different port. Well-known ports are used by system applications and their protocols. Services running on other ports are typically user applications.

Name Resolution

We fallible humans use a name system to identify computers on the network since it is harder for us to remember sequences of numbers. Computers, on the other hand, prefer numbers, which they handle mathematically and procedurally much faster. The original developers of TCP/IP hit upon an effective mechanism to resolve this issue: simply have both and translate between them. This translation process between a network name and its representative numerical address is known as *name resolution.*

Most network protocols today provide some form of name resolution. Computers have *node names* and *node addresses* and belong to specific *network domains* or areas of authority. In plain English, each computer is part of a network (a subdomain) within an organization (the domain). Domains are logical groupings that do not necessarily have to reflect a specific local area network. However, we use the term *virtual network* or *domain* to refer to a group of computer nodes that is not part of the local network.

For each network protocol that supports node names, there is a system service known as the *network name resolver*. In TCP/IP this is known as the *Domain Name System* (DNS) service. NetBIOS maintains a name table for each interface; name resolution is based on broadcasting a query to all members on the network and waiting to receive a response from one of the nodes.

Most name translations are one to one; that is, each node name translates to one node address. Name resolution can be *static*, where each name always translates to the same address. Or it can be *dynamic*, where a name can translate into different addresses at different times. In TCP/IP there is also the concept of *virtual names* or *addresses*, where a single node name can translate to multiple addresses. Virtual names allow multiple mapping, and the resolution system has to decide whether to give one address or multiple ones.

Routing

Routing is the process of directing network traffic between the source and destination of a network connection. When you establish a network connection between nodes, you need to define how these packets are to travel from one machine to the other. This is usually a function of the network protocol layer.

As indicated earlier, there are two ways to establish a connection. On one hand, you can decide, when initially establishing the connection, how the data is to flow and the path it is to flow along; that is, you establish a circuit between the two machines. On the other hand, you can set up the connection and simply provide the destination address and all the options on how the data is to flow with each and every unit of data; that is, you set up packet communications between the machines.

On an abstract conceptual level, both forms of connections perform routing, but in practice, a circuit-based connection is said to be *switched*, while a packet-based connection is said to be *routed*. It takes less effort to deliver information on a switched network since the network nodes, which deliver the information, do not have to process each and every piece of data, unlike the routers of a packet network. However, packet networks do not have to dedicate a portion of their bandwidth to a circuit, leaving more for other connections.

Routing in packet networks is usually based on including the source and destination nodes' addresses within the packet. Each device along the network path, called a *router*, examines this information and decides where to send it based on a predefined set of rules or *routing policies*. A router normally looks at the network ID portion of the node's address to decide where to send it. If it recognizes this network ID as its own, it will send it to a machine that is directly connected to the router over a LAN.

On the other hand, if the router sees that the network ID is elsewhere, it checks its routing policies to determine which other router to send the packet to. The other router then sends it to a directly-connected node on its own network. This way, routers forward packets from one network to another until they reach their appropriate destination.

Routers can be manually assigned routing policies, or they can attempt to discover new routes themselves. Manually assigned routes, or *static routes*, are directly entered into the routers' policy or table of route entries. If a network does not change very much, then static routing works well. However, if the network has been reconfigured in any way, each of these static routes has to be changed manually to reflect the new configuration.

To avoid this, you can set up *dynamic routing*, which automatically takes care of discovering routes between sites. Dynamic routing uses special routing protocols to distribute the routing information about each network. Since static route tables are cumbersome to maintain and lack means of fault-tolerance, there are dynamic routing protocols that allow routers to automatically inform others of their network route information.

There are two levels of dynamic routing protocols: *interior* and *exterior gateway protocols*. An interior gateway protocol distributes routing information within a single intranet or company network. In routing terminology, this intranet is referred to commonly as an *autonomous system* (AS) and these protocols are called *intra-AS protocols*.

When you have a network system such as the Internet, where there are lots of separate independent networks connected together that are owned and controlled by separate companies and organizations, you need to set up dynamic routing systems at each point where you connect with another organization's network. Since you have no control over the network configuration within the other organization's network, you have to resort to dynamic routing protocols to receive routing information from them as well as to share your own routing information, so that nodes on your network can communicate with nodes on theirs, and vice versa. Between such large networks there are exterior gateway protocols, which allow communications between individual AS networks with more bandwidth and in an administratively efficient manner.

Quality of Service

Quality of service (QoS) is an old concept in networking but is only now being implemented in some network protocols. A QoS system absolutely guarantees that computers on a network will be able to communicate with each other at a certain security, management, route, or speed level. QoS implies that some communications on the network will run at a higher priority than others.

IBM's System Networking Architecture (SNA) implements QoS at various levels, but most other protocols, including TCP/IP and IPX/SPX, are *best-effort* delivery systems. In a best-effort system, the delivery of network packets is not guaranteed, and the computers and the networks make the best possible effort to deliver packets from the source to the destination. Best-effort networks don't even guarantee that a packet will be delivered at all. A packet may encounter trouble somewhere along the network path, which results in it getting mangled or lost. Network protocols that support best-effort often have to rely on higher-level constructs for redelivering lost packets. For example, IP is a best-effort protocol that does not guarantee reliable delivery of a packet; however, using the TCP transport-layer protocol, a session between two endpoints can check to see if any packets have been lost along the way and redeliver them if necessary.

Service quality focuses on optimizing several vectors: *secure delivery, predetermined routes, priority delivery,* and *delivery management information collection.* With secure delivery, the idea is to encrypt the contents within each packet so that they cannot be viewed by any user or computer other than the intended destination. With predetermined routes, you guarantee that the data will travel along only the authorized network path. This comes in handy in TCP/IP, where routers can send packets along multiple paths to provide their best effort service, even for the same network connection. Priority delivery implies that the information on one network channel should be delivered before that on others. Finally, delivery management information collection makes sure that when data is delivered, all the statistics for delivery times, paths, and quantity are collected for later analysis.

Not all these QoS features can be implemented easily. Since networks are a limited resource that cost money to operate, implementing QoS may mean upgrading computers and routers on a wide scale. On the network protocol level, QoS can require changes to the fundamental structure of the protocol, or it can be implemented in a best-guess fashion based on delivery history between two endpoints. IPv6, for example, is a new version of IP that implements QoS by changing the overall structure of the network protocol packet and requiring that every router on the network services these changes appropriately.

QoS has also been implemented over the current generation of TCP/IP using the best-guess method. Since the protocol is in such wide use, it is unlikely that you will be able to get everyone to agree to change to something like IPv6 in a short period of time. Thus, based on the unreliable delivery of IPv4 (the current generation), a secondary protocol known as the *Resource Reservation Protocol* (RSVP) keeps track of delivery history and negotiates with routers along the network path to try to provide the best QoS possible under the circumstances. You would think this method would fail, but it actually works very well for an intranet. It's when you have to consider delivery over the Internet that it starts becoming unreliable.

There are several different ways to implement QoS in your network. The first method involves implementing QoS features into the routers on your network, called *network-centric* or *network-only QoS*. This allows routers to define QoS parameters between connections. End nodes connected to the router can rely on a certain level of QoS from the network. The second method requires implementing QoS in the operating system and possibly the NIC of each client, as well as in all the routers. Since this implies that each node can provide direct QoS to every other implemented node, this is called *node-to-node QoS*. A third level implies implementing QoS directly at the application level at each node, as well as within the OS and the network. This means developing code that uses QoS APIs within the operating system to establish QoS down to the point of the application. This method is known as *application-to-application QoS*.

Network Booting

Network booting is the ability to boot the operating system of a client stored on a server elsewhere on the network. This process usually involves two phases. In the first phase, the client has to create a temporary identity and broadcast a request to find a *boot server*. The boot server then contacts the client and assigns a full address identity. In the second phase, the client downloads (or the server sends to the client) a copy of the boot image of the operating system for the client.

The network boot process requires enough software on the client to send out a network boot request. This is usually implemented in a pre-OS, a miniature system application that is either embedded directly onto a network card or stored on the local hard drive or floppy drive. Since network boot clients typically have either small hard drives or none at all, the most common options are either a boot PROM directly on the NIC or a special boot floppy disk.

A network boot request comes across only once per client, when first turned on. Clients typically do not periodically check with the server to see if the boot image has changed. However, in some cases, the address information supplied by the server may expire and may need to be renegotiated.

Windows Network Architecture

The Windows networking architecture is built on the OSI model but the actual layers overlap each other quite often (see Figure 4.2). This is due to the fact that Windows supports many different networking protocol families, which may or may not implement similar concepts in a network. In addition, there is backward compatibility support on many levels so that older Windows network applications will run within the existing framework.

Windows supports all the protocols shown earlier in Figure 4.1; that is, it supports TCP/IP, IPX, NetBEUI, AppleTalk, and SNA, using either default built-in components or optional products and packages. In NT 4.0, there is a lot of reliance on NetBIOS services running on top of other protocols. With Win 2000, there has been a move away from relying on NetBIOS, which suffers in performance in larger networks, and toward TCP/IP, which has been successfully deployed on the largest network in the world, the Internet. Similarly, there has been a move away from the use of NetBIOS-associated presentation protocols and toward the non-protocol-family-specific Windows sockets system.

According to Figure 4.2, there are basically five groups of protocols or layers: the *data-link layer*, the *network/transport/session layer*, the *presentation layer*, the *application protocol layer*, and the *applications* themselves.

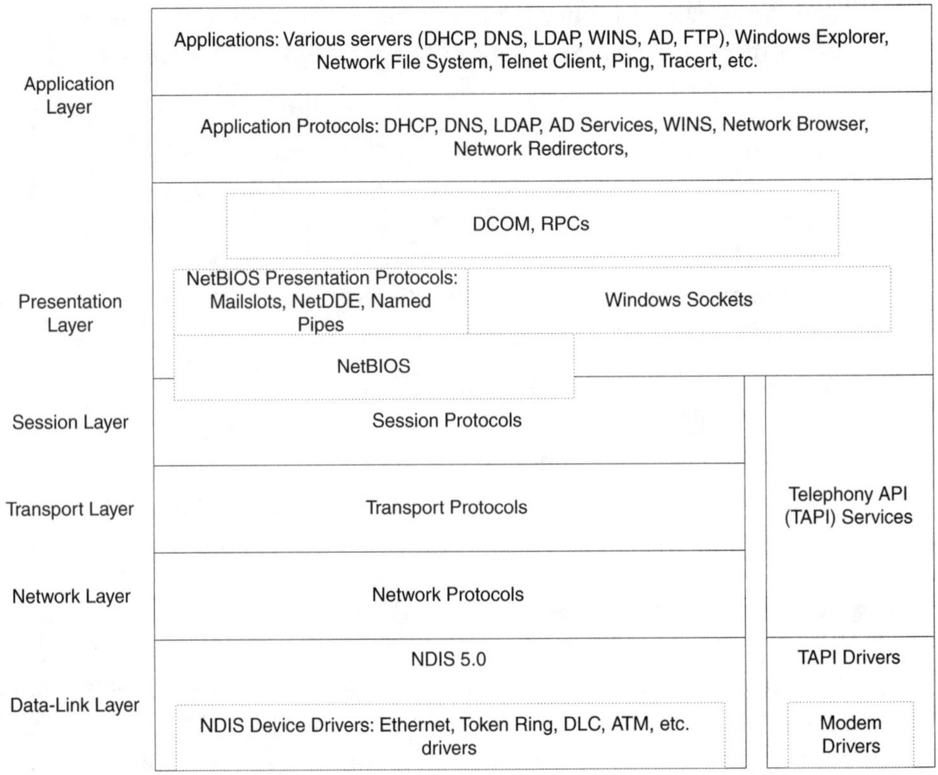

	Applications: Various servers (DHCP, DNS, LDAP, WINS, AD, FTP), Windows Explorer, Network File System, Telnet Client, Ping, Tracert, etc.	
Application Layer	Application Protocols: DHCP, DNS, LDAP, AD Services, WINS, Network Browser, Network Redirectors,	
	DCOM, RPCs	
Presentation Layer	NetBIOS Presentation Protocols: Mailslots, NetDDE, Named Pipes	Windows Sockets
	NetBIOS	
Session Layer	Session Protocols	Telephony API (TAPI) Services
Transport Layer	Transport Protocols	
Network Layer	Network Protocols	
Data-Link Layer	NDIS 5.0	TAPI Drivers
	NDIS Device Drivers: Ethernet, Token Ring, DLC, ATM, etc. drivers	Modem Drivers

Figure 4.2 Windows network architecture.

Network Device Drivers

Network device drivers under Windows implement the Network Driver Interface Specification (NDIS). This allows the OS kernel to communicate with the different device drivers written for each NIC through a common interface. NICs support a variety of different network signaling protocols, including Ethernet, Token Ring, Fibre-Channel, ATM, and even modems (although technically they aren't NICs). Each of these signaling protocols works differently and has different capacities, but in the end all do the same thing: They take data contained in memory buffers, format it into a packet, add network-protocol-specific information, and deliver the information. Receiving data works similarly except in reverse. The kernel needs to check the NIC to see if it is ready to deliver more information, or if information is waiting for it.

There are actually two competing standards for this network driver interface. A third type of driver standard, known as *packet drivers*, is no longer significant under Win 95, NT, or Win 2000. Other than NDIS, Novell also created its own driver system, known as the *Open Driver Interface* (ODI). These other drivers are primarily used for NetWare clients and servers but work under Windows just as well. The architecture of the device driver is different, but ODI serves the exact same purpose. Some NIC vendors claim better performance under ODI than NDIS.

The only difference that comes into play is when the protocol stack is looking for a specific type of driver. NetWare's IPX/SPX stack will typically look for an ODI driver, while Microsoft's TCP/IP and NetBEUI stacks look for NDIS drivers. Microsoft has also implemented its own IPX/SPX stack, called *NWLink*, which runs on top of NDIS drivers.

In any case, each driver specification can emulate the others through a *shim*. If you install a protocol stack that needs an alternative driver interface, you can install a shim that emulates that interface on top of your current driver specification. So far, ODI can emulate NDIS drivers up to version 4. NDIS version 4 drivers can similarly emulate ODI drivers. Under Win 2000, which uses NDIS 5.0 drivers, you can emulate the appropriate ODI drivers as well, but there is yet to be an NDIS 5 shim for ODI, since it is so new.

NICs that implement standards such as Ethernet and Token Ring use low-level addresses that have been preassigned to the NIC. These are called *hardware network addresses* and usually conform to an address format defined by the NIC manufacturer. The IEEE has standardized this level of networking and has organized the format of these addresses into the *Media Access Control* (MAC) layer; each addresses is known as a *MAC address*. If you are familiar with Ethernet addresses, then you have seen at least one type of MAC address. The IEEE MAC address format is 48 bits long and usually is represented in a hexadecimal format, for example, 02:a2:b2:38:90:2f.

MAC address information is used to identify on the hardware level individual computers on a LAN. Each computer maintains a mapping between a MAC address and a network protocol address in various ways. For example, TCP/IP uses the Address Resolution Protocol (ARP) and Reverse ARP (RARP) to translate between MAC and IP addresses. The IPX protocol, on the other hand integrates the MAC address directly into its network-layer protocol address, which allows NetWare client systems to automatically configure their address information.

MAC-layer address information is nonroutable and valid only within a specific LAN. Although uncommon, it is possible to reassign the MAC addresses at the operating system level, which sometimes leads to having the same MAC address on multiple networks. Once a higher-level network protocol traverses a router, the MAC address information is no longer pertinent.

Network Protocol Families

Win 2000 supports a number of protocols, in particular, IP, NetBEUI, IPX, AppleTalk, and SNA DLC. In addition, Microsoft has a separate application that is part of the BackOffice Suite, called *SNA Server 4.0*, that provides greater support for the SNA protocols. This book primarily discusses connectivity through the IP protocols, but we will also look at some of these other protocols and how they interact with different applications.

TCP/IP

TCP/IP or IP version 4 (IPv4) is the current king of protocols on the Internet and in most enterprise networks. Developed originally for the U.S. Department of Defense, TCP/IP has been part of UNIX for decades now. On Windows systems, it only started becoming the preferred protocol once Microsoft released a protocol stack for their Windows for Workgroups product. It is now the standard network protocol for most Windows networks, and even Win 2000 is moving away from using other non-IP-related transport, presentation, and application protocols.

Unlike protocols such as IPX and NetBEUI, IPv4 addresses are not based on the MAC hardware address. IPv4 follows a 32-bit addressing scheme for every node. Theoretically this would allow up to 2^{32} or 4 billion or so different addresses. Each address is normally noted in 4 sets of 8 bits written in decimal numbers for readability, for example, 216.19.15.10 or 198.102.68.2. Although computers still just see this as a 32-bit value, this *dotted decimal notation* is much easier to remember by us lowly humans. This partitioning into 8 bits also has a historical significance in how addresses and routing used to work on the Internet.

Addressing and Routing IP

When IP was originally designed, IP networks were divided into several classes, defined by these first few bits. This broke the flat address space into one level of hierarchy. Every node would have a network ID and a node ID. This allowed each company or organization to have its own network of addresses that it could assign node IDs from. The Internet Addressing and Naming Authority (IANA) would be responsible only for assigning the network ID to the organization. The network ID was further partitioned into *classes*, which gave varying numbers of node IDs or addresses to an organization.

The three most popular classes, A, B, and C, each had different capacities for the number of networks and node addresses there could be. Companies requesting Internet addresses would be assigned a Class A, B, or C network based on the number of nodes they needed to support. Table 4.1 shows the distribution of addresses across these classes.

The class-based method of addressing isn't used on the Internet anymore since they were running out of addresses due to the inefficiency of this address distribution system. For a time some vendors offered *network address translators* (NATs) as the general-purpose solution. Each company would install its own NAT, which would keep a private address space that would not be valid on the general Internet address. When communicating with computers outside the private space, the NAT would translate the private address into a valid public address. Each company would then get only a small Class C network of public addresses. This made some sense because not every computer within a company needs access to the Internet. However, this still didn't solve the problem in the case of an Internet service provider (ISP), which would need to allow practically every address within its space with a public address to satisfy its customers.

Replacing the class-based system is the *classless interdomain routing* (CIDR) system, which partitions the address space more efficiently. Under the old system, companies would get large blocks of addresses in Class A or B and end up never using all the addresses, leading to a lot of

Table 4.1   The Old Class-Based IP Addressing Scheme

CLASS	BITS IN NETWORK ID	TOTAL NETWORKS	BITS IN NODE ID	NODES PER NETWORK
A	8	128	24	16,777,216
B	16	16,384	16	65,536
C	24	2,097,152	8	256

wasted address space. With CIDR, the address space is partitioned by bits. For example, a company could be assigned a /16 CIDR block, indicating that the first 16 bits constitute its network address and the next 16 would be individual addresses for nodes. This is technically the same as a Class B network.

With CIDR, on the other hand, the network space can be partitioned more effectively. For example, a small 10-person company could be assigned a /28 block, indicating that they have about 4 bits of addressable nodes, that is, 2^4 or 16 addresses. An ISP for a small city might get a larger block of size /18, giving them a total of 2^{14} or 16,384 addresses which they can in turn subpartition to their own Internet customers. The customers might get small subpartitions of anywhere between a /31 and a /19 block, giving them a total of 2 to 8192 addressable nodes, respectively, that they borrow from the address space of the ISP.

With CIDR address partitioning, routing of addresses becomes more complicated, however. With the old system, there were three classes and every router had to check three bits at the very head of the address space to determine the network class and then match the network number against a table. On the Internet, this had a side effect. The tables of information that each router had to maintain started growing to huge proportions which, in turn, slowed down overall routing on the Internet and required ISPs to purchase larger and larger expensive routers.

With CIDR partitioning, each router keeps a list of *aggregate routes*, that is, all the possible routes to networks and addresses within its block. For example, an ISP with the address 192.168.0.0/16 block owns the aggregate space of addresses below it, that is, all the addresses between 198.32.0.0 to 192.168.255.255. Top-level routers of the Internet simply maintain the highest-level blocks of addresses between /3 and /8. This keeps the total number of entries within their tables to a lower amount of at most 256. Compare this against the 42,000 entries or so that they used to have to maintain back before 1996.

CIDR essentially breaks up the responsibility of routing more evenly across all the routers on the Internet. If your company has an external router that links to the Internet, you most likely have a CIDR block of your own. If the internal network space is not kept private or firewalled from the outside Internet, then it's possible that each desktop node on your network has a legal Internet node address.

Within a private network, you can also define further subnetworks using the *subnet mask*. This was developed originally with the class-based system to allow a company to further subdivide its address space. The mask essentially works the same as CIDR blocks, although it is notated differently. A mask is a set of bits that differentiates one subnetwork from another in dotted decimal notation, indicating which bits designate the network ID.

For example, a 192.168.0.0/22 block, which has a total possible address space of 1024 nodes, could be broken up into 4 separate subnetworks of 256 nodes each or 16 separate networks of 64 nodes each. To break it up into 4 networks, the subnets would have masks of 255.255.252.0 for the first one, 255.255.253.0 for the second, 255.255.254.0 for the third, and 255.255.255.0 for the fourth. Subnet masks do not mean anything to networks and nodes outside of the CIDR block since addresses within any of the subnets simply fall into the same block. External nodes simply send packets to the main router for that CIDR block and let it deal with them appropriately. The reason to use subnet masks rather than CIDR blocks is that they use simpler protocols.

There are several dynamic routing protocols for IP used in intranets, and a different set for the Internet. The *Routing Information Protocol* (RIP) distributes the contents of routing tables between routers. This way each router sends routing information on networks that it services to its adjacent routers. The routers each maintain routes to networks and routers immediately adjacent to them but not necessarily any beyond those. Using the information in routing tables, routers are able to send a packet to its destination by forwarding it to the next closest router along the network path. RIP packets are broadcast every 30 seconds or so, so that adjacent routers will know if a network or router goes down or is unreachable. Version 2 of RIP enhances the standard by replacing the broadcasting system with direct *multicasting* between routers, if multicast IP is installed on the network. This transfers route traffic more efficiently across the network. Furthermore RIPv2 also supports CIDR blocks and net masks, and password-based authentication, which are both expected of most modern routers.

The *open shortest path first* (OSPF) routing protocol is more advanced than RIP, in that it maintains a map of the network at every router. This map, stored on the *link-state database*, defines how packets can travel from one network to another in the shortest calculated route. This is an advantage over RIP, which does not provide any services for declaring shortest routes and may inadvertently suffer from endless loops within the network created across several routers.

OSPF uses an algorithm known as *shortest path first*, which establishes an optimal route between one network and another by going to the nearest router (the one with the least delay) first. It uses this principle to try to create a map of routes between the two networks; when all the routes are defined, it selects the route with the least overall amount of delay. This algorithm works very quickly for small intranets but can take a lot of time or processing to determine optimal routes on large networks.

OSPF-routed networks are defined within an *autonomous system* (AS). This normally marks the boundary of responsibility for the network within one company. It is subdivided into separate *areas* and *backbone areas*, for each internal LAN or network, and each backbone network for routers, respectively. The areas are interconnected by means of *area border routers* (ABRs) to a backbone area.

Both OSPF and RIP are intranet or *interior gateway protocols*, and they are ineffective on something the scale of the Internet. OSPF can work on larger networks more effectively but requires more computation resources than RIP. These protocols may even be ineffective within your network if you have a particularly large one. For these cases, there are *exterior gateway protocols* that aggregate entire networks at a time and send their information to their peer routers on the Internet. This is a fairly complex topic which is beyond the scope of this book. You may wish to read good network routing books such as *Interconnections, 2nd Edition*, by Radia Perlman (Addison-Wesley, 1999).

Packet Disassembly, Reassembly, and Fragmentation

On the application protocol or presentation protocol level, data is not necessarily stored in sizes that fit into IP packets. For most cases, the largest possible IP packet is 64KB. However, if you need to send 1MB, you are certainly going to need a larger payload size than that. The protocol stack thus decides to disassemble the 1MB file into numerous smaller packets of 1500 bytes each for transmission on an Ethernet, for example. An identification number exists within each IP packet to denote its portion of the entire message. The node on the receiving end lines up the packets by identification number and then reassembles the entire message.

To ensure that the header information of a packet has not been scrambled due to some error along the way, each packet has a *header checksum* that acts as a parity value for the header. When a node receives the packet, it computes a mathematical function to generate a checksum and compares it against the header checksum value. If the values match, the packet is fine; if not, the packet is discarded. The receiving node, however, does not ask the sending node to retransmit the packet and leaves this function to higher-level protocols.

IP packets, however, are not of a fixed size. In fact, packets can be broken up into smaller packets and later reassembled to their original size. This process is known as *fragmentation*. It occurs because networks of different types can send out different sizes of packets. An Ethernet packet can contain up to about 1500 bytes of data, whereas a dial-up modem line typically sends out 256-byte packets; other WAN links have similar differences in packet sizes.

A packet traveling from a source to a destination node may traverse several different types of networks. Rather than supporting the smallest size of hardware network packet that is most likely to always get through in one piece, it is easier to dynamically break up or assemble packets while en route. When the packets reach the router on the other side of a section of the network path, the router checks the packet size of the next segment of the network and may decide to combine several of the smaller pieces together or cut them down even smaller. This fragmentation process works on a lower level than data payload disassembly and reassembly.

Higher-Level and Other IP Protocols

IP itself is only a network protocol capable of delivering packets of information between one machine and the next, in a nonguaranteed fashion. The *Internet Control Message Protocol* (ICMP) was designed as a sort of management and control protocol to determine the state of IP networks. It is actually a special type of the IP protocol that uses different headers and does not normally include a data payload. ICMP is used in applications such as *traceroute* and *ping*, to determine the network path between the source and destination nodes and the amount of time it takes for packets to travel between them, respectively.

Several higher-level protocols are also part of the IP family: TCP and UDP. The *Transmission Control Protocol* (TCP) is a connection-oriented protocol between two IP nodes. It establishes a session and guarantees the ordered delivery of packets between the two nodes by keeping sequence numbers for every packet it sends. If packets arrive out of sequence, they are simply rearranged before the actual data payload is reassembled. In addition, if some packets are lost along the way, the destination node informs the source of the missing sequences and they are retransmitted by the source. Every packet in a TCP session travels from one endpoint or port to another. These port numbers define separate sessions between two nodes, possibly by several applications or users communicating between the nodes.

To set up a TCP session, the initiating client first opens its port and sends out a *connection synchronize* packet to the receiving server, containing the initial sequence number of the packets that it will be sending. The server then responds with a *synchronize packet received* message, sends a sequence number for packets coming from its direction, and opens the port on its side. When the client receives this message, it recognizes that the connection has been established and starts sending the packets sequenced as both sides have agreed.

To close a TCP session, the client first sends a *session close* message to the server and waits to receive an acknowledgment from the server. When the server receives this close message, it sends an close acknowledgment. The client receives this acknowledgment and waits for a short period of time until the last sequenced packets sent before the close was initiated have been received. When these packets have been sent by the server, the server port sends one last acknowledgment and then closes its side. Upon receiving this last acknowledgment, the client closes its side, as well.

The *User Datagram Protocol* (UDP) is a connectionless and nonguaranteed delivery mechanism that serves as a very basic application data delivery system. In essence, UDP exists simply to create one level of separation between the network and application layers. UDP is technically sessionless but still has port numbers to differentiate between different UDP applications. Applications that use UDP must create their own session-based protocol, if needed.

Above TCP and UDP, other presentation and application protocols can exist, such as the sockets system or the Telnet protocol, but technically these are not part of the IP protocol family, which focuses on network and transport protocols. You can have a TCP/IP protocol stack that does not implement these higher-level protocols, but in every case, the product must implement at least TCP, UDP, IP, and ICMP. Nonetheless, some of these protocols have been defined and standardized by the Internet Engineering Task Force responsible for all IP protocols.

If you wish to learn more about the details of TCP/IP protocols, pick up *TCP/IP Illustrated*, volume 1 by W. Richard Stevens (Addison-Wesley 1995), or *Internetworking with TCP/IP*, volume 1, 4th Edition by Douglas Comer (Prentice Hall, 2000). They give a detailed description of exactly what TCP/IP packets look like, as well as how they work.

IPv6

IP version 6 (IPv6) is the newest version of this protocol family. It has been worked on for several years, and there are implementations of IPv6 protocol stacks available for a number of platforms, but it is far from becoming popular despite its potential.

IPv6 significantly improves the structure of the basic IP protocol. First, it increases the overall address space available in a TCP/IP network. Under the older 32-bit address structure, the total address space available across the Internet is somewhere along the several hundred million addresses range. Believe it or not, we are actually approaching an exhaustion of this address space. IPv6 expands the address structure to 128 bits, allowing for trillions of trillions of trillions of addresses; the actual number allows for thousands of IP network devices per square foot of space on Earth.

The IPv6 address format is notated slightly differently from that for IPv4 addresses simply because it is shorter than dotted decimal notation. IPv6 addresses are notated in 8 pairs of 16-bit numbers, and each 16-bit value is notated in hexadecimal. For example, the value:

01BB:1B28:7004:3110:DA10:D3B1:C61C:0122

would be the equivalent of:

1.187.27.40.112.4.49.16.218.16.211.177.198.32.1.34

You can also denote IPv4 dotted decimal numbers within the IPv6 format as follows:

::198.32.1.34

The two colons before it indicate that it is an IPv4 address.

Although the address assignment policy for IPv6 has been changing since 1996, several of the first few bits have been reserved. Unlike the problem with IPv4 classes, taking 4 to 8 bits out of 128 will not cause a significant shortfall in address spaces, at least hopefully not for several generations from now.

IPv6 introduces new options that allow protocol stack vendors and router manufacturers to implement QoS. The IPv6 packet header is an extensible to include other optional headers for establishing per-packet security, defining network path or flow control, embedding routing protocols, or embedding other network protocols within IPv6.

It is unlikely that you will use IPv6 in the next few years. Although it is available for UNIX systems and Windows, a tiny fraction of a percent of the Internet implements it. You are free to try to implement it within your intranet, but the procedures for assigning address space in IPv6 have not yet been determined. In addition, you may be stuck with a lot of experimental software implementations for your routers and computers, and find support from vendors lacking.

NetBIOS and NetBEUI

The *NetBIOS Environment User Interface* (NetBEUI), also called the *NetBIOS Frames* protocol, was developed by IBM in the 1980s as a basic networking system for small LANs. NetBIOS itself is a presentation-layer programming interface and uses NetBEUI or other protocols as the transport and network layers.

NetBEUI was designed for small LANs. It provides automatic addressing of computers on the network using MAC addresses. The protocol is non-routable, and although it can be bridged across larger networks, it uses up a lot of network bandwidth. It is usually hard to consider NetBEUI as a protocol by itself since it exists only to support one higher-level protocol, NetBIOS. Thus we consider them both together here.

NetBIOS maps on top of the transport- and network-layer protocol by using *LANA numbers*. These numbers originally identified which NIC was to be used for a given NetBIOS session. The NetBIOS 3.0 specification, the last one defined, indicates that only two LANA number values, 0 and 1, can be used. This is because the original IBM networking system only supported up to two NICs. With the use of other protocols, Microsoft has extended the meaning of the LANA number from identifying a NIC to identifying a transport- and network-layer protocol. It is now possible to have up to six LANA numbers (three network protocols with two adapters each).

You can have up to 254 separate connected sessions per each LANA number. The NetBIOS *local session number* (LSN) identifies each of these sessions separately. The LSN is very much like the concept of a port in TCP/IP.

NetBIOS name resolution maintains a name table for each LANA number that maps 16-byte names to appropriate network-layer addresses. To resolve an unknown name to an address, an application broadcasts the NetBIOS command NCBFINDNAME on a LANA interface and waits for an answer. The node that has registered that name responds. If more than one node responds with the same name, then it is up to the application to decide on the appropriate computer to connect to. On large-scale networks, this system generates much more traffic that it really needs to.

This broadcast name lookup method is fairly inefficient but still exists in NetBIOS systems set up as *broadcast nodes* (B-nodes). To replace this method, Windows has a NetBIOS name service system, the Windows Internet Name Service (WINS). Each client or *peer node* (P-node) is configured to query the WINS server for the name mappings, just as IP hosts query a DNS server. Most Windows clients are configured as *hybrid nodes* (H-nodes) when they first attempt to resolve a name through the WINS server, before they try the broadcast method of name lookup.

IPX/SPX

When Novell created its NetWare operating system, it also built the Internet Packet Exchange (IPX) protocol family as the network, transport, and application protocol mechanism. It served as the protocol system of choice up to version 4 of the operating system. With the release of version 5.0 in 1998, NetWare has moved over to TCP/IP in the network and transport layer with new IP-based implementations of its applications protocols.

Still, the majority of NetWare networks run IPX. Windows can use IPX as its default protocol mechanism and run its NetBIOS application services on top of it. With Win 2000 this is no longer as significant, but there is a strong likelihood that you may need to integrate NetWare clients and servers into your Windows network, as well.

IPX is a network-layer protocol designed for the LAN. It uses MAC addresses within its full network node address format, allowing IPX clients to be automatically configured with network address information. Like IP, it provides nonreliable delivery of data at the network level between nodes and supports routing across multiple networks.

IPX packets have been traditionally set to a fixed size of 576 bytes, 30 bytes of which constitute the IPX header. This is a throwback to really old networking hardware systems that only supported sending packets of this maximum size. The IPX header included the source and destination network address, the node address, and the socket number. The network address is an assigned number for each IPX network, whereas the node address is actually the same as the machine's MAC address. Unlike IP and more like UDP, IPX includes the port or socket number within the network-layer protocol. This allows programmers to use IPX directly to establish communications with a network application on another node. Thus, IPX can also be considered a transport-layer service for nonguaranteed data delivery.

On top of IPX is the Sequenced Packet Exchange (SPX), which builds sequenced guaranteed packet delivery services on top of IPX. It supports creating a session between two computers and allows for retransmitting lost packets. An SPX connection can send session-control commands within the session through a variable called the *data stream type*. This determines not only the packet type (system application, user application, etc.) but also control signals for closing the circuit.

Routing in IPX is based on keeping tables of all the IPX networks connected. Each IPX router communicates its network information with adjoining routers using the *Routing Information Protocol* (RIP). Based on this information, routers can determine the distance, measured in hops, between routers, as well as the time delay it takes to get to a node on another network. The IPX router looks at the destination address information within the packet and compares it against the routing table. If the node is directly connected, it sends it out on the locally attached network; if not, it forwards it to the next router along the path.

Another protocol, known as the *NetWare Link State Protocol* (NLSP), provides route information between networks similarly to OSPF. It distributes information directly between routers (unicast as opposed to RIP broadcast), the metrics needed to define an optimal route.

IPX supports a common *service advertising protocol* (SAP) that indicates to a client where different services are located. It describes where print servers, file servers, job servers, archive servers, gateways, time synchronization servers, NetWare access servers, and so forth are all located. When a server joins the network, it broadcasts an *SAP identity packet* informing other servers on the network what kind of services it provides. When a client joins the network it can query for available services by sending out an *SAP query packet*. Unlike the TCP/IP system, where there are separate name resolution and service lookup protocols, SAP provides a distributed mechanism that works very well on LANs.

Finally, at the top level for user authentication, file access, printer access, administration services, and, in general, communicating between clients and servers, the IPX family includes the *NetWare Core Protocol* (NCP). Most system network applications and administration services use NCP.

Unfortunately, the IPX family's use of broadcasting in RIP and SAP is far too noisy on a large WAN and would generate unnecessary traffic in networks that did not require it. This is what particularly limits its use on larger networks and is one of the reasons why Novell has since moved over to using TCP, UDP, and IP as the network and transport protocols rather than IPX and SPX. Novell still uses SAP and NCP at the top level but has left RIP for the routing protocols available in IP.

AppleTalk

AppleTalk was developed by Apple Computer, Inc., for communications between Macintosh computers in a LAN. The current version, AppleTalk Phase 2, has been the leading protocol since the early 1990s. The protocol runs on top of standard LAN networks such as Ethernet and Token Ring, but also supports a proprietary networking hardware system, called *LocalTalk*, that essentially provides high-speed serial connections between machines.

AppleTalk uses the network-layer protocol known as *Datagram Delivery Protocol* (DDP), which works similarly to IPX in that it implements not only network-layer functions but also endpoint to endpoint communications through sockets. Under the new Open Transport protocol system in Macintoshes, higher-level AppleTalk protocols can now also use TCP, UDP, and IP as transport- and network-layer mechanisms.

Addressing in AppleTalk, used in DDP, consists of a network number (the network ID), a zone name, a node ID, and a socket number. The network ID is a 16-bit value, allowing up to 65,536 separate AppleTalk LANs within a single internetwork of LANs. The zone name allows AppleTalk networks to be subdivided into groups or subnetworks of machines of arbitrary size. The node ID is an 8-bit value, allowing up to 256 nodes per AppleTalk network. Finally, each node can have up to 254 endpoints or socket connections.

A *zone* is actually independent of the networking infrastructure. Nodes on multiple networks can be part of the same zone. If you look at it from a company's divisions, a zone could map to a single division, which may contain many separate LANs of AppleTalk machines. If a division has multiple departments, you can use zones to identify departments instead. Departments could physically share AppleTalk LANs, but ZIP will differentiate nodes on the network.

AppleTalk routing is based on looking up network and zone information. If a packet is intended to be broadcast to an entire zone (e.g., a client queries the zone for available network printers), it will be sent to the AppleTalk router. The router will then look up all members within that zone and broadcast the packet to each member.

Routing information distribution requires the services of two protocols: the *Zone Information Protocol* (ZIP) and the *Routing Table Maintenance Protocol* (RTMP). ZIP provides the distribution of Zone information between AppleTalk routers. When a new printer or server is added to the zone, for example, this prompt a ZIP broadcast to AppleTalk routers that serve that zone. Routers in the same zone also periodically send updates to each other to maintain identical information.

RTMP is used to manage routing table information within an AppleTalk router. It updates routers within the internetwork of AppleTalk LANs with information on each network within. Each router keeps a table of network ID entries and the number of hops to that network.

AppleTalk defines a number of higher-level protocols for establishing communications. The *AppleTalk Transaction Protocol* (ATP) creates guaranteed delivery services on top of the network layer. It doesn't really provide transaction services, only reliable transport; a transaction system implies that any action that is performed is done so as a single operation that can be undone if needed. ATP is used by the *AppleTalk Session Pro-*

tocol (ASP), which defines a sequenced session connection between two nodes. The *AppleTalk Filing Protocol* (AFP), which handles network file sharing, uses ASP to communicate with other file servers and clients. ATP and ASP are both connectionless protocols. The *AppleTalk Data Stream Protocol* (ADSP) is the closest thing to TCP. It provides guaranteed connection-oriented services within sessions between nodes.

AppleTalk uses the *Name-Binding Protocol* (NBP) to advertise application services. A network application registers itself within the zone using NBP. Each registered application is referred to by its *entity name*, which is a combination of an *object, type,* and *zone* name. This institutes a mailbox protocol similar to that in NetBIOS for accessing objects. Each node maintains an NBP table of all registered entity names and the addresses currently available or in use within that node. When an application needs to find a service, it broadcasts an NBP command within the specified zone; the node that recognizes the needed service responds to the requesting node with its information. The application then uses ADSP, ATP, or other AppleTalk protocols to establish a session to the service provider node, and both nodes mark their NBP tables.

SNA

IBM's System Network Architecture for connectivity between mainframe devices has changed since its original conception in 1974. The original network structure required central controller devices that managed the network connections between all devices (workstations, terminals, printers, etc.) and the central processors (the mainframe itself). It has since been modified to allow some of these devices to work independently of each other, just as how each TCP/IP node is independently controlled by itself.

SNA focuses on two concepts: *nodes* and *links*. A node, as defined earlier, is an implementation of the set of hardware and software network protocols needed to communicate with others. It can be a computer, a terminal, a printer, a front-end processor, a mainframe processor, and so forth. A link is a network component that attaches nodes to each other. This includes switches, routers, and hubs.

SNA Nodes and Network Types

In SNA, nodes are categorized into four types: *Type 5* (T5), *Type 4* (T4), *Type 2.0* (T2.0), and *Type 2.1* (T2.1). Each of these nodes performs different functions on the network, categorized under *hierarchical roles* and *peer-to-peer roles*.

T4 or T5 nodes are called *subarea nodes* and serve the purpose of controlling all network connections within a subarea of the network. Typically, these include older-generation mainframe central processors and front-end processors, such as S/36s and S/390s. Within a subarea, various end nodes called *peripheral nodes* (T2.0 and T2.1) connect to these subarea nodes. These include workstations, printers, and terminals. Devices that work within subareas fit under the hierarchical role system. In fact, this is the original SNA networking scheme, now commonly referred to as *SNA subarea networks* or just *SNA subareas*.

In peer-to-peer roles, each node is an independent peer of the others and does not rely on any controlling device such as a subarea node to establish a session with another peer node. This form of networking more closely resembles how TCP/IP nodes communicate. Known as *advanced peer-to-peer networking* (APPN), it forms the basis of more modern IBM mainframe networks. To distinguish it from the older type of SNA, this is commonly referred to as *SNA/APPN networking* or simply APPN.

Under APPN there is a separation between *end nodes* (ENs), which create and operate sessions, and *network nodes* (NNs), which handle the routing of sessions. There are two types of end nodes: the *low-entry node* (LEN) and the *APPN node* (APPN EN). Standard T2.1 peripheral nodes are LENs; this allows older devices from SNA subarea networks to be integrated into newer SNA APPN networks. T2.1 peripheral nodes that implement the APPN protocols are known as *APPN ENs*. Any LEN sessions to other nodes must be predefined since LENs cannot really create a session by themselves, although they can operate a session—that is, send data over it. An LEN requires the help of the NN to create sessions. APPN ENs, however, can create as well as operate sessions.

LENs include older terminals, workstations, and printers built for SNA subarea networks. APPN ENs are newer versions of these devices as well as distributed processors such as AS/400s, designed with APPN protocols in mind.

Newer-generation central processors and front-end processors (T5s and T4s), such as the ES/9000 series, also implement APPN protocols and thus can act as APPN ENs, LENs, or even NNs. Those T4s and T5s that support both APPN and subareas can act as *interchange nodes*, which help in routing between newer and older protocols. Most newer-generation SNA routers such as the 372x and 374x series serve as NNs.

In reality, SNA networks are more complicated than what is explained here, but for our integration purposes you won't need to know too much more. If you are interested in learning more about it, please read the *Illustrated SNA* by Mark Pataky (John Wiley & Sons, 1998), or *Introduction to SNA Networking* by Jay Ranade and George Sackett (McGraw Hill, 1995).

SNA Protocols

The SNA protocols as displayed in Figure 4.1 can be grouped together into two categories: the *transport network* (the lower three layers containing physical, data link control, and path control services), and the *network accessible units* (the upper four layers containing the transmission control, data flow control, presentation, and transaction services).

The transport network layers perform similar functions to those in other network protocol families such as TCP/IP. The physical layer performs physical network signaling; the data link control layer performs the formatting of network packets and the establishment of links between nodes; and the path control layer performs the routing of information across the network.

The network accessible units (NAUs) use the transport network services to establish sessions between nodes. NAUs on nodes communicating with each other are known as *session partners*. The links between one node and its session partner form the *route* of the session.

There are three categories of NAUs: *physical units* (PUs), *logical units* (LUs), and *control points* (CPs). PUs come from the older-generation subarea networks and are responsible for activating and deactivating links between nodes for a session. LUs provide services for end-user applications to communicate with applications on other nodes. CPs provide network control and management functions for the nodes and resources within their domain.

LUs are essentially high-level application protocols and form the basis of communications between SNA applications. There are several types of LUs designated by number as shown in Table 4.2, each used by different IBM mainframe and minicomputer applications. NAUs provide session, presentation, transaction, and control services that are used by these LU types to provide their application protocol services.

Table 4.2 Logical Unit Types in SNA

LU TYPE	DESCRIPTION
1	Interactive or batch mode applications that use the Document Content Architecture stream protocol. Example: a database client connecting to a database server.
2	Interactive terminal access protocols that use the 3270 stream protocol. Example: a 3270 terminal connected to a mainframe.
3	Applications and printer protocols that use the 3270 stream protocol. Example: a 3270 user directing a print job to a printer.
4	Data-processing and word-processing application protocols for interactive or batch sessions. Example: a user accessing information from a CICS database.
6.1	Application protocols for distributed data processing. Example: an application running on the IMS/VS operating environment communicating with a CICS database.
6.2	Transaction protocols for distributed data processing. Example: a 5250 terminal accessing information from an AS/400 database.

SNA Routing

Connectivity between Windows, UNIX, and IBM mainframe systems today mainly uses the APPN protocols, so we will focus on APPN routing only. Routing in SNA in general takes more of a circuit-based approach. When you establish a session between an APPN EN and another one, the LU protocol contacts the NNs along the route to the other EN and registers the session. This, in fact, creates a circuit running across the network in which each network node is actively aware of the connections that are taking place.

An LEN requires special attention. Since it is not capable of creating its own sessions, you must use an NN to establish the session ahead of time. For example, a printer by itself may not know how to advertise its services on a network; the network node that the printer is connected to can preestablish a link to the printer and advertise the printer's presence. When the workstation wants to connect to a printer it communicates with the network node and establishes a session with the printer by way of connecting to the NN.

All this works within the confines of a single network or subnetwork. SNA also provides a way to connect sessions between networks using the *SNA Network Interconnection* (SNI) protocol through a common *gateway*. The gateway consists of T4 and T5 nodes whose sole purpose is to perform address translation and to LU-to-LU session interconnections between the two networks.

ATM

Asynchronous transfer mode (ATM) is actually a hardware network protocol on the level of Ethernet and Token Ring. However, ATM supports many of the features of higher-level protocol systems at the network, transport, and even session layers. Still, when compared against other network- and transport-layer protocols, ATM seems out of place. It can be thought as both a hardware protocol simply signaling between machines and used as such, or it can be used by presentation-layer protocols such as Windows Sockets to build connection-oriented sessions between applications.

ATM is a circuit-based protocol. When two ATM devices are to communicate, they build a circuit between themselves, define the circuit session parameters, deliver the data, and close the circuit. Because of this feature, ATM can provide guaranteed QoS between computers across a circuit. The ATM uses *switches*, as opposed to routers, since it essentially switches circuits like the telephone system rather than deciphering packets and routing them.

ATM Cells and Circuits

At the same time, ATM uses individual *cells* to contain the data for delivery. The word *cell* is used rather than *packet* just to prevent confusion between the ATM delivery component and what it is actually carrying (like the ATM cells carrying IP packets.)

Each cell is 53 bytes long; 5 bytes for a cell header and 48 bytes as data payload. The header contains a *virtual circuit identifier* (VCI) and a *virtual path identifier* (VPI) that allow the cells to be distinguished and sent to the appropriate interfaces along the circuit. Processing this short header is very quick and requires very little intelligence at each point for delivery.

The ATM cell can contain any sort of data payload as long as it can be encoded digitally. You could have digital voice data, IP packets, and even, although redundant, Ethernet packets if you really wanted; the delivery mechanism is independent of the type of data to be delivered. The circuit itself does not know what the payload is, just how to deliver it. The payload size is kept fixed and small so that it can be delivered very quickly.

When carrying other network protocols, ATM has to resort to reducing the data into appropriate sizes that can fit into its small cells. For example, IP packets vary in size and most are significantly bigger than 48 bytes. This means that the IP packet will need to be broken down, or *shredded*, as a common ATM joke goes, into little 48-byte cells, delivered, and then reassembled at the other end.

There are two ways to build a circuit when it comes to ATM. If you predefine a set of parameters and class and administratively create a set of circuits across your ATM network, you essentially build what is known as a *permanent virtual circuit* (PVC). This term may be familiar to those who have T1 or fractional T1 frame-relay connections. A PVC is usually defined just once, at the time of installation of the circuit, and retains this type of circuit until you cancel your WAN service from your provider. On the other hand, a *switched virtual circuit* (SVC) is established when you run a specific network application and exists only as long as your application uses the services network. The network equipment (the ATM switch) builds a dynamic connection upon request with the given requirements.

PVC hardware is much easier and cheaper to build than that needed to support SVCs, since less intelligence is required on the switch to maintain connections. Although SVCs are a required part of the ATM specification, not all equipment can provide SVC connections; however, this is becoming less and less the case. You can have circuits of any of the service classes as PVCs or SVCs depending on how you wish to deploy a network. If, for example, you do not have any computers that have direct ATM connectivity, all you may need is a PVC. One of the problems with PVCs is logistical or administrative. Since most PVCs are configured manually, you have to either know ahead of time what the values for your traffic and QoS parameters should be or make educated guesses at them. Naturally, more customers are looking forward to SVCs, where the network performance of circuits is automatically determined by the switch, possibly saving significant costs in monthly traffic transmission, as well as providing more balanced and optimized services to network users.

ATM Classes of Service

ATM provides several classes of service, with distinguishing behavioral differences depending on the type of information that is to be transmitted. The ATM specifications are defined by two major groups, the *ATM Forum* and the *International Telecommunications Union* (ITU). The ITU uses an alphabetic labeling of the classes. The ATM Forum has accepted the more popular, descriptive name-based labels. Keep in mind that the alphabetic class labeling of the ITU does not exactly match that of the ATM Forum for all of these service classes, although there is close approximation. To avoid confusion, we adopt the more popular ATM Forum designations, which is how most vendors describe their products' capabilities.

Constant bit rate (CBR) service provides a continuous time-synchronized stream of data traffic. This is most appropriate for time- and loss-sensitive applications such as high-quality digital video transmission and private branch exchange (PBX) interconnections. This is an expensive option since the bandwidth is guaranteed between two points even if the line is idle; if no real data is being sent, the link will continue to send idle or blank cells at the same rate, effectively still using traffic when it really isn't necessary.

Real-time and *non-real-time variable bit rate* (rt-VBR and nrt-VBR) allow data to be delivered in bursts. The delivery of data may be synchronized, but it isn't necessarily guaranteed at a certain level. Using VBR, you can share the same link between more applications at the same time; this works best when applications have idle frames that could be used by other applications instead. VBR can be used for videoconferencing where the loss of one frame or two won't really affect the result of the output significantly, especially when you consider that the typical TV signal runs between 30 to 60 frames per second. Real-time VBR provides for precise delay control between the two endpoints. Delay issues are not as critical for non-real-time VBR. Essentially, one provides a better quality of service than the other.

Unspecified bit rate (UBR) is what most of us experience on the Internet. The service makes no guarantees on delays or whether cells are delivered in sequence or at all. It leaves all these features up to higher-level protocols, such as the IP, to handle. When you lose cells, it is quite possible that an entire sequence of cells that constitutes an IP packet (this can be a maximum of 64KB and consequently has to be chopped up to fit the many small 48-byte cell payloads) will be useless. The entire sequence of cells is tossed, and the higher-level IP protocol needs to signal the source that the whole packet must be resent. This procedure is known as *early packet discard* or *tail packet discard* and was added to UBR after its definition, leading some vendors to designate it as *UBR+*.

Available bit rate (ABR) is similar to UBR in that it can vary the transmission rate of cells at any time. However, it differs in that it offers better quality-of-service guarantees. ABR is what most hope will replace the UBR-like behavior of IP.

There are three important parameters for the different service classes available for ATM. The *peak cell rate* (PCR) determines the maximum rate at any moment at which cells can be delivered across the circuit. A circuit cannot surpass the PCR under normal circumstances. If its rate increases beyond the PCR, the cells may be dropped along the way, and an error recovery situation will fall into place. The *sustained cell rate* (SCR) is the continuous average rate at which cells are available to pass through a circuit; it is a suggestive parameter for determining service configurations. Finally, a *minimum bit rate* (MBR) indicates the minimal amount of bandwidth that has been reserved for the circuit. The delivery rate does not ever fall below the MBR under normal circumstances. If source has nothing to deliver to the destination, empty cells might be sent instead. In addition to the traffic parameters, there is another group of parameters that describe the level of quality of service needed for a connection of each service class. Even among service classes, you can indicate what the maximum *cell transfer delay* (CTD), *cell delay variation* (CDV), *cell loss ratio* (CLR), and *cell error ratio* (CER) are allowed to be before any connection is terminated for unavailability at the rates and parameters indicated. Grouped together, they act as quality-of-service parameters.

The CTD is the amount of time that it takes for a cell to be taken from one endpoint to the far endpoint (with however many ATM switches in between). The CDV is the maximum change of individual CTD amounts that is allowed. The CLR describes how many cells out of the total can be dropped in case of congestion. And finally, the CER describes how many cells out of the total can be dropped in case of transmission error.

The traffic parameters define the acceptable bandwidth rate and service class of a connection. The QoS parameters define how well the connection should perform. Not all parameters are used by all service classes; on the contrary, there are other parameters that also affect these classes that are beyond the scope of the current discussion.

CBR service typically has the same values for the PCR and SCR. The CLR, CTD, and CDV need to be defined per the requirements of the equipment that you will interconnect. High-performance digital audio or video transmission has much stricter and often higher demands than, for example, ordinary telephone calls between two sites.

Rt-VBR uses the PCR, the SCR, and another parameter called the *maximum burst size,* which is the total number of cells transmitted at the peak cell rate. This class usually results in traffic that averages around the SCR, with small bursts at nonperiodic intervals. Applications that are somewhat time-sensitive but can afford some degree of freedom or loss (such as videoconferencing and even some audio applications) are best suited for this. The audio would be the equivalent of what it is for good FM radio transmission, where losses of one or two seconds occur, although rarely.

Nrt-VBR is similar to rt-VBR but is lower quality and therefore less suited for time-synchronous applications like video or audio. This would be better suited for pure connection-oriented data services. Frame relay over ATM is one good example of its use. It uses the same parameters, but only an average CTD and CDV are specified, rather than a maximum CTD.

UBR, as previously mentioned, is similar in effect to the connectionless nonguaranteed data transfer mechanisms of the current Internet. With UBR the cell rate QoS parameters are not typically implemented; only the basic traffic parameters are used. To get any form of level of quality in your network service, you have to properly configure your network architecture. The SCR is specifically set to 0 since there are no minimum guarantees on bandwidth. The PCR is set to the maximum amount of bandwidth allowed on the connection; this upper limit is absolute according to the standard, and even if the physical link can afford larger bandwidth, the circuit will not go beyond the PCR.

And finally we get to ABR. This is another connectionless data transfer system except with provisions for QoS. Most of the future development is on Internet performance and on the next-generation Internet protocol, IPv6. Specifically, there is concentration on how higher-layer protocols such as IP can establish the QoS parameters of the lower-level ATM network.

ABR uses the minimum cell rate indicated earlier. Effectively, the PCR, SCR, and MCR identify a high, average, and low level that the bandwidth can be adjusted to on a dynamic basis. The ABR class looks quite a bit like the VBR service in concept; the difference lies in the fact that the extra unused bandwidth on the link is redistributed in a way that is more fair than that for VBR.

Presentation Protocols

The Windows platform offers seven different presentation-layer mechanisms: *NetBIOS, Windows Sockets, remote procedure calls, mailslots, named pipes, network dynamic data exchange,* and the *Distributed Component Object Model.*

NetBIOS is the original presentation-layer interface for application communications on a Windows network. It was first designed for DOS networking and relied on NetBEUI as the transport protocol. Windows for Workgroups and LAN Manager used NetBIOS and NetBEUI as their default networking and presentation protocols. Microsoft has since replaced NetBEUI with TCP/IP as the preferred networking protocol, but NetBEUI still maintains a fairly important role in small networks of Windows for Workgroups or Win 9x machines.

NetBIOS now primarily runs over the TCP protocol as NetBIOS/TCP (NBT). NetBIOS can also run on top of IPX (NBIPX) and is known as NetBIOS on NetWare (NWNBLink); this form of the protocol allows NetBIOS applications to run on a Novell NetWare-only LAN.

Windows Sockets (Winsock) originally began as a standard presentation layer to build TCP/IP applications over the different TCP/IP stacks once available for Windows. Although most Windows platforms now use the standard TCP/IP protocol stack included with the system, Winsock still provides a useful function. It has since been enhanced to become a general presentation-layer interface to a number of different protocols for the Windows platform, including TCP/IP, IPX/SPX, AppleTalk, and DECnet.

A Winsock socket is conceptually similar to a Berkeley socket on UNIX and can communicate with the other with no problems. Even the code between the systems looks similar. However, Winsock sockets can also provide other services and features that are not available in TCP/IP, as well as those particular to the Windows environment. This makes it a more flexible construct at the price of some source-code-level compatibility.

Remote procedure calls (RPCs) offer an alternative to the sockets mechanism by providing program code stubs that an application on one machine can call to execute on another. RPCs form the basis of protocols like the network file system. However, Windows RPCs are a derivative of the *distributed computing environment* (DCE) RPCs and not the RPCs developed by Sun Microsystems called *open network computing*

(ONC) RPCs. This latter form is what is implemented in most UNIX systems. Although available, the RPC mechanism in Windows is compatible only with other Windows systems.

Named pipes provide a connection-oriented communications service between two applications over a network with reliable data delivery. Every data item delivered between the two endpoints is acknowledged when received intact. Named pipes offer a level of security by allowing an endpoint to impersonate the security identity of the other endpoint (as discussed in Chapter 6).

Mailslots provide connectionless communications between two applications. A mailslot essentially allows one application to send a request to another without having to check that the other application is running. Windows uses this mechanism to register a machine within the workgroup or domain. This identifies the presence of the machine to all others on the network using a simple broadcast mechanism.

Dynamic data exchange (DDE) is a used by applications to interact with each other within the same system to exchange information. Network DDE (NetDDE) is an extension that allows applications to communicate with those on other computers. NetDDE uses the NetBIOS protocol as the network delivery system. In concept, NetDDE isn't too different from sockets; it just grew up in a different protocol family. NetDDE is still used by many Windows applications but is being supplanted in favor of the next system, DCOM.

The Windows environment supports a distributed object communications protocol known as the *Distributed Component Object Model* (DCOM). This system is an extension of an earlier technology, simply called COM, that allows object-oriented applications to communicate and interact with each other within the same system. DCOM creates a programming-language-neutral interface to application objects so that they can communicate. This allows, for example, a C++ application object to call a Visual Basic object. DCOM takes this to a network level, allowing objects to be accessed from remote machines.

A competitor to DCOM is the *Common Object Request Broker Architecture* (CORBA) designed by the Object Management Group, a consortium of more than 500 software companies working on object technology. CORBA works independently of the operating system platform, providing similar technology to allow application objects written in different programming languages to interact with each other. CORBA is available for both UNIX and Windows platforms. Although some vendors have made announcements that they will port the Microsoft COM and DCOM environment to UNIX, this has yet to happen, which leaves DCOM a Windows-only solution.

Application Protocols and Services

A number of different application protocols and services are implemented for the system. This section discusses the most important ones used, particularly those used in relation to TCP/IP. These include the Domain Name System (DNS) for mapping IP addresses and hostnames; the Dynamic Host Configuration Protocol (DHCP) and Windows Internet Name Service (WINS) for assigning IP addresses; the Routing and Remote Access Service (RRAS) to provide routing services, remote access, and virtual private networking; and the quality of service (QoS) system to provide network communications service and performance guarantees.

Domain Name System

The Domain Name System is the default name resolution system used to translate IP hostnames into addresses. Prior to this system, name resolution on IP networks was based on a table of names and addresses stored in the *Hosts* file of every node on the network, as shown in Figure 4.3. You can see that this eventually became cumbersome as the number of nodes within networks grew to thousands, and, on the Internet, tens of millions. The DNS protocol now serves as the default name resolution system, with static tables per node as a backup system still often in use.

Windows NT's networking system, which is derived from the older LAN Manager product from Microsoft, also uses static files to resolve names.

```
# Loopback address for the local host so that it can talk
# to itself through TCP/IP
127.0.0.1      localhost

# This node's hostname and address
192.168.2.2    bohr.atollsw.com      bohr

# Other nodes in this network
192.168.2.3    einstein
192.168.2.4    feynman
```

Figure 4.3 A sample IP Hosts file.

The system, however, allows for deferment to other nodes for further address mappings, as shown in Figure 4.4.

The INCLUDE statement allows you to add the mappings stored on another server. The BEGIN_ALTERNATE section defines a secondary node that contains an identical mapping file to the preceding INCLUDE statement. The LMHosts file is used for statically defined NetBIOS over TCP/IP name lookups.

Standard DNS provides only static hierarchical mapping between names and addresses, assigned based on predefined name database files. The new *Dynamic DNS* (DDNS) protocol enables hostnames to be dynamically mapped to addresses and is supported in Win 2000. DDNS is an extension to the existing protocol and keeps the original protocol's structure for distributing name resolution queries and the global hierarchy of DNS addresses.

On the Internet, DNS mapping is maintained by a number of top-level or *root* servers that contain overall mapping information by domains. Each Internet service provider maintains its own level of DNS servers, which map address information for the networks within their domain. Corporate DNS servers link to the Internet root servers as well as the ISP's DNS servers to perform name resolution for addresses not within the corporate DNS database. The private corporate DNS servers maintain mapping information for end nodes within their own network.

For every IP network, there need to be DNS servers providing the name resolution service. Depending on the number of nodes within the network and the anticipated load, a company can have multiple name servers. Each company needs to have at least one *primary DNS server* and can have multiple *secondary DNS servers*. The primary name server

```
#PRE There is no Loopback address
192.168.2.2     bohr
192.168.2.3     einstein
192.168.2.4     feynman       #PRE #DOM:NUCLEAR

#INCLUDE \\feynman\config\lmhosts
#BEGIN_ALTERNATE
#INCLUDE \\einstein\config\lmhosts
#END_ALTERNATE
```

Figure 4.4 A sample LMHosts file.

contains the authoritative information for all nodes served under its network. The secondary name servers exist to optimize access to the information contained within the primary server, and provide load balancing of name service calls. If the network is to be further subdivided into multiple hierarchical levels, each of these levels can also have its own primary and secondary name servers. A final type of DNS server, known as the *caching-only server*, only keeps a cache of mappings for a particular node or a subnetwork to speed name resolution services.

Each primary name server has a *zone* file (see Figure 4.5) that contains a *start of authority* (SOA) record. The SOA defines the domain name (the zone) that it services, the primary contact or e-mail address for name service problems, the list of all name servers for the domain, the list of mail servers for the domain, and various parameters for distributing information between name servers. This is followed by other records defining address mappings.

```
@            IN        SOA        atollsw.com. root.atollsw.com. (
; The following are parameters for distributing name mappings
; information with other name servers
             9822981   ; Serial
             3600      ; Refresh
             300       ; Retry
             3600000   ; Expire
             3600 )    ; Minimum

; These define the name servers for this domain
             IN        NS         10              ns1.atollsw.com.
             IN        NS         100             ns2.atollsw.com.

; This defines the Mail Exchanger or server for this domain
             IN        MX         10              mailhost.atollsw.com.

; These define the forward (host -> address) mapping
bohr         IN        A          192.168.2.2
rutherford   IN        A          192.168.2.4
sagan        IN        A          192.168.2.7

; This defines an alias for the host 'bohr'
mailhost     IN        CNAME      bohr

; These define the reverse (address -> host) mappings
192.168.2.2  IN        PTR        bohr
192.168.2.4  IN        PTR        rutherford
192.168.2.7  IN        PTR        sagan
```

Figure 4.5 A sample DNS zone file.

There are usually two sets of mapping tables—one for mapping a host-name to an address, known as the *forward resolution* or *lookup table*, and the other for mapping an address to a hostname, the *reverse resolution table*. You always need to have the first set of mappings. The second is optional, but security software on many systems will reject connections if there is no reverse mapping from an address to a hostname.

Both these tables can be stored within the same file, but many DNS servers allow you to keep separate files containing the information to aid user readability. Forward tables are usually stored by the domain name they serve. Reverse tables are normally stored by the IP address number of the network, with a separate file for each network.

On Windows NT and 2000 Servers, you do not have to manually write these files, as you do on most UNIX-based DNS servers. The DNS administration tool (**dnsadmin**) provides the interface for creating and defining all the necessary files. The system stores the files under \Winnt\System32\DNS. Aside from the zone file for each domain you support, each DNS server has a configuration file defining the type of name server it is, the location of the local cache of mappings, and, if the zone information is partitioned into multiple files, the location of these files.

Microsoft went a separate way with NT 4.0 for mapping dynamic addresses. They created the *Windows Internet Name Service* (WINS) to provide mapping between hostnames and IP addresses on a static or dynamic basis. WINS improves on the static tables implemented in earlier LMHosts files and is used primarily by the NetBIOS system.

Address Assignment

TCP/IP address information can be dynamically assigned to client PCs using the *Dynamic Host Configuration Protocol* (DHCP). This system is based on assigning temporary or semipermanent leases to clients at boot time to provide them with address information. When the lease expires, the client needs to either renegotiate the lease or ask the server for a new one, if it wishes to continue using the IP network.

The benefit of using DHCP to assign addresses is that it saves having to manually distribute the information across all your clients. Instead, client PCs are configured to broadcast a request when they boot and are assigned a lease by the server. The client maintains the same hostname at all times, but is assigned an address through DHCP; initially, this hostname is stored on a boot PROM on the NIC or on a floppy disk.

If the network that the client is on does not have a DHCP server, it may have a *DHCP relay agent*. This is typically a router that takes the broadcast DHCP request message from the client and forwards it to a particular predefined DHCP server node on another network. A DHCP server may also relay the request to another DHCP server if it cannot serve that request because of exhausted addresses within its pool.

The DHCP server is responsible for keeping track of address assignment. Each client PC may be assigned the same address every time on a semipermanent basis until the PC is shut down. This accomplishes the same thing as manually encoding the address information directly into the PC, except on a server-assigned basis. This method is known as *server-assigned static addresses*.

On the other hand, a client may be assigned an address from a pool of available addresses on the server. This dynamically maps an IP address to a client with a given hostname. The network name identity (the hostname) remains the same for the client but the address may change with each boot session. These addresses are known as *server-assigned dynamic addresses* or simply *dynamic addresses*.

Dynamic addresses will confuse a DNS server that does not have the dynamic address-mapping features of DDNS. The DHCP server may be separate from the DDNS server but has to communicate dynamic address assignment information to it.

DHCP is an extension of the Bootp protocol for remote booting. It uses the same packet format but further defines the section on optional extensions. The two protocols are not necessarily compatible. A DHCP server may also function as a Bootp server in many cases, but it depends primarily on what the client needs. Windows clients do not support Bootp with the default Microsoft TCP/IP stack.

Routing and Remote Access

Windows offers a *Routing and Remote Access Service* (RRAS) system that combines functions for multiprotocol routing of TCP/IP and IPX, as well as remote access facilities such as remote login and authentication onto a network. One portion, the Windows *Multi-Protocol Router* (MPR) supports static routes, RIP version 2, and OSPF for IP, and RIP and SAP for IPX. In addition, it can also act as a DHCP relay agent, forwarding DHCP packets between clients on one network and a DHCP server on another.

There are two main scenarios for remote connections. First, there's the remote office that is in another location, state, or even country. The remote office usually has several computers or even a few LANs and connects to the main offices over a dedicated or on-demand WAN link. Since many computers are involved, the remote office typically needs a way for each of these to communicate independently with others at the main office. One method is to have the link directly between the offices. Another more recently popular method is to use a public network infrastructure like the Internet, and establish security mechanisms to connect between the offices. Whichever method is used, there is usually a router or a bridge to serve all the computers that interconnects the two offices.

The second scenario is the independent remote machine that needs to connect to the main office from a mobile location. This is usually a laptop or home computer that connects to the main office either by dialing directly into the network or, again, by using the Internet. There is no need for a router with these individual systems, since they involve a direct point-to-point link from the remote computer to the main network.

The differentiating point for the remote access for the client side is if it is a dedicated or permanent link, or if it requires dial-in connectivity. They both may use the same connectivity technology, but a dial-in connection often uses more dynamic authentication and networking methods. A dedicated connection that is a permanent link between the two sites usually involves a telecommunications circuit such as T1, Frame Relay, DDS, ATM, and so forth. These circuits are maintained by the network service provider or telecom company for you. In most cases, these circuits are private to your own network (i.e., not shared with any other companies), and thus do not need encryption or authentication protocols.

A dial-in connection, however, requires that you connect either manually or automagically from the remote site each time you need to access the main network. Thus, you need to authenticate your account, set up the direction of traffic, and possibly encrypt the traffic each time. The dial-in services are usually open to allow users to connect in from any location or any number. In some cases, they may even be shared with other customers or companies at your service provider.

Remote clients can be configured to automatically dial and connect to a network over a modem line when packets are sent to that network. This means that when a user tries to access a file or a network service on another computer, the system will automatically dial out to that network with preconfigured information. If the client is also preconfigured with login information, it will also log them in seamlessly. A more advanced form of this system, known as *demand dialing*, connects remote nodes to a network only when there is traffic ready to be delivered. It then disconnects until further network traffic is ready. This could be traffic on either side of the network. Demand dialing often requires the administrator to configure how much network traffic to buffer at each location, which affects the feel of interactivity with the remote node. This system makes most sense when it is significantly costly to connect to a remote node—for example, over long-distance lines, where every minute is being billed.

Both UNIX and Windows systems have standardized on the Point-to-Point Protocol (PPP) as the means to establish a direct link for remote access. As part of PPP, there are directions on how to authenticate the remote user, and how to format and deliver traffic.

There are several authentication methods for PPP, some fairly insecure, others quite robust. At the insecure end is the basic clear-text account and password authentication, where all the information is passed over the connection unscrambled. The downside of this method is that a cracker snooping the network or the remote connection may be able to intercept and copy these authentication parameters. This method is generically known as the *Password Authentication Protocol* (PAP).

A second method uses an algorithm known as the Message Digest 5 (MD5) hash, which generates a unique string each time for a given password. This is sent over the connection to the remote access server, which then calculates a similar hash for its own copy of the password and compares the two to see if they match. This is called the *Challenge Handshake Authentication Protocol* (CHAP).

The remote access portion of RRAS provides a number of functions for remotely connected clients, including dialing services, authentication protocols, virtual private networking, data encryption, RAS user profiles, multiple connection linking, and bandwidth allocation.

RRAS implements a number of different authentication protocols: PAP, Shiva-PAP (a proprietary version of PAP), CHAP, Microsoft's version of CHAP, the RADIUS authentication system, and the Extensible Authentication Protocol (EAP). Most of these provide authentication using different security information. The RADIUS system is the most popular for cross-platform authentication. CHAP uses a system like Kerberos in that it generates tickets based on the original password and never actually sends the password over the network. Most of the other systems encrypt the password in one way or another. The EAP is a programmable protocol to allow developers to create their own authentication system.

RRAS supports encryption of any data before delivery over a network protocol using either 40-bit RC4, internationally, or several 128-bit public-key encryption systems, within the United States.

Every user who will need to access to the RRAS system has to have a user profile. This profile defines the authentication protocols, encryption systems, and network parameters that the user must use to communicate with RRAS servers. This profile is also manageable through the MMC.

Multilink PPP is an Internet standard that allows you to aggregate several separate communications lines together to make them all seem like one single network hardware connection. The two nodes in a multilink PPP connection have to negotiate the number of links within, and how traffic is to collect traffic from each of these links together into the same network queue or buffer. This system is most often used to create a higher-bandwidth connection using several smaller and cheaper network connections; for example, you can connect four 56-Kbps modems on each node to create a multilink connection of 224 Kbps between the two machines.

The *Bandwidth Allocation Protocol* (BAP) works with the multilink system to dynamically add or drop one or more connections within a multilink connection to optimize traffic flow. This protocol allows nodes to negotiate on bandwidth and, combined with the demand dialing feature, saves on overall operating costs.

Virtual Private Networks

Virtual private networking is implemented in RRAS using Microsoft's proprietary *Point-to-Point Tunneling Protocol* (PPTP) and the *Layer 2 Tunneling Protocol* (L2TP). PPTP is used by remote clients to communicate with Windows servers over the Internet. The protocol is an extension of the industry-standard PPP for direct connection over serial or WAN lines. Essentially, what PPTP does is negotiate an PPTP/IP connection over the public network, and then embed PPP frames within the transport layer (TCP). PPTP runs directly between IP and TCP as a sort of control layer.

L2TP works by actually embedding Layer 2 (data link control) frames such as Ethernet within an IP packet for delivery over the network. This allows two networks to be connected together as if they were on the same physical LAN, creating what is called a *virtual LAN*.

These protocols are used when a remote node or network has to first connect to an ISP, tunnel over the Internet, and connect through the other network's ISP directly into the other network. Both protocols can embed any of the other protocols Windows supports within an IP VPN. L2TP is most useful for networking protocols that cannot be routed, such as NetBEUI, or when some nodes on either side of the network do not do IP at all, such as with SNA-, IPX-, or AppleTalk-only nodes. Only Windows clients and some remote access server products implement the PPTP and L2TP system, in particular products from Cisco and 3Com. Most UNIX systems use an Internet standard known as the *IP Security* (IPsec) *protocol*.

Windows 2000 directly supports IPsec for building secure VPNs. IPSec is a public key-based secure delivery protocol for IP that provides authentication of the packet header and encryption of the packet data payload for each packet. Before a connection is established, both nodes send public keys that identify the identity of the node, very similar to the method in Kerberos. IPsec defines a standard key-exchange protocol known as the *Internet Security Association Key Management Protocol/ Oakley version* (ISAKMP/Oakley) but Win 2000 by default uses the Kerberos system instead. The nodes then build either a transport mode or a tunnel mode IPsec connection.

A *transport mode* IPsec connection implies that the security information for IPsec is directly included into each IP packet as part of the header. This type of connection is typically available only in IPv6, which has optional extension headers for security. A *tunnel mode* IPsec connection embeds a secure IP packet within an unsecure one. The unsecure IP packet is used for general delivery over a network or the Internet. The secure packet contains the actual data payload encrypted and authenticated according to the information in the security header.

Tunneling mode also allows you to implement a firewall or security encryption gateway or proxy on your outgoing network connection. Within the intranet, every node can communicate either in the open or using security. However, to communicate with remote nodes or networks over the public Internet, the security gateway encrypts all outgoing data and decrypts incoming data.

Win 2000 Security Policy for networks defines how a node can communicate with others using IPsec. This security policy defines which other nodes it is willing to communicate on unsecure and secure modes; the negotiation policy for which authentication algorithm it will use for each packet header and which encryption algorithm it will use for the data payload; and the key-exchange protocol it will use to establish the connection.

Quality of Service

Win 2000 supports four different types of QoS protocols as well as a general QoS API. The first type, *IP precedence*, uses 3 bits within the IP protocol header to define the precedence of each packet. This allows for up to eight different levels of priorities to deliver packets. Although included within the IPv4 packet header since its inception, this field has not been actively used very much, and not all routers necessarily implement IP precedence.

A second method works down at Layer 2, using the standard IEEE 802 frame used in Ethernet, Token Ring, and other hardware networks. The *IEEE 802.1p protocol* standard defines a 3-bit priority level for IEEE 802.1q virtual LANs. This type of virtual LAN defines groupings of machines within the IEEE 802 frame, using a special identifier for each group. Machines are grouped at Layer 2, effectively putting them directly in a LAN of their own even when they may be physically connected to a different LAN. The 802.1p system works very similarly to IP precedence at a lower level. Both are fairly new, and not all network products implement either of these Layer 2 protocols. Unlike IP precedence, this system will provide priority services for any network protocol.

A third method uses the Internet-standard *Resource Reservation Setup Protocol* (RSVP) to set up a QoS connection between two nodes and within all the network nodes or routers along the way. RSVP is particular to the IP protocol only. When establishing a connection, the application informs the system how much bandwidth it will need and other QoS parameters. The system then sends out an RSVP packet between the node and the remote node it wants to communicate with. Each router along the network route reads the information within the RSVP packet and negotiates the level of QoS it can provide with the source node. This way, the entire route will define how much network traffic and what kind of QoS is available. The application can then decide if it is willing to work within the parameters provided by the routers or if it will wait for another time. If it agrees, it sends another RSVP packet to each router and the destination node to confirm this, and the connection is established. If it does not, the application responds with an error message saying that the network resources are not available.

Subnet Bandwidth Manager (SBM), or *RSVP Proxy*, is the last type of QoS protocol offered by Win 2000, to serve routers, hubs, and network devices that do not implement RSVP. In essence, a separate software component, either on a server or on a router known as the SBM, monitors the usage of these legacy devices and decides for them how bandwidth will be used. A client requesting an RSVP session with a server first sends an RSVP packet to the SBM to find out if the legacy device can allocate the information. The SBM decides based on existing connections through the device if it can allocate more QoS sessions. If so, the SBM informs the client, and continues passing the message along the route. This way, the legacy device does not have to implement anything new at all. However, the clients have to know that an SBM exists on the network and the legacy network devices it serves.

Summary

Win 2000 supports a large number of different protocols although bases communications with other Win 2000 systems primarily on TCP/IP. Nevertheless, many of these protocols still play an important role in corporate networks and thus must be considered alongside IP. The next generation IP protocol has been designed but its implementation still lags in available tools, platform implementations, and support by vendors. It's a good sign that Win 2000 includes IPv6 within as this will accelerate its use in desktop and server systems.

Win 2000 also adds new security and quality of service management features. IPSec and these QoS features will constitute an important part of future TCP/IP networks. Now that one of the leading OS platforms includes these services by default, they are likely to be deployed even faster across corporate networks.

Although Win 2000 tries to be completely independent of NetBIOS, there still are some left over portions to support backward compatibility. Thus, NetBIOS will continue to exist until the last application that uses it disappears. The new protocol communications structures that solely use IP and the new system services that do not rely upon NetBIOS information will eventually replace this aging system.

Amongst the new system services, the Active Directory service plays one of the most important roles, as we will see in the next chapter.

## CHAPTER 5

Windows 2000 Active Directory Services

T he newly introduced Active Directory system is probably one of the most interesting changes to Win 2000 overall. It has changed how user accounts and domains are created, accessed, and managed as well as providing a common infrastructure for directory services for applications. A directory is a common store of information about objects on the system that applications can access. Directory services provide the backbone of administration tools, user account management, and resource location services. In Windows 2000, this is provided by the Active Directory system and the Active Directory Services Interface (ADSI) programming libraries.

This chapter introduces the Win 2000 Active Directory system that serves as a database to contain system, application, and user information. We romp through a comparison against the existing NT domain system on older Windows servers, followed by an explanation of the new concepts introduced with Active Directory. We then take a look at the architecture of an Active Directory-based service for your network and a description of the tools for AD management.

Features and Services Offered

Active Directory (AD) takes elements of the system registry and the domain system in NT 4.0 to create a more manageable and flexible system.

User accounts that were once stored in the system registry can now be a part of the Active Directory system, allowing users to easily move between departments and supporting single enterprisewide login services.

AD can support a better hierarchical view of users, groups, and machines with up to a million different objects, a much greater capacity than individual domains in older NT systems. It creates a globally distributable directory service that can be integrated with multiple directory service providers such as NetWare Directory Services (NDS) and Internet Lightweight Directory Access Protocol (LDAP) servers, and can still be administered through a single console.

Some of the particular features that hold promise are:

- A hierarchical view that supports many different kinds of objects: users, groups, computers, applications, application services, system services, and so on.

- Support for distributing objects across multiple servers and multiple sites with automated replication services between servers.

- A transaction-based database of all objects to allow manipulation of the objects and directory structure to be performed in a single operation or atomically, as well as undoing an operation.

- Access and interoperability with NDS, NetWare 3.x, NT 3.51, and NT 4.0, and LDAP directory servers.

- Per-object security through access control lists.

- All servers can be managed from anywhere on the network. Portions of the directory can be managed separately through delegated administration to individual system administrators.

- A cache of partial views of all objects in the directory speed access on an individual server level.

- Multilanguage searching and sorting of objects in the tree to support international character sets.

The Previous NT Domain System

In NT 3.51 and 4.0, the domain model is much simpler. Essentially there are two types of devices, the *primary domain controller* (PDC) and the *backup domain controller* (BDC). These domain controllers only hold information about user accounts and groups, unlike the Active Directory system of Windows 2000. The PDC is the authoritative holder of all account and group information, which is replicated to multiple BDCs spread around the network to enhance performance. There is only one PDC per domain. If the PDC should fail, one of the BDCs can be promoted to PDC status until the main controller is brought back online.

Domains in the older NT systems are assigned a domain name. Although similar in concept, it does not correlate to the domain name of Internet hosts. Each NT workstation or server has its own machine name within this domain. You can have two machines with the same name in different domains but not within the same one. Machines from one domain can still access those in other domains by first contacting the PDC of the other domain to search for the particular machine and then contacting the machine.

Essentially, this older structure provides only a single level of hierarchy, which can be quite limiting to large networks. The new Active Directory system, which we will discuss shortly, is superlative to the older NT domain system. Older NT 3.51 and 4.0 machines can still be part of the Active Directory system but are referenced through special providers that translate the function calls. Objects (accounts and groups) have the same status as those created in Win 2000 systems, but domain applications and other objects are left behind.

To overcome some of the limitations of the old NT domain system, *trust models* and *global groups* were introduced. A trust model defines how objects from two or more domains can be converged into a single set. Essentially, one domain defines the other domains that it trusts. If trust is established, users from other domains can access resources of the first inherently without any complicated intermediary login procedures for each access. Each user must have an appropriate account within a domain. To avoid recreating all the accounts of other domains simply to allow them access, the NT domain system has global groups. These groups define accounts belonging to foreign domains that the current domain trusts.

To further create the model of a single enterprise structure, there are several domain *trust relationship* models. In the basic *single domain model*, only one domain exists, and there is no need for any trust relationships. This model is unrealistic when you consider the complicated structure of most companies and organizations.

If you have multiple domains, as is more likely the case, you can certainly build trust relationships between each and every domain. However, even as little as five or six domains in a company require you to maintain a whole lot of trust relationships between all the domains. A better model is the *master domain model,* which allows each domain to build a trust relationship to one domain in particular, known as the *master.* This master contains global groups of accounts and resources within all the other domains that can be used by individual domains to authenticate foreign domain accounts and resources. This trust between the member domains and the master is all in one direction, toward the master.

In some organizations, even the master domain model isn't enough. These organizations can have offices in multiple locations with similar departments and organizational structures, each serving a regional area. To reduce the problems of performance in working long distances, you need the *multiple master domain model,* where there are several masters serving the domains at each location. In turn, the masters from each location build trust relationships with each other. You can create an even higher master that brings each of these masters into one entity, but this is usually inefficient, given the performance considerations between sites.

The Active Directory system replaces these trust models in all but the multiple master scenario. It provides a more complex hierarchy to determine resource and account access, which obviates the need for trust models and maintaining the complications of PDCs and BDCs in each domain. Instead, AD servers can service portions of an overall tree of all objects and information can be replicated across multiple servers and sites automatically. Take a look at Table 5.1 to understand the NT 4.0 domain system in the context of Windows 2000's Active Directory.

Understanding Key Active Directory Concepts

Entries within Active Directory are known as *objects.* An object can be a number of different types: a user account, a group of users, files, printers, a group of computers, an entire division network, and so on. On the programming level, each AD object supports several COM interfaces that provide access to the object and information about the object.

Objects of the same type have similar properties. A user object, for example, includes the following properties: first name, surname, user account name, e-mail address, telephone number, and so on. One special type of object is known as the *container.* It does not represent a specific

Table 5.1 Conceptual Translations between NT Domains and Active Directory

NT 4.0 DOMAINS CONCEPT	CLOSEST EQUIVALENT ACTIVE DIRECTORY CONCEPT
Account	Account object
N/A	Container
Local group	Domain-local group
Global group	Global group or universal group
N/A	Directory information tree
Domain	Organizational unit or naming context
Trust relationship	NT 4.0 domain trust relationship or AD transitive trusts
Master domain	Domain tree
Multiple master domains	Forest
Primary or backup domain controllers	AD server
N/A	AD site

instance of information by itself, but is instead a collection of other objects of the same type.

Objects and containers are hierarchically organized in a tree format to describe their role in the entire network. The trees start at the very top, representing the overall computer network, down through departments and divisions, to workgroups, and finally to individual users. All objects are unique in the structure; even a copy of an object is considered a unique, separate object with all the same values for its properties as the original, as long as it doesn't belong in the same location as the other object within the tree hierarchy. A visual representation of objects, containers, and the tree, as well as other objects we will discuss shortly, is shown in Figure 5.1 on page 160.

To maintain object uniqueness, every object has a *name*. This name differentiates it from all other objects. The *distinguished name* (DN) is the full identity of a unique object as defined in the overall hierarchy. For example, a DN might look like the following:

```
/O=John Wiley & Sons/OU=Computer Books/CN=Authors/CN=Rawn Shah
/O=Internet/DC=Com/DC=AtollSw/OU=San Diego/CN=Tom Duff
/O=Internet/DC=Com/DC=AtollSw/OU=PC LAN/CN=Einstein
```

The forward slash separators indicate nodes within the tree hierarchy that might branch out to other groups of objects. To avoid the repetition of these fairly long names, you can also use a *relative distinguished name* (RDN), which refers to other objects within portions of the overall hierarchy. For instance, in the first example, there might be a separate branch of the tree for editors, and our very distinguished editor, Bob Elliot, might have an RDN of the form /OU=Editors/CN=Bob Elliot. Similarly, the UNIX computers in the Atoll Software (AtollSw.com) network might be referred to as /OU=UNIX LAN/CN=Feynman (where *Feynman* is the name of the computer itself).

Although there is a defined tree structure to how global systems like the Internet and its domains are organized, there isn't a single global definition of what a tree should look like for every organization. The AD system is flexible enough that you can define your own vision of the objects on your network. This definition, called a *schema*, shows how objects are grouped together within the tree. The schema also defines the structure of individual objects in the directory.

The *namespace* refers to the set of names within a portion of hierarchy or to the entire hierarchy itself. The scope of a namespace defines the limits of that namespace and all the names that can be seen under it. For example, within the scope of /CN=Authors there are various authors including /CN=Rawn Shah and /CN=Tom Duff. Within the scope of /O=Internet/DC=Com are all the Internet domains that end in *.com* (that's a fairly huge list of companies and their domains) and all the objects that belong to these domains; we're not even going to hazard a guess as to how many such objects there may be.

Furthermore, the DN of any object can change if the object is moved to another location. To maintain an identity for its entire lifetime, irrespective of its location in the AD tree, each object has a *globally unique identifier* (GUID). This string array is assigned during object creation time and can be used to look up a name in the same way as a DN.

Active Directory also defines *naming contexts*, which are the equivalent of partitions of the hierarchy that are placed in a set for replication services. All objects within that context are replicated across the Active Directory servers as specified by the network administrator. Essentially, it takes a particular scope of the objects within the Active Directory and places them within a dataset, ready for replication.

Active Directory changes the notion of the *domain* as instituted in earlier versions of NT. An AD domain is a single area of security containing any number of AD objects. Such an area can be an organizational unit (OU) defining all user accounts in the Sales department, for example, or it can be any group of AD objects that share the same security policy. Each domain has a security policy defining how objects outside the domain can interact with those within. An AD domain can be the equivalent of multiple NT domains and most closely resembles the master domain model. The hierarchical structure of a single AD domain is known as the *domain tree*.

It is very possible to build separate trees for different divisions or locations of your company. For example, you can build a domain tree with multiple domains for all personnel, computers, and objects at your New York division that is separate from those of the offices in San Francisco, London, Johannesburg, or Singapore. Multiple domain trees can also be connected into a *forest*, so that network administrators for large organizations can have separate systems for each location but still create a single view of all objects belonging to the company. Domains within a forest have an inherent bidirectional trust of each other known as a *transitive trust*.

An AD *site* is a location holding AD servers. Defining sites for AD makes it easier for administrators to set up replication between servers and configuring systems by physical location. When users log in, the AD-capable machines look at the local site for AD servers capable of authenticating the user, for a reliable and fast connection.

Figure 5.1 displays how contexts, sites, domain trees, and forests relate to one another. In this example, there are two domain trees labeled Alpha and Omega that are part of the overall forest called simply MyForest. Domain tree Alpha has two main naming contexts spread across two sites. Naming context 1 is replicated across site A and site B, while naming context 2 is located only on site A. Each naming context is located on its own server. Site C contains all of domain tree Omega. This domain tree has only one naming context. Although labeled similarly to one in the other domain tree, this naming context 1 is entirely different from the one in domain tree Alpha.

AD redefines the meaning of groups in NT. A *group* compared to a container has member objects of the same or different types. A group is not a conceptual structure of AD objects but a type of AD object in itself. Groups exist in many forms. For example, you can have a group of users that have a common set of security rights. You can have a group of users as part of an e-mail distribution list. You can have a group of application

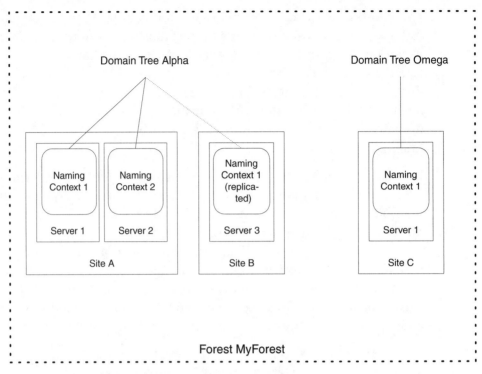

Figure 5.1 Contexts, sites, domain trees, and forests.

objects all belonging to a particular software suite. Groups can be within the same domain tree or they can span domain trees across the whole forest. A *domain-local group* contains only objects within a single domain tree and can be accessed only by other objects within the same domain tree. A *global group* contains only objects from one domain tree but the group is recognized in other domain trees and anywhere in the forest. Finally, the *universal group* can contain objects from any number of domain trees in the forest and can be accessed anywhere in the forest. Grouping helps reduce the number of AD calls that must be used to identify multiple object access to the group.

Understanding the Architecture of Active Directory

Active Directory is built on the structural model of ISO X.500 directory services. The model defines a schema containing all objects and descriptions of object classes. It defines how object properties are accessed and how objects relate to each other. AD stores the schema describing the directory in a special location within the directory. This allows managers to dynamically change or update the object classes and the schema.

AD consists of several components as shown in Figure 5.2. It has a *directory service agent* (DSA) that manages the storage and access services for the local directory and the way DSAs interact with each other. The DSA is part of the Local Security Authority subsystem discussed in Chapter 2 and later in this chapter.

The schema defines the structure of the AD and all objects contained within. It also provides a set of object classes that define how these

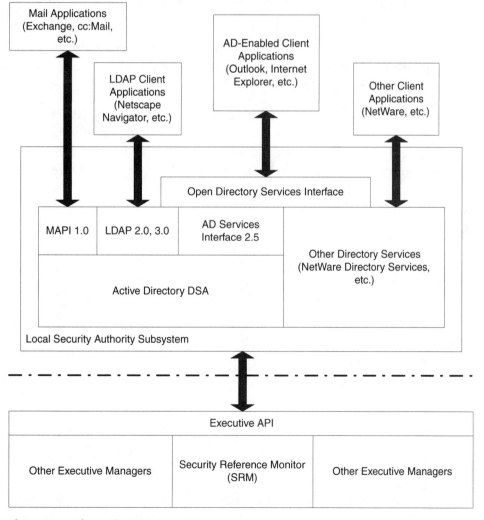

Figure 5.2 The Active Directory OS components.

objects are located and serviced. Applications use the schema to understand the callable methods and how to use an object. The schema itself is stored on an AD server, which means that it is also built of objects. There are three types of schema objects: classes, properties, and syntaxes. *Schema class objects* help create a programmable interface to manage and control the schema. You can use *schema property objects* to retrieve or set the current state of schema class objects. *Schema syntax objects* define how AD providers (which we will discuss in the next section) interact with the schema. In short, the schema defines what objects look like within an AD server, how they behave, and their place in the hierarchy of objects. Unless you have detailed knowledge of how Active Directory works as a whole, we advise you to stay away from modifying the schema.

The *directory information tree* (DIT) is the formal hierarchy of objects stored in the Active Directory (see Figure 5.3). It defines how each object relates to other objects in parent-child or sibling relationships.

Within the DIT there are at least three naming contexts or partitions to contain the schema, the configuration of the AD server, and the domain of objects within the directory. As indicated earlier, a naming context is a subtree of objects that can be replicated across multiple AD servers.

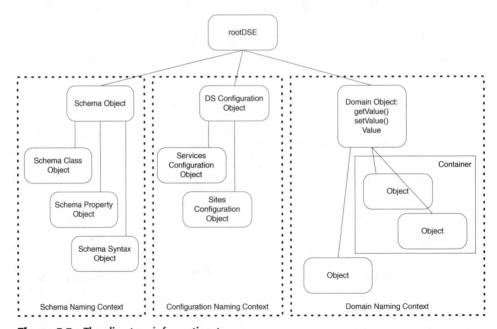

Figure 5.3 The directory information tree.

The *schema naming context* contains the schema of all objects that are part of the entire domain tree. The *configuration naming context* contains two subtrees: services and sites. The services subtree contains objects defining all the system services running, with four children subdivided into Windows NT, network services, remote access services, and other services. The sites subtree contains information about AD sites of multiple servers. The subtree is further subdivided by the subnet that the site belongs to and the individual sites within the domain tree or forest. These individual sites contain sitewide license settings, directory service settings, file replication services, and the settings of individual per-site server settings. Finally, the *domain naming context* is where all the objects reside in the DIT.

The *rootDSE* (root directory service entry), which serves the root point of the DIT, contains properties about the directory server (see Table 5.2). The rootDSE is specific to each AD server and contains global variables used by the access and replication services built into AD. The rootDSE is unique on each server and can always be accessed by specifying just the object name *rootDSE* at the server.

The core interface to AD is implemented in the AD Services Interface (ADSI). ADSI provides the programming API for retrieving, modifying, and managing AD objects. Originally, Microsoft envisioned the Open Directory Services Interface (ODSI) to provide a neutral interface for multiple directory systems including AD, NDS, and any LDAP server. However, even Microsoft admits that ODSI is mostly implemented in ADSI and often uses the terms interchangeably.

Accessing AD Services

Access to AD is structured on ADSI *providers* and *clients*. A provider connects a client to an AD object with a specific protocol. Currently supported providers support LDAP, MAPI, WinNT, NDS, and NWCompat. The Lightweight Directory Access Protocol (LDAP) versions 2 and 3 provide platform-independent network directory service. The Windows Messaging API (MAPI) provides support for application-neutral messaging and mail services. The WinNT provider allows clients to connect to primary and backup domain controllers on NT 3.51 and 4.0 networks. The NDS provider connects to objects in Novell's NetWare Directory Services. Finally, the NWCompat provider connects clients to objects on older NetWare 3.x servers.

Table 5.2 The RootDSE of an Active Directory Server

ROOTDSE PROPERTY	DESCRIPTION
ConfigurationNamingContext	DN for the configuration container.
CurrentTime	Current time on this server.
DefaultNamingContext	DN for the domain that this AD server belongs to.
DnsHostName	DNS hostname for this server.
DsServiceName	DN of the settings object of the AD server.
HighestCommittedUSN	Highest update sequence number used by this AD server, for replication purposes.
LdapServiceName	LDAP service principal name for this server.
NamingContexts	DNs for all the naming contexts stored in this server.
RootDomainNamingContext	DN for the root domain of the forest that this domain belongs to.
SchemaNamingContext	DN for the schema container.
ServerName	DN for the server object in the configuration container.
SubschemaSubentry	DN for the subschema object that contains properties that define how all object properties in the schema are accessed.
SupportedControl	Object IDs for ActiveX/COM controls associated with this directory.
SupportedLDAPVersion	List of all LDAP versions supported by the server (current LDAP 2 and 3).
SupportedSASLMechanisms	Security mechanisms for LDAP.

To allow ActiveX Data Objects and older object linking and embedding (OLE) applications to use ADSI objects, there is an OLE database provider within ADSI that emulates existing OLE DB providers. The OLE DB providers are used to connect services such as the Open Database Connectivity (ODBC) system, a neutral software interface to multiple database products.

A client using any of these providers may be a user application or the operating system. In fact, applications developed for Win 2000 will most likely be clients in one form or another, directly or indirectly. AD function calls are normally COM interfaces to free the client application of the underlying network API calls. This allows clients to be written in several programming and scripting languages. Those written in scripting languages such as Visual Basic, VBScript, JScript, Active Server Pages, and Java/J++ use the automated COM services. It is also possible to access these providers through nonautomated COM services in low-level languages like C and C++. Figure 5.4 shows how clients communicate through ADSI providers with the respective servers.

Although AD is based upon X.500 it doesn't implement the complete standard. It implements the schema and subsets of some of the protocols needed to provide and distribute directory services. For retrieving information from the directory server or for saving to it, applications use LDAP or the native function calls in ADSI. X.500 has other protocols that AD does not implement for accessing and distributing objects between

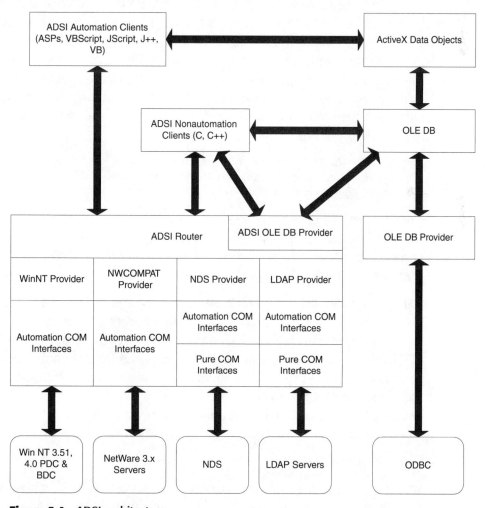

Figure 5.4 ADSI architecture.

DSAs. LDAP provides most of the same functions provided by these other protocols.

Searching across a large directory tree can be time consuming. To facilitate this, the local AD server maintains a *global catalog* (GC), an index of all names in the directory, organized according to their naming contexts. The index contains the names of the objects and only a partial set of its properties that are needed to locate the object. The catalog is automatically built and distributed by the AD server replication system. It is limited to one AD domain tree; each separate domain tree in a forest maintains a separate global catalog.

AD services and objects can be accessed directly from a server through a naming convention known as *ADSPaths*. This follows the style of LDAP access to objects on a network. The path usually consists of a service type (LDAP, GC, WinNT, NDS, etc.), a hostname (e.g., einstein .atollsw.com), and an object path. With some protocols such as LDAP, there may even be a port number after the hostname to indicate the specific network port for the client to connect to. The object path can be in various forms; it can be a distinguished name, a globally unique ID, or even a file path. For example:

```
ldap://atollsw.com:999999/CN=Tom Duff,OU=San Diego, DC=AtollSW,DC=Com
WinNT://einstein/<GUID=9a3c0110f7e1f161a6bb8aaf842b9cfa>
GC://einstein.atollsw.com/CN=Tom Duff,OU=San Diego,DC=AtollSW,DC=Com
```

Another way to access these services is through *serverless binding*. In this method, you don't specify a hostname to connect to. The local AD server will attempt to locate the most plausible server on the network that complies with the object name you specify.

AD is integrated with the *Domain Name System* (DNS) used commonly on the Internet to translate hostnames to Internet addresses. It uses DNS as the location service for AD servers and client machines. Unlike NT 3.51 and 4.0, AD domains are now the same as DNS domain names. AD servers are located through a special DNS table configuration known as the *Service Resource Record* (SRV RR). The DNS Start-of-Authority file, defining how a particular domain is structured with respect to name services, contains this resource record. The SRV RR is of the following form:

```
<service protocol>.<network protocol>.<domain> SRV RR PRI WGHT ADServerName
```

where PRI is a numerical priority for the server, WGHT is a secondary numerical weighting for a particular server in an AD site, and ADServer-

Name is its hostname. For example, the SRV RR for the domain atollsw .com could be as follows:

```
ldap.tcp.atollsw.com.  SRV RR 1 1 ldap1.sandiego.atollsw.com.
                        SRV RR 1 2 ldap2.sandiego.atollsw.com.
                        SRV RR 2 1 ldap2.tucson.atollsw.com.
```

AD Security

AD implements secure access to each object in the tree using the access control lists within the operating system. Each object has a *security identifier* (SID) that is part of its GUID, and an ACL. Access control entries, within the ACL, can be applied to each object directly by the administrator or they can be inherited from its container.

The AD system also allows specific users to be given rights to portions of the AD tree. The user is granted access and is allowed to perform designated actions to the identified objects and branches in the tree. This process of *delegated administration* allows network managers to assign specific administrative tasks to their subordinates.

When AD objects are accessed, they are normally passed in unencrypted form. When writing a network client application, it is advisable to use the authentication and encryption options. If the authentication flag is set, the network user must first be authenticated before it is allowed access to the object the first time. The client application can also be set to prompt users for their credentials through a system dialog box. The object data can also be encrypted using public-key cryptography in the secure sockets layer (part of the networking and security system), for transmission over a network.

AD Replication

Since a domain tree might have multiple naming contexts, some of which may be needed on multiple servers or even sites for the sake of performance, it makes sense to build a replication service directly into AD. The form of replication available with AD is known as *multimaster replication*. This means that the each naming context can be modified by client applications within a server independently of the other copies. The replication system keeps track of these changes and propagates them across the various copies of the naming contexts. This replication process is automatic and coordinated with the help of *update sequence numbers* (USNs).

The USN is a 64-bit number stored in the rootDSE of each AD server. When an object is modified on the server, the USN is incremented. Each AD server maintains a table of USNs of other servers with replicated naming contexts. When the server finds that it's time to replicate, it requests the current USN of each of the other servers and compares it against those stored in its table. If the USN of any of the other AD servers is higher than what is in the table, the AD server requests the other AD servers for the changes to its naming context and updates the local copy appropriately.

There is still the chance that two of the AD servers might have changed the same object before the replication step. During such a *replication collision*, the first AD server cannot tell simply from the USN which is the correct state for the object across the entire domain tree. For this reason, each property of each object has a *property version number*. This number is used to determine which is the proper state for that property of that object across the entire domain tree.

Each object originates from one of the AD servers. All copies of the naming context that the object belongs to must adhere to the value of the object on the originating server. When a write is performed on the originating server (known as an *originating write)*, this is the state that the object and all its copies must be set to. The originating writes are the only ones that actually increment the property version number. During a replication collision, all changes to object properties on replicated servers are held off until the originating write to the object property is first synchronized with all the replicated servers. This means you can't change the value of an object unless everyone agrees with the original first.

The propagation of changes through the replication system can be a linear path from one server to all others or it can be looped across multiple servers. A propagation loop allows for full redundancy should any of the servers go down. However, you must be able to prevent the propagation from continuing endlessly through the loop. For this, AD performs what is known as *propagation dampening,* based upon the USNs of originating writers. Each server keeps a list of server-USN pairs as its *up-to-date vector*. If the USN of an originating writer is higher than that of the current server, the data does not need to be propagated to that server. This vector list is secondary to the USN list for replication and is used only to determine propagation.

Finally, replication differs between servers within the same site and those between two or more sites. When servers need to replicate with others within the same site, they use remote procedure calls that are part of ADSI. When a server needs to replicate to another site, which may be as close as the next room or on the other end of the country, it can use the RPC mechanism or it can send its replication data through the messaging APIs. AD is integrated with Microsoft Exchange 5.0 to provide these messaging services. To put it simply, the replicated objects can be sent over e-mail specifically to the remote AD servers.

Publishing Objects

Publishing is the step of creating an object within AD. When you create new user accounts, you effectively publish their accounts to the AD, which registers them with the security database. Published information is structured as a set of properties defining the object. This information is relatively static and is not a temporary object.

Application data can be published in AD in three ways: as a new object in the AD tree, through *application-specific objects*, or by using *connection points*. A new object is recorded in the schema and becomes a child somewhere within the tree. It is assigned a new GUID and a distinguished name. Application-specific objects are created when an application is installed and contains the current configuration settings of the object. When we modify an application to suit our needs, it changes the properties of these application-specific objects. Finally, connection points are named objects that may be short-lived. For example, RPC, Winsock, and some COM interfaces are part of the connection point known as the *service administration point*. Other COM interfaces particular to applications can have their own connection points.

Summary

Active Directory greatly increases the versatility of the Win 2000 environment in large companies. By distributing user, application, and other information in a directory service, any machine is thus able to access the required information, given proper permissions. The structure of the system is complex enough to support hundreds of thousands of users and is capable of distributing this information across many servers and sites. This makes it ideal for large companies. At the same time, the model is simple enough to create a small directory just for a local office, making it useful for small businesses as well.

Novell was among the first to successfully implement directory service as a core component of their network operating system but Active Directory holds much promise for the Windows environment. The compatibility issues with LDAP may give rise to some problems eventually but for the most part, it can interact with other applications that are independent of Active Directory. There are tools for ensuring full compatibility and cross-directory communications but current work in standards groups are trying to tackle the problem by integrating directory services with the eXtensible Markup Language (XML). In the future, you will be able to access any of the directory information from any operating systems platform.

Active Directory is what allows Win 2000 to scale to large networks. Most prominently it helps with managing user accounts and account authentication as discussed in the next chapter.

Windows 2000 Security

The security system in Windows 2000 has gone through a significant overhaul. New security services for network login, certificate-based trust models, and cryptographic APIs have been added to the mix. Win 2000 still uses some of the internal data structures for describing an object's security level, but the external components for connecting to the system have changed. Most importantly, the new security model is integrated with Active Directory allowing it to scale to enterprise size networks.

In this chapter we introduce the existing and new features built into the Windows 2000 security model. We follow this with a description of the various system objects and security components and objects such as login and authentication, file and application access, and account privileges, and how they work and interact with each other.

New Security Features

The design of NT and Windows includes security monitoring at multiple levels. In the UNIX model, security is simply a matter of the user identifier, group membership, and file access privileges, which, in turn, determine the runtime security privileges of applications. NT was designed for security at all levels of the system. Security objects determine who has access, the type of access, and at what level.

The security architecture of Win 2000 is tightly integrated with Active Directory when on a network. Although standalone machines can have their separate accounts and security settings, in any network larger than 10 machines it makes more sense to use the integrated structure within AD. Think of AD as providing the distributed database services for storing account and security information.

In total, Win 2000 introduces a number of features to security services in particular:

- Accounts now reside on Active Directory and can be spread across multiple servers and sites. Replication of account information speeds authentication and the stability and reliability of the information.

- You can now group accounts into logical organizational units to match your corporate structure rather than a flat account namespace in NT 4.0 domains.

- You can have system administrators who are delegated a particular organizational unit to manage only accounts within their area of responsibility.

- Trust relationships between Active Directory servers is simplified through transitive trusts between all organizational units within a domain tree. You no longer have to manually set trust relationships between domains.

- User authentication on a network is now based on Kerberos 5, an Internet and common UNIX standard certificate-based authentication system. Account passwords are never transmitted over the network; only certificates are.

- A single sign-on service allows users to log in anywhere on the network and still be authenticated within their organizational unit, maintaining a unique identity anywhere on the network.

- New security protocols such as Transport Layer Security (TLS) and Secure Sockets Layer (SSL) 3.0 provide strong client application authentication using public-key certificates.

- Microsoft CryptoAPI and Certificate Server provide centralized certificate management services for the enterprise.

- Encryption services are now part of the operating system (CryptoAPI) to provide new types of user and application services such as an encrypted file system.

- Security properties of an object can now be inherited from its parent automatically.

Understanding Key Security Concepts

Before we discuss how the security mechanisms in Win 2000 work, there are several key concepts and data structures that you should understand. The Windows security model takes the concepts of user accounts to a new level. Compared to UNIX, the security identity of each user session is more detailed.

When a user logs into a UNIX machine through a terminal connection, there is usually a set of information that is assigned to the new process created for the session. This includes items like the terminal device number, the process identifier, and the user account name and number. The system views the security and access level of that user based upon the user account number and group number. In Windows, all user session security is based on an access token that defines the security level allowed to that session. The token contains a number of items including the basic user and group identifiers, a specific set of account privileges, their default access security setting (similar to the umask in UNIX), and a list of restrictions. All this is apart from other information about users' sessions such as their terminal device and memory usage.

Each object on the system also has a security descriptor indicating which users and objects can access it. The closest concept in UNIX is that of file permissions, although on Windows, it isn't restricted to the file system. Windows also implements access control lists, which can identify precisely, down to the user or group, who is allowed access to the object and how.

The Security Identifier

The security identifier (SID) is how objects are uniquely identified on a system. It is a set of numbers that define the type of object (with respect to security), where it belongs, and whom it belongs to. The basic format is as follows:

```
S-1-5-21-118821091-1102943891-238368926-1022
```

The SID always starts with the letter *S*. The first number indicates the SID version number. For NT 3.1 through 5.0 (Windows 2000), the value is always 1. The second number is called the *identifier authority*. The third is the *identifier subauthority*. In fact, all the number sets after the second one are simply called identifier subauthorities until the final number (in this example, 1022), which is known as the *relative identifier* (RID).

There are several common values for the SID that are predefined within the system. These values, as shown in Table 6.1, are used to define the SID of objects that always have the same identity. These SIDs may be complete or have additional identifier subauthorities as indicated.

The RID value is used to identify specific user accounts. Most built-in user accounts for the system start at RID value 500 (see Table 6.2). All non-built-in user accounts start at the RID value 1000.

Account Privileges

Every user account has a set of rights or privileges that dictate what that account is capable of. These include simple user privileges, such as being allowed to interactively log in, and range to administrator privileges, such as being allowed to create a backup of the system. The NT system had several built-in groups for user accounts, which still exist in Windows 2000. These built-in groups often have preassigned privileges, as shown in Tables 6.3 and 6.4.

Impersonation

Impersonation allows server processes to execute commands on behalf of and using the identity of clients, somewhat like the SetUID feature in UNIX. It is used in client/server communication within one machine or between multiple machines on a network. Impersonation, however, does not allow a process to execute an entire program in the context of another user; it allows only specific actions by the server process on its socket, remote procedure call, or named pipe object. To execute an entire application, the client must log on and create a session in which to run the application.

There are four levels of impersonations: delegation, impersonation, identification, and anonymous. The *delegation* level allows a server process to completely assume the identity of the client on the local and remote computers. *Impersonation* allows the server to identify the client and impersonate it on the local machine. *Identification* allows the

Table 6.1 SID Identifier Authority Values

SID PREFIX	DESCRIPTION
S-1-0-0	The Null SID. This group has no members and this SID is used when an actual SID is not known.
S-1-1-0	The World or Everyone SID. This group includes all users on any system.
S-1-2-0	The Local SID. This group indicates users who are logged into the console or through Windows Terminal Server.
S-1-3-0	The temporary owner SID of a new object. This is replaced by the actual SID value of the creator of the object, once it has finished being created.
S-1-3-1	The temporary group SID of a new object. This is replaced with the actual SID value of the creator's primary group, once the object has finished being created.
S-1-5-0	The NT Authority SID. This is used only by objects that belong to the NT security authority.
S-1-5-1	RAS Group SID. All users who connect through the remote access modem dial-up services have this SID.
S-1-5-2	Network Group SID. All users who connect through an LAN have this SID.
S-1-5-3	Batch Group SID. All users who execute an application through a batch queue facility have this SID.
S-1-5-4	Interactive Group SID. All users who log in interactively have this SID.
S-1-5-5-x-y	Login session SID. All login sessions start with this SID. The SID has two other numbers, x and y, that are different for each session. This is different from the interactive group SID, since a single user may be logged in several times through multiple sessions.
S-1-5-6	Allowed Login SID. All accounts that are authorized to log in have this SID.
S-1-5-18	System account SID. A special SID and account used only by the operating system.
S-1-5-32	Built-in Domain SID. A special SID and domain owner used only by the operating system when no NT 4.0 domain is specified.

Table 6.2 RID Values

RID VALUE	DESCRIPTION
500	The Administrator account. The default account for the system administrator on any NT or Win 2000 system.
501	The Guest account. The default account for guest users on any NT or Win 2000 system.
1000 and above	User accounts. Any RID above 1000 is an account created by an administrator for any user.

Table 6.3 Default Account Groups

GROUP NAME	DESCRIPTION
Administrators	These accounts have complete access to the system. By default, at least one account, simply called *Administrator*, always exists in this group.
Server Operators	These are NT 4.0 domain accounts that have access to the Domain Controller administration facilities.
Backup Operators	These accounts have limited administration capabilities that are related to drive backup duties.
Account Operators	These are NT 4.0 domain accounts that are only allowed to create regular user accounts.
Replicator	This is a system account used by the AD system for AD replication purposes only.
Print Operators	These are NT 4.0 domain accounts that are allowed to perform the print queue management tasks.
Power Users	On NT Workstation or Win 2000 Professional, these users have the ability to reboot the machine if necessary.
MTS Administrators	These are Win 2000 accounts trusted to perform administration tasks in regard to the Microsoft Transaction Server system.
MTS Impersonators	These are Win 2000 accounts that are allowed to use the MTS system.
WBEM Users	These are Win 2000 accounts that are allowed read-only access to the Web-Based Enterprise Management system.
<Domain>	This is a special account that changes according to the NT 4.0 domain that the system belongs to. The account name matches the domain name. This account is only used by domain controllers to exchange domain information.
Users	These are ordinary user accounts.
Guests	These are guest accounts that allow anonymous login and have very limited privileges.
Everyone	All accounts belong to this group.

server to retrieve the identity of the client only. *Anonymous* prevents the server from identifying or impersonating the client.

The Access Token

All users have an owner SID for their user account object. This SID is then used to create an *access token* to establish that user's identity and all the privileges the user's account has. During the login process, the

Table 6.4 Account Privileges by Default Group

PRIVILEGE NAME	PRIVILEGE DESCRIPTION
Assign Primary Token	Log in to system.
Audit	Create entries in audit logs.
Backup	Back up files and directories.
Change Notify	User applications are notified of changes to files and directories.
Create Machine Account	Create and manage user accounts.
Create Pagefile	Create a system memory page file.
Create Permanent Object	Create a permanent object such as a file or directory.
Debug	Debug a process in memory.
Increase Base Priority	Increase the priority of a process.
Increase Quota	Increase the disk quota of a user.
Load Driver	Load and unload device drivers.
Lock Memory	Lock portions of memory for specific use.
Profile Single Process	Gather profile information on a single process.
Remote Shutdown	Force shutdown of the system from remote.
Restore	Restore files and directories.
Security	Manage audit and security log files.
Shutdown	Shut down the system.
System Environment	Modify the configuration settings in hardware non-volatile RAM on systems that use this.
System Profile	Gather profile information on any process on system.
System Time	Change system time.
Take Ownership	Take ownership of files.
Trusted Computer Base	Privilege holder is part of a subsystem of the OS.
Unsolicited Input	Read unsolicited input from a terminal.

owner SID is used to determine other group SIDs that belong to the account, as shown in Figure 6.1.

The *Token User* property in the token is currently the same as the Owner SID property and indicates which user this is. The *Group SIDs* property indicates all the groups that the user is a member of. The *Privileges* property is a list of all privileges that user has. The token can be of varying sizes depending upon the number of group SIDs or privileges the account has. The *Owner SID* is the actual SID of the user. Every user

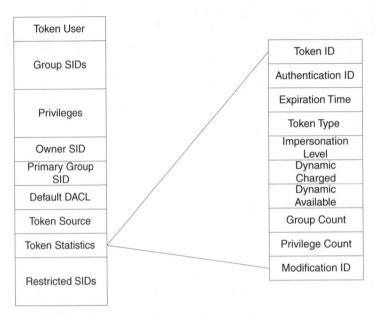

Figure 6.1 The access token.

account has a *Primary Group* that it belongs to. The token defines the *default discretionary access control list* (DACL), which we will cover in the next section. The *Token Source* is a character string describing who created this token.

The Token Statistics structure contains a number of properties that define the token identity, as well as some token modification statistics and information. The *Token Identifier* is a *locally unique identifier* (LUID) created by the system to keep track of the token within the operating system. The *Authentication Identifier* is another LUID created by the Local Security Authority to keep track of the login session that this token originated from. It serves as a session identifier to keep tokens separate between multiple logins by the same user. The *Expiration Time* is a preset time limit counter for how long this access token is valid. According to Microsoft, this last property has not been used, although technically this could be used to limit how long a user is allowed to access a system at any one time. The *Token Type* differentiates between a primary token and an *impersonation* token. If it is an impersonation token, then the *Impersonation Level* indicates the method of impersonation in use.

The *Dynamic Charged* property is the amount of memory allocated for storing the default DACL and primary group SID. The *Dynamic Avail-*

able property is the amount of memory not being used by these two items. These two properties exist because the amount of memory allocated for them is fixed. The *Group Count* indicates the number of group SIDs within the token. The *Privilege Count* indicates the number of privileges in the token. The *Modification Identifier* is an LUID that is changed each time the properties of the token have been changed.

Finally, the *Restricted SIDs* property is a list of SIDs of objects that the token is allowed to access. If the token has this list, then the user can interact only with other objects that are in both the group SIDs and the restricted SIDs. The user can always access any object it owns (i.e., those that have the same SID as the owner).

The Security Descriptor

The access token is compared against an object's *security descriptor* to determine whether the owner of that token can access the object. The descriptor contains ownership information and access control lists that describe who is allowed to access the object and how. There are a variety of objects that use security descriptors, including NTFS files and directories, local or remote printers, other computers, local or remote system services, network shared drives, registry keys, communications objects (mailslots and named pipes), kernel objects (semaphores, events, mutexes, timers), processes and threads, and memory-mapped file objects.

The descriptor, as shown in Figure 6.2, has a number of data structures. The version number describes which version the descriptor format follows. Currently this is still set to 1. The *control flags* indicate special options (see Table 6.5 for a full description), such as what memory layout the descriptor uses, and whether the descriptor contains a discretionary access control list (DACL) or a *system access control list* (SACL).

The *owner SID* and the *primary group SID* are those assigned from the SID information of the owner or creator of this object. The *DACL pointer* and *SACL pointer* are used when the descriptor is not a single contiguous block of memory and they hold references to where the DACL and SACL are stored in memory.

The DACL and SACL are two lists of permissions showing how objects can be accessed by other objects and what to do when an access happens. The DACL contains access rights, while the SACL contains auditing instructions on the type of access used.

Version Number
Control Flags
Owner SID
Primary Group SID
DACL Pointer
SACL Pointer
DACL
SACL

Figure 6.2 The security descriptor.

Access Control Lists

The access control list (ACL), as described in earlier chapters, is a set of entries that identify user or group accounts that are allowed to interact with an object. Each entry, known as an *access control entry* (ACE), can be an *access allowed ACE*, an *access denied ACE*, a *system audit ACE*,

Table 6.5 Control Flags in the Security Descriptor

FLAG NAME	DESCRIPTION
DACL Auto Inherited	In Win 2000, DACL is inherited from parent or creator object.
DACL Defaulted	A default mechanism sets the DACL when accessed.
DACL Present	DACL is present.
DACL Protected	In Win 2000, this indicates that the DACL cannot be modified.
Group Defaulted	A default mechanism sets the group SID when accessed.
Owner Defaulted	A default mechanism sets the owner SID when accessed.
SACL Auto-Inherited	In Win 2000, SACL is inherited from parent or creator object.
SACL Defaulted	A default mechanism sets the SACL when accessed.
SACL Present	SACL is present.
SACL Protected	In Win 2000, this indicates that the SACL cannot be modified.
Self Relative	All descriptor information is in a contiguous block of memory rather than using pointers to other memory locations.

or a *system alarm ACE*. The first two indicate whether an SID is allowed or denied access. The system audit ACE indicates that this type of access is to be logged as an information event in the event log utility. The DACL is a list of ACEs of the first two types. The SACL contains system audit ACEs.

Every ACE has a *trustee*—that is, an account name or an SID that the access entry applies to—and a set of *access rights*. The trustee can be a local account name, an NT 4.0 domain account name, a built-in group name, or one of several other predefined names (the current user, the owner or creator of the object, the group of the owner or creator of the object). In Active Directory, an AD object can have an ACE for accessing the object as a whole, an ACE for each set or group of properties, or an ACE for each property in the object.

There are four types of access rights: generic, standard, SACL, and object-specific. The generic access rights are Read, Write, Execute, and All. The standard access rights are described in Table 6.6. The SACL right indicates that the object's SACL can be accessed or modified by another object. The use of object-specific access rights varies depending upon the type of object. These rights have meaning only in the context of the type of the object.

System Policies

Windows 2000 allows administrators to define strict system policies to regulate how the system is used. System policies allow the administrator to configure portions of the user and system environment so that they are not misused. Both an administrative and a security feature, system policies allow you to regulate the following:

Table 6.6 Standard Access Rights

ACCESS RIGHT	DESCRIPTION
Delete	The right to delete this object.
Read Control	The right to read the information in the object's security descriptor but not its SACL.
Synchronize	The right to use this object in thread synchronization.
Write Discretional Access Control	The right to change this object's DACL.
Write Owner	The right to change the owner of this object.

- *Account policy* determines how often passwords need to be changed, at what times a user is allowed access, how the desktop environment appears, and if the person has access to shared network resources.

- *Local policy* determines how user privileges are assigned and which system events are to be audited, as well as systemwide security options configuration.

- *Event log policy* determines who is allowed access to the system, security, and application logs.

- *System services policy* defines which system services are allowed and how they are configured.

- *File system policy* defines how to configure and analyze security descriptors for file system objects.

- *Registry policy* determines how to configure and analyze security descriptors for registry keys.

- *Restricted group policy* determines which accounts are members of restricted groups and in what ways they are restricted.

We will discuss system policies at length in Chapter 17.

Understanding Windows 2000 Security Architecture

Windows 2000 has several components in user and kernel space that work together to provide system security. In user space, the Local Security Authority Subsystem (LSASS) provides user authentication services and the creation of access tokens. The CryptoAPI, another user-space component, provides central cryptography services for several system components. The Active Directory system plays a very important part in storing information on object security. In kernel space, the *security reference monitor* (SRM) handles requests by processes to evaluate or confirm access security. On the application level, the Kerberos system application acts as a network authentication mechanism for a network of computers.

User Authentication

Win 2000 revises part of the user authentication system in NT 4.0. Multiple *security service providers* to authenticate users and maintain information on user accounts have been available in earlier NT systems, but in Win 2000, we see two parallel authentication mechanisms, by default.

The Local Security Authority from NT 4.0 still provides standalone Win 2000 systems with a built-in authentication system as well as supporting the older NT 4.0 domain network login system. Win 2000 also supports other security providers such as the Kerberos network key authentication system and the Secure Channels authentication system. These other SSPs integrate into the LSA through the *Security Support Provider Interface* (SSPI). The role of the SSPI is to provide a programmable interface that allows the login system to use any number of different authentication mechanisms. The SSPI router handles the task of sending the login request to specific providers.

The Kerberos system is intended to replace the older NT 4.0 domain network login, with better security mechanisms and tighter integration with the Active Directory and management systems. Kerberos, as experienced UNIX administrators will know, provides a means to authenticate users on multiple machines across a network. It uses *public-key cryptography* (PKC) techniques originally designed by RSA Datasystems, which is the leader in PKC technology on the Internet. The Kerberos system in general can actually use several types of cryptographic authentication methods including PKC, the Data Encryption System (DES), Triple DES, and RC-4, depending upon the preference of the network administrator and what is available at the location.

Figure 6.3 shows what the new security system in Win 2000 looks like displaying the traditional Local Security Authority (LSA) and the new Active Directory/Kerberos-based network authentication system. The authentication process through each mechanism is explained in the next section.

The Login Process

The user account authentication or login process begins when a user contacts the operating system to initiate a login. If you are directly on the console, this is done with the *secure attention sequence* (SAS), or by pressing the Control-Alt-Delete buttons on the console keyboard at the same time.

Activating the SAS presents the login window, WinLogon.exe, which requires you to enter a user account name and a password. This window itself is a special dialog window created by the Graphical Identification and Authentication (GINA) library. GINA looks for the SAS in the keyboard form (Ctrl-Alt-Del) or in other forms such as a smartcard, voice

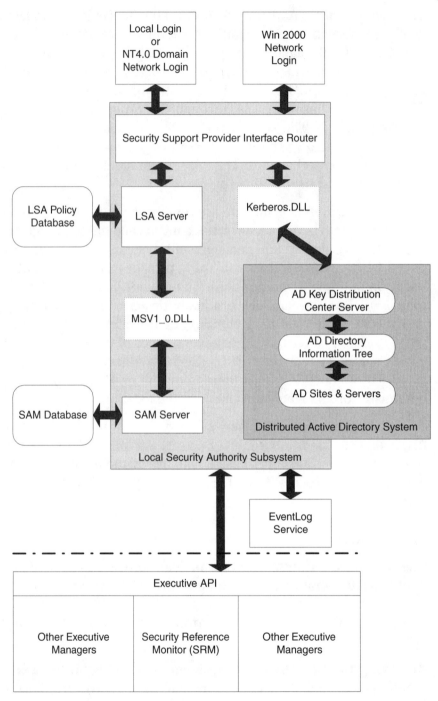

Figure 6.3 User authentication components.

authentication, and fingerprint authentication, and takes the authentication parameters. Microsoft provides the default GINA called *msgina.dll*.

WinLogon then passes this account name and password to the Local Security Authority Subsystem (LSASS.exe). At this point, the system has to determine how to handle the account. GINA allows a user to perform either a local or a network login, and the processing for each is handled through a different mechanism.

Local Login

Win 2000 still keeps available the local account system from NT 4.0 that allows a machine to maintain a set of accounts within itself and not as part of the network. The local account system also provides backward compatibility with NT 4.0 domains, where you have accounts maintained on NT 4.0 domain controllers. Win 2000 also offers a new secure network login through Kerberos, as we indicated earlier.

If it is a local or NT 4.0 domain login, the LSA server, a subcomponent of the LSASS, hands it off to the account verification code, which is, by default, contained in MSV1_0.dll (Microsoft Verify 1.0).

This verifier first checks whether it is a local login or an NT 4.0 domain login. If it is a local login, the verifier contacts the security accounts manager (SAM) server (in samsrv.dll) to check against the local SAM database. The SAM database is a protected area of the system registry that corresponds to \HKEY_Local_Machine\SAM\SAM. This is directly mapped to the SAM registry file \Winnt\System32\Config\SAM.__. This part of the registry cannot normally be seen by even the administrator and seems to be empty when you look at it from the registry editor. The format for the database is undocumented and subject to change.

The system compares the authentication parameters given by the user against the list of accounts with the SAM database and extracts that user's SID. This SID is then passed back to the verifier, which in turn passes it back to the LSA server to look up what privileges this account has.

The LSA server at this point checks the given SID against the *NT Security Database*. This file is stored in \Winnt\System32\Config\Security.__. and maps to the system registry key \HKEY_Local_Machine\Security. The Security database contains the list of all privileges that have been assigned to this account and all the groups that this account is part of.

The LSA then creates an access token based upon the user SID, group SIDs, and privileges that can be used by the system and any applications to track and identify this user while logged in.

NT 4.0 Domain Login

If MS Verify 1.0 determines that this is an NT 4.0 domain account, it uses a subcomponent library known as Netlogon (netlogon.dll). This subcomponent looks up the NT 4.0 domain by the domain name given by the user when entering the login parameters. It contacts the domain controller for the given domain and sends this information over the network to the domain controller.

At the domain controller, its own Netlogon component passes the information up to MSV1_0.dll, which checks it through the SAM and Security database on the controller. These steps are the same as if making a local login directly on the domain controller. This SID information is then relayed back to the original machine the user is logging into and is passed up to its LSA server to create the access token.

Kerberos Login

The Kerberos system does not use MSV1_0.dll at all. In Win 2000, all network accounts are stored in Active Directory. The user logging into a workstation specifies the AD domain login. The Kerberos system contacts the AD system to determine a public key and uses this key as a means of identifying the user. The user can then be logged into a network server based upon this key.

The LSA server passes the authentication parameters to kerberos.dll if it determines that this is a Win 2000 network login. The Kerberos system creates an initial ticket or *ticket-granting ticket* (TGT), which is an encrypted hash of the user's password and the local workstation's public key, and caches the TGT in a local cache. It then sends the TGT to the nearest AD Key Distribution Center (KDC). The KDC checks the format and attempts to decrypt the ticket using the private key of the workstation that the KDC already has a copy of. If the decryption works, the KDC takes the unencrypted user password and compares it against the copy of the user password that it has stored.

The KDC then creates a *session ticket* based upon the TGT. This session ticket can also be used with any of the other machines in the same domain. When the machine receives a session ticket from a workstation, it decrypts the ticket and determines that it was generated with the help of a known KDC server. The user is thus logged into a network server.

Session tickets normally have a limited lifespan and are used only when users are interacting with a machine (i.e., while they are logged in). The lifespan is determined by the security policy set for the entire AD domain and, by default, is eight hours. If the session ticket expires while a user is still logged in, the machine the user is connected to generates an expiration error, which causes the workstation the user is logged into to request another session ticket, and the whole process repeats.

The session ticket can be used to specifically log into any of the servers that are part of the AD domain as long as the user has the correct privilege to access the server. Once the user is logged in, the server contacts the Active Directory system to determine the user's SID and load the group SIDs and privileges. The owner SID, group SIDs, and privileges are now stored as part of the Active Directory system and, as part of the AD system, they can be distributed across multiple AD servers and sites. The network server the user logs into then takes this SID information set and creates an access token to be used by the local operating system executive.

We presented this scenario as if the user's workstation and the network server were two separate machines, but this is not necessarily so. They can be the same machine and yet still use this same network login process. The speed at which this process completes depends upon the design of your AD system and how the object information is distributed to the various AD servers and sites. As a whole, this is a more secure system that never passes account passwords in the clear and even passes encrypted passwords only once between the client workstation and the KDC.

Kerberos introduces authentication *realms* focused around the KDCs. Each realm can have one or more KDCs provide authentication for a number of machines within that realm. Very often, the realm follows the AD domain. However, in a large AD domain, it is better to have multiple KDC realms supporting the individual organizational units within.

Users can be authenticated between realms as well. When the user specifies a different realm to log into, it contacts the local realm KDC first and obtains a session ticket for the remote KDC. The user then contacts the remote KDC and creates another session ticket that is recognized by the servers in that realm.

Summary

The big shift from domain controller based login to Kerberos based login separates the authentication task from the directory service. Under this new model in Win 2000, system security and authentication is now performed by a separate service that may run on separate servers. However, authentication is still tightly wound into the Active Directory service as the authentication server has to check user identity and attributes against that stored in the directory. AD allows per-object level access control lists that need to be compared to the user's identity and this is again compared to the user's security token once logged in.

The Kerberos system makes it easier to manage login authentication by reducing the workload on the important Active Directory servers. It also adds much greater security by not passing passwords across the network at all, only certificates. Someday all Internet logins will be based upon this certificate method. Win 2000 thus brings Kerberos into mainstream use.

Once logged in, the user will face the new Win 2000 user interface which, not coincidentally, looks very much like that of Windows 98.

## CHAPTER 7

The Windows 2000 User Interface

I f you are going to work with multiple platforms, you have to know the ins and outs of the primary user interfaces of each system. You may be used to the shell interface on UNIX or to your choice of window managers. Windows, however, allows a total (non-) variety of one GUI and one command line interface, which means you have to live with what you get.

The Windows GUI went through a major change between Windows for Workgroups 3.11 and Windows 95. The style is more like the Motif Window Manager, but only in its visual aspects. The structure and use of this GUI differ quite a bit. Win NT and 2000 also offer an emulation of the 16-bit DOS shell to maintain backward compatibility. This chapter discusses the Windows GUI and Command Shell interfaces and how they can be used to your best advantage.

Using ActiveDesktop

For a while Microsoft was jumping up and down and shouting about the wonders of its new ActiveDesktop system. This combination of Internet Explorer, Windows Explorer, and the desktop that first appeared in portions in Win 98, is by no means a revolutionary idea, but nonetheless is the most popular implementation that mixes the metaphors of local and network resources.

Basically, it combines the file manager views to your local system and your LAN with direct access to Web sites as part of the desktop. ActiveDesktop (see Figure 7.1) combines the concept once forwarded by Pointcast Network and other push technology vendors with the *portal* concept evident in sites like Yahoo! and MSN, and slaps them both onto your desktop. Resources are now commonly addressed by the Universal Resource Location (URL) scheme that is apparent in any Web site address, although all the old methods still work. The new shell also improves on existing features such as the task bar and the start menu, all of which are discussed in detail in this section.

About the Task Bar

The Windows task bar is the equivalent of the Icon Manager window under the Motif Window Manager on UNIX systems, but it includes other useful features. The task bar on Win 2000 (at the bottom of the screen in Figure 7.1) has four areas: the start menu button, the shortcut buttons, the window icons, and the tray.

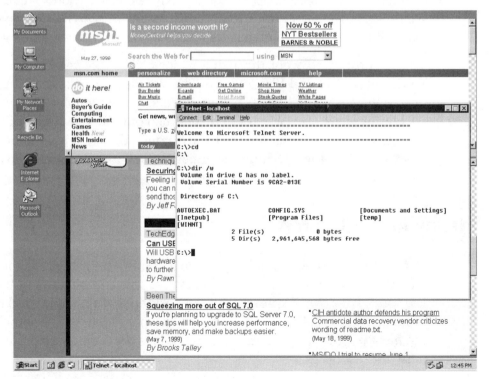

Figure 7.1   The Windows 2000 ActiveDesktop.

The Start menu is a quick access to common commands for the desktop such as Login/logout, Run an application, or Find an item. You can access settings for the system and the most recently accessed documents through this menu. In addition, the **Start menu** shows icons for all Windows applications installed on the system. It is a hierarchical menu that is split into two parts: the system hierarchy and the user hierarchy. The system hierarchy cannot be easily modified by the user and is controlled by the GUI shell itself. The user hierarchy is where the user can place icons to allow quick access to applications or documents. This area is modifiable by the user by clicking on **Start**, **Settings**, **Task Bar**, or right-clicking on the **Start menu** and selecting **Properties**.

The shortcut buttons menu was added to the task bar with Internet Explorer 4.0. They allow you to define icons for shortcuts to applications or documents that can be started immediately. It does sort of duplicate the role of the start menu, but users found that the start menu becomes easily cluttered when you have large numbers of applications installed. Unlike the start menu, this one only shows icons; however, if you move your cursor over to rest on the icon, a pop-up window will show the name of the icon. The shortcut buttons allow you one-click access to very commonly used applications and some additional desktop functions. In particular, there are always buttons for the Explorer application and Hide All Windows button. This menu is also resizable and scrollable, so you can display a small number of icons at a time and allow the user to scroll through the list to get to others. To add new buttons to this menu you can either right-click on properties and define a new shortcut to an application or just drag and drop a shortcut onto it.

The application icons portion of the task bar shows individual running applications as icons and names. Rather than displaying just minimized application windows, the task bar shows an icon for every window, with the current active window as a highlighted icon. You can bring to the front, display, or minimize windows by clicking directly on their icons. These icons dynamically resize themselves to show individual icons for every running application. As they resize to become smaller, the names of the application displayed in the icon are abbreviated. Running more than 10 applications on a 1024×768 screen will leave very little of the name, so you can either not do it, remember what windows match to which icons, or simply increase the size of the task bar.

The desktop tray is a small window of icons in the task bar that shows applications or applets that are currently running on the system in the background. The differentiation between these applications and others is that these do not require opening a Window to run the application. They may be preloaded at boot time, as is the case with virus checkers, the system lock, the system agent, or the audio volume control applet. They may also be launched by the user during a login session such as the dial-up connection applet.

Single- or double-clicking these icons may bring up a configuration window or just present an About box. These applets are usually preconfigured to execute a task that either saves the output to a file or does not require any visual output. In some cases, the icons may even be animated to display action or modified to indicate a different state.

These tray applets are specific to the user and his or her current workstation. A server system will also show these icons as present, but only during the active login session of a user directly on the console. One common application on the Internet, for example, called ICQ (a clever play on "I Seek You"), appears entirely as a tray applet. However, this applet can also bring up full applications for chatting, messaging, or directory searches.

The task bar as a whole can be resized or moved around the screen. You can increase the size of the pane of the task bar by dragging the edge facing the center of the screen. You can even hide the task bar away almost completely if you need that extra desktop space by dragging it away from the center of the screen. This leaves a thin line at the edge, which marks where the task bar went. And for the next magic trick, you can make the task bar completely disappear and reappear whenever you move the cursor toward where it is supposed to be, by setting an option under **Start**, **Settings**, **Task Bar**.

To move the entire task bar, click on any area of the task bar and drag the cursor to any one wall of the screen. The task bar will only sit at the edges of the screen and cannot be free floating on the desktop.

Using Explorer

The Explorer file manager application that originally came with Windows 95 has been extended to merge with Internet Explorer (IE), Microsoft's Web browser. In Win 2000, this is based upon IE version 5.0. Explorer is a combination of file, program, network access, printer access, dial-up connection, desktop, Internet, and control panel managers. You can access or configure files or devices in each area through this same application.

Disk Functions

Explorer can browse drives, directories, and documents within trees. Drives are listed individually, sometimes with an icon indicating the type of drive it is. Following each drive is the volume name (if assigned during format time) and the drive letter. Unfortunately, the drives will not show what type of file system is installed on the drive.

Keep in mind that each of these drive devices is a logical drive and does not necessarily represent an entire physical drive. As discussed in Chapter 2, you can have multiple logical drives on a single physical drive or you can combine several physical drives into a single logical drive. In addition, the drives could also be mapped to others on the network.

Removable media drives such as floppy disks, CD-ROMs, ZIP drives, or DVD-ROMs installed on the system should always appear in Explorer. However, until actual media are loaded into the device, any action to access the device will result in a *Device Not Ready* error. Basically this is the way Windows says that it does not see an appropriate file system in the drive. If such an error appears on a hard drive, then there is either a physical or a file system problem with the drive.

CD-ROM and DVD-ROM drives are automatically recognized by the system and displayed as such. If the CD or DVD contains software applications, it may show a special icon for the main application on the system. The Windows system will attempt to automatically run an application when one such disk is placed in the drive. This facility, with information contained in a file called *Autorun* in the root directory of the CD or DVD, will start either an application or the installation process for the package.

Right-clicking on a drive will bring up other properties or actions that can be performed on the drive. In particular, three commands—**Format**, **Sharing**, and **Properties**—will perform actions on the overall drive. The **Format** command will attempt to reformat the drive either by completely wiping off all the data or by wiping off only the file system on-disk structures. The first method rewrites random data over the entire physical drive, while the second method wipes the file system structures but actually leaves the files and directories still in place. With special utilities, you can recover a drive accidentally wiped this way.

The **Sharing** and **Properties** commands bring up a general dialog box describing the properties of the disk and how the drive is shared on the network, as well as some tools for drive error checking, defragmenting, or checking the status of the last backup of this drive. Each of these launches a separate system application to execute the actions.

File and Folder Functions

As mentioned in Chapter 3, folders are different from directories. A directory can be a folder, but a folder is not necessarily a directory. Some folders run special applications or views of the system, for example, the Control Panels folder and the Desktop folder. These folders do not show actual files or applications that reside somewhere on the file system but, rather, system applications and folders that can be visually represented as such.

You can view files within Explorer in four modes: as a file list, as a detailed file information list, and as small or large icons. The individual files themselves can be arranged by their name, extension, size, or the date when the file was created. When in icon view, a toggle option for autoarranging files will place the files in preset positions so that you don't have to worry when you move an icon around; it helps clear up space, too.

By default, not all files are shown. The system files such as dynamically linked libraries, virtual device drivers, and configuration files will not show up until you select an option under **View**, **Options**, **Show All Files**.

Data file icons are shown by the program associated to open that file. For example, a Microsoft Word document would show a Word document icon; a Web page will show an Internet Explorer icon, and so forth. These associations are stored within the registry and map to the extension of the file. Unfortunately, this isn't entirely a smart system. Two applications that use completely different data file formats but the same extension (e.g., .sav) cannot both have their own permanent associations to that file. This means that double-clicking on the data file will launch one application or the other based upon the association, even if it isn't the correct one. Even if you right-click on a file icon to bring up other options for opening the document, you will only see the default **Open** command, which launches the associated executable program. To ignore this association, when you hold down the **Shift** key and right-click on the icon, you will see a second option called **Open With** that lets you select an alternative executable application.

Desktop Functions

Aside from the task bar and application windows, the desktop itself holds icons and has default properties. The main icons that always appear on the desktop are called, by default, *My Computer, My Documents, My Network Places, Recycle Bin*, and *Internet Explorer*. Double-clicking on any of these will launch Explorer, but with a different view of each.

The first, *My Computer*, displays the top level of the local system showing all connected drives, the *Printers* folder, the *Control Panel* folder, the *Scheduled Tasks* folder, and the *Network Connections* folder. *My Documents* is the default folder where new documents are stored. This folder is stored on your system disk within each user's personal profile directory. The *My Network Places* icon shows all other systems on your LAN that are reachable from your machine. This is not the same as the *Network Connections* folder that displays configuration files and the status for dialup connections and LAN connections to the machine. The Recycle Bin and the Internet Explorer icons should be fairly obvious and are described in other sections.

The icons are, by default, arranged at the left side of the screen starting at the top, but this placement can be changed. The default icons cannot be removed from the desktop and are controlled by the predefined profile for the *Default User*.

The desktop itself is viewed as the root folder for all other folders and directories in Explorer. When you *explore* the file systems, the very top node is the desktop; immediately under this, you have each of the icons seen on the desktop either as a folder or a file. The actual desktop, like all other folders, is defined within the registry. However, each user has his or her own desktop view. The default icons are always present, but each user may have his or her own desktop icons for applications and files also showing. These, on the other hand, are not special settings but either files or directories that are stored under the user's personal directory (e.g., \Documents and Settings\AllUsers\rawn).

The properties dialog box for the desktop will show six tabs: *Background, Screen saver, Appearance, Web, Effects*, and *Setting* properties. The Background properties tab defines the kind of wallpaper that you use for a background—either a picture, a pattern, or a single color. The Screen saver properties tab defines which screen saver is to be used, the properties of that screen saver, how long to sit idle before it goes off, and whether the screen is to be locked with a password when the saver goes off. If you have an energy-saving monitor, this can also be used to access power management features of the monitor.

The Appearance properties tab defines the color and font scheme used on your desktop. This includes titles for windows, icons, menus, and dialog boxes, as well as sizes for window border widths, scrollbars, and spacing between icons. The Web properties tab is discussed further in the next section. The Effects properties tab allows you to change the bitmap image and color depth used for default icons, as well as setting transition effects between windows, smoothing screen fonts, and determining whether contents of a window are displayed when it is dragged around and whether the navigation underlines for menu commands are hidden until the Alt keyboard button is pressed. Finally, the Setting properties tab defines the color and screen resolution of the desktop; the *Advanced* button in this tab gives access to more tabs for managing the device drivers for the graphics card, monitor frequency settings, advanced desktop control functions, and so on.

Browsing and Internet Functions

It's a system browser; it's an Internet browser; it's a dessert topping all in one! Well, probably not the last one, but the versions of Explorer in Win 98 and 2000 are both desktop system browsers as well as Web and Internet browsers. In Win 2000, the desktop Explorer is interfaced with Internet Explorer 5.0. There are two ways of doing this: You can have a desktop view to Web sites or you can launch independent Explorer application windows to each site.

By interfacing the desktop shell with Internet Explorer, you can now view any resource accessible by a URL directly on your desktop wallpaper. These seem to appear as special application windows on your desktop but actually run as part of the shell. These windows have a Confederate gray outline and title bar as opposed to the default Union blue of application windows. They cannot be iconized, although they can be minimized to a smaller box on your desktop, or you can hide them completely by toggling the window name under the right-click pop-up menu. They also cannot be terminated, since they are effectively part of the shell. You can have multiple desktop Web windows to view different Web sites at the same time, although they become overlapped with application windows.

If you right-click on the desktop to bring up the menu, then choose **Active Desktop**, you will see options to add Web sites and to toggle them into and out of view. Other menu options allow you to lock the content to their position on the desktop, add new Web content views, and toggle the desktop icons.

There is some utility in having such default desktop views. You can have a permanent backdrop of your favorite Web site or portal, or a direct view of your file system at all times. If you have applications that run within Internet Explorer, such as ActiveX components, you can keep them viewable on your desktop at all times. With the help of the **Show Desktop** task bar toggle button, you can show and hide all regular applications when you need to turn back to the desktop.

We did mention that there is another way of browsing with the Internet Explorer interfaced desktop. In this mode, it appears to run just like any normal application in its proper window. Since this is both the desktop and Web Explorer, you can type in a file or directory name to view local resources, or you can type in a Web URL to go out to the network somewhere. This browser window can be launched directly from the **Launch Internet Explorer Browser** task bar button.

Your folders themselves can be either viewed as Web pages for yourself or exported on the network for others to access. If you set **View, Folder Options, General, Enable Web Content in Folders** (which is the default), every folder is viewed as a Web page with icons for each file or subfolder. The view is split with the left-hand column describing the details of the folder or a selected file. For instance, if you are at C:\, it will show a 3D pie chart of disk usage; when you select a file, it details what kind of file it is, when it was last modified, the file size, and its attributes. If it is an HTML or a graphics file in particular, it may even show a thumbnail view of what the document looks like before you open it.

Each Explorer folder can have a special file called *folder.htt* (take a look at the one in \Program Files) that presents the folder as an HTML page along with special functions to access the files or subfolders as icons. As with any other Web page, you can also add in other text, images, or plug-in applets to add more definition or pizzazz to the folder, but typically this is used to add script functions that execute when you select files.

Do *not* change the folder.htt files that are in the system areas such as under \Program Files or \Winnt. These can drastically affect the way the browser interacts with the folder and its contents. There are a number of such files under \Winnt\Web that define how your exported drives and local resources are viewed by others if you share them to the Web. Slap any hands with a splintered ruler when they try to approach these unless the brain that's guiding them knows exactly what they do.

Printer Functions

The Printers folder in Explorer is a special application that displays available printers as objects in a folder. In reality it does not correspond directly to a directory on your drive but it does exist as a folder within the registry. The objects in this folder include the default **Add Printer** script, followed by icons for any printers you might have defined. Clicking on **Add Printer** executes a printer wizard to help configure a local or network printer that can be accessed from this system. The printer icons will usually indicate whether the printer is being shared with others (the hand holding the printer in the palm) or whether it is the default printer (a check mark in the top left corner). A printer definition that is incorrect or a printer that is currently malfunctioning will have its icon grayed out.

If you select a printer then click on the **More Info** link in the Explorer column, it will bring out a special Web-based printer control program. This shows all print jobs currently queued for the printer, how to view its properties, and how to pause, resume, or cancel documents. The program is very much like the printer application that pops up as a tray icon whenever you have a print job running.

Network Connection Functions

The Network Connections folder, like the Printers folder, shows available connections from your computer to the network. This may display modem connections, LAN connections, wireless connections, and so on. There is at least one icon in this folder: the **Make a New Connection** wizard. If your system does not have any network connection devices, then this will be blank, of course. Otherwise, a separate connection profile will show here.

When it is connected, the icon will appear and link directly to the connection dialog box for that device. If you right-click for the menu and select **Properties**, you can bring up the device configuration properties of the LAN, modem, or other network device it is associated with. Each connected network device can also be displayed as a tray icon in the task bar; clicking on these tray icons will also show the current status of this connection. Disconnected devices are grayed out in the Network Connections folder.

A special button, called **Network Identification**, in the column within the Folder window will bring up the similarly named tab in the system control panel applet. This shows the hostname and workgroup or domain name to which this computer belongs.

Control Panel Functions

The Control Panel folder is another special nondirectory that exists in the registry. It contains applets that control the installation or configuration of almost all system functions. Depending upon the applications and services you install on the system, there can be anywhere from 20 to 40 different control panel applets. Table 2.6 briefly described the common Control Panel folders.

Now, actually being able to run them is another matter. Control panel applets change the behavior of the system or applications and, thus, typically most of these applets will only work for those who have the proper administrative privileges. Others that control the user environment, such as the video or default sound properties, may be accessible by ordinary users, unless, of course, these too are closed off by the administrator.

The Windows Help Utility

The help system under Windows has been standardized into a common framework and application tool. The original help system isn't too far from the basic HTML pages for the Web. It has text, images, and links that take you from document to document, with a more proprietary tinge, however.

The help application orders information in sets of books or volumes that can contain any level of chapters and subsections and any number of pages. Once you start the help program by clicking on a help icon, or from the start menu, the system does a basic check to see if you have any prebuilt help indexes that facilitate faster searches. It then presents the browser window that shows the volume(s) contained in that help file. Two other tabs show the raw index of all possible keywords in the file

(Index) and the text search interface to the volumes (Search). A graphic view of WinHelp is shown in Figure 7.2.

The difference with help under the ActiveDesktop system is that you can now link keywords directly to URLs on the Web. This uses the Internet Explorer browsing facilities in the system to access the documents and feed them to WinHelp.

The Windows Update utility, introduced with Win 98, allows you to download and install new components to the operating system directly from Microsoft. The system is a combination of a Web site (http://windowsupdate.microsoft.com), an Update client, and update packages. A registered Windows user can download free or paid updates delivered by Microsoft over the Internet and have them install themselves.

As with any installation procedure, Microsoft recommends that you have your system running at minimal use so as not to create any sort of conflicts. Although Microsoft has implemented a component into the operating system that minimizes what are called *DLL conflicts* (dynamically linked or shared system library conflicts), this does not work all the time, nor does it work perfectly. Properly developed applications for Win 2000, on the other hand, should not have this specific problem.

Microsoft hopes to make Windows Update a regularly used feature of their newer operating systems to allow for software distribution. Although they currently don't sell software this way, they have already said that after Win

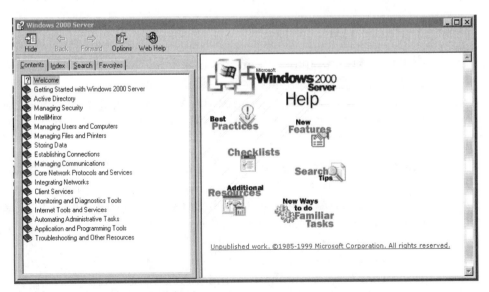

Figure 7.2 The Windows help tool.

2000 they will consider selling only major updates to the operating systems rather than a whole new packaged OS every few years or so. Get with it, but be careful. Although the system is secure for authorized software delivery, the paranoid and the (ahem) unregistered Windows users out there may want to be afraid of the fact that Microsoft may just be watching you.

Using the Command Shell

Windows NT and 2000 provide a command line interface similar to DOS called the *Command Shell* (CMD.EXE). This gives you an 80×25 character window that allows you to type in text commands and create shell scripts for execution manually or by means of another program.

Unlike the 16-bit DOS shell (Command.COM), the Command Shell is a full 32-bit application that runs directly on the system as an application. To offer full 16-bit backward compatibility, Windows includes the *Windows on Windows* (WOW) system within the Win32 environmental subsystem. You can run the old DOS shell within WOW as *Virtual DOS Machine* (VDM). If you launch the Task Manager, you can see the individual processes associated with the Command Shell and Command.Com and can notice the difference between the two.

Although not as complicated as UNIX shells such as KornShell or Bash, the Command Shell provides basic features needed to create a scripting and text command environment. It supports environment variables, but on a systemwide basis (as opposed to per-user environment variables in UNIX); it has line editing tools for typing or repeating commands; it provides some language structures such as labels, conditional structures, loop structures, goto commands, and early program exits; it can call other executable programs to run.

Shell scripting in the Command Shell is actually downright ugly. At best, you could make spaghetti code with it, but even then, without using other executable programs you wouldn't be able to make much more than a tiny morsel of it. The language structures are the same as they were in DOS; they were created years ago as an afterthought more than a design. The basic list of all internal commands is shown in Table 7.1.

There are a number of other text commands that come standard with Windows 2000 and, although they are not internal commands, they are very commonly used in shell scripts. These are basically the ones they left out when they last expanded Command.COM and decided not to stuff into the shell any more (see Table 7.2).

Table 7.1 Command Shell Internal Commands

COMMAND	DESCRIPTION
ASSOC, ASSOCIATE	Associates a file's three-character extension with a file type.
CALL	Executes another program or script.
CD, CHDIR	Changes the directory position to another location.
CLS	Clears the screen.
COLOR	Sets the colors for the Command Shell window.
COPY	Copies a file to a different name or location.
DATE	Shows or sets the date.
DEL, ERASE	Deletes a file.
DIR	Shows the listing of the current directory.
ECHO	Echoes the following string to the text screen.
ENDLOCAL	Closes the scope area for environment variables.
EXIT	Exits the script.
FOR	Repeats a block of commands in a loop.
FTYPE	Associates a file type with an executable application to be launched when it is double-clicked.
GOTO	Jumps to another location in the script.
IF	Starts a conditional command.
MD, MKDIR	Creates a new directory.
MOVE	Moves a file from one directory to another.
PATH	Shows the full command execution path.
PAUSE	Pauses the script until the user hits a key.
POPD	Saves the current directory location before you move to another.
PROMPT	Changes the text prompt.
PUSHD	Retrieves and goes back to a directory location saved earlier.
RD, RMDIR	Removes an empty directory.
REM	The following text on this line is just a comment or remark that is not to be executed.
REN, RENAME	Renames a file in the current directory.
SET	Sets an environment variable.
SETLOCAL	Defines the start of a scope area for environment variables.
SHIFT	Shifts position of input parameters on the command line to left.
START	Executes DOS or Windows application in a separate window.

Table 7.1 *(Continued)*

COMMAND	DESCRIPTION
TIME	Displays/modifies system time.
TITLE	Changes title of the Command Shell in window mode.
TYPE	Shows all content of a text file (nonpaged).
VER	Shows the current version numbers of the executing shell.

Command Line Editing, History, and Macros

The command prompt has the usual editing functions using the left and right cursor arrow keys, the Delete key, the Backspace key, the Home key, and the End key. More advanced functions are provided with the DOSKEY command. It provides functions for aliasing or renaming commands and keeping a history of typed commands, as well as several special macro keys.

In Win 3.1 and 95/98, DOSKEY is a separate command that needs to be executed before any of these advanced functions are made available. In NT and Win 2000, these functions are built into the Command Shell (see Table 7.3). DOSKEY still exists in NT, but only as a control interface to change properties of macros or other advanced functions.

DOSKEY can be used to set up macros for commands. This is directly parallel to the alias system in some UNIX shells such as csh, KornShell, and bash. For example:

```
C:\> doskey ls=dir /w $*
```

This will create an alias that maps the familiar UNIX *ls* command to the actual DOS equivalent of *dir*. The */w* flag indicates a wide format display, a *dir* option, and the *$** characters matches any input parameters as those to the aliased command. You can predefine such macros into a text file, similar to the UNIX .aliases, .cshrc or .profile, and load them at start using the following command:

```
C:\> doskey /macrofile=mymacros.mac
```

Any application that accepts input from the command line can have its own set of macros, which is set by the following command:

```
C:\> doskey /macros /exename=mycommand.bat
```

Table 7.2 Command Shell External Commands

COMMAND	DESCRIPTION
AT	Schedules a program to be launched at a certain time.
ATTRIB	Changes file attributes.
CHKDSK	Checks disk format properties.
CHOICE	Provides user with yes/no command choice.
DELTREE	Deletes an entire tree below a directory.
DISKCOPY	Copies floppy disks.
DOSKEY	Changes advanced line editing features.
EDIT	Launches text editor.
EXTRACT	Extracts tool for Microsoft Cabinet archive files.
FC	Compares two files.
FIND	Searches for a text string in a file.
FINDSTR	Does advanced search for text strings in files.
FORMAT	Formats a disk.
LABEL	Labels a disk.
MEM	Shows DOS memory usage.
MODE	Shows/modifies DOS devices (LPT:, COM:, CON:).
MORE	Shows a file a page at a time.
NET	A group of commands for Windows networks.
SORT	Sorts lines of text.
SUBST	Maps a virtual drive letter to a directory.
XCOPY	Advanced Copy utility.

This will load the current list of defined macros. Or you can enter them one at a time:

```
C:\> doskey /exename=mycommand.bat ls=dir /w $*
```

One last item is command or filename completion. Although this is available, it is disabled by default. To enable it, you have to modify the assigned key for command completion that is defined in the registry entry:

```
\HKEY_CURRENT_USER\Software\Microsoft\Command Processor\CompletionChar
```

It is normally set to the Null character (0×0), which does not map to any defined keyboard key. You can set it to any character, but be mindful which one you pick. The most favored choice is the TAB character

Table 7.3 DOSKEY Special Macros

MACRO KEY	DESCRIPTION
F1	Shows another character from previously entered command.
F3	Shows entire line last entered.
F4	Deletes characters in current line up to the next typed-in character.
F5	Deletes entire line.
F6	Types in end-of-file character.
F7	Shows command history list.
F8	Recalls commands in command history list, scrolling upward.
F9	Recalls specific item in command history list.

(0×00000009), although this might make for a confounding prank on some-one on April Fool's Day. The completion process maps filenames and the default DOS commands, so, yes, you still have to type in some of it.

Some Scripting Details

We won't go into the full details of DOS shell scripting. However, we will point out some useful basic features that can help you use it better. First of all, there is a way to send the output of one command to another or to a file. The nice thing is that it is very similar to the way they do it in UNIX.

The pipe character, a vertical bar (|) is used to send the output of one command to that of another, if it is text. You can have multiple levels of pipes from one command to another, just like in UNIX.

The redirect characters in UNIX also exist in the Command Shell. You can redirect output from a command using the *greater-than* sign (>). You can also append the redirected output to the end of a file using the >> sign. You can input data from a file using the redirect input character, the *less-than* sign (<). To send any command error output you use the for-mat 2>*file* after the command. You can direct both command output and command error output to the same location using the format 2>&1 *file*.

You can string together multiple commands on the same line and even provide conditional execution of them using the &, &&, and || characters. To simply list a number of separate commands to one line, a single ampersand character (&) between the two commands will do. Unlike UNIX, where the single ampersand typically means execute one command in the background then the other, there is no differentiation. The first command executes to completion before the second one starts. You can use the double ampersand to denote that the first command has to complete successfully before the second one can start or the shell will abort it. Using the double vertical bar, you can denote that the second command will execute if the first one did not complete successfully.

Several special filenames are available for DOS that can be used in creating commands and scripts, as shown in Table 7.4.

For example, if you want to copy the input data at a command prompt or script to a file you can use the following (remember to type **Ctrl-Z** and hit **Enter** when you are done):

```
C:\> copy CON: myfile.txt
```

If you want to discard any error output from a command or script, you could use:

```
C:\> command parameter 2>NUL:
```

You could even type a text message and have it sent to the printer directly, without ever creating a file, with this command:

```
C:\> copy CON: LPT:
```

With these basic details of shell commands and methods, you can perform most tasks, short of writing full scripts. A detailed instruction on how to develop shell scripts is, unfortunately, beyond the limits of this book. The scripting system is simple, but, with the help of command line programs, you can accomplish a surprising amount.

Table 7.4 Special DOS Files

SPECIAL FILE	DESCRIPTION
NUL:	The null file or the bit bucket, where everything that goes in disappears.
CON:	The Console or Command Shell window.
CONIN$:	The input file version of CON:.
CONOUT$:	The output file version of CONOUT$:.
LPT:	The DOS printer port. Can also have a number after LPT to signify a specific printer.
COM:	The COM or serial port. Can also have a number after COM to indicate a specific port.

Summary

The Windows environment has evolved with the coming of the Web. Internet Explorer is now closely integrated with the desktop as seen first in Windows 98 and now Windows 2000. Although the look and feel remains the same as that of Windows 95 and NT 4, there are subtle changes that have altered the layout and structure of the environment. In particular, now every folder on the system can be viewed and used as a Web page. This transforms the concept of local disks and folders into network objects that can be viewed from any machine. Active Desktop and Internet Explorer similarly bring any network object, such as Web pages, straight to your desktop and file browser. It's a short step to completely virtualizing the user's file system environment from local to distributed across the network.

Despite the focus on a graphical environment, the DOS shell environment is still in common use for writing quick scripts. In fact, scripting is still the favored way to run commands for large numbers of iterations and thus, this shell will continue to exist for many years to come.

Here ends the first part of the book focused on the environment of Windows 2000 and UNIX. The next part moves on to planning for integration between these two environments.

## PART TWO

Planning for Integration

## CHAPTER 8

Selecting System Hardware

G etting the right equipment in place may save you from being stoned to death by your users. The PC hardware is the last point of failure after the application and operating system. Sometimes, it can be the first point of failure as well. The idea is to select a reasonable system for your budget that will perform as well as you hope.

This chapter goes through the different configurations for PC hardware, both in desktop systems and in PC servers. We then cover network interfaces and hardware connectivity that can be used in the PC environment. This will give you the background you need to determine what kind of computers and network will be appropriate for specific applications.

Selecting PC Hardware

Anyone can go to a Web site by Dell, Compaq, or some other PC vendor and pick out a cool machine. However, this does not mean that you will be picking out the right one for your needs. In fact, you may already have what you need sitting somewhere in the office that can do what you want with just a little fixing. Of course, if you have the moola, feel free to spend the money on new computers; just spend it wisely.

We hope that, with the background information on PC hardware in this section, you will be able to make such new purchase decisions, question the vendor on available configurations, or perhaps purchase parts at a cheaper price from third-party vendors.

Selecting New Hardware

Hardware features play an important part in the performance of PC clients and servers. Unlike UNIX workstations, where the historical pri-

How to Buy

Making a purchasing decision is like three dogs, all pulling at the same raw steak. The first dog whom the steak was tossed at, the IT staff, wants a system that it trusts to run well and cause the fewest problems. The second party, the administrative staff, wants the server with the best price-to-performance numbers for the task it will undertake. Finally, the third dog, the vendor sales reps, just wants to pull more meat away from the other dogs and for you to buy their deal on the latest or best models. A frail little fourth dog, who usually just gets the leftover scraps, is the employees who will end up using the equipment.

The best method that we can think of for arriving at the type of device to purchase is based upon a combination of the needs of the user(s) and the amount of performance that you can get from a device to support the user(s). These needs and performance variables are different depending upon the type of equipment as well as the application that they will run. To further break this down, you can fix one variable (one of the items) and then determine all the others. Let's say you have a very server-dependent application. The decision is relatively easy:

1. Fix the amount of money you want to spend on the server.

2. Consider the performance values and configurations published by reliable trade magazines on how many users can run the application on a single server.

3. Determine the actual cost to support the number of users you will have.

4. Determine an appropriate vendor with server products falling into that price range and with a service and support contract you can agree with.

5. Purchase appropriate clients for running that application on the client side from that vendor.

If the application is more client-centric, you can determine the system configuration you will need by following the application vendor's suggested requirements (multiplied by 1.5 to 2 times in most cases) for a particular system.

Always keep in mind that the goal in our situation is to create an integrated network. The actual integration cost will be higher than whatever price you determine for the hardware system because of the need for additional software, licenses, administration, and so on, even if a copy of Windows comes with the system.

mary focus has been on the CPU, the shape of the PC has constantly been changing and evolving over the years. To determine appropriate hardware, you should know about the various important components of the system that affect system performance and usability.

In this section we discuss the details of PC processors, system chipsets, caches, system buses, memory systems, and disk systems. The discussion covers old and new information so that you can decide what kind of equipment to look for, what is worth keeping, and what can be used as a shot-put at a track meet.

Choosing Processor Models

It seems like a new processor model is coming out every other month or so these days. Actually, that isn't too far from the truth. Most new models include incremental increases in the speed of the processor, but every year or two a new member of a processor family appears, especially when it comes to desktop computing.

The UNIX market is more recalcitrant when it comes to new processors. But then, most UNIX vendors base their merits on the performance of their total operating system more than on incremental performance increases. Although almost all UNIX vendors now also offer the parallel developments of Intel-based products, each of the major vendors—IBM, Sun, SGI, and Compaq/Digital—continue to release workstations and servers based upon their own processor and board designs. Most of these vendors now focus on 64-bit processors, such as the UltraSPARC family, the HP PA-RISC, and the IBM Power Series, for their UNIX computers. At the high end of the server market, 32-, 64-, and even 128-processor UNIX servers dominate; it will take quite some time for Intel-based processors running Windows to catch up.

Until the release of Intel's 64-bit Itanium (formerly called 'Merced') processor, the Windows market will remain a 32-bit family. However, the Itanium is radically different in structure to the Pentium processor family, and thus will run older 32-bit applications in emulation mode. AMD has their own plans for 64-bit processors but will continue to focus on the architecture of the current Pentium II compatible processor, extended to support 64-bit addressing. Theoretically, this should allow AMD to run both 32-bit and 64-bit applications on the same system without using an emulation system as Intel does. Although Microsoft and some of its developers are approaching completion of the 64-bit versions of their products, it won't do them any good to release them beforehand.

And since Microsoft will no longer develop Windows NT or 2000 for the Alpha platform, the Intel-compatible processors will solely support 64-bit Windows when it is released. There are five classes of processors (see Table 8.1) these days: the handheld or PDA processor, the mobile processor, the low-end desktop, the high-end desktop or workstation, and the server. The processors for handheld devices and mobile computers need very careful management of power usage, in addition to operating at lower voltages. The low-end desktop processor was created with less cache within, to reduce the overall cost of the chip. The aim of the workstation processor is to create faster paths to memory with a reasonably sized cache and to support, at minimum, dual processor configurations. Finally, the server chips have large caches and can be combined in larger multiprocessor configurations.

Of all the chips, most are familiar with the Pentium, Pentium II, and Pentium III chips. The Pentium and all earlier Intel chips are surface socket-mounted chips. All current Pentium chips fit into the Socket 7 standard, although older models fit into Sockets 3 and 5. Essentially, this socket interface defines what chips you can plug into the system. AMD has also made their own processors fit into the Socket 7 model all the way up to the K6-3. Some of the Celeron processors also fit onto socket interfaces.

Socket mounts are cheap to produce but not very friendly, even with innovative designs like that of the Zero Insertion Force socket. In addition, Intel was planning to change the interface to improve connectivity and space usage on the motherboard. There is also reason to believe that Intel moved to a new CPU interface to stay ahead of the competition. Thus, they came up with the slot-based Pentium II packages. Each "chip" is enclosed in hard plastic and is really a small daughterboard with the

Table 8.1 Classes of Processors

CATEGORY	PROCESSOR
Handheld	Sharp, Motorola DragonBall, Hitachi
Mobile	AMD K6, K6-2 and K6-3, Intel Mobile Celeron, and Pentium II
Desktop	IDT Centaur, Cyrix 6x86, AMD K6 and K6-2, Intel Celeron
Workstation	AMD K6-3, AMD Athlon, Intel Pentium II and III, Intel Pentium II and III Xeon (512KB cache)
Server	Intel Pentium II and III Xeon (1-2MB cache), Intel Itanium*

* Not yet released.

Pentium II chip core on one side and the L2 cache on another. The hard plastic protects the chip and cache from physical damage and serves as a cooling surface as well. The Pentium II and III (non-Xeon models) use the Slot-1 interface. Some of the Celeron chips also use the Slot-1 interface but are not enclosed in the same plastic overgarments as the Pentium II and III. The Xeon models of these chips use a wider Slot-2 interface. The Itanium chip will use an even wider Slot-M interface. The AMD Athlon (formerly the "K7") uses a slot-based interface called the Slot A, based upon the interface used by the Compaq Alpha processor.

Choosing Chipsets and Caches

The *system chipset* consists of one or more chips that focus on handling the traffic and connections between the processor, memory, system bus, and peripherals. PCs with different memory systems, system buses, and processors are likely to have different chipsets. Many chipsets will support more than one combination of these components.

First of all, the chipset defines the system bus speed. Each processor has its own internal rated speed, varying from the 8.3 MHz Intel 80286 chip to the 800 MHz Pentium III. However, Intel first stepped away from matching processor-internal and system bus speeds with the 90 MHz Pentium. Since the processor can perform multiple tasks internally compared to the traffic on the system bus, there is no reason it has to twiddle its thumbs while it waits for the bus. The system chipset negotiates these different speeds between the processor and the bus.

When multiprocessing came around to PCs, a new problem emerged. The system chipset now had to handle multiple CPUs trying to communicate with devices over one system bus. The dual-, quad-, hexa- (8-CPU), and decaheptaprocessor (16-CPU) systems out there all rely on the capability of the system chipset to effectively provide communications with the system bus(es).

The system chipset controls the path between main memory and the Level 2 (L2) cache memory that is directly accessed by the CPU. L2 caches speed access to commonly used portions of memory by the processor. They come in varieties of 256KB and 512KB for most desktop and some server processors. The Intel Pentium II and III Xeon server CPUs support larger L2 caches of 1MB and 2MB. The Pentium Pro and some Pentium III's have caches of 256KB directly on the same silicon as the processor, making them even faster. The Intel CPUs already have an

L1 cache of about 16KB directly on the silicon. CPUs of these sorts can still have external L2 caches, but in reality these should probably be called L3 caches.

Every chipset will support a limit on how much memory the system can hold and how this memory is accessed. Desktop systems have memory controllers in the system chipset that typically can support up to 512MB of dynamic random access memory (DRAM). Workstations and low-end servers can access up to 1GB. Midrange servers can support up to 4GB. Until Windows 2000, this was the maximum possible addressable physical memory for the Windows platforms. With Win 2000, there is support for new memory controllers from Intel that will support up to 64GB of RAM. This chipset, currently known as the Intel Corollary chipset, will also support 8- and 16-CPU SMP machines.

The system chipsets of today also implement the controllers for the system bus. Although PCI is the standard today, we still see machines with the industry standard architecture (ISA) bus hanging around for several more years. Most chipsets support both types of buses, although in separate components. The accelerated graphics port (AGP) slot requires chipsets that directly support it; AGP is essentially just a PCI slot at double the speed, which we will discuss in a later section.

The controller for integrated drive electronics (IDE) drives is now commonly integrated into the system chipset. The drives on the IDE bus (the floppy drive, hard drives, some removable drives, and tape drives) communicate directly with the controller at slower speeds of 8 to 33 MHz. Some chipsets may even implement SCSI controllers, but these are usually done in a separate chipset.

Two final features that desktop and server chipsets support are plug-and-play and the universal serial bus (USB). Almost all chipsets after 1997 implement support for plug-and-play devices. The USB, which is targeted to replace the much older serial connections for mice and keyboards, also supports plug-and-play and, hence, requires an adequate chipset.

Mobile systems absolutely need careful management of power utilization by the various devices within the computer. The system chipset regulates power to individual devices such as the drives, the processor, and PC cards. Some newer desktops now also feature automatic sleep modes, as most laptops do, to save on power consumption. Another feature is wake-on-network, where the system can be booted up if any traffic comes over the modem or the network. A separate chipset monitors for wake-on-LAN calls, but the system chipset is responsible for powering up the rest of the system.

Tables 8.2 and 8.3 show details of the system chipsets needed by various popular Intel-compatible processors for the older Pentium and the newer Pentium Pro, II, III, and Celerons, respectively. We don't include anything

Table 8.2 Chipsets for the Intel Pentium Generation

CHIPSET	CPU SUPPORT	NUMBER OF CPUS	MAXIMUM MEMORY	MEMORY TYPE; MODULE TYPE	SYSTEM BUS	OTHER BUSES AND COMPONENTS	PLUG-AND-PLAY, POWER
Intel 430LX (obsolete)	60–66 MHz Pentium	1	128MB	FPM; SIMMs	50, 60, 66 MHz	PCI	No, no
Intel 430NX (obsolete)	60–133 MHz Pentium	2	512MB	FPM; SIMMs	50, 60, 66 MHz	PCI	No, no
Intel 430FX	60–133 MHz Pentium	1	128MB	FPM, EDO; SIMMs	50, 60, 66 MHz	PCI, IDE	Yes, no
Intel 430HX	133–266 MHz Pentium	2	512MB	FPM and EDO; ECC SIMMs, DIMMs	50, 60, 66 MHz	PCI, USB, IDE	Yes, no
Intel 430VX	60–266 MHz Pentium	1	128MB	FPM, EDO, SDRAM; SIMMs, DIMMs	60, 66 MHz	PCI, USB, IDE	Yes, no
Intel 430TX	60–266 MHz Pentium	1	256MB	FPM, EDO, SDRAM; SIMMs, DIMMs	60, 66 MHz	PCI, USB, IDE	Yes, yes
VIA Apollo VP2	60–266 MHz Pentium	1	512MB	FPM, EDO, SDRAM; ECC SIMMs	66, 75 MHz	PCI, IDE	Yes, no
SiS 5598	60–266 MHz Pentium	1	512MB	FPM, EDO, SDRAM; SIMMs	50, 55, 60, 66, 75 MHz	PCI, USB, IDE	Yes, yes
SiS540	60–366 MHz Pentium, all AMD K6-2	1	512MB	EDO, SDRAM	66, 83, 90, 95, 100 MHz	PCI, USB, Ultra66 IDE, AGP2x, 10/100 Mbps Ethernet, VGA, DVI, Integrated Audio	Yes, yes

Table 8.3 Chipsets for the AMD K6-2, and K6-3, and the Intel Pentium II and III Generation

CHIPSET	CPU SUPPORT	NUMBER OF CPUS	MAXIMUM MEMORY	MEMORY TYPE; MODULE TYPE	SYSTEM BUS	OTHER BUSES AND COMPONENTS	PLUG-AND-PLAY, POWER
Intel 440KX (obsolete)	Pentium Pro	2	1GB	FPM; SIMMs	60, 66 MHz	PCI, IDE	Yes, yes
Intel 440FX (obsolete)	Pentium Pro, 233–333 MHz Pentium II	2	1GB	FPM, EDO, BEDO; SIMMs, DIMMs	60, 66 MHz	PCI, IDE, USB	Yes, yes
Intel 440LX	233–333 MHz Pentium II	2	1GB EDO, 512MB SDRAM	EDO, SDRAM; SIMMs, DIMMs	60, 66 MHz	PCI, AGP, IDE, USB	Yes, yes
Intel 440EX	266–466 MHz Celeron	1	256MB	SDRAM; DIMMs	66 MHz	PCI, AGP, Ultra33 IDE, USB	Yes, yes
Intel 440BX	333–450 MHz PII, 450–550 MHz PIII	2	1GB	SDRAM; DIMMs	100 MHz	PCI, AGP Ultra33 IDE, USB	Yes, yes
Intel 440ZX66	266–533 MHz Celeron	1	256MB	SDRAM; DIMMs	66 MHz	PCI, AGP, Ultra33 IDE, USB	Yes, yes
Intel 440ZX	333–450 MHz PII, 450–800 MHz PIII	1	256MB	SDRAM; DIMMs	100 MHz	PCI, AGP, Ultra33 IDE, USB	Yes, yes
Intel 440GX	400–450 MHz PII Xeon, 450–800 MHz PIII Xeon	2	2GB	SDRAM; DIMMs	100 MHz	PCI, AGP, Ultra33 IDE, USB	Yes, yes
Intel 440NX	400–450 MHz PII Xeon, 450–800 MHz PIII Xeon	4	8GB	EDO, SDRAM; DIMMs	100 MHz	PCI, AGP, Ultra33 IDE, USB	Yes, yes
VIA Apollo MVP4	233–450 MHz PII, 400–533 MHz PIII, all AMD K6-2s, K6-3s	1	768MB	FP, EDO, SDRAM, DDR SDRAM, ECC SDRAM	66, 75, 83, 100 MHz	33–66 MHz PCI, AGP, Ultra66 IDE, USB, Integrated Audio	Yes, yes

Table 8.3 *(Continued)*

CHIPSET	CPU SUPPORT	NUMBER OF CPUS	MAXIMUM MEMORY	MEMORY TYPE; MODULE TYPE	SYSTEM BUS	OTHER BUSES AND COMPONENTS	PLUG-AND-PLAY, POWER
VIA Apollo Pro	233–450 MHz PII, 400–533 MHz PIII	1	1GB	FP, EDO, SDRAM	66, 100 MHz	PCI, AGP, Ultra33 IDE, USB	Yes, yes
SiS620/ 5595	233–533 MHz PII, PIII, 366–533 MHz Celeron, all AMD K6-2s, K6-3s	1	1.5GB	EDO, SDRAM	66, 100 MHz	PCI, AGP2x, Ultra66 IDE, USB, VGA, DVI	Yes, yes
SiS630	233–533 MHz PII, PIII, 366–533 MHz Celeron, all AMD K6-2s, K6-3s	1	1.5GB	EDO, SDRAM	66, 100 MHz	PCI, AGP2x, Ultra66 IDE, USB Integrated 3D Audio, 10/100 Mbps Ethernet, SVGA	Yes, yes

in the 486 or older family, which you shouldn't be running on anyone's desktop anymore unless you feel a little punishment is necessary.

Intel has introduced a new generation of chipsets with even greater integration of function. In fact, with these new chips, you don't even need a video card. It can support both analog (VGA style connection) and digital video (DVI) interfaces for connecting to monitors. This new series known as the 828x0 family, is more well-known simply by the last three digits: 810, 820, and 840 chipsets. These chipsets support dual or quad speed AGP, which radically improves graphics performance by increasing the bus access speed of the graphics slot. Quad speed AGP (AGP4x) can transfer graphics data at 1GBps and requires very fast memory to work with as well. Thus, the 820 and 840 are the first to support RDRAM memory for the Intel architecture platform. The 840 has two separate RDRAM channels and can thus transfer data from memory twice as fast, when accessed separately. They do support SDRAM running at 133MHz as well.

AMD also has a new chipset to support their Athlon processor but at the time of writing had only released their desktop chipset. This chipset does not support multiprocessing or large memory sizes as yet although

VIA also has a chipset for the Athlon that can handle up to 2GB of RAM. Table 8.4 shows these additional chipsets from Intel, AMD, and VIA Technologies.

Choosing Memory Systems

Dynamic random-access memory (DRAM) is a generic name for RAM memory chips. There are other types of memory, such as static RAM (SRAM), nonvolatile RAM, flash RAM, read-only memory (ROM), programmable ROM (PROM), electronically erasable PROM (EEPROM), that serve different purposes. Every system has some type of ROM or flash RAM to contain the system BIOS, the hardware configuration information of the motherboard. SRAM is costly and is used mostly to implement a fast cache. When people commonly speak of RAM or memory chips, they mean those of the DRAM variety.

Table 8.4   More Chipsets for the Intel Pentium III and AMD Athlon Generation

CHIPSET	CPU SUPPORT	NUMBER OF CPUS	MAXIMUM MEMORY	MEMORY TYPE; MODULE TYPE	SYSTEM BUS	OTHER BUSES AND COMPONENTS	PLUG-AND-PLAY, POWER
Intel 810	366–600 MHz Celeron, 450–800 MHz PIII	1	1GB	100MHz SDRAM,	66, 100 MHz	PCI, AGP2x, Ultra66 IDE, USB, VGA, DVI	Yes, yes
Intel 820	450–800 MHz PIII, PIII Xeon	1-2	1GB	100–133 MHz SDRAM, RDRAM	100, 133 MHz	PCI, AGP4x, Ultra66 IDE, USB, VGA, DVI	Yes, yes
Intel 840	450–800 MHz PIII, PIII Xeon	1-2	2GB	100–133 MHz SDRAM, RDRAM	100, 133 MHz	33–66 MHz PCI, AGP4x, Ultra66 IDE, USB, VGA, DVI	Yes, yes
VIA Apollo Pro133A	450–800 MHz PIII, 366–533 MHz Celeron	1	1.5GB	66, 100, 133MHz SDRAM	66, 100, 133 MHz	PCI, AGP4x, Ultra66 IDE, USB,	Yes, yes
AMD-750	550–1000 MHz Athlon	1	768MB	100MHz SDRAM	200 MHz	PCI, AGP2x, Ultra66 IDE, USB	Yes, yes
VIA Apollo KX133	550–1000 MHz Athlon	1	2GB	66, 100, 133MHz SDRAM	200 MHz	PCI, AGP2x, Ultra66 IDE, USB	Yes, yes

There are a number of different varieties of memory chips and packages that are used in PC systems, but, for the most part, they use two core types of chips, in two common package types. A *memory chip* is an implementation of some memory technology in a single semiconductor chip and with a certain capacity; almost no one uses memory chips by themselves (not since the days of surface-mounted chips in the late 1970s). When most people talk about memory chips, they normally mean the *memory chip package* or *module*. These modules contain eight, nine, or more individual chips directly mounted on a small strip of board that has connectors on one edge.

Memory chips come in two modes: parity and nonparity. Parity chips contain extra bits that help maintain the consistency of individual bytes of data. Nonparity chips do not. A higher level of parity, called *error-correcting code* (ECC), actually checks sections of memory and corrects errors of individual bytes based on other extra bits of information.

These packages are also commonly referred to as SIMMs or DIMMs. A *single inline memory module* (SIMM) contains a number of chips mounted on one side. A *dual inline memory module* (DIMM) contains chips on both sides of the strip. SIMMs typically come in 30- or 72-pin modules, indicating the number of connectors that are present on the edge. DIMMs come in 144- and 168-pin modules. The most common types these days are the 72-pin SIMM and the 168-pin DIMM.

Within the DRAM family, there are a number of separate technologies indicating how the internal architecture of the RAM chip is implemented. DRAM is also the name for the original type of architecture used in constructing these chips. The first improvements over these were called *fast page mode DRAMs* and provided marginally faster accesses—which used to be really worth it, too, in the late 1980s. *External data out (EDO) RAM* is the next generation, providing up to 20 percent faster access and operating at 50-, 60-, 70-, and 80-nanosecond speeds. However, you have to be careful not to mix and match these different speeds on your motherboard to save the poor machine's state of mental health. Today, the 50-ns variety is most common (but you should still check with the vendor). Another variety, known as *burst EDO DRAM*, allows for data to be sent out in larger bursts; unfortunately, this technology was short-lived and cannot handle a system bus faster than the 66 MHz still used in the Celeron and the 233 to 333 MHz Pentium IIs and older chips.

Synchronous DRAM (SDRAM) broke out of the original mold of DRAM chips and went off the slower main system bus to its own faster private bus to the CPU. SDRAM had its own separate clock chip (at 100 MHz and more) and bus interconnect that ran more slowly than the actual speed of the CPU itself (166 to 550 MHz), but still synchronized with it. SDRAM is an estimated 50 percent improvement over EDO.

Memory modules plug into several *slots* or *banks* of slots directly on the motherboard. A slot holds only one module, and a bank can have two, four, or more slots within. Before SDRAM, you needed to plug memory modules in pairs into the banks; to add 32MB of memory to the system, you had to plug in two 16MB modules or it wouldn't work, and, yes, that is confusing. SDRAM left that behind, and single SIMMs or DIMMs could be plugged into slots. Although some older motherboards still support banks for both 30- and 72-pin SIMMs, most have gone to all 72-pin banks. Others will support SIMMs and DIMMs in separate banks, but only one of those banks will be actively used.

One feature of some system chipsets for servers works better with EDO RAM than with SDRAM. Known as *memory interleaving*, the memory controller can access 2 or more banks at the same time, effectively doubling or quadrupling memory access. It started with being able to access 2 and 4 banks, but this will be increasing to 8 and 16 with newer system chipsets. This is why you will find many high-end servers that support only EDO RAM, rather than SDRAM

SDRAM was the first successful technology in PCs to introduce a separate memory bus. This created a much faster access technology than the older asynchronous DRAM types (DRAM, FPM DRAM, EDO DRAM). These memory systems use a memory controller, embedded into the system chipset, for communicating with the CPU(s). Most newer memory technologies focus on implementing better bus technologies to access memory. SDRAM also has to communicate with the general system bus for direct memory access (DMA) transfers from boards like network cards. Thus they also have to be rated for the speed of the system bus. There are three varieties in use today, known commonly as PC66, PC100, and PC133, indicating the various system bus speeds. A higher-rated module can run in a lower-speed system, but it is better to buy those with matching speeds. The new generations of RAM chips go even faster. *Double-data-rate SDRAM* improves on the original by performing two accesses on each clock cycle, effectively doubling the speed of access from 100 to 200 MHz. This effectively doubles the transfer rate for data. In fact, SDRAM implementations have been hobbled by having to support system boards slower than 75 MHz, and DDR SDRAM is the speed SDRAM ought to be.

Synchronous link DRAM (SLDRAM) extends the available number of memory slots from 4 to 16, increases the data path size to 64 bits from 32 bits for everything earlier, and raises the clock speed to 200 MHz. Since it does double accesses like DDR SDRAM, the effective speed is 400 MHz. The total theoretical bandwidth for SLDRAM is 3.2 Gigabytes per second. Finally, *Rambus DRAM* (RDRAM), developed by a company called Rambus Technologies, runs at 800 MHz and provides access speeds of up to 1.6 Gigabytes per second between main memory and the CPU via the memory controller. Rambus memory comes in several varieties, but most PCs implement Direct RDRAM. Table 8.5 lists some details of the various DRAM technologies.

Intel decided to move to RDRAM as the memory type of the next generation. However, RDRAM systems have just come out in 2000, and were in

Table 8.5 DRAM Technologies in Detail

MEMORY TYPE	MEMORY SPEED	SYSTEM BUS SPEED	LATENCY	MAXIMUM BANDWIDTH	PACKAGE
Fast page mode	66 MHz	50, 60, 66 MHz	70–80 ns	66 MBps	30-, 36-pin SIMM
EDO	66 MHz	50, 60, 66, 75 MHz	50–70 ns	66 MBps	30-, 36-, 72-pin SIMM
SDRAM	66–133 MHz	66, 75, 83, 100, 133 MHz	6–12 ns	100–266 MBps	72-pin SIMM, 144- and 168-pin DIMM
DDR SDRAM	166–200 MHz	100+ MHz	6–12 ns	200 MBps	72-pin SIMM, 144- and 168-pin DIMM
Direct RDRAM	800 MHz	100+ MHz	n/a*	1.6 GBps	168-pin RDIMM
SLDRAM	266–800 MHz	100+ MHz	5–10 ns	0.8–1.2 GBps	168-pin DIMM

* These technologies are still in the works at the time of writing and some specific information on them is not yet available.

short supply. Many vendors who did not want to go the expense of switching over to completely new memory systems chose to stick to the improved 133MHz SDRAM. Thus both kinds of systems are now currently on the market with SDRAM based systems at a slightly cheaper price because of greater memory availability and cheaper manufacturing costs.

Choosing Disk Systems

In choosing system configurations, you should pay particular attention to drive types and management features. Most PC desktops are still running IDE, although a much faster variant than the original. The current top IDE standard, called Ultra-66, ATA66, or UltraDMA-66, can transfer data up to 67 MBps. Practically every PC built today, no matter the kind or size, will support IDE drives, whether they have them or not. Table 8.6 shows the different IDE, SCSI, and Fibre-Channel disk drive buses available for PCs.

Most PC workstations and servers have gone to SCSI platforms, whether SCSI-2, Ultra2 SCSI, or Ultra3 SCSI. The basic disk provided by most vendors is a 4GB Ultra2/Narrow SCSI drive running at 7200 rpm. That serves the purposes of most small applications in terms of speed and throughput. Hot-plug drives become necessary at the departmental level as you start supporting large groups of people on different floors or in different buildings. In terms of cost, the amount of time spent manually replacing non-hot-plug drives simply costs more than the price of the drives themselves or the cost of upgrading a non-hot-plug system.

Workgroup servers are often simply full tower enclosures and can incorporate between 3 and 6 drives. Departmental servers can usually handle

Table 8.6 Different Drive Bus Standards

STANDARD	MAXIMUM BURST TRANSFER RATE	LATENCY	DATA PATH SIZE	DRIVE SIZE	DRIVES PER CHAIN	MAXIMUM DISTANCE	NOTES
IDE, ATA	8.3 MBps; 4.2 MBps (DMA mode)	18–30 ms	16 bits	10–512 MB	2	18 in	Obsolete
ATA-2, Fast ATA, Fast ATA-2	16.6 MBps; 16.6 MBps (DMA mode)	9–20 ms	16 bits	10MB–4GB	2	18 in	Disks > 504MB require BIOS enhancement
EIDE	16.6 MBps; 16.6 MBps (DMA mode)	9–20 ms	16 bits	10MB–4GB	4 with dual adapters	18 in	Disks > 504MB require BIOS enhancement

Table 8.6 *(Continued)*

STANDARD	MAXIMUM BURST TRANSFER RATE	LATENCY	DATA PATH SIZE	DRIVE SIZE	DRIVES PER CHAIN	MAXIMUM DISTANCE	NOTES
ATA-3	16.6 MBps; 16.6 MBps (DMA mode)	7–11 ms	16 bits	512MB –8GB	4 with dual adapters	18 in	Self-Monitoring Analysis and Reporting Technology (SMART) features
Ultra ATA, Ultra DMA, ATA-33, DMA-33	16.6 MBps; 33.3 MBps (DMA mode)	7–11 ms	16 bits	>8GB	4 with dual adapters	18 in	Includes SMART
Ultra DMA 66	16.6 MBps; 67 MBps (DMA mode)	7–11 ms	16 bits	>8GB	4 with dual adapters	18 in	Includes SMART 2
SCSI	5 MBps @ 5MHz	11–30 ms	8 bits	Any	8	6 m	Obsolete
Wide SCSI, Wide SCSI-2	10 MBps @ 5MHz	6–15 ms	16 bits	Any	16	6 m	-
SCSI-2, Fast SCSI, Fast SCSI-2	10 MBps @ 10MHz	6–15 ms	8 bits	Any	8	3 m	Low-voltage differential (LVD) version extends range to 12 m; high-voltage differential (HVD) extends range to 25 m.
Fast-Wide SCSI-2	20 MBps @ 10MHz	6-15	16 bits	Any	16	3 m	A "very wide" 32-bit path SCSI-2 exists but not popular with PCs; LVD extends to 12 m; HVD extends to 25 m.
SCSI-3, Ultra SCSI	20 MBps @ 20MHz	6-11	8 bits	Any	8	1.5 m (recommend use LVD)	LVD extends to 12 m; HVD extends to 25 m.
Wide SCSI-3, Ultra Wide SCSI	40 MBps @ 20MHz	6-11	16 bits	Any	16	1.5 m (recommend use LVD)	LVD extends to 12 m; HVD extends to 25 m.
Ultra2 Wide SCSI	80 MBps @ 40MHz	6-11	32 bits	Any	8	12 m (LVD only)	-
Ultra3 Wide SCSI	160 MBps @ 80MHz	6-11	32 bits	Any	8	12 m (LVD only)	-
Fibre-Channel Arbitrated Loop (FC-AL)	100 MBps	varies	32 bits	Any	126	30 m (copper); 500 m (short-wave fiber); 10 km (long wave fiber)	Multiple loops can support more devices; higher-speed FC supports 200–400 MBps but not common in PC servers.

up to 10 drives. Enterprise and datacenter class servers usually rely upon secondary drive systems to contain the drives and usually keep only a few open drive slots within the chassis. Vendors like IBM, Dell, and Compaq provide such storage enclosures to house hundreds of gigabytes of data. You can also link several of these enclosures to the main server enclosure to reach a terabyte of storage.

As you go up the chain to 9GB, 18GB, or 25GB drives, and shift from 7200 rpm to the blazing 10,000-rpm systems, the prices per disk double, triple, or even quadruple. The SCSI standard supports speeds from 10 MBps in narrow SCSI-2 to the latest Ultra2 Wide SCSI systems delivering 80-MBps throughput. The upcoming generation, Ultra3 SCSI-3, will support 160-MBps transfers once vendors start shipping products. As you go to faster SCSI buses, the actual length of the bus shortens and unreliability increases due to increased electromagnetic interference. To avoid lengths much shorter than 1 m, there is a second variation known as *differential SCSI*, which uses multiple voltage signals over the SCSI bus to provide greater reliability over longer lengths. Differential SCSI, which is a type rather than a version (there are differential SCSI-2, SCSI-3, Wide SCSI-2, etc.), comes in *low-voltage differential* (LVD), supporting up to 12-m ranges, and *high-voltage differential* (HVD), supporting up to 25-m ranges. High-voltage, in this case, isn't like what you see on signs outside power plants or electric fences; it's just a higher voltage than the low-voltage type.

In the meantime, to go even faster, you need to switch over to Fibre-Channel (FC) systems. Starting at speeds of 100 Mbps, Fibre-Channel brings you into the realm of *storage area networks* (SANs) and distributed storage systems. These can store hundreds of gigabytes to several terabytes of data in separate enclosures, each with its own independent storage system.

Fibre-Channel creates a separate network system intended only for disk subsystems and not for traffic like TCP or UDP packets on a regular LAN. It is a Layer 1/Layer 2 protocol in that it handles physical signaling between a storage device and the controller. But it also handles a simple form of routing and addressing. In fact, it is flexible enough to have other disk/peripheral bus protocols like SCSI, the *High Performance Parallel Interface* (HIPPI), and IBM's Enterprise Storage Connection (ESCON) for mainframes run on top of FC.

Fibre-Channel, as the name implies, started out as an optical fiber-only system. It now also includes copper transmission systems as well. Running at speeds from 100 Mbps to 4 Gbps (hopefully in the future), it's faster than the main buses on many systems. What's more, bandwidth can be guaranteed. Initial Fibre-Channel runs are in the 2- to 10-km range, but with future repeaters this can be extended to 20 to 40 km. For a campus area network, this is a great solution.

RAID Data Balancing

Redundant arrays of independent disks (RAID) provides a means of distributing data across multiple drives so as to speed access or improve reliability or serviceability. RAID is often defined by separate levels, each supporting a different feature. Table 8.7 introduces each of these levels in brief detail.

RAID 0 isn't really redundant in any form. It takes the data and stores it in small stripes across the drives. This makes it faster to access data since the physical limitations of accessing data on a single drive are minimized by accessing data in parallel across several drives. RAID 0 offers no protection of data whatsoever.

RAID 1 creates a duplicate of all the contents of one drive on another. This protects the data since a failure of one drive means that the data is still available live on the other. Read access is faster since the data can be obtained from either drive, but writing data is slower since you need to write the data twice.

RAID 0 + 1, also called 1 + 0 or 10, combines the elements of RAID 0 and 1 to provide striping and redundancy at the same time. Basically you have two sets of drives that are mirrors of each other (RAID 1), and within these sets, the data is striped across the drives to speed access.

RAID 2 is practically nonexistent now. The technique was developed by one-time massively parallel vendor, Thinking Machines, Inc., which built those very cool looking black refrigerators with hundreds of red lights for complex parallel calculations like determining weather patterns and the behavior of an atom within a nuclear explosion. RAID 2 protects the accuracy of data by encoding each byte or block using a technique known as the Hamming code. This uses multiple drives, which correspond to each other in a manner similar to that of the Mirror concept of RAID 1, but does not entail having one-for-one mirrors; hence, fewer drives are needed.

RAID 3 protects data accuracy by using a different data-mapping technique known as *parity bits or bytes*. In RAID 3 every bit or byte has a

Table 8.7   RAID Levels

LEVEL	NAME	DESCRIPTION
0	Striping	Data written across multiple disks in stripes to speed data read/write access.
1	Mirroring	Data written in duplicate on multiple disks to provide redundancy of data and speed read access.
0 + 1, 1 + 0, 10	Mirroring with striped subsets	These three RAID levels are the same thing. Data is set up in a mirror and individual drives in each mirror subset are striped. Combined, this provides faster read/write access as well as redundancy of data.
2	Hamming encoding	Data is encoded for accuracy using the Hamming code technique. This RAID level is mostly unimplemented, since it is much slower and more expensive than other techniques.
3	Striping with single parity disk, bit/byte parity	Data striped across multiple disks, with parity bits/bytes for each data bit/byte to provide accuracy of data. All parity information is stored on a single drive separate from the data drives.
4	Striping with single parity disk, block parity	Similar to RAID 3 but parity is organized by blocks (e.g., 1KB, 4KB, 8KB), which improves access.
5	Striping with distributed parity	Data and parity striped across multiple disks to provide read/write access and provide accuracy of data. Parity blocks distributed across all disks allows any single disk to be recreated.
6	Striping with distributed parity, double parity bytes	Similar to RAID 5 but two sets of parity blocks for each data block are stored, allowing drives to be replaced without suffering any resyncing delays. Read access performance is the same as RAID 5 but write is slower since twice the parity information has to be written twice.
"7"	String with asynchronous single parity disk	A proprietary scheme similar to RAID 3 but with asynchronous disk write operations and multiple cache banks.

companion parity bit or byte, which ensures that an error on the system has not changed the value of the bit or byte in some form. It does this using a simple mathematical function known as the *XOR*. The deal with XOR is that if you take one value and XOR it with another twice, you will get back the original value. This method only works with a certain second value (the parity value) for each original value. If the original value changes because of an unknown error, the parity value is no longer valid for it, indicating that the original is now erroneous; the value can then be changed back to its original state. All the parity bits or bytes in RAID 3 are stored in a separate drive known as the *parity drive*. All RAID 3 operations are also synchronous, meaning that any operation has to wait for all drives to complete reading or writing before it is retrieved or stored. This can slow down the system.

RAID 4 expands the RAID 3 concept by moving from individual bits and bytes to blocks of bytes. Since most disks read data in blocks rather than in individual bits or bytes, this makes for better performance. Every drive made for North America and those in parts of Europe read in 512-byte increments (one sector); in Asia, it is 1024 bytes. Beyond this, data is accessed from drives in different block sizes depending upon the operating system. Typical sizes range from 512 bytes to 8KB. By creating a parity block for the entire block size, the actual per-block processing is reduced (there are fewer accesses and XOR comparisons), thus reducing the overall retrieval and storage time. However, write operations create bottlenecks. Since every parity block has to be calculated (it takes longer to calculate parity for a block than for a byte) and then written to the parity drive, and all drives are synchronized, the operation is much slower. As a result of this, it is less popular.

RAID 5 takes the block parity system of RAID 4 and distributes it across all the drives. Hence, all the parity information for one drive is stored on all the other drive members. This means that if one drive goes bad, it can be replaced and its data recreated from the other drives. This involves a period of resynchronization of the data when access may be slow or unavailable. In RAID 5, the parity is no longer bottlenecked to a single drive.

RAID 6 works like RAID 5 but creates two sets of block parity. This allows up to two drives to be swapped from the array should they fail. The benefits of RAID 6 are only partially greater than those of RAID 5 with hot-swap since resyncing a drive does not take very long and it is much less likely that two drives will fail at the same time. Hence, not many such products have been shipped.

RAID 7 is a proprietary architecture created by Storage Computer Corporation, which is similar to RAID 3 in that the data is striped across the array with a separate disk for parity; however, RAID 7 allows the drives to operate asynchronously, unlike RAID 3. This means that all the disks do not have to wait for one drive to finish writing before they can continue operations. It achieves this by maintaining multiple levels and banks of cache in the controller for separate operations. RAID 7 might as well be called *Asynchronous RAID 3*.

Table 8.8 shows how RAID levels compare to each other when it comes to performance in one particular aspect. Basically it shows which level is better (using the greater-than sign) in that aspect. Some levels have equivalent performance. Left out of the table is RAID 2, which is practically extinct, and RAID 7, which is far too new.

Solaris and AIX implement most of the original six RAID levels (0, and 1 through 5). NT only provides host-based support for RAID 0, 1, and 5. But just because the host OS does not support the RAID level this doesn't mean that you can integrate other RAID levels into your server storage system. Read on to see the difference between host-based and controller-based RAID.

Host versus Array Controller RAID

Storage demands weigh heavily on a processor. Executing all the read and write operations on the disk system can result in a huge number of I/O interrupts. If these were to be processed by the server's CPUs, then the server really would be doing little else on a heavily used file server system. To this end, storage vendors and motherboard designers have contemplated alternative methods of processing I/O.

When the server CPU and OS handles all the I/O interrupts itself, you have a host-based RAID or storage system. An immediate alternative to this is to stick an I/O processor directly on the storage controller to handle most of the I/O to its connected drives, in which case you would have a controller-based RAID. In the former, all the RAID functions are han-

Table 8.8 Comparative Performance among RAID Levels

PERFORMANCE VECTOR	COMPARISON
Random read speed	1, 0 + 1 > 6, 5 > 3, 4 > 0
Random write speed	1, 0 + 1 > 0 > 5 > 3, 4 > 6
Sequential read speed	0, 0 + 1 > 1, 5, 6 > 3, 4
Sequential write speed	0 > 0 + 1 > 1 > 4 > 3 > 5 > 6
Redundancy	1, 0 + 1 > 3, 4, 5, 6
Availability	0 + 1 > 6 > 5 > 1 > 0, 3, 4
Accuracy	6 > 5 > 4, 3 > 0 + 1, 1 > 0
Cost	0 + 1, 6 > 1 > 3, 4, 5 > 0

Is RAID *Inexpensive* or *Independent*?

"Independent," you say. "Inexpensive," says the next guy. What does the *I* in RAID really stand for?

This has to be one of the most common mistakes of the computer industry. When University of California at Berkeley researchers Patterson, Gibson, and Katz first presented a paper on the topic in 1987, they proposed the redundant array of inexpensive disk (RAID) system as an alternative to the single large expensive disk (SLED) systems being developed by vendors at the time. Since disk storage was still fairly expensive (remember, in 1987 a 1GB drive was about $15,000 and about the size of a 15-inch monitor), the use of these SLEDs was limited to large companies. Using cheaper 100MB drives (then around $1000), the researchers showed ways not only to combine disks for larger storage capacities but also to introduce concepts of data reliability in the less reliable smaller drives. So the word *inexpensive* really did apply in a relative sense. Today, when the price difference between a 6GB and an 18GB drive is about $100 and no one uses the term *SLED* anymore, it doesn't seem that important. Over the years, the term has become less associated with cheaper drives and more with several separate physical drives combined to form a larger storage space. In the early 1990s, most RAID systems were based upon SCSI drives rather then the more common IDE drives in PC systems. SCSI has always been a better performer than IDE, but it was also more expensive. RAID disks also became hot-swappable and this meant custom connections so that they could be removed and plugged in fairly quickly and safely. Soon RAID systems were no longer considered cheaper, although the benefits in redundancy and data reliability were not contested. Hence, the use of the term *independent.*

I prefer to use *independent,* but choose whichever you prefer, since, in a sense, they are both correct anyway.

dled directly by the file system and device drivers of the host operating system. In the latter, most of the RAID functions are passed on to the controller to manage. There still is I/O between the host CPU and the controller, but a significant portion of this is reduced in the latter scenario.

Intel has also developed a new design for server motherboards known as the *intelligent I/O system* and commonly referred to as I_2O. In this design, the server has a separate I/O CPU directly on the motherboard, which takes over the responsibility of handling I/O interrupts for devices connected to it. This allows vendors to design simpler and cheaper I/O controllers since much of the work is being done by the I_2O processor. Unfortunately, I_2O has been underutilized by the industry. Although I_2O

is available on a number of motherboards, few I/O controllers have been designed to support I_2O. What's more, the only OSs that support I_2O right now are Novell NetWare and Wind River System's IRTOS (an embedded OS). It's not even supported in Solaris or NT yet. Microsoft plans to support it in Win 2000, but Sun has made no promises.

Without an I_2O-compatible controller or OS, you have only a third of a solution, which essentially works no differently than if the I_2O processor wasn't even there. One other factor is that I_2O is starting to be eclipsed by the upcoming work on NGIO from Intel and Future I/O by a consortium of other vendors. These two next-generation I/O systems radically change the PC server architecture and overtake the speed and scaling limitations of the existing PCI bus.

Egad! EDAP

The next step in storage system evolution involves a concept called Extended Data Availability and Protection (EDAP). Created by the RAID Advisory Board in 1997, EDAP introduces a classification system for the resilience of the entire storage system and not just disk-based storage. The participating vendors decided that they needed to agree upon a common description for their storage systems that they can use in their literature (mostly in brochures, proposals, and articles such as this chapter).

EDAP defines the properties of disk systems and controllers with respect to the level of reliability they can provide. There are two sets of definitions, one for disk systems and the other for array controllers, but the definitions for each are the same; it's just the context and the acronyms that differ. Table 8.9 lists these acronyms and their associated reliability-level definitions.

There are several terms that need to be explained. First of all, *write hole* is a term used to describe an error condition that can occur when another error in the system, such as a brownout or a physical disconnection, occurs in the middle of a write operation. Since a write operation across multiple drives requires careful coordination, a disruption when it is occurring results in data errors. The storage system should be able to recover from the disruption and complete the write operation properly.

An FRU is a *field replaceable unit*. This can be a single drive, a power supply, a cooling fan, or the little magic disk elf—practically any physical unit that can be replaced as a whole by a system administrator

Table 8.9 EDAP Classification for Disk Systems

EDAP CLASS	EDAP CRITERIA
Failure Resistant Disk System (FRDS)	1. Protection against data loss and loss of access to data due to disk failure.
	2. Reconstruction of failed disk contents to a replacement disk.
	3. Protection against data loss due to a "write hole."
	4. Protection against data loss due to host and host I/O bus failures.
	5. Protection against data loss due to component failure.
	6. FRU monitoring and failure indication.
Failure Resistant Disk System Plus (FRDS+)	Items 1–6 and
	7. Disk hot swap.
	8. Protection against data loss due to cache component failure.
	9. Protection against data loss due to external power failure.
	10. Protection against data loss due to a temperature-out-of-operating-range condition.
	11. Component and environmental failure warning.
Failure Tolerant Disk System (FTDS)	Items 1–11 and
	12. Protection against loss of access to data due to device channel failure.
	13. Protection against loss of access to data due to controller failure.
Failure Tolerant Disk System Plus (FTDS+)	Items 1–13 and
	14. Protection against loss of access to data due to host and host I/O bus failures.
	15. Protection against loss of access to data due to external power failure.
	16. Protection against loss of data access due to FRU replacement.
	17. Disk hot spare.
Failure Tolerant Disk System Plus Plus (FTDS++)	Items 1–17 and
	18. Protection against data loss and loss of access to data due to multiple disk failures in an FTDS+.

continues

Table 8.9   *(Continued)*

EDAP CLASS	EDAP CRITERIA
Disaster Tolerant Disk System (DTDS)	Items 1–16 and
	19. Protection against loss of data access due to zone failure (at most 1 km distance between zones).
Disaster Tolerant Disk System Plus (DTDS+)	Items 1–15 and
	20. Long-distance protection against loss of data access due to zone failure (at least 10 km distance between zones).

Source: RAID Advisory Board.

without involving overly complicated removal procedures or software magic.

Finally, a *zone* is a term used when you have wide area or non-local distribution of your disk system. In such a case, you may have a storage system in one room in one building and a second one down the street or even across the country. The catch is that, on the software side and from a server point of view, they have to be part of the same storage system or network. Zones come into play in storage area networks and when you have huge storage systems for your servers and mainframes that need redundancy or separation for technical, security, or business reasons.

There are basically three main classes: failure resistant, failure tolerant, and disaster tolerant. A *failure-resistant* (FR) system has protections from error conditions and can rebuild the consistency of data once the failure has been handled. A *failure-tolerant* (FT) system will maintain the consistency of the data even when a failure has occurred and will continue to be operational while it is being fixed. A *disaster-tolerant* (DT) system will continue to be operational even if all the devices at one particular physical location have failed, since they are backed up with an identical storage system at another physical location. You can probably guess which one is the most expensive and which is the least.

The acronyms for EDAP can get confusing, so just keep in mind that in general DT > FT > FR, and the pluses simply mean *greater protection*. Hence, the EDAP classes in Table 8.9 can be thought of as:

DTDS+ > DTDS > FTDS++ > FTDS+ > FTDS > FRDS+ > FRDS (for disk systems)

DTAC+ > DTAC > FTAC++ > FTAC+ > FTAC > FRAC+ > FRAC (for array controllers)

Fibre-Channel Supplements Your Disk Diet

Fibre-Channel has got to be one of the most interesting developments in the storage market. It provides a new connectivity, signaling, and framing protocol system that can be deployed as a network. Although FC is not particular to storage networks, this is where it has been received with open arms. FC itself is only a communications protocol like Ethernet, Token Ring, FDDI, or ATM. It can be used to deliver any sort of packet from SCSI to IP. Did I just say SCSI over FC? Yes, one storage access protocol over another. To understand the differences between SCSI and FC, read Ron Levine's article in the March 1999 *SunWorld* (www.sunworld.com/swol-03-1999/swol-03-fibre-scsi.html).

When most people talk about FC, however, they really mean Fibre-Channel Arbitrated Loop (FC-AL), one wiring system for it that uses optical fiber cabling. FC-AL is a loop network just like Token Ring and FDDI. It provides a bandwidth of up to 100 MBps (actually 1.062 Gbps) in half-duplex mode, or twice that in full-duplex mode. Raw-speed-wise, that is the same as with Gigabit Ethernet. The 1Gbps is limited only because of current technology. The next step is to produce 4Gbps FC networks.

Like Ethernet, FC has hubs and switches. An FC loop can have up to 127 separate addresses for devices. When compared to SCSI's 7-address limit, this makes a lot of sense and saves dollars when it comes to the multidisk enclosures of storage systems. Theoretically, it is possible to network up to three levels of addresses, setting a maximum device limit of around 16 million. FC loops can connect with two forms of optical cabling: multi-mode fiber (50- or 62.5-micron wavelength fibers) or single-mode fiber (9 microns). Similar to the cabling used for ATM networks, the multimode cables allow a maximum device distance of up to 1 km, while single mode can go to a distance of up to 10 km, without any signal repeaters.

Although FC is fast becoming *de rigueur* for high-end storage systems, it is also being considered for creating clusters of servers. The actual devices are already available and vendors simply need to work on developing the device drivers and OS software to create FC-based clusters. Some of these technologies, such as the new InfiniBand bus architecture for PC systems, can use FC for clustering as well as storage connections.

Storage Area Networks and Network Attached Storage in Action

Two acronyms are now the darlings of enterprise storage management: SAN and NAS. The first stands for *storage area networks*, where several storage systems are connected into their own network and then private channels are linked directly to bus adapters or storage controllers on hosts that need to access them. With the second, *network attached storage*, each storage system is directly connected to the LAN that the hosts are on, and their drives are exported using NFS or CIFS. The difference in implementation is far different. With SANs, the storage system requires each connecting host to have a fairly expensive host bus adapter with Fibre-Channel or SCSI; however, this provides high-bandwidth links directly to the storage system. With NAS, the host only needs to have an Ethernet card, which can communicate with the NAS unit using standard network protocols such as TCP/IP. The complete similarities and differences between the two technologies are described in Table 8.10.

You can see from Table 8.10 that each technology has its own merits and can be used for different purposes. When you need fast online storage, such as for digital video services, huge databases, search engines, huge FTP sites, or the like, a SAN model might be appropriate for you. When you need mass storage but cost saving is more important than high speed, then NAS would probably be a better choice. SANs for one will also require more management because of the separate network cabling system (two networks are harder to manage than one).

Vendors such as EMC, Compaq, IBM, Data General/Clarion, Sun, and StorageTek are working on SAN products from host bus adapters (HBAs) to storage systems. On the NAS front, two vendors are the most prominent: Network Appliances and Auspex. The multi-billion-dollar storage market has sufficient room for both product types, as evidenced by the numerous start-up companies working on components and products for both technologies.

Choosing System Buses

Most server systems don't need too many PCI cards. Features like SCSI and basic video adapters are often built directly onto the motherboard.

Table 8.10 Storage Area Networks Compared to Network Attached Storage

SAN	NAS
Large storage capacities (in the terabyte range).	Large storage capacities (in the terabyte range).
Storage system may have internal RAID.	Storage system may have internal RAID.
Supports hot-swap disks.	Supports hot-swap disks.
Provides access to multiple servers.	Provides access to multiple servers.
Can be a hierarchical storage system with tapes, optical drives, etc.	Can be a hierarchical storage system with tapes, optical drives, etc.
Can have hubs, switches, and routers between storage system and host connection (with SCSI or FC).	Can have hubs, switches, and routers between storage system and host connection (with Ethernet, WAN lines, etc.).
Can provide failover at storage system level.	Can provide failover at storage system level.
Can provide failover at switch/router level.	Can provide failover at switch/router level with some networks.
Can provide failover at host bus adapter level.	Can provide failover at host bus adapter level with some cards.
Can provide high-bandwidth connections (up to 2 Gbps-duplex Fibre-Channel).	Can provide high-bandwidth connections (up to 1 Gbps-Gigabit Ethernet).
Each connection is dedicated per host (a full 2 Gbps to a host).	Each connection is not normally dedicated to a host (1 Gbps is shared between hosts).
Requires host bus adapter card for connection (expensive).	Requires LAN network card for connection (cheaper).
Host bus adapter is intelligent and has large on-board cache (smarter and faster processing).	LAN adapter is simple and usually has no significant on-board RAM (not so smart).
Low overhead storage system communications protocol (SCSI or FC).	High overhead network and application protocols (NFS or CIFS over UDP or TCP over IP).
Always on separate storage network (no unnecessary network traffic).	Can be on same network as hosts or on separate private network (can have unnecessary network traffic).
Does not really have an internal operating system (less overhead).	Has its own internal operating system (more overhead but possibly smarter operation).
Does not have its own internal file systems (file system is host-dependent).	Has its own internal file system (file system is NAS-dependent).
Software security dependent upon host.	Internal software and system security.
High overhead to connect additional servers.	Low overhead to connect additional servers.

In such a case, the only other cards that should go into your slots are RAID, Fibre-Channel, or network interface controllers. Keep in mind that you may need multiple RAID or network controllers as your server grows, and you should therefore place them close together.

Almost all PC servers are equipped with 32-bit PCI at 33 MHz as standard these days. Some models at the low end may come with ISA (EISA isn't common available anymore) slots as well, which you should leave unused. Some 64-bit PCI slots have started showing up in enterprise-class devices, although very few cards work with them. These cards can fit into and work in 32-bit slots (with part of the connector hanging off of the end of the slot) and the 64-bit slots can work with 32-bit cards as well, providing backward compatibility. High-end servers may also sport dual-peering PCI buses. This means the slot is wired to two separate PCI buses and PCI controllers, effectively providing a backup path should one fail. The next generation may also feature 66 MHz PCI slots, effectively doubling the throughput from 133 MBps to 266 MBps. These will work at full 66 MHz only when all PCI cards on the bus operate at 66 MHz. If a 33 MHz card is plugged in, the others will also drop down to 33 MHz. A full 64-bit, 66 MHz PCI bus can transfer at 532 MBps. Full details of these buses are shown in Table 8.11.

Intel and other PC vendors are also looking to push another generation of system buses, taking it into the gigabits-per-second range and putting it in competition with UNIX servers. Three new technologies—PCI-X, NGIO, and Future I/O—will compete for different server markets. PCI-X is an extension of current PCI into a 133 MHz, 64-bit system offering an overall shared bus of 1 GBps.

Next-Generation I/O (NGIO) from Intel and Future I/O from a group led by IBM, Compaq, and HP are switched fabric systems, which allow direct communication between individual ports and the processor bus or memory bus. These two competing standards are merging into a single standard known as InfiniBand. By compromising on a common standard the specifics of the standard were not available at the time of writing of this book and thus we provide descriptions of both systems.

Notice that we did not mention hot-plug PCI as an option for the system bus. Hot-plugging cards into the system can be very dangerous, especially if the card is poorly designed. Plugging a card into a standard PCI slot is difficult enough, without having to worry about power running through the system. Cards for UNIX servers are usually designed with

Table 8.11   Various PC Bus Architectures

BUS	BUS TYPE	SPEED	DATA PATH	MAXIMUM DATA TRANSFER	NOTES
ISA	Bus	8.3 MHz	16-bit	16.6 MBps	—
EISA	Bus	8.3 MHz	32-bit	33.3 MBps	Has mostly been replaced by PCI.
Micro-channel	Bus	8.3 MHz	32-bit	33.3 MBps	IBM standard; has mostly been replaced by PCI.
PCI-33	Bus	33 MHz	32-bit	133 MBps	Standard PCI.
PCI-33/64	Bus	33 MHz	64-bit	266 MBps	—
I20	Bus	33 MHz	32-bit or 64-bit	133 or 266 MBps	Intelligent controller for DMA transfers.
PCI-66	Bus	66 MHz	32-bit	266 MBps	—
PCI-66/64	Bus	66 MHz	64-bit	532 MBps	—
PCI-X	Bus	133 MHz	64-bit	1 GBps	—
InfiniBand	Switch	n/a*	64-bit	est. 2GBps	Data transfer is actually duplex 1 GBps in each direction; works over copper or fiber; supports internal and external enclosures (up to 300 m distant) for cards.

* Technology still in development.

lock-in tabs and slide paths, making them easy to install. The majority of cards for PCs don't have anything of that sort; many don't even have standard form factors. This means that, depending upon the internal layout of your PC server, a full-length card may not be able to plug into just any PCI slot due to obstructions (yes, this still happens). Another thing to consider with a newly added card is that the system BIOS may rescan all interrupts and I/O addresses and reassign them if the card isn't an exact duplicate of the old one; even minor revisions between cards can affect the system.

Replacing Existing Hardware

Purchasing new systems to replace your current system is always a losing proposition. You may need the new hardware, but buying a PC at any time always means obsolescence from the day you purchase it. That has been the general agreement in the industry for years, but it may be time for the power of PCs to have caught up to their usage.

You can always find reasons to buy the top models, especially as a safeguard against obsolescence. However, the PC industry has created powerful enough client systems to warrant careful consideration of buying the latest and the greatest. In fact, chip, operating system, and hardware vendors (we won't name them) are even promoting new technologies for which most people don't have a dying need, just to sell higher-end equipment.

In general, anything older than a 90 MHz Pentium should be replaced. Also, systems with ISA-only or EISA-only bus architectures are going the way of the dodo; these should be replaced with comparable PCI-based systems.

Server technology, on the other hand, is poised for serious growth over the next few years with the emergence of new bus technologies, RAM, and processors and their chipsets. In fact, it is very likely that new server products developed in 2000 will show significant improvement over the models selling earlier in year.

Selecting a New Client Station

Client stations are what most people equate with beige-box PCs sitting on your desktop. There are several classes of clients, several configurations for drive systems, and video graphics that affect the performance of the machine. This section discusses the differences between processors for clients, their drive systems, video cards, and monitors. A later section focuses on network interface cards for your client.

Processors and Motherboards

There are typically three classes of desktop systems these days: the low-end (typically under $1200), the midrange (under $2000), and the high-end (over $2000). The low-end machines run the Intel Celeron, AMD K6, or other low-end processors; these processors have reduced cache sizes and typically run on slower system buses of 66 or 75 MHz. The midrange includes the Pentium II and some Pentium III chips. These have larger caches, which enable them to interact faster with applications. At the top end are the fastest Pentium III chips. These have larger caches, which enable them to interact faster with applications. At the top end are the fastest Pentium III chip systems, which qualify as Intel-based workstations. Aside from supporting dual or even quad processors, they also support SCSI disk systems by default and support better memory controllers that increase application speed even more.

The Pentium III class machines, intended for the midrange users, may be priced under $2000, but unless you are doing lots of heavy-duty work, you are spending more money than you need to. Intel introduced the Celeron processor systems to compete with AMD's K6-2 processor-based systems, at half the price of the higher-end machines. One interesting fact that may sway you is that a major PC trade publication noted that 400 MHz Celeron systems run less than 10 percent slower than a 400 MHz Pentium II. Save your money; buy Celeron or K6-2/3 systems.

Low-end and midrange desktop clients often have a limited number of slots for memory modules. In fact, at the very lowest end, sometimes they have only one slot. In the midrange there are usually at least three SDRAM slots or one bank of EDO RAM slots. This means that you have to be careful when initially purchasing a new client and configuring memory. Sure you can buy a 32MB module now and worry about upgrading later. However, when it comes to upgrading, which you are most likely to do en masse for desktop clients, you may just end up with a small mountain of 32MB modules that aren't of much use any more. Most clients will do fine with 64MB with Windows 2000. Higher-end workstations should have 128- to 256MB RAM.

Most desktop clients have IDE drives, so you should check to see that the motherboards on these systems support the latest IDE standard, UltraDMA 66. This will allow them to run the fastest, as well as supporting the largest IDE drives on the market. If you don't have support for this, anything larger than 8GB will not be accessible by your hardware. Either you would have to wait for a BIOS upgrade from your system or motherboard vendor or you might want to buy an add-in PCI card that supports this. With new drives up to 40GB falling in decent price ranges, there's no reason you should go for an older system.

Drive Systems

Speaking of drives, most PC clients can survive with one large hard drive, one CD-ROM, and a floppy drive. Here is one point of advice:

Ignore DVD-ROM drives. Until the industry shapes up to standardize on an appropriate DVD-RAM (read and write capabilities), you will have nothing but an expensive CD-ROM drive. Not much software comes in DVD format at all. The only things that really use DVD are movies, so unless you plan to stock a library in your office and hold periodic showings of *2001: A Space Odyssey*, they won't be of much use to you.

Although vendors are also advocating the Iomega ZIP or other similar superfloppy drives (100MB per floppy disk or greater), media for these devices come at an appropriately higher cost. Unless you anticipate that your users will be transferring a lot of data between machines using floppies, you won't really need these. One exception is the Imation SuperDisk drive, which supports both traditional floppies and super-floppies.

With the huge sizes for IDE drives at low cost these days, you shouldn't need more than two hard drives per machine. At current maximum, that would put at least 50GB on the desktop. A user could get lost in there. Keep in mind that IDE supports only four physical drives at the maximum. With one hard drive and a CD-ROM drive, you will have used up two slots. A superfloppy drive may use up another. Workstations that need larger and more drives usually come with UltraSCSI support, which allows them up to eight internal drives. If you really need more than that, some vendors also provide external drive enclosures that attach as a separate SCSI chain. You could go on to terabytes this way.

Video Cards and Monitors

Video cards are fairly important for the desktop. Telepathy with the system unit may work for some people, but the rest of us still have to use our eyes. If they could have it, every user would want a top-of-the-line 100-million-polygon-serving 3D card with TV input, along with the best new 21-inch LCD monitor. Unless you are inclined to spend $6000 or $7000 on making everyone screen-happy, you should agree on basics.

First of all, unless the desktop will be doing computer-assisted design (CAD) work or be thoroughly engaged in games, you shouldn't have a burning need for a 3D-capable card. Most office applications are 2D; even those with presentation graphics do more 2D work than anything else, so the idea is to optimize what they see most of the time.

All new client systems come with support for the accelerated graphics port (AGP), which is essentially a special PCI slot for your video card that runs at twice the speed as the normal PCI bus. This gives the video board a fast path to the processor and memory and greatly speeds up all graphics. The new generations of AGP should arrive soon, supporting four times (2×AGP) and eight times (4×AGP) the speed of the regular PCI bus. Keep in mind, when the PCI bus is speeded up from 33 MHz to 66 MHz, the AGP port will also increase incrementally.

Video cards have their own video RAM (VRAM) separate from main memory, which is used by the card to store images and screen frames before they are displayed. Since the card does not need to go over the slower PCI bus or AGP slot to access memory for temporary use, this speeds up the graphics drawing process. There are a number of different types of specialized and nonspecialized VRAM. The nonspecialized variety is EDO or SDRAM running at higher frequencies placed on the card. Both versions are described in Table 8.12.

Table 8.13 shows the type of resolution you need to support and the amount of video RAM the video board will need to support that resolution at true 24-bit color (over 16 million colors). You could go for lower 16-bit resolution (over 65,000 colors) to save on buying more expensive video boards with larger frame buffers.

If, on the other hand, you do plan to use these systems for high-end video graphics applications, there are a number of options available to you. High-end graphics cards today have 3D rendering engines to assist the display of graphics. The common API for accessing the capabilities of

Table 8.12 Video RAM Technologies

VIDEO RAM TYPE	DESCRIPTION	BANDWIDTH
Video RAM	Original VRAM based upon FPM RAM.	80 MBps
Window RAM	Also FPM but with multiple access.	80 MBps
EDO RAM	EDO at higher frequencies.	100 MBps
SDRAM	SDRAM at higher frequency.	200 MBps
Synchronous graphics RAM	SDRAM with a wider data path.	400 MBps
Rambus DRAM	Same as RDRAM for main memory.	1.6 GBps

Table 8.13 Video Cards and Monitors

MONITOR SIZE	RESOLUTION SUGGESTED	MINIMUM VRAM FOR 2D COLOR DEPTHS		MINIMUM VRAM FOR 3D COLOR DEPTHS	
		16-BIT	24-BIT	16-BIT	24-BIT
13–14 in	800×600	1 MB	2 MB	3 MB	5 MB
15 in	1024×768	2 MB	3 MB	5 MB	8 MB
17–19 in	1280×1024	3 MB	4 MB	8 MB	12 MB
19–21 in	1600×1280	4 MB	6 MB	12 MB	18 MB

these 3D cards is OpenGL, although many Windows based systems still use Microsoft's Direct APIs only.

3D video cards often have large banks of video memory to store images used for texture mapping. This allows the card to render 3D texture mapped screens like CAD, games, and other software, much faster. If you use large monitors and require 3D viewing as well, then such cards with 16MB and above will be more suited to your needs. You also need to make sure that your 3D card can also support 2D applications like office productivity, database and most other applications. Although many 3D cards also have this capability, some don't or are very weak at it. Since 2D applications constitute nearly all business applications, it is important that you look for this quality in a video card first. Today it is possible to get high-quality 2D/3D cards under a couple of hundred dollars so it may not break your bank to have them installed for future-proofing your equipment.

A special note on digital monitors and LCD screens: If you plan to put these onto your users' desktops, we're pretty sure you will win the Cool Guy of the Office award. Perhaps purchasing may not vote for it, but the rest will. In any case, you should be aware that standards for "video boards" for digital monitors are not widely available. We use the quotes since this technology is fairly different from the analog video boards for tube monitors that have to convert video digital signals from the computer into analog pictures for the tube. Digital boards do not have to worry about this at all and do not lose resolution. Unfortunately, some of the earlier digital monitors used analog video connectors, thus losing some of the effectiveness; in such situations the video information gets converted twice and, along with this process, loses some clarity. The digital video interface (DVI) standard is now accepted by most monitor manufacturers as the common video interface for digital connections on both the monitor and the card. However, DVI has still lots of catching up to do on most video cards. If you do buy an LCD monitor, make sure you get it from the vendor you are purchasing the system unit from and make sure they have a tested video card that works with the monitor, or at worst case supports both digital and analog connections.

A final tip for those who need more than one head (the monitor, we mean). It used to be the case that you could not put two video cards into one PC and expect it to display on two screens. There are a few cards, however (notably those from Appian), that will allow you to connect two or four monitors directly to one computer. These cards use their own special video drivers that allow you to combine several monitors into a much larger desktop. We only assume that you have an adequate desk that won't collapse from the weight of four monitors. Use two smaller desks; it's safer.

Windows 98 and 2000 both can support multiple video cards in the machine to support two or more monitors and spread the desktop across them. However, you should note that one video card may run faster than the other, since only one of them can be in the AGP slot at a time. To put two video cards into a PC you would need one card to be AGP capable and the other, designed for the PCI bus. Although technically the former is just a souped up version of the latter, the physical bus interface is slightly different. Some video board vendors will sell separate AGP and PCI versions of the same board for this function. When possible you should get the boards from the same vendor, preferably the same model with different interfaces. This will minimize compatibility or performance differences between the screens. Keep a note of this when purchasing video cards for creating multiheaded PCs.

Selecting New Server Hardware

Selecting a new server hardware platform is largely a function of how the server is going to be used, the number of users, the applications to be installed, and the demands of the network environment. Information for designing servers for specific applications can be found in many of the popular trade magazines. Each application-specific server has its own special needs in terms of memory usage, disk usage, network interfaces, and management accessibility.

Since we cannot possibly guess at every configuration of server hardware per application, we have gone toward creating a common design for hardware platforms. First, we group the systems into four categories: the workgroup, the department, the enterprise, and the datacenter. Each of these categories defines the size of the application server.

A workgroup server is intended to provide basic functions and common applications to a small group of users, somewhere between 5 and 25; a departmental server should work for a larger population of 25 to 100 users; an enterprise server should be able to handle between 100 and 250 users; and a datacenter server should be able to handle up to 2000 users.

This last configuration pretty much hits the limits of single-box, Intel-based servers. Beyond this level, you have to create clusters of servers. You should probably use at least failover servers starting at the departmental level, meaning that to support 100 users, you would have to pay for two boxes with identical configuration, either load-balancing between themselves or with the second as a backup unit in case of failure of the first.

Pricing Intel Servers

Table 8.14 shows systems configured to support the four population sizes: workgroup (5 to 25 users), department (25 to 100 users), enterprise (100 to 250 users), and datacenter (250 to 2000 users). It assumes that each person, on average, uses 16MB of RAM and 525MB of disk space; that's 500MB of user disk quota and an additional 25MB for the system per user. The

Table 8.14 Server Configuration Scenarios

SERVER TYPE	PROCESSOR TYPE	NUMBER OF USERS	NUMBER OF CPUS	TOTAL RAM	TOTAL STORAGE
Workgroup	400- to 550-MHz PII	5–25	1–2	256–576MB	4–14GB
Departmental	450-MHz PII-800-MHz PIII	25–100	2	512MB-1.5GB	14–54GB
Enterprise	450-MHz PII Xeon-700-MHz PIII Xeon	100–250	4–8	1.5–4GB	54–260GB
Datacenter	500–700-MHz PIII Xeon	250–2000	8–16	8–32GB	260–520GB

base Windows 2000 system will need approximately 96MB of RAM and 500MB to itself. The RAM and disk storage have been rounded up (always up when possible—never down!) to the closest approximate drive size.

In the case of RAM, we have taken typical SDRAM sizes and followed the general practice to use the same size DIMMs whenever possible (e.g., three banks of 128MB SDRAM DIMM equals 384MB) and the next closest DIMM size whenever not possible (e.g., a 128MB DIMM plus a 256MB DIMM equals 384MB). Most memory manufacturers advise against using disproportionately different DIMMs within the same bank of memory slots (e.g., a 256MB DIMM with a 32MB DIMM) for the sake of performance. We have never seen any serious performance effects, but perhaps they know something we don't. Finally, Intel Xeon servers work better with EDO DIMMs than with SDRAM DIMMs because of memory interleaving at RAM sizes over 512MB.

Drive Systems

Servers often come with hot-swappable drive cages that allow you to pull out any drive while the system is running. Of course, this could disrupt any disk activity that is going on, but then you shouldn't be pulling them out unless there is something wrong with them, should you? Hot-swap drives are a good idea when you are using your drives in a RAID configuration. If the drives are not being used in a RAID configuration, pulling out a drive removes that drive volume from usage completely. Never, ever, put your system disk among the hot-swap drives; there is just too much of a chance that someone will accidentally remove it and crash the entire machine. Windows NT and 2000 support hot-swap capabilities in RAID 0, 1, and 5 configurations.

Per-User RAM

The 16MB per user estimate is reasonably high, but it covers all types of applications; we're not being cheap here. That's the amount of memory you might require when running separate user applications directly on the server, such as with a terminal server system. Some servers, such as Exchange, won't need more than 1 or 2MB per additional user. Others, such as SQL Server, will want as much as you can feed it. Low amounts of memory (64 to 256MB) are reasonably cheap so that you should go for the maximum if your budget will allow it.

To help you out, the CD includes an Excel worksheet to help you determine more exact pricing, in \Chapter8\ServerPricing.XLS. You can use this worksheet for your own calculations to determine more exact pricing. Depending upon the server scenario, you should change the number of users, the CPU model, and the number of CPUs per scenario. This should help you arrive at an estimated price that you should expect to pay for this configuration of server. This file is also on the companion Web site and will be periodically updated to reflect current estimates.

If you wish to change the general industry pricing environment, change any of the values colored in bright yellow. As always, the industry is constantly changing, resulting in different configurations, which we cannot predict, and certainly different pricing. By 2000, servers may come with a different peripheral bus system (e.g., the System I/O bus) and also will start including RDRAM by default. At the time of this writing, none of these servers are available; hence, no pricing information is available. You can plug into this model the pricing for new types of buses, RAM, and servers at the appropriate locations. The direct information contained in this worksheet mode may not be relevant, but the calculations and structure will help your IT department formulate its own future version.

If you run out of internal drive space, as is common in many PC server models, most vendors will provide external drive enclosures that hook into your external SCSI port. If you add a Fibre-Channel card to the server, you can connect to these enclosures at the much higher speeds for FC, allowing for faster transfers. Each of these enclosures may have its own internal SCSI chains for the drives and support up to eight drives each.

For huge archival systems containing terabytes of data, you should consider a *hierarchical storage management* system. These units keep most of the data on tape or magneto-optical disks and they have robot-arm-driven systems that load and unload these cartridges onto drives such that you have automatic access to any of the information at all times, with some delay when swapping between volumes. These things are mesmerizing to watch, although there are cheaper forms of amusement.

Power Management

Nothing is more important than having a reliable power system for your server, because without it, it's just a large, ugly end-table. At the very low end, such systems come with a single power supply unit that goes up to 400 watts. However, a single power supply unit is fairly risky. Most midrange PC servers include dual or triple redundant power supplies.

This means that the system can always run as long as one of the power supplies is still working. With dual power supplies you still have the risk that the remaining one might fail while you are getting the failing one fixed. Triple redundant power, also called *N + 1 redundancy,* will save your skin in 99 percent of power supply failure cases but usually comes only in the high-end servers.

Uninterruptible power supply (UPS) systems are almost a necessity in the case of any server. These are basically large batteries that will keep your system running for a short time while your building power is out. Single low-end and midrange PC servers can run up to 30 minutes (even loaded ones) on a 1400-kWh UPS that fits neatly next to your server. It's when you have rows and rows of drives or servers that you start needing the washing machine-sized 3000- to 6000-kWh units.

NOTE

There's a reason that there are separate power cords for each power supply. It's so that you can plug each into a different wall outlet or UPS.

Other Important Server Hardware Features

The hardware management features of a server are often overlooked. It's easy to mistakenly assume server management software tools will do it all for you. You need hardware monitoring devices on your servers to warn you ahead of time of any hazards to the system. If a component on the server is about to fail, you can plan for a hot-plug change or bring down the server as necessary. An ounce of preparation goes a long way toward saving time and money.

An *external management port* (EMP) is invaluable. On UNIX systems, you can often hook a console serial port into a terminal server and manage the hardware system remotely. PC servers are now beginning to sport similar devices, either as specialized serial ports or built-in modems. This approach allows sysadmins to connect directly to the server from any phone line and manage the box or even reboot the system if necessary. Nothing is more frustrating than having to run someone to a box simply to power cycle it while the phone rings off the hook with calls from angry users. Make sure your EMP device can be attached to both a network and a private modem line (not part of the general dial-up user modem pools) and make very sure that a server password (different from your NT administrator password) is enabled on the port.

Finally, you often have the choice between pedestal-based and rack-mounted cases. Pedestal cases make sense for smaller workgroup-class machines and even for some departmental systems. In many cases, the environment in which they will work is not a climate-controlled network operations center, but more often a corner in an office or inside a closet somewhere. These environments place greater physical demands and wear and tear on these devices. Very often, they become dusty and have to be cleaned every few weeks. In some cases, the pedestal-based servers consume slightly more power for better cooling systems. A rack-mounted system is designed for industry-standard 19-inch racks, some-times with slidable arms on each side so they can be pulled out of the rack for inspection or maintenance.

TIP
PC servers do not need flashy graphics or sound cards. Everything they need usually comes with the system. 'Nuff said.

Selecting Network Hardware

If you are setting up a new network for desktop PCs, you should know about what network technologies PCs currently support. This section defines the different networking technologies in common use, as well as pointing out which one is more suitable for different types of PC systems.

Switched versus Shared Networks

Standard Ethernet and Token Ring are both shared networks; that is, the total amount of bandwidth available is shared between the total number of nodes connected to it. So if you have 200 nodes on a 10-Mbps Ether-net (eww!), you will have less than about 0.05 Mbps of throughput per machine; that is about 6KB of data per second. That is what we in the industry call *absolutely pathetic*. Most network administrators these days are smarter and plan for much smaller networks of 20 or so nodes.

A switched network, on the other hand, goes full speed for every port connected to it. It is like having an entire Ethernet LAN segment to yourself. If only one device is connected to the port on the 10-Mbps switch, it is communicating at full 10 Mbps with every other port. Within the Ethernet switch, the actual collapsed backbone runs significantly faster. A 24-port

100-Mbps Ethernet switch, for example, might internally be able to push data around at 2 Gbps. Most switches, however, are rated by the speed of the external ports. A fast Ethernet switch can have 8, 16, 24, 48, or even 96 separate ports, each running at a full 100 Mbps. You could also hang a standard Ethernet hub off of a switch port, thereby splitting the total bandwidth of that port across however many nodes are within that segment.

Switched networks are becoming commonplace, especially for groups or clusters of servers. The servers are directly connected to the switch; one port of the switch is then connected to another switch or hub that connects to all the actual desktop nodes. On the other hand, switches also have one or two even faster uplinks that connect to an even faster network hub, router, or switch. We will discuss this in a following section on ATM networks.

Some switches come with several different port speeds. For example, you can find Ethernet switches that provide a number of 10-Mbps ports, a few 100-Mbps ports, and one or two 1-Gbps ports. Keep in mind that each port is separate; having a mixed-speed switch like this will not limit you to the lowest common denominator as it would with a shared hub.

Network devices such as Ethernet hubs and switches are normally valued at the *price per port*, that is, the overall cost of the device divided by the number of ports that it contains. This lets you compare devices with different numbers of ports on an even level. Of course, you shouldn't compare the price per port of a hub with that of a switch; the switch gives significantly more performance value than the hub; it's like comparing Volkswagens and Ferraris.

Server NICs

When it comes to servers, you should select a NIC specifically designed for this environment. These NICs are two to four times the cost of regular NICs but typically have much better performance or offer additional services particular to the server environment. In fact, you might even want to think of multiple NICs in your server. Here's why.

Some server NICs implement two important features: *trunking* and *failover*. Trunking is the ability to combine the bandwidth delivery of multiple cards into a single larger bandwidth pipe; you simply take two server NICs and pump up traffic over them using the same network protocol address. Some NICs provide *symmetric trunking* and can both send and receive traffic over multiple cards. Other NICs with *asymmetric trunking* can only send traffic out over multiple cards but receive incoming data over one card. This is usually because it can get confusing when you have multiple NICs with the same network protocol address.

If you are wondering what the point of trunking is if there is a limit to what the PCI bus can transfer, you may have missed the fact that many higher-end Intel servers have multiple separate PCI buses. Each of these dual- or triple-peer PCI buses can take a card and each has a direct path for the system to transfer data. These make most sense in SMP machines where you aren't bottlenecked by one lonely, overworked processor.

With NIC *failover*, you can set up multiple cards in the server and designate one or more as the backup card. This card is typically not in use by the node and the network, and simply waits until the primary card fails. This is particularly important when you need to set up a fail-safe system where the server never goes down because of a failed network port or NIC.

In both cases, you also need a network switch that is aware that these features are being used. That way no one gets confused and the packets do not get misdelivered.

Ethernet and Fast Ethernet

Although 10-Mbps Ethernet is still the most common form of LAN in the world, 100-Mbps Fast Ethernet is rapidly approaching the same price range. Essentially you can buy an *autosensing dual-mode* 10/100-Mbps Ethernet hub that supports both speeds of Ethernet networks for about twice the price of a 10-Mbps Ethernet hub by itself, while yielding a near tenfold increase in speed. Keep in mind that this kind of hub runs at 100 Mbps only if all the nodes connected to it run at Fast Ethernet speed.

NICs still come in 10, 100, and 10/100 varieties, although the last one is pretty much all you see these days. They are commodity products now, meaning that one card is almost identical to that of another in performance capabilities. Some NICs, particularly the well-loved 3Com Etherlink family, have a good reputation for performance over others. Under Win 95, 98, and 2000, cards practically automatically configure themselves when first installed. You may run into problems when you have multiple NICs but nothing that isn't too hard to resolve. Furthermore, most cards come with some form of diagnostic utility to check the overall performance of the device.

Table 8.15 shows some pricing on what NICs, hubs, and switches cost these days; it is a far different picture from that of the $300 10-Mbps Ethernet cards that one of the authors had to buy years ago. For servers, a full 100 Mbps is the least amount that you need per server. This means an Ethernet switch, of course. The cost per port isn't that much more, so there is no reason not to do it.

Gigabit Ethernet

 Gigabit Ethernet is a completely different story. At one point in 1997, vendors claimed that it was going to be just about *the* greatest thing since sliced bread. Unfortunately, prices for Gigabit Ethernet devices are still very high and, for the most part, they are not widely available. Actually, one of the primary problems for Gigabit Ethernet isn't the networking system but the server itself. Non-Intel-based UNIX operating systems have been able to use a major portion of the bandwidth available with a Gigabit Ethernet connection, but Intel-based hardware still has a number of limitations.

First, the peripheral buses on most Intel servers are still slow. Until the widespread adoption of InfiniBand, or some other system, most buses

Table 8.15 Prices per Port for Various Ethernet Devices

DEVICE	PRICE PER PORT
10-Mbps NICs	$5–$25
100-Mbps NICs	$20–$75
Dual-mode 10/100-Mbps NICs	$25–$90
Dual-mode 10/100-Mbps server NIC	$100–$500
10-Mbps Ethernet hubs	$7–$12
100-Mbps Fast Ethernet hubs	$15–$25
Dual-mode 10/100-Mbps hubs	$17–$35
10-Mbps Ethernet switch	$35–$55
100-Mbps Ethernet switch	$60–$80
Dual-mode 10/100-Mbps Ethernet switch	$60–$90
Gigabit Ethernet NICs	$500–$2000
Gigabit Ethernet switches	$800–$3000

can only deliver up to 266 Mbps over the fastest port. Unfortunately, this is reserved for the graphics card. In higher-end servers with 64-bit PCI cards running at 66 MHz, you can reach speeds of 1 Gbps in bursts, but this is across the entire shared bus and for all the cards.

Second, no matter what Microsoft claims, Windows NT and 2000 have not been able to push anywhere near 1 Gbps (assuming that the peripheral bus is not a factor). In fact, NT has had a troubled history of falling near 20 percent of maximum throughput of networking systems like Gigabit Ethernet and ATM.

If you buy a Gigabit Ethernet card, you should first check with the vendor for performance test results on how much data Windows can push over the vendor's card and device drivers. Always use the drivers supplied by the vendor; actually, that's pretty much all you can use for Gigabit Ethernet.

ATM

ATM cards for Windows machines have been available for several years. It's just that not many people buy them. For desktop machines, there are two kinds of ATM hardware over copper wiring: 25-Mbps Desktop ATM, as promoted and led by IBM, and 155-Mbps OC-3c ATM. Both of these are limited in distance between the switch and the desktop unit. You can guess that 25-Mbps ATM is cheaper than 155-Mbps ATM; in fact, it is about a quarter the price.

The switch that immediately connects to your desktop is called the *edge device*. Aside from full ATM-based edge devices, you will also see 100-Mbps Ethernet switches as edge devices, too. These boxes connect to your PC using 100-Mbps Ethernet protocols (not ATM) and connect elsewhere on the network through ATM cells. However, with the proper protocol software installed on your desktop, you can make them join an ATM virtual LAN just like a real ATM node. If you don't recall the point of virtual LANs, go back to Chapter 3—do not pass "GO"; do not collect $200.

If you plan to pull fiber directly to your workstations, then use multimode ATM fiber connections beginning at 155 Mbps (OC-3c) and ranging up to 622 Mbps (OC-12). Multimode fiber is intended for the LAN and comes at a cheaper price than long-distance single-mode fiber.

Even Faster ATM

You should check whether your server hardware is able to push much more than OC-12. For most servers before 1999, there really isn't any point to looking at higher-speed cards. The system and memory bus cannot handle transfers of data much higher than this. With emerging standards for new system and memory buses, this will cease to be a problem. UNIX systems with better peripheral buses can actually support up to 2.4-Gbps (OC-48) connections.

Summary

Computer hardware was what people used to think of as the Cost of Computing. However, with falling prices, and improvements in technology, the purchase price of a system is now much less than the support cost for it. Cheaper, however, does not always mean better. Choosing the proper platform can save you a significant amount of hard dollars in maintenance costs and the cost of managing hardware obsolescence.

One item we cannot take into account in this book is the internal design of the PC system. Some systems are designed well for maintenance purposes, while others look that they have all been squeezed into a unit that is never meant to be modified. Thus when looking at a system for purchase you should also take a look at the inside of the system and read the manufacturer's instructions on how easy it is to fix or modify the units.

The meat of this chapter focuses on how to compare technologies and what constitutes a comparable system for your needs. Unfortunately, computer systems hardware is in constant flux. Even during the writing of this book, not only have a number of new chips emerged, but whole new technologies. With that in mind, you should keep up to date with what is currently being offered. The accompanying Web site to this book will attempt to track some of these upgrades, so use it to your benefit.

## CHAPTER 9

Selecting Integration Packages

There are quite a number of packages that use different approaches to solve the UNIX and Windows integration puzzle. You have software that allows Windows machines to behave like UNIX systems and vice versa. Since they both speak a common network protocol, TCP/IP, it is a lot easier to combine such environments.

The usefulness of these packages depends on how well they're suited to the type of integration needed by your network. Nothing is worse than finding out after hours of work that a newly purchased package falls short of what you expected. Thus, this chapter takes a look at the various categories for such integration packages and shows what to expect. More so, this chapter looks at the different approaches to integration and how to choose between them.

What Integration Means

The word *integration* implies that there are at least two systems that are not natively compatible with each other and need to be brought together into one environment. This is because they either don't speak the same language, don't work the same way, or don't look alike. In our case, we are considering integration between Windows and UNIX platforms.

These are two historically different operating systems with very different internal architectures. DOS and Windows users were satisfied with software that ran only for single users and with the simplicity of their environment compared to the competition's. UNIX users laughed off the fallibility of the DOS/Windows operating systems and their lack of support for a secure, robust environment. For many years, it seemed that never the twain would meet, and, indeed, people (vendors) even suggested that the systems should not be integrated. Eventually, reality crept in and vendors began introducing TCP/IP network services for PCs, making them more effective than the text terminals of UNIX systems. Soon PCs could use UNIX systems as file servers. E-mail became a necessity, and the e-mail services for TCP/IP started to overtake other proprietary mechanisms. To support real graphics, UNIX vendors began to support the X Windows graphical desktop on their systems, effectively one-upping Windows until the late 1990s. Eventually, integration came to life and the software started evolving into different species of integration products.

Levels and Types of Integration

There are different *types* and *levels* of integration that define just how closely combined the environment is. An *integration level* for an operating system follows the structure of modern OSs. For example, integration at the network protocol level means that the software on two machines can communicate over the network. Integration on the application service level means that the software on Windows machines can access server applications running on a UNIX platform or vice versa.

These levels (see Table 9.1) define the similarities between the different OS platforms. It begins at the bottom, with hardware and OS emulation, and works its way up to the very top, where even the user environment looks the same. The levels are not always inclusive; you do not need hardware coprocessor boards to allow a UNIX machine to understand the Windows file system. Instead, the UNIX system implements a software equivalent of the other file system.

An *integration type* describes which system component is being integrated. For example, file sharing is one type of integration in which the operating systems know how to exchange files and their formats so that they can be read by one side or both. Both file and printer sharing fall

Table 9.1 Levels of Integration

LEVEL OF INTEGRATION	TYPE OF INTEGRATION
Hardware integration	Hardware coprocessor boards.
OS system/subsystem emulation	System emulation software.
Network protocol integration	TCP/IP implementation.
Application protocol integration	RPCs and sockets.
Application development integration	XML, CORBA, and Java.
Application service integration	Name service, e-mail service, file sharing, and printer sharing.
User management integration	Account translators and domain controllers.
Application access integration	Terminal applications, X11, Webtops, and Windows terminals.

under the same level (i.e., application service integration) but are two distinct types of integration. The integration type is normally viewed from one platform or the other.

Most NT-UNIX integration packages approach the problem from one platform and build a solution that works on the other. They build a package that executes on an NT platform and runs or accesses UNIX services or vice versa. For example, PC-X is an implementation of the X Windows protocol (the traditional UNIX graphical user interface) on a Windows box; on the other hand, Samba is a Windows NetBIOS system service that executes on UNIX servers and provides access to Windows file systems and printers.

Table 9.2 shows the integration direction from PC systems to access UNIX servers and applications. We differentiate these categories of products by noting that these packages add native UNIX communica-

Table 9.2 PC Client Access to UNIX Resources

TYPE OF INTEGRATION	INTEGRATION PACKAGE
Windows applications	Native, Windows terminal software.
UNIX applications	Terminal applications, PC-X, Webtop, UNIX emulators, and remote script execution.
UNIX files and file systems	(PC)NFS and NetBIOS sharing.
UNIX printers	(PC)NFS, NetBIOS sharing, and UNIX 1pr emulation.
UNIX tape drives	Windows RMT.

tions and features to PC clients or add native PC features to the UNIX server, all so that PC clients can access UNIX resources. A PC client in this case can be either a desktop PC or a server, since they are all clients to a UNIX server.

On the other hand, there are packages that allow UNIX systems access to PC applications and resources, as shown in Table 9.3. These packages provide a UNIX client with native PC features or a PC server with UNIX features so that the UNIX client can access PC resources.

Not all concepts in one platform have an equivalent on the other; hence, there is a lot of translation and approximation of ideas going from one direction to the other. Many objects and applications are not truly bidirectionally compatible. When developers have tried to unite concepts in both environments, the result has often been a new kind of application programming system that is not compatible with the majority of software available for one platform or the other. Developers of other applications have to rewrite their code and recompile it to the new environment, which is not practical on a commercial scale.

The problem with the unidirectional integration method is that it focuses on the features of one platform rather than leveraging the strengths of each platform to its best ability. Until recently, this has not been a very difficult choice to make for developers, since the concepts and features of the UNIX system have been established for years, providing a model for similar software on PCs. The source code for many UNIX tools is easily available on the Internet, giving developers a head start on taking these tools to the Windows platform. Hence, most of the integration software you find runs on PC systems and connects to UNIX systems.

Microsoft's attitude toward building proprietary protocols has shifted toward supporting more commonly accepted systems. With Windows

Table 9.3 UNIX Client Access to PC Resources

TYPE OF INTEGRATION	INTEGRATION PACKAGE
UNIX applications	Native, X11.
Windows applications	Windows terminal software, Windows emulators, and hardware coprocessing.
PC files and file systems	NFS and NetBIOS sharing.
PC printers	Windows LPD.
PC tape drives	Not available.

2000, Winsock and TCP/IP become the flagship protocols, with lesser reliance on older NetBIOS applications. In the Service Packs for NT 4.0, Microsoft application suites, and this release, IP application protocols such as DHCP, FTP, NFS, SMTP, POP, IMAP, LDAP, and so forth have all become regular features of the operating system.

Integration Architecture

The architecture of how these platforms communicate with one another is crucial to their successful deployment. This architecture includes a plan on how the hardware interconnects, how the operating systems communicate, and how applications and users interact between the two platforms.

The simplest form can be seen in a single direct communication between two machines. This communication can be at any integration level. In such an instance, you have an integration package that runs on the Windows or UNIX platform that accesses the services of another machine. The machine that accesses the services is known as the *client* and the machine that provides the service, the *server*. Hence, what you have is the very basic and commonly known *client/server* architecture. To be more correct, this is a *single-tier* client/server architecture since the client communicates directly with the server. The data may traverse a number of routers and network nodes, but just like a phone conversation can go through many switches, it is still a one-on-one conversation between the two end-points.

Most integrated networks work this way since this is all that their software allows them to do. The problem is that it forces the system on which the integration package is installed to work like something it is not. If the software is not designed well, the users will most likely be forced to learn a new interface or access method that they are not familiar with. This is not necessarily the fault of the integration package or the developers who created it. After all, vendors are limited to the constraints of the protocols and standards for the other platform. For example, there simply is no analogue to a window manager in the Windows environment, and users may have never seen a virtual desktop that provides multiple separate desktop screens where application windows can sit. Such a system is fairly common in X Windows systems for UNIX, however.

The good thing about single-tier client/server communications is that it is easier to establish, communicate through, and troubleshoot, since there are only two end-points to deal with and it does not go through a translator. The downside is that if one end-point changes how it communicates, you have to modify the other end-point to accommodate this change. Thus, if the server is re-written or upgraded and expects different input, all the clients have to conform to the change and be modified as well. To avoid this problem, adding another layer in between can help.

Multi-tier Integration

Sometimes it is more difficult or simply isn't possible to directly integrate software tools between multiple platforms. The need for an "integration glue" to bind the two different types of platforms forms the basis for many application server systems; thus, the rise of multitier integration services.

To illustrate, a PC database client trying to access a mainframe-based Customer Information Control System (CICS) database requires several layers of integration. First, the client has to be able to communicate with the mainframe on the network level. Next, the client has to be able to send jobs to the mainframe to process at the session level. Finally, there has to be a conversion between the data format of the PC database client and that of the CICS database, at the presentation level.

Even between a Windows and a UNIX system, there may need to be multiple tiers of indirection. For example, a Windows terminal desktop that is only able to access a Windows NT or 2000 terminal server would need to go through the NT system to access drives or printers on the UNIX system via a platform-neutral network sharing protocol.

Multiple tiers allow more flexibility to the modification of a system. The multiple tiers create focus between the access sources (the desktops) and the destinations (the servers). Rather than installing an integration tool at every source client desktop, introducing an intermediary tier can make upgrades, migration, or other transformations much easier. You not only have potentially fewer systems to perform the upgrades to; you may also have additional security within the tiers that is independent of individual client services.

The cost of creating multiple tiers is that there are more hardware and software assets involved, which may make the initial network design process more difficult. If you use packaged multi-tier integration products, you may save yourself a significant amount of time and trouble designing custom interfaces or software for your specific needs.

Some packages are naturally multi-tiered. For example, Microsoft Proxy Server is an intermediary between client desktops and servers on the Internet. The proxy service is always a middle tier no matter how you look at it. SCO's Tarantella Web-browser-based network access software is also a middle-tier product providing any Java-capable browser clients with access to UNIX and Windows server-based applications.

Microsoft's general attitude toward servers is that they should be fixed to a single function. A SQL Server system should be running only the database and not Windows Terminal Server or the Exchange e-mail server. The network system services provide the glue to bind them together. Some argue that this is because NT and Windows 2000 do not perform very well running several server applications at a time, although this has been disproved in some cases by installations that combine Web, database, e-mail, and remote access services in one system, as are often used by Internet service providers.

In this respect, multiple tiers are almost a fact of life for Windows networks. This contrasts with how many UNIX servers are used for any number of server applications. Many UNIX sysadmins find it hard to come to terms with the fact that a single Windows server should be running only a single service. Even PC-based UNIX systems can often run multiple services. The benefits of single-function servers lie in the reduced complexity of managing these systems. With the costs for server hardware so low these days, even the purchase cost is friendly enough to make it possible.

Cross-Platform Service Integration

Cross-platform service integration is the process of linking server applications that are running on two or more different platform types. Such integration processes work only when there is a common standard that server applications on both platforms understand. The common problem is that Microsoft tends to adopt many standards, such as those from the Internet Engineering Task Force (IETF), the World Wide Web Consortium (W3C), and others, and then extends them for its own environment, as many know. The net effect is that the system works, in cross-platform environments, but not quite as well.

For example, the Domain Name System is designed to work identically across a number of operating system platforms. This is what is called a successful standard. Windows NT worked with DNS services on UNIX machines fine, but Microsoft needed an addressing system for its Net-BIOS-based protocols and thus created the Windows Internet Name Service (WINS). However, with Windows 2000, the addition of Dynamic DNS required a new type of server application to support a dynamic information environment. Active Directory and DHCP in Win 2000 both rely on DDNS, running either on the NT server or on an external server. On UNIX systems you have to run a DNS server that supports these dynamic updates, such as Bind 8.1.2 or CheckPoint MetaIP.

RAWN RANT

This kind of extensionist attitude is for the depraved. It sometimes is the case that there is a valid reason to introduce such extensions. However, it is more often the case that these extensions are introduced because of other services the vendor tries to meld into the original one. They keep changing the parts until what was once a car might look more like a hydrofoil-blimp-roadster. It is detrimental to users, since most reasonably sized networks involve mixed-platform computing and services, and such changes mean that services won't work the way users expect. Vendors do this to try to establish a technical advantage over others. What's worse is vendors who claim to be standard and then introduce such extensions. You know who you are. Stop it!

Cross-platform service integration is a common issue for services that relate to the network and to interapplication communications. This covers many aspects, including addressing, name services, sessions and connections, data format exchange, and remote access.

Protocol incompatibility in cross-platform services can cause a discontinuity in the behavior of user applications across your client systems (see Table 9.4). The general policy is that a person trying to use the same type of service across should be able to expect the same kind of responses from all the servers. You don't want your users to have to remember the differences in the environment of each of the servers. For example, retrieving e-mail from the mail server should work the same even if you replace or add to the mail server hosts.

The worst kind of problem is propagation of errors through cross-platform services, when a client connects to a multitier service system and the data or behavior of the system changes as it moves between the tiers. This can introduce intermittent unpredictability in the service that is especially difficult to trace.

The reality is that it is not possible to achieve platform-neutral services in all cases, and your users will have to be prepared to deal with the vari-

Table 9.4 Protocol Differences between Windows and UNIX

CLIENT SOFTWARE	WINDOWS	UNIX
Telnet	Standard; assumes VT52 or VT100 emulation.	Standard.
FTP	Most commonly used FTP commands; no Proxy FTP support.	Most commonly used FTP commands; some implement Proxy FTP.
Web (HTTP)	Supports HTTP 1.1 and 1.0.	Supports HTTP 1.1 and 1.0.
Web (HTML)	Extensions to HTML in DHTML.	Third-party software extends HTML.
nslookup (DNS)	Standard; Win 2000 also supports Dynamic DNS.	Standard; Bind 8.1.2 server handles Dynamic DNS.
LDAP	Win 2000 supports LDAP v2 and v3; supports non-standard ACL security within queries and nonstandard directory replication methods.	OpenLDAP and other third-party packages support standard LDAP v2 and v3.
Time (NTP)	Standard.	Standard.
X Windows	Variety of third-party packages and support; many X11R6.3 versions, but not with complete support.	Standard.
Databases (SQL)	Superlative of standard; contains several additional SQL Server-specific operations. Differences vary depending upon application, as well.	Varies; standard implementations are available.
Mail access (SMTP/ESTMP)	Standard.	Standard.
Mail access (POP)	Standard POP2 and 3 supported.	Standard.
Mail access (IMAP)	Third parties provide full IMAP implementation.	Third parties provide full IMAP implementation; also available as freeware.
Net connection (PPP)	Standard PPP; alternative authentication with MS CHAP.	Standard PPP; uses CHAP or PAP.
Virtual private networking	Uses PPTP and L2TP rather than IPSec.	Standard IPSec; various encryption protocols (DES, 3DES, RSA, RC4).

continues

Table 9.4 *(Continued)*

CLIENT SOFTWARE	WINDOWS	UNIX
File sharing (NFS)	Implements standard (PC) NFS with both UDP and TCP.	Implements standard (PC)NFS with both UDP and TCP.
File sharing (SMB)	Standard.	Third-party package Samba implements standard SMB file sharing.
Printing (LPR/LPD)	Third-party LPR Client support.	Standard.
Remote procedure calls (RPCs)	Uses extended version of DCE RPCs; incompatible with Sun RPCs.	Usually supports Sun RPCs; DCE RPCs also supported.
Proxy services	MS Proxy can support Socks.	Socks and other protocols in third-party software.

ations. Your sysadmins and logbooks should also note which systems are affected by these differences should a future change to the setup suddenly start causing other inadvertent problems.

When to Integrate

The need to integrate depends on the specific situation. The circumstances might dictate that you should give your desktop PCs access to UNIX applications rather than invest in building these same applications for the PCs. On the other hand, you may already have a partially integrated environment for some services and need to work on how to get other services running for both groups. It is best to consider the cost of integration versus the alternatives first.

There are always alternatives to integration. One obvious choice would be to completely abandon one platform in favor of another. This is practical when you have few machines on one platform and the same software is available on the other platform. There is the cost of purchasing new machines, but this may work out much better than trying to jerry-rig a solution onto an existing one. However, maintaining dual systems for every user is not very cost efficient on anything more than 20 machines.

Another option would be to build the same features on the other platform. With some programming skill you can recreate the services and features as they would be on the original platform. However, this may be costly and involve a bit of development work. What's more, it is not a trivial task to build a new system simply based on the user interface. Without access to the source code of an existing package, the project may take too much time, energy, and money to be justifiable.

If you already have an integration solution in place that doesn't seem to be scaling very well to the number of users you have, you may wish to take a look at other similar integration products or investigate different solutions. The first, most obvious thing to do would be to ask your current vendor what you can to do expand the role of the system and scale it to a larger environment.

With cross-platform integration there are often several ways of accomplishing the same task, and one might work better for you than another.

Choosing between Integration Packages

Many integration packages overlap in the features they support. They operate in different ways, so it becomes difficult to directly compare them based simply upon their technical capabilities. The choice becomes easy when everything you are looking for shows up on the ingredient list of just one package, but this is a rare occurrence. When it comes down to it, what matters most is how much implementing the package will cost, not just the sticker price. This includes:

- The cost of software licenses, and distributing and managing these licenses to all the systems that will use the product including servers, and client stations.

- The platform support cost, which is the cost per annum of keeping sysadmin staff on hand and managing the platform(s) on which the product will run. This may include the need to support more than one type of hardware and operating systems platform. If you already have existing staff to support these platforms, include the incremental cost of adding the product to the platform, if any.

- The user support cost for maintaining help desk staff to aid users and troubleshoot user problems with the product. This should be measured separately from that of user support for the platform and other products.

- The cost of vendor technical support for the product per annum, including how much the base technical support costs, the cost per incident, on-site service costs, and the cost of shipping products back to the vendor.

- The cost of any custom development needed to make the product work towards the need of your specific computing environment.

Choosing among the various integration packages means measuring the cost versus benefits of each product for all of these items. You may only have estimates for the costs of a number of these items, but educated guesswork at the start is better than surprise expenses when addressing these issues after deployment. The next chapter takes these costs into account in looking at the overall project deployment plan.

Based upon the integration approach you choose, you should try to prioritize your choice based upon vectors such as cost, scalability, and manageability of the entire system. You won't be able to determine performance at this point, but examining similar configurations of the product at other sites might give you an idea of how well it will work. Sometimes a solution may provide everything that your users need but becomes far too expensive to implement on a large scale. This is why reading trade magazines that give examples of other successful projects of the same kind is so helpful.

Summary

Choosing how you want to perform an integration is a philosophy of its own. Many packages attempt to bend your will toward their method, but with the wide-ranging choices available you should be able to pick something that falls more in sync with your own ideas. Think of the level of integration you want to perform, and then choose an appropriate type of integration. Watch out for the dangers of cross-platform integration. You may be faced with unseen problems with slight incompatibilities that vendors do not advertise on their packages. Furthermore, you may even get caught in a Catch-22 paradox when it comes to support, as each vendor blames the others' products for the source of your problems. Look for third-party integrators or solution providers that have worked with both environments for the proper expertise and a history of dealing with such problems. Finally, you should think about a multitier approach since this provides intermediate levels that allow either the client or server endpoint to change its integration methods more easily. This allows flexibility without the loss of features.

## CHAPTER 10

Developing an Integration Strategy

Before you go out and buy an integration package, you should first be aware of how your network is implemented and what computers are already on your network. You should also have a well-defined approach to integration. This will go a long way toward saving you time and money during the integration process and will help you explain to your boss what you intend to do to the network, how you intend to do it, and why.

Staging Your Integration Project

Although this is not a book on project management, some consideration should be given to how you approach an integration project. For some, this may be as simple as installing a new application or server. For most, however, it will involve careful coordination between several different groups, a defined technical implementation plan, and training of IT staff and users.

This chapter looks at project planning and implementation issues from the perspective of integrating Windows and UNIX systems, mostly from a technical viewpoint.

Any well-planned project will go through several stages that build toward successful completion:

- *Investigation.* In this stage, you define the scope of the project and assess the needs of the business and the users. You then proceed to an examination of the existing system before deciding on the approach in the next stage

- *Design and proposal.* In this stage, you take the information about the existing system and the strategic goals and develop a tactical plan on how it can be accomplished, the costs involved in completing the project, a time schedule, and the deliverables of the project.

- *Procurement.* Once the project approach has been outlined, you can approach vendors with a formal request for proposals that defines what equipment and services are needed to accomplish the project.

- *Implementation.* When you have selected one or more vendors, the actual project implementation gets underway. This will most likely take the majority of the time involved with the project.

- *Training.* Once you have implemented the new system, the IT staff and users must be brought up to speed on how to handle the new system. This is also a good time to develop policies on the technical administration of the system.

- *Maintenance.* This stage pretty much lasts till the end of the lifetime viability of the project and involves the active technical and business management of the project by assigned staff members. With the information collected during the monitoring phase, you may refine or redefine the project itself, or set a new project underway to accomplish tasks that were not anticipated in this one.

A final stage, which can be considered part of maintenance, is sometimes called *postmortem* (when the project fails) or *project completion assessment* (when it seems to be working). In this stage, the project management group looks over the original goals defined for the project, the problems encountered during the various stages, and the results after a certain period of time in the maintenance phase. It's simple enough to say on the completion date that the project is a raging success or an abysmal failure, but the real truth of it comes out several months after the project is completed, when users have generally accepted the new system.

For the technical crew, the work starts at the first stage, all the way through the last. Many sysadmins tend to think that their involvement comes only in the implementation stage. This is what leads many projects astray, as the technical considerations for the project get left behind during the initial project specification phase, and this continues through the stages.

If you look over the chapters of this book, you might see a parallel between the project development process and the organization of the chapters. Part One provides background information that can help during the investigation stage. Part Two, Chapters 8 to 10, provides more background information on hardware and software issues of integration that could help you choose an integration path. The present chapter also contributes to integration but continues on toward the design and proposal and the procurement stages. All of Part Three, Chapters 11 through 15, makes up the implementation stage. In Part Four, Chapter 16, on management strategies, brings into play the training process. Chapter 17 focuses on maintenance, and monitoring your integrated system. Finally, Chapter 18 focuses on how to determine the success of your project.

Investigation Stage

Projects begin when someone (practically anyone) promotes an idea to management that may improve the business in some fashion, and gets validation for the idea. This initial idea must then be expanded to give it life in the form of the various people, systems, and business groups that work on the project. Once the motion to pursue the idea has been given the go-ahead, the investigation stage begins.

This stage attempts to define the scope and the objectives of a project. It takes the needs of the business, the users, and the technical group and attempts to find a balance between the three that will accomplish the goals of the project. In the process of this investigation, you have to find out what existing systems you can use, and how your users work with them currently. These systems include the hardware platforms, the software operating systems, and the applications. With this information in hand, you can start on a requirements specification document that states in nontechnical terms what the users need and what the applications need.

What Does My Project Need?

The scope of a project is usually determined by a group of people brainstorming on the central idea. The project manager, business managers, and IT managers must get together and hash out what they plan to do with the project. The scope defines what areas of the business and technical sides will need to be involved. It outlines who will need to be involved in the project and how. The scope goes hand in hand with the objectives of the project. The objectives describe what the end result of the project will be. This could be a new product, a new communications system, a new business process, a new method to access resources, and so forth. These objects are goals initially set for the project that will be refined over the life of the project to become its strategic goals.

Actual integration between Windows and UNIX platforms usually arises out of the scope and objectives of the project. As indicated in Table 9.1 in Chapter 9, there are a number of different levels and forms of integration. The integration might be the main focus of the project or an adjunct that needs to be completed so that the project itself may be completed.

There are two sources for impetus for an integration project: *business needs* and *technical needs*. A business need might be that you need a mixed-platform network to develop a new product. Another might be that your company is looking to reduce costs (there's that total cost of ownership issue again) by moving to a cheaper platform.

A technical need might be that the existing equipment is becoming obsolete. This could be because the vendor is removing your equipment from its product line, the cost of maintaining the equipment far outweighs the benefits of keeping it, or new products needed for your business project are being developed on an alternative platform. Another technical need might be because some platforms perform significantly better than others but still require the assistance of those others. Finally, there is the very obvious need that the required software is available only on a different platform.

Reviewing the Existing System

Examining the existing system of technical components allows you to pinpoint which components will be involved in the project either in its existing form or in an upgraded or modified form. To do this, you need to know where things are now and how they work together.

With a proper survey or audit of your network, you should be able to tell exactly the hardware and software components of any computer on your network. You might even be able to tell what asset value the computer has, when it was purchased, who it was purchased from, and what form of service contract it is under.

A full network audit can be performed with the help of commercial tools, or you can simply send your technicians to each and every computer and record its configuration. The commercial-tool mechanism is certainly faster, but many packages cannot track every single platform and configuration type. Furthermore, it comes at a price. With human labor, it takes significantly more time, but skilled technicians should be able to figure out what type a computer is and what is running on it; if they can't, you should seriously ask yourself why it is even on your network. Depending upon your network size, one method may be more affordable than the other. For networks larger than 500 nodes, it is a really good idea to get a software-based system, in spite of the cost. In the long run, it will save you more.

A network audit means collecting information on your network layout and network nodes (routers, switches, hubs, remote access devices, etc.), on each computer connected to the network, and on each user account to be used on the network.

Existing Hardware and Operating Systems

The first step is to have recorded information about all your computer hardware and operating system assets. When performing an audit of your computers for the purposes of network integration, you need to know a whole bunch of stuff: the type of box; its peripheral devices; the type of the drive system and installed drives; the peripheral cards installed; the version of operating system; the configuration of file system(s); the installed application software; the network protocol configuration; the account database (if it supports multiple users); the primary user of the system (if it supports multiple users); the primary user of the system (if it is a desktop system); the physical location, network location, and network hardware connection type; and what network connections and other interactions with devices it has.

To help you out, the CD includes a sample asset information document, in \Book \Chapter10\Asset Record Sheet.doc. You should take this, customize it to your own needs, and use it. There is also an Excel spreadsheet file that you can use to create a database of all the entries of the assets.

The very last item, network connections and device interactions, you should pay particular attention to. Forgetting this element is the source of many problems that pop up on other parts of the network when you modify a particular computer. You should record a reference to all other computers that this computer establishes a client connection to, and which other computers connect to this one, and for what reasons. No LAN computer is an island, or else it wouldn't be on the network now, would it? These relationships between two computers can be of any kind: drive sharing, database connection, shared user accounts, e-mail services, and so forth. If one computer communicates actively with another computer, you should write it down.

Surveying Users and their Habits

Surveying users helps define what processes they use and how this use maps to the technical system. This helps create a model of general user behavior according to their assigned tasks.

As part of the survey, you need to determine each user's job function, the machines they use on a regular basis, the operating system they are most comfortable with, the kinds of applications they use on a regular basis, and the things they have the most problems with. This allows each user to give their perspective on what their role in the company and the computing infrastructure is. Surveying users will help outline the most common elements of use and of difficulty.

The needs of users to accomplish their tasks as cogs in the great wheel of the business machine are the heart of the matter when it comes to technical infrastructure. Contrary to popular belief among sysadmins, users aren't supposed to conform to the needs of the machine; the machines have to conform to how users work. Actually, a balance between the two is what is really needed (despite many interesting stories the alternative can provide; see www.bofh.net).

User habits are exceptions to the general behavior of your users. The work that users are assigned to do isn't always the same as what they actually do. They may have a complete sheet describing each and every technical process and still go about it in their own fashion. User habits are harder to detect because people usually don't like to admit that they have been doing something other than what they were assigned. Still, you can slide in a few questions or phrase them in such a way as to detect how they actually go about their business. Habits aren't necessarily bad, but the fact that the user may use an alternative method to what you recommend means that if you change the existing environment in some way, their processes might break. All of a sudden you get a user coming back to you with problems you never thought you had or could get into. On the other hand, good user habits might even help you. For example, a user might be meticulous about documenting in detail any problem they notice with the system. Such notes can help you debug the problem faster.

Approaches to Integration

The approach that you take to changing your environment to integrate alternative platforms is just as important as the implementation of the system. First, you have to take into account how the change will affect people. Some changes do not directly impact the end users at all, while others require that you retrain all your users in a new mixed environment.

When you integrate different platforms, there are three ways of looking at the setup of the environment:

1. You can add in new services independently of the old ones, and simply allow some of your users to access and utilize them separately from the existing ones.

2. You can overlap the existing and new services, but provide mapping between the old and new services such that the users can access both services through different means.

3. You can add in new services slowly and start to take out the existing system piece by piece, such that the users can continue to access the service without noticing the difference in transition.

Integration of new services into your computing environment may mean quite a bit of change for your users. In some cases, when the new software works very much like existing systems, the change may mean a slight change in which resource is to be used (e.g., an NFS drive exported to Windows appears just like another network drive), or it could mean complete changes to the applications people use or the user environment they are familiar with (e.g., switching from Windows to X Windows user interfaces).

Any sort of change will result in a degree of temporary lost productivity until people get used to it. The idea is to minimize this loss so that business can return to normal as soon as possible and, hopefully, even accelerate due to the changes. You can classify the changes in several categories:

- *Administrative change.* There is a change to how some administrative operations are conducted, but not those of a technical nature.

- *Back-end technical change.* There is a change to the technical systems, but it is not apparent to the users at all.

- *Front-end technical procedural change.* There is a slight change to the system that affects how people will use the system but does not require learning a new method or technique.

- *Front-end technical overhaul.* There is a change to the system that requires people to learn or train for a very different environment.

This book doesn't focus very much on administrative changes that affect the workflow of your business. They are nontechnical in nature and beyond the scope of this book. The other three we do have to worry about.

Back-end technical changes occur when you add new system or network management features, or do minor hardware upgrades that are non-application-related. User application and application service changes do not normally fall into this category. Users may notice a slight difference (hopefully an improvement) in the system, but in most other respects, the way they work or the things they do are not affected. With a back-end change, you do have to inform your system administrators, however. This may mean distributing new policies or system administration procedures, or it may even involve new training for them. Most IT managers prefer this sort of change if it can solve their problems, since, relatively speaking, the number of people in the IT staff is significantly lower than the number of users affected by the change. This, in turn, translates into relative savings in lost productivity due to the change.

Front-end technical procedural changes are basically small alternations of how people use the system. For example, if you add a new faster network printer that works exactly like an older one and tell everyone that they can use it, you have a procedural change—people should know how to use the printer since it does not involve learning something new, and since the older printer is still around, people can continue using it until you slowly transition everyone. A procedural change may or may not allow the user to go back to the older system. For example, if the older printer was to be taken offline permanently, users must remember to switch to the new one and how they are supposed to do that.

Such procedural changes may involve a little bit of work and, certainly, some monitoring of the users that are still using or trying to use the old system. Usually they do not involve general user retraining. These changes certainly affect the system administrators, whose responsibility it is to maintain the systems where the changes occur. Their job is not only to facilitate the change but also to answer questions, help users, and remind users of the change.

The most expensive of the lot is the front-end technical overhaul, where the system that people are used to is being replaced with a new one. Although some of the users may be familiar with the new system, in general, most of them will have to train, educate, and familiarize themselves with it. This means an expensive loss in productivity, and the cost of user retraining. This sort of cost can be one-time, where you endure the pain with a move over to the new system. It can also be spread out over time, where there is less pain in making the move by moving small components or portions of the system or users at a time. In small companies and workgroups, the short and painful method might be better, but for a large company, you simply have to endure it over a long time due to the huge penalty the alternative would impose.

From an IT staff point of view, this involves long planning, extensive user support, and, potentially, quite a bit of troubleshooting. User support comes particularly in answering questions for users who do not know or don't recall something about the new systems. A frequently asked questions list posted prominently and distributed to every user can go some distance toward reducing the number of tech support calls your department has to handle. Since a major overhaul can involve many complex systems, it isn't possible to anticipate every single problem, so a bit of footwork may be involved. This could take the form of virtual steps within your server systems to analyze application or system conflicts, or you could be catching up on all that jogging you have been missing by going from user desk to user desk.

This brings up an important point. Changes can be central to a handful of systems, such as servers, or they can spread across every desktop that you have. The former is easier to handle, but any change may affect a large number of users at a time, so you have to time it and execute it carefully. Changes to individual desktops may affect only one or two users but are quite time consuming, mostly in fairly unimportant tasks such as walking around, getting a hold of the user, opening up computers, or tracing network lines.

One important tool that can help reduce the time-consuming factors of moving from station to station is remote management products. Although some such products offer only monitoring services, others, such as software delivery and distribution products, can greatly improve the time it takes to distribute configuration changes. There's no avoiding hardware changes with this software, unfortunately. In any case, several software distribution products are listed in the CD-ROM and Web site for this book.

Independent New Systems

With this approach, you start by adding new systems in parallel to your existing ones and moving a subgroup of your users at a time over to the new system. This essentially creates two separate groups using the two separate systems in parallel. As time progresses, you can increase the capacity of the new system and start moving more users over to the new group. If you move all your users over to the new system, you don't really have an integration scenario, more a migration one.

The benefit of this method is that you can work with transitioning small groups of users at a time. This means smaller training group sessions, a lower likelihood of problems to be resolved, and fewer new systems to add at a time. The downside, of course, is that you have to manage both environments in parallel. The integration aspect comes with the different client stations and user training for dual environments that you have to manage.

Overlapped Systems (Existing and New)

Overlapping systems means that you take it upon yourself and your department to maintain both types of services either because of a continuing need for the old system as well as the new one, or because the cost of moving over to a full-fledged replacement is far greater than your budget will allow in the short term. This is a difficult process that makes the most sense when you are attempting a front-end overhaul as described earlier.

Overlapping Windows and UNIX systems in a network is certainly possible for the long term. The services accorded to UNIX applications are now also available for Windows machines, and although the details may vary, the utility can stay the same. For example, let's say you move from dedicated X terminals per person to giving some of them a PC. This raises the issues of having to support both X terminals and PCs, and, in addition, the PCs will most likely also need X Windows application support. Although both systems use X Windows to access the server-based applications, the issues involved in managing the X terminals (fairly minimal but expensive to fix or replace) are different from those for PC X stations (some work but cheap to fix).

Adding parallel PC systems alongside UNIX systems adds not just one more platform issue to manage (the PC) but two—the PC and how the PC and UNIX systems behave together on the same network. You can isolate the two networks into separate segments, but at the server endpoint they may contact each other in any case.

Phased Replacement of Older Systems

Taking out existing systems that have been around for a long time requires a little bit of finesse. The first step would be to determine how much the system is still being used. Glance through the log files (you do have log files, don't you?) for the kind of system activity it has had over past weeks or months. It is usually safe to say that anything that has not been used in three months for any significant purpose can be gracefully removed.

Graceful removal means taking careful precautions to check with every user of the system and to warn everybody before beginning to take it down. Check all users allowed access to the system. Then check all other systems that interact with it in any way. A server system, for example, may sit idle for a while but periodically interact with another machine.

The best idea is to initiate a *closedown period* during which all users of the system are notified of the coming shutdown of the system. Give them a final deadline on responding to the sysadmins, and post notices in newsletters or on tech-support bulletin boards. If you can, put an active network packet sniffer at the edge of the machine to watch all network activity to and from the machine. Almost all of it should be your own activity of checking on the machine.

Even more complicated is when you intend to replace the old system with a new model. Similarly to the closedown period just described, you can initiate a *transition period*, during which all users are informed of the coming switchover to the new system. It is likely that you will need to put out a list of frequently asked questions and answer them accordingly to help users understand how the new system will function.

Feasibility Study

A study on the feasibility of the project can give a strong rationale for why the project should or should not be carried out. The duty of the reporters is to examine the project objectives and the status of existing systems and users, and define how this project will affect them. Such a study should be conducted by someone not partial to either proponents or opponents of the project and knowledgeable enough about the technical and business systems that may be involved in the project to make an informed determination. The study can also be broken up into technical and business feasibility aspects and given to two different individuals to produce. An IT manager who is aware of the status of the technical systems involved might be appropriate for the technical aspect. A business manager who is aware of how the company uses those technical services might take the business side.

Design and Proposal Stage

The goal of the design and proposal stage is to produce a document that can be sent to the management group and the sponsor for the project within the company to decide whether to invest in the idea wholeheartedly. The proposal contains four aspects: a *definition* of the project, its scope, objectives, and any background information; a *design* of what processes are involved in carrying out the project; a *plan of action* on how the implementation, training, and maintenance phases of the project are to be carried out; and an estimated *budget* laying out all the expenses for the project.

Project Proposal and Definition

The proposal is the overall document that is sent to those involved in the project and to the decision makers and sponsors of the project. In its simplest form, it puts down on paper the need for the project, its scope, and the strategic goals that were outlined in the brainstorming sessions during the investigation stage, followed by the design, the plan of action, and the budget.

Since not everyone may understand the implications of the project, the rationale for it, or some of its aspects, a background document defining the history of the systems involved in the project and how they currently interface is of immense help. A feasibility study can also help build the case for the project. The definition section of the proposal must indicate those individuals and systems that must be dedicated to the project, how much of this resource will be dedicated, and for how long. For example, programmers and sysadmins count as resources whose involvement you can specify in personnel-hours; a server system can be dedicated to the task or shared between its current role and its new role in the project.

Project Design

Documenting your plan of action will present a clear and concise method of approach, the steps needed to accomplish the project. It takes the resources described in the project definition, defines tasks that need to be accomplished, and shows the relationships between resources, tasks, and the end products.

Taking an object modeler's point of view, you can define these resources and end products as individual objects—the tasks show the relationships between the two in simplified form, or they can be broken down into multiple objects and subtasks that define the path from beginning to end. There are several different methods of modeling objects and their relationships, but a common unified expression of these methods has been adopted by the industry. This is called the *Unified Modeling Language* (UML).

Although it is often thought of as a tool for designing and implementing software, UML can be used to define any sort of project as long as you can identify individual resources and relationships. It helps you to turn the concept of hard resources and tasks into abstract data constructs and processes that can be manipulated much more easily. With the help of the language, you can also broadly define processes and leave the details of the individual steps for others to refine, thus allowing you to divide and conquer the work of defining the design. Object modeling is a complex subject in itself and isn't discussed in this book. We do recommend that you take a look at it in books such as *Instant UML* (P. A. Muller, Wrox Press, 1997), *Object Solutions: Managing the Object-Oriented Project* (G. Booch, Addison-Wesley, 1995), and *The Object Advantage: Business Process Reengineering with Object Technology* (I. Jacobson, M. Ericsson, A Jacobson, Addison-Wesley, 1995).

With object-modeling and project-planning software tools, you can draw up a complete design and schedule for the project such that it can be visualized and understood by others—and nothing is more helpful than if the other person can imagine what you can imagine.

Action Plan

The action plan takes the objectives and definition of the project and the design of how the project is to be carried out and creates a schedule and task allotment plan. It takes into account real-world issues of timing and scheduling to arrive at a formal description of which resource goes where, what it is supposed to do, and when it is supposed to be completed.

Scheduling and Deliverables

The *schedule* is a cornerstone of the proposal document. It defines the time, personnel, and other resources that are dedicated to aspects of the project as defined. A schedule clearly outlines the project as broken down into *phases* and *tasks*, each with a start date and an end date; the individuals, groups, or departments involved; what each task is to accomplish or deliver; and what relationships each task has with other projects. A phase is a grouping of individual tasks.

Throughout the phases in the schedule there will likely be milestones for the project. A *milestone* is typically a recognizable event indicating that one major aspect of the project has been achieved. Milestones can occur at the end of certain tasks or at the end of a phase, but with each one there is an associated *deliverable*. A deliverable is a measurable output of a task, such as a document, a piece of code, an integrated platform, a user list, and so forth, that is either used by another task or phase of the project or is the final output of the project itself. Almost anything that you can point a finger at and identify as the result of a task can be considered a deliverable, as long as it is something you expected. Unexpected results either are side effects of a task, phase, or project or are incorrect output from a task that is designed or executed poorly. They are bad news, but even bad news has a purpose: It can point to what went wrong.

Schedules and milestones need to be set realistically. If you are very unsure whether a task can be completed in the allotted time, then you should either not set the time limit, reschedule it, or revise the definition of the task and its associated deliverables.

The stages of a project as described earlier in this chapter directly map onto the project's phases and tasks. In fact, you might even say that the schedule is a calendar for the project stages.

A schedule can be denoted in a number of different formats, but the most popular schedule notation is the *Gantt chart*. Figure 10.1 shows a simple sample Gantt chart for an NFS disk-sharing project.

The project is broken up into different tasks and phases. Some tasks depend on other tasks and thus start only when the former is complete; they are indicated by arrows linking the tasks. Phases of the project are identified in bold and cover the entire time period allotted to the tasks in the phase. When phases or tasks run in parallel, they are likewise indicated by parallel bars that start at the same time reference and possibly even end together at another time reference. The dates across the top give an idea of the time references and scheduling of the tasks and phases.

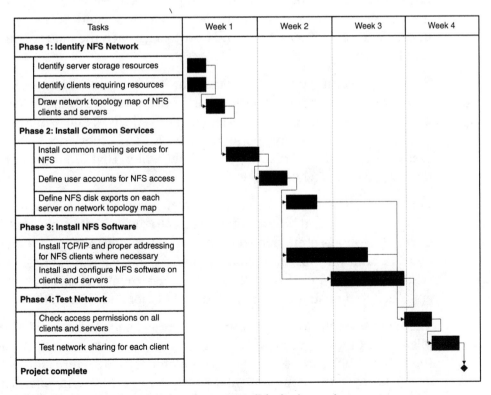

Figure 10.1 Sample Gantt chart for an NFS disk-sharing project.

Consultants and Outside Help

When do you need outside help? When you don't know what to do or don't have the time to do it, of course. But seriously, planning a project is pointless unless you can dedicate the time and energy of your crew to work on it. This is when you bring in help from outside the firm to do the project.

You can also bring in a consultant when you need their experience and expertise in a particular area. This is particularly relevant when considering Windows-UNIX integration. Often you have IT departments that have experienced staff for one side (let's say Windows) but only a handful of people for the other (UNIX). Having your Windows staff learn about UNIX just so that they can get around to figuring out how to integrate the two platforms will probably take too long. Rather, you should bring in a team that has worked with both platforms together.

If you are lucky enough to find one that can do both, so much the better. If, on the other hand, you have two people or two groups with experience in only one area, you might be in a fix. It only helps if the two sides know something about each other's topic area, even if they do not have significant experience in the matter. What they need is the ability to understand each other's work and how to approach the matter in a cohesive fashion.

When a consulting group indicates that it has x years of experience in Windows and y years of experience in UNIX, you have to look closer and ask if it has had z years of experience in mixed UNIX and Windows environments and how many people it has with such experience. With UNIX platforms, you should also try to find out which UNIX vendor's product they are knowledgeable about.

This book is intended to help UNIX system administrators learn about the Windows system and how to integrate it into their existing systems. It can also help you learn enough to figure out when consultants are trying to pull a fast one on you. Although we cannot possibly cover every single current item in this area, it is still enough to ask them questions about their approach to the integration plan and find out just how much they know.

There are several ways of breaking up a project such that it can be accomplished by different groups. You can either: (1) do it yourself, (2) design the system but hire someone to implement it, (3) hire someone to design the system but implement it yourself, or (4) hire someone to design and implement the whole thing. You can add another level for managing the project as well, but in any case, it is a differentiation between who does the job, your IT staff or outside help.

The cheapest (all else being equal) would be to design and implement the whole thing yourself. If your staff does not have any time, then you should consider farming out the whole project to a consulting firm. If the details about the project or your current environment are significantly complex and customized, you might be better off designing the project yourself but hiring outside staff to implement it. On the other hand, if you do not have enough experience but do have the time to do it, you might hire a consultant to figure out how the new system will fit together, and then assign your staff to do the actual implementation.

As you can see, the design and implementation can be done by separate groups, either within your company, by one consultant firm, or between several consultants. Managing a project is normally handled by your staff or by a project management consultant. The consultant can be used to locate appropriately experienced outside help to design or implement the project.

Project Budget

Here comes the scary part of the proposal document: how much the whole darn thing costs. Budgeting a project is an imprecise science. No matter what you can think of now, you won't know the exact costs until you actually do it. Some tasks may be easier and cheaper to implement than you previously thought, and others may simply lay waste to your soul. However, the point of budgeting is to give a description of where the costs of the project lie and their relationship to the goals of the project. A small portion of the project that has significant cost must show how this cost maps to an appropriate benefit to the company or how it contributes toward the goal of the project. The budget is not about the raw numbers themselves so much as the value of the individual aspects of the project. It allows the project sponsor and corporate decision makers to outline their expenditure strategy for the company and make comments on how the project may be restructured if certain elements or objectives are either put in or taken out; unfortunately, it is more often the latter than the former.

Based on the resources dedicated to the project outlined in the earlier portions of the document, you can allot an estimate either by phase, task, or resource. Phase and task allotments define the estimate on costs when the deliverable for the phase or task is achieved. It goes down in factors by the level of detail. Allotting an estimate for an entire phase gives a great deal of flexibility in how the actual budget is allocated in that phase, but does not provide a high degree of detail on costs. As you go one level down to the tasks, you get more detail, but lose some flexibility on how to reassign the budget between tasks. Going down to the individual dedicated resources, you get the highest degree of precision, but lose almost all flexibility.

Flexibility in the budget is an all-too-important feature. Too much of it means that the project is not very well defined or the project management group does not have a good handle on how it will progress. This could turn hideous as the project overruns its schedule and budget, usually resulting in heads getting chopped. Too much rigidity means that the project management group thinks that it is aware of all the costs but cannot tolerate any failure or delays in the project. This, in turn, can run into delays in other aspects of the schedule and result in overruns in costs as well, taking you back to the guillotine scenario.

Projects undergo reviews every so often to see if they are on track and within budget. The project manager needs to share this information with the sponsor group and other management personnel in the business so as to maintain the validity of the project or explain shortcomings. Reviews also give the project manager an opportunity to present a revised or updated version of the project with new budget estimates. Of course, you have to rationalize why a revision is needed. The new budget estimates might be lower than the original, in which case you may see shiny, happy faces. Significantly higher budgets will bring out the frowns and glares. But more realistically, they will be higher in some parts and perhaps lower in other parts of the project. Every estimate change has to have its associated rationale.

Procurement Stage

The procurement stage involves defining what kinds of products or services will be needed from an inside or outside source, how to approach vendors that provide these services, and how to make a selection on which vendor to go with. The primary document associated with this stage is the request for proposals.

Any request for proposals is customized to the specific environment of a company. Similarly, the choice that you make to go with a particular vendor is also entirely yours. All we can provide is advice in the form of sample documents, descriptions of what many companies do in such situations, and where to go for more factual information directly pertaining to your project.

Creating a Request for Proposals Document

A request for proposals (RFP) document clearly identifies a solution that you are seeking from one or more vendors. Essentially, it is a series of parameters that describe your existing systems, the type of computing environment you want to go to, and the type of performance you expect to see. An RFP states for everyone to see what you expect the vendor to deliver: equipment, support contracts, and services.

The better you describe the problem, the more your vendor may be able to help. However, you have to give leeway to the vendors and speak in general terms unless a specific item is an absolute requirement. Not all of them may be able to provide the solution you are looking for.

The actual document format is fairly short and simple. The longer it is, the more overbearing it becomes. Although it is likely that the solution you need is complex, you should give vendors freedom to choose how they wish to implement it. Some vendors won't be too happy to read through a 20-page document only to realize that the dollar value of the project is much smaller than expected.

 To help you out, a brief skeleton of what an RFP may look like (bereft of all the style and grace you could add to it, of course) is provided on the accompanying CD-ROM to this book, in \Chapter10\RFP.doc.

With the RFP prepared, you should prepare a short message briefly stating the topic of the project, include a response deadline for the RFP, and ask the vendors to confirm that they have received the RFP document immediately. To be fair, you should send out the RFP to all the vendors at the same time.

Choosing and Buying a Vendor Solution

Once the RFP is out, you should be getting some telephone calls, e-mails and other responses. Vendors are likely to want to give presentations on their products if they have not already, or at minimum will send you brochures and details on their product line. Their hope is that you will see in their products something you don't in the others and will pick their solutions despite the cost. Brochures and product data sheets are fine, but you should strongly consider the merits of the entire proposed solution before going with one vendor.

The criteria for choosing a vendor solution always depend on your particular project needs, but in general are as follows (in no particular order):

- Fits all major project requirements and options
- Price
- Support services and contract
- Years of practical viability
- Upgrade possibilities
- Vendor size and respectability

No solution is really worth it if it doesn't do what you want it to. The real problem is deciding what to do when a solution provides most of what you are looking for but not all of it. By categorizing your needs into groups of absolute needs and optional wants, you can define limits for the solution. You should always keep the needs to as short a list as necessary. Basically, they should state what the overall solution must accomplish in general terms. For example, "We need a solution that allows NT servers access to UNIX volumes." This states what is needed, and for what platform. You can go one step further and get more precise: "We need a solution that allows NT 4.0 servers access to disk volumes on Solaris 2.x, AIX 4.x, and IRIX 5.x, using the Windows file-sharing protocol." This defines exactly the kind of platform support you are looking for and refines it further with another vector (Windows file-sharing protocol). However, the next phrase might be too much: "We need a solution that allows NT 4.0 servers to access Solaris 2.x, AIX 4.x, and IRIX 5.x disk volumes through the Windows file-sharing protocol, and that will automatically convert Microsoft Word documents into LaTeX documents and create associated font and style templates." This might be too complex a need that should probably be broken down into separate issues. Or it might not. It depends on your needs and what you know vendors can do.

An item should be identified as an option if it is something that you desire and hope to use in the future but can do without in the meantime. You can live without it, but part of your long term goal is to move toward a system that uses the option. If it isn't provided as part of the solution now, it isn't a deal-breaker, since you can start a project in the future where it is a requirement.

Vendors may be able to provide what you are looking for but at a price beyond what you expect. Giving an expected price range for a project is not always kosher, although the vendor will appreciate it. It will, however, eliminate those that are too expensive for you almost immediately, even if they are the perfect choice in all other respects. If you give an expected range for the cost of the project, then you should always give a fairly wide range between the minimum and maximum estimates; a 50 to 150 percent above the minimum estimate might provide sufficient range.

The maximum estimate should be 5 to 20 percent over your actual budget maximum. This will accomplish two things. If most of your vendors are near the maximum, within the 5 to 20 percent superlimit, you should reconsider your budget. Your actual budget maximum may be a determining factor for vendors that nearly tie on all scoring except for the price. Keep in mind that the lowest- and the highest-cost figures may not be the best solution for you.

Some of you may be wondering why we bother even suggesting to put down a minimum. This helps define the limit of quality you expect. In most cases, quality goes up with price. Putting down a minimum will state to vendors what you expect of them quality-wise. Of course, if vendors' solutions fall below the minimum, they will pad their prices to be at least 10 percent more than the minimum; they don't want to look like the cheapest solution (meaning lowest quality), after all. Giving a range makes the vendors think about the solution more.

Expect vendors to fall into the 20 percent delta of the price that you are thinking about (which may or may not be your actual budgeted amount) unless you do not have a general feel for the price of such a solution at all. Very few companies are not concerned with the price of a solution; after all, they have to rationalize their budgets.

When we talk about *support services* here, we mean those that will be provided from the vendor as part of their solution. Support services are a must with any product. Few computer products are built like the Sony

Walkman, whose use and function are trivial to learn. This is because the overall function of a computer product cannot be so easily defined or categorized. Software relies on the application, operating system, and hardware environment to function properly. Should anything go wrong with these other components, then the software may fail. It is up to the troubleshooter to determine if these outside influences are causing the problem or if it is an internal problem because of bad design, unanticipated errors or bugs, or unanticipated input. Although you would hope that they be infallible, the operating system and hardware environment also fall into such a position, at rarer times.

Support services can include telephone technical troubleshooting, parts or component replacement, expert on-site diagnosis and fixes, remote or on-site management by the vendor, customer education or training, and custom development. Some of these services, such as telephone technical troubleshooting and parts replacement, are provided de facto by all vendors since they have become the basic industry standard. However, this does not necessarily apply for the other types of services. When choosing a vendor for its support services, you may wish to check if it can provide a predetermined level-of-service guarantee. This works for some technical components, such as bandwidth and uptime on network connections. Server vendors are also starting to provide a minimum level of uptime on their hardware and approved operating systems. However, this does not normally apply to integration software, or any application software, for that matter.

Although it is not easy to determine the length of time that a specific project will be viable for use due to the rate of change of technology or the evolution of your business, planned obsolescence has become part of the hardware industry, especially when it comes to PC products. There has been a leveling off of the actual power a desktop provides, and although PC client hardware is getting cheaper, server hardware remains the same or is even getting more expensive as it gets more powerful. The biggest variable is what your business will be doing a few years from now. Some businesses remain unchanged for years, despite the onslaught of technology. The availability of long-term support services from a vendor even after the product has been declared outdated and is no longer part of its product line is what you want to look for. Of course, the costs are going to be high. Some vendors are not willing to sign long-term support contracts for more than a certain number of years since this requires them to maintain the resources to keep supporting such software. Depending on the difficulty of the integration, you may not want to try to go through it again within a certain period of time.

This is why keeping track of upgrade possibilities with a vendor comes in handy. If a vendor cannot tell you where the product can go two years from now, it most likely has no idea of how long it will support the product and whether the product itself will still be functional in two years. Upgrades keep software and hardware technology in step with that of your competitors, but they can hurt your business if they occur too regularly. This pain shows up in system downtime due to upgrades, productivity loss due to user confusion, increased troubleshooting due to mismatches in software capabilities due to multiple versions, increased custom development for supporting multiple versions, and generally increased maintenance costs.

Vendors will almost never promise upgrades that they haven't already planned. However, once they actually have one, they will most likely come to you with fanciful documents and demonstrations on the wondrous new features that you, your uncle, and his pet hamster must have. Try to figure out how to translate a new feature into dollar amounts, either in savings or in revenue. This amount will determine the value of the upgrade compared to its cost and the cost of implementing it.

The Windows Update feature may be an interesting part of the Win 2000 system, but without coordinated and tested upgrades, you may end up with a whole mish-mash of minor OS revisions that are hard to track. This is a feature you should definitely disable for ordinary users on workstations.

Finally, you have to know your vendor's reputation. It may be one of the top vendors for the product category, but if it has a history of slow responses to customer needs, or low-quality products, it will probably be more of a hindrance than a help. With the large vendors, it may be easier to find out their reputation. Trade magazines periodically do surveys and analyses of services from product vendors. Look in magazines that pertain to the product, or even search the Web for articles on vendors with the best services. In particular, magazines intended for resellers and integrators, such as *VARBusiness*, *Solutions Integrator*, *Smart Reseller*, and *Computer Reseller News*, often contain this kind of information.

For smaller companies that don't make the headlines as much, you have to go with product review articles, analyst recommendations, and word of mouth. When a magazine reviews a product, it often also tests the support services provided by the vendor. Although this is not necessarily indicative of the general customer experience, it can give you some highlights on what to expect. Analysts often also test products and services for particular market segments and publish their results, but at a high cost. Believing an analyst's report depends on their reputation for accuracy and fidelity. The same, of course, goes for word-of-mouth reports from associates in the business.

Magazines also do case studies of integration projects that can be helpful, although they do not always provide the details you might like to have (project costs, for one). Such case studies may also cover a customer's experience with a particular solutions provider or consultant organization.

Summary

An integration strategy rationalizes your project. It should outline the goals, the approach, the deployment plan, and the support plan. The strategy indicates how the project is to be carried out with the least amount of interference to the activities of the business. The biggest output of this phase of the project is documentation. Once the concept has been investigated and the goals of the project are outlined, you need to draw a formal document that describes it. It should give an outline for the different phases of the project, the people involved, and when each phase is to be completed. Once you have the project designed and documented, you then need to contact vendors and inquire about their solutions. To this end, you need a request for proposals document that explains to the vendor in as much detail as possible the technical side of the project, and what kind of support you are looking for. These documents will then help you carry out the actual implementation of the project.

## PART THREE

NT Installation and Network Configuration

## CHAPTER 11

Integrating Network Services

W hen John Gage came up with the slogan, "The Computer is the Network," for Sun Microsystems way back in the mid-1980s, he must have had a personal genie or magic crystal ball. Today it is almost impossible to run a medium-to-large corporate computing system without all the networking services.

The network appears to be the grand unifier for computers, allowing any platform to communicate with any other. Those of us who run the network systems, however, know that that level of equality is unrealistic. Despite the many common standards for network protocols and services, vendors always come up with one addition or modification that changes the perspective and often complicates the compatibility issues between the platforms. Nonetheless, the services must go on.

In this chapter we look at the different core components of network services in Windows 2000 and how they interact with UNIX systems in a mixed environment. This includes network addressing, name services, remote access, routing, and network protocols.

Network Addressing and Name Services

The children's story of the Ugly Duckling offers a very important lesson in personal identity and the network of individuals one hangs out with. Every computer faces this issue of knowing what it is, but it doesn't have to be alone in this. That's exactly what the sysadmins strong guiding hand is for.

Every node in a network needs its own name and that of the group it belongs to. From an Internet and UNIX point of view, this is called the *hostname* and the *domain name*. From a Windows point of view, this is also called the same thing but it means something very different in terms of technological innards. By standardizing on TCP/IP on both platforms, the two different approaches combine into one, although they still hold onto their alternate identities in some respect.

Each UNIX or Windows machine has an IP address and a hostname assigned to it, either manually or automatically from a server. These machines can communicate with others, but they need facilities to contact them (name services) and to send traffic to them (routing). Thus, it is very important to create an environment for name services and routing that can serve both environments at the basic level but can also support the specific needs of one or the other.

The difficulty is caused more by Windows than by UNIX systems, particularly because of Active Directory. Many of the network services in Windows integrate closely with AD and thus have to be running to support the Windows domain environment. This takes some of the options away from running these services under UNIX.

Network Information and Configuration in Windows 2000

With Windows 2000, network connections have been moved into a new special folder known as *Network and Dial-up Connections*. Each interface is shown as a separate connection object, rather than each network protocol. There are five types of connection objects: dial-up, local area connection, virtual private network, direct, and incoming connections. These refer to the function of the connection rather than the actual hardware interface. A *dial-up connection* can apply to analog modems, ISDN, or even cellular dial-up services. *Local area connections* include Ethernet, cable modems, DSL, wireless LAN, and even some WAN systems such as T1s and frame relay. A *virtual private network* (VPN) connection uses the Point-to-Point Tunneling Protocol or the Layer 2 Tunneling Protocol over any hardware networking standard. The *direct connection* works by connecting the serial ports of two computers or with infrared between the two machines. Finally, an *incoming connection* can be any of the interfaces that allow connections into the machine.

By right clicking on a connection object and showing its **Properties**, you can see each of the protocols and services that service the connection. This dialog box also allows you to configure, add, or remove protocols and services. These differ depending upon the type of connection, but mostly they include commonly known protocols such as TCP/IP, IPX/SPX, AppleTalk, and ATM. Services include file and printer sharing over Microsoft networks (i.e., NetBIOS services), gateway and client services for NetWare, and AppleTalk services.

Furthermore, on a Win 2000 server platform, there are a number of different snap-ins for MMC that manage network services: DHCP Manager, WINS, Routing and Remote Access Services Manager (RRAS), DNS Management, and Internet Authentication Service (IAS). Each of these management interfaces and their corresponding services are discussed in separate sections throughout this chapter.

Managing the Dynamic Host Configuration Protocol

The Dynamic Host Configuration Protocol (DHCP) is a handy service for automatically assigning address information to TCP/IP hosts from a central server. With Win 2000, this is, in fact, the default setting when you first install the machine. You have to specifically choose to install addresses by hand after the OS installation is complete.

The DHCP server should be installed from the **Windows Components**, **Networking Options** section. Once installed and the service is started, start up the DHCP Manager snap-in from the administrative tools. It will have Dynamic DNS updates configured by default. If you are not using the Win 2000 DNS server or some other DNS server that supports dynamic updates, you should right-click on the server, then on **Properties**. In the **Dynamic DNS** tab, uncheck the box that says **Enable dynamic update of DNS client information**.

The DHCP server files are stored under \Winnt\System32\dhcp. These include the database file that contains the permanent DHCP assignment information and the audit file that contains the currently leased DHCP information. Neither should be edited manually in any way.

The *DHCP scope* defines a grouping of client machines that will share the same DHCP properties. Clients in the same scope are assigned DHCP leases or reservations from a defined range of addresses. DHCP scopes can be within the same LAN subnet or on other subnets that can communicate with the DHCP server through a *relay agent* that is DHCP-aware such as a router.

To assign DHCP addresses, you need to define the scope that clients will belong to, their address range, and the different DHCP options for that scope. These DHCP options define where the client should look for other network services such as DNS, NIS, and Network Time Protocol.

When planning for a DHCP-assigned network, you need to take a look at your network map and outline all the clients in the various LANs that will get their addresses from DHCP. Next, you need to identify the routers that can act as DHCP relay agents. A typical DHCP server can handle several thousand clients, but those clients that are isolated (without relay agents) will need a DHCP server on their LAN or they will have to go the manual assignment way.

Clearly defining and naming each of the DHCP scopes will make it easier to identify connectivity problems. Scopes should never overlap on the same server or between multiple DHCP servers. This not only confuses the client but also makes it harder to troubleshoot. A scope can have fewer addresses in its assigned pool than the actual number of clients. However, this method should be used only when the number of clients in active use is always fewer than the total number of clients—for example, when you have shift workers with separate cubicles or offices. During the day shift, the night-shift desktops will not be turned on and will not be using the network, and thus the total number of assigned addresses needed will be the total number of active desktops in the day shift or night shift, whichever is more.

Most sysadmins use DHCP as a means to deliver permanently assigned addresses from a server rather than to dynamically assign a client a different address each time. Dynamic assignment is helpful only to desktop machines that do not run server applications. Until the development of Dynamic DNS, this was the only option since each client would be assigned a different IP address with each lease, thus causing a mismatch between hostnames and IP addresses over time. Server machines can use DHCP to assign the addresses at boot time, but these addresses must be reserved for the particular server, or, in other words, that server hostname must always be mapped to the same IP address. This gives the benefit of easier management through DHCP server assigned addresses, but bypasses the problems with dynamic assignment. If you have a DHCP server that works with a particular Dynamic DNS server (as in Win 2000), you can still dynamically assign the server addresses from a pool, but there seems little point to it. Such a DHCP-DDNS dynamically assigned address is most handy when you have large numbers of servers, with several hot spare servers waiting to take over a failing server.

Windows-Specific DHCP Services

DHCP between Windows and UNIX client machines varies in the types of server options that can be assigned to them. Other than that, both can participate in a mixed-platform environment and run with UNIX or Windows DHCP servers. Windows DHCP clients will also need assigned information on NetBIOS parameters such as the nearest NetBIOS name server (WINS server), the NetBIOS node type, or NetBIOS scope information. UNIX DHCP clients also have some specifics that do not apply to Windows clients, such as the location of the swap server (for diskless UNIX workstations), the location of NIS domain servers, the root path for the client's root directory, and the X-windows font and display properties.

The Win 2000 DHCP server supports each of these DHCP options, as well as older (now extinct) options such as the location of Imagen servers, IEN name servers, cookie servers, and resource location servers. These other options are associated with IP network protocols that are very rarely used anywhere anymore. The Win 2000 DHCP server also allows you to define other options not already listed in there so any vendor-specific DHCP options needed by a particular set of clients (within a defined scope) can be added in the future.

Active Directory has to authorize DHCP servers within this domain of Windows machines, so that it knows the list of official DHCP servers on your network. Rogue DHCP servers, set up on the network independently of those managed by the sysadmins, can cause havoc by trying to assign improper or illegal addresses to clients. For DHCP servers to operate within an Active Directory domain, they have to either be running on the same machine as an Active Directory controller or be a member of that domain. They then have to be authorized by the Active Directory server to operate in the domain. On the Win 2000 DHCP server, right-click on the server's icon, select **Browse authorized servers**, then click on **Add** when the dialog box appears, and type in the host-name or IP address of that server. That DHCP server will then be added to the list of authorized servers within Active Directory (under **\Config-uration\Services\NetServices\DHCP**).

Win 2000 DHCP servers work slightly differently from others. When they first start up, they broadcast a message to look for the Active Directory root. This then responds with vendor-specific DHCP options indicating the (proprietary) domain-relevant DHCP information. Since the Active Directory domain controllers should be the first to come to the network, they build a list of valid DHCP servers this way, and then continue to periodically check on the status of the DHCP servers. Any Win 2000 DHCP server that does not see itself on the DHCP server authorized list in the directory will automatically shut itself down.

This authorization process increases the security of the domain by force-fully shutting down rogue DHCP servers. However, it can render other non-Win 2000-based DHCP servers unable to service that domain due to interference by the Active Directory domain controllers. If your DHCP server can be set to ignore messages from particular machines (say, the Active Directory controllers), you should be fine. If not, you have the option of either running everything through a Win 2000-based DHCP server or running separate DHCP servers for the UNIX and Windows portions of your network.

Other Windows DHCP Tools

The Windows 2000 Resource Kit contains two additional tools for DHCP, called **dhcpcmd** and **dhcploc**. The former can issue any DHCP command to a particular DHCP server directly for the command line, making it very handy when developing scripts. The latter is a location service for checking out the status of DHCP assignments within the existing domain. Both have to be installed as part of the Resource Kit and run only by privileged accounts, since they allow access to important network information.

Managing Domain Name Services in Win 2000

Domain Name Services (DNS) now play a more important role in Win 2000 systems because of their link to Active Directory. The actual DNS service has been expanded to include dynamically changing the name service information, as well as new resource records describing specific service information.

A Win 2000 server can be set up as a DNS server for any heterogeneous network of UNIX, Windows, or other hosts. However, Active Directory requires special use of DNS services resource records and thus can affect the behavior of a locally installed DNS server. This type of Active Directory-enabled DNS server may still be used by any DNS client to look up information, but should be run only as a primary DNS server. It can be run as a secondary DNS server only if there is another Active Directory-enabled Win 2000 DNS server acting as the primary for the same domain. You do not have to run a DNS server on every Active Directory domain controller just as long as you have one that supports its needs for that domain. More information on Windows-specific DNS appears in a later section.

Aside from these special Windows concerns, most Windows clients are just as happy working with a UNIX-based DNS server, and vice versa. As with any DNS client system, the IP addresses of the name servers must be assigned to the machine during network installation time. In all Windows systems, this is under the **Network** properties section for each interface.

The DNS Snap-in

The DNS Management snap-in for MMC covers all areas of configuration for IP domains. It is organized first by servers, followed by a section each on forward lookup zones, reverse lookup zones, and cached lookups. The cached lookup zones appear only if you select the advanced view (right-click on top DNS icon, select **View**, then the **Advanced** option). Within each of these zone folders are the individual DNS zones and all the information they contain.

To create a new zone, right click on the forward or reverse lookup folders and select the **Create a New Zone** option. This runs you through the zone creation wizard, which creates all the necessary files for the domain, including both forward and reverse zone files.

To add specific entries or aliases for hostnames, click on the DNS server machine, then right-click on **Forward Lookup Zones**, **New**, and then **Host** for a hostname or **Alias** for an alias (also called a canonical name or CNAME). This pops up a dialog box where you enter the hostname and address or alias. An option exists to create a matching reverse lookup name or pointer record (PTR) in the reverse lookup zone. This currently fails to work on the beta versions of Win 2000, so be sure to check the **Reverse Lookup Zone** matching that forward zone, to see that the entries have popped up. If not, you should add a PTR directly.

The DNS Management snap-in handles all the issues of changes to the DNS zone information, the version control data (the zone serial number), and the time intervals for refresh, retries, and expiration that coordinate between the primary and secondary DNS servers. The traditional form of DNS zone management using text files and editors is still available, and, in fact, all the DNS snap-in does is present a wizard interface to creating these files. These DNS files are normally stored in \Winnt\ System32\DNS.

One small note about the reverse zones is that they ask you to fill in the network ID and subnet mask for the zone but allow only the first three octets to be modified. They do not take into account CIDR-style addressing that can go to fewer addresses than a Class C block. For example, a CIDR block of 192.168.20.0/28 would have a netmask of 255.255.255.224. Unfortunately, the wizard does not allow you to enter that netmask-only 255.255.255.0—as the smallest. This has a slight chance of causing confusion in reverse DNS lookups. There currently isn't a workaround for this, other than that you do not specify addresses outside your range.

Windows-Specific Considerations for DNS

Windows DNS services use an alternative scheme for domain names known as UTF8, a Unicode format, so that other non-ASCII characters can be used in DNS names. Although this is a valid extension to internationalize DNS names, it is not yet standardized by the IETF, and thus may cause problems with other DNS servers and client applications attempting to resolve names. The strict RFC format for DNS names allows the first character to be an ASCII alphabetic character, followed by any number of other alphabetic characters, numbers, or hyphens. No other characters or symbols are allowed. This has been around for a long time and will probably persist for many years to come. We can only advise you to use the standard format for now. To force strict RFC names, right-click on the DNS server, choose **Properties**, and then select the **Advanced** tab. In the drop-down list for **Name Checking**, choose the **Strict RFC** option. Additionally, keep hostnames to under 16 characters—just the host part of the name, not including the domain name—so that they can also be used as NetBIOS names.

Windows DNS servers exchange their data by combining multiple resource records into the same packet and compressing it. This allows the servers to exchange the information at a much faster rate. They can also be configured not to use this compressed format to be more compatible with other DNS servers. For UNIX DNS servers, **bind version 4.9.4**, and newer versions, also work with this compressed format. To disable this feature, go to the DNS snap-in, bring up its **Properties**, click on the **Advanced** tab, and under **Advanced server options** unselect the **Bind Secondaries** option.

To support Dynamic DNS on your UNIX DNS servers, you need to upgrade to at least **bind 8.1.2**. If you run a different DNS server product, check to see that it can support the Service Resource Record (SRV RR) described in RFC 2052 and dynamic updates of RFC 2136. Active Directory needs the former to define information about its objects, and DHCP needs the latter to work with dynamic naming.

If you cannot upgrade these DNS servers for one reason or another, you may have to create a subdomain for your Windows systems that use Active Directory and run the Windows DNS server for that subdomain. For example, if your domain *straypackets.com* is handled by a UNIX DNS server, then you can create a subdomain called *win.straypackets.com* and use this as the namespace for all your Windows machines. The Windows DNS server for this subdomain should then defer to the main root DNS servers running on the UNIX host to access other areas of the domain.

You may also want to create multiple Windows subdomains under the top-level UNIX DNS servers. To keep these Windows subdomains as part of the same Active Directory forest, you need to define two special domain server names: *msdcs* (for directory delegation control) and *_ldap._tcp* (for LDAP lookups). For example, if we want to define two AD domains, *bluewin.straypackets.com* and *greenwin,straypackets.com*, under the root domain *straypackets.com*, then we need to define two additional hostnames, *msdcs.straypackets.com* and *_ldap._tcp.straypackets.com*. These two hostnames should point to the main Windows DNS server.

Other DNS Tools

All the tasks involved in creating and managing IP domains are part of the DNS snap-in. However, you might also find some of the command line tools such as **nslookup** and **dnscmd** useful.

nslookup is used to resolve any IP hostname or domain information. It works exactly as it does in UNIX, resolving forward (IP hostname to address) as well as reverse (IP address to hostname) domain name resolution. It does not accept any command line options, but if you launch the application without any parameters, you can then type in commands for how **nslookup** is to behave (see Table 11.1). For a full list of **nslookup** commands, simply type **?** or **help** at this prompt.

dnscmd is useful for writing scripts where you need to issue DNS commands to other Windows machines directly from the command line. It is an additional command provided with the Windows 2000 Server (or Professional) Resource Kit and stored under \Support\Reskit. It can be used to create or delete DNS zones and records dynamically and thus is both powerful and dangerous. There are still a number of these commands that are helpful and somewhat safe to use (see Table 11.2). For a full list of all the commands that this tool allows, try **dnsadmin /? |more**.

Managing Windows Internet Name Services

Although NetBIOS plays a reduced role in networking under Win 2000, it isn't entirely gone; thus, you still need to run the Windows Internet Name

Table 11.1 Helpful **nslookup** Commands

NSLOOKUP COMMAND	COMMAND SYNTAX
Show all information about a host or domain.	set type=any
Set the current default domain.	set domain=\<domain\>
List all addresses in a domain.	ls -d \<domain\>
Save listing of all addresses in a domain to a file.	ls -d \<domain\> > \<filename\>
Set a search list of name servers.	set srchlist=\<nameserver1\>/\<nameserver2\>/ . . .

Table 11.2 Safe and Semisafe **dnscmd** Commands

DNS COMMAND	COMMAND SYNTAX
Get general information on server.	dnscmd <server>/Info
Get server statistics.	dnscmd <server> /Statistics
List all DNS zones.	dnscmd <server> /EnumZones
List all records in a zone.	dnscmd <server> /EnumRecords=<zone>
Restart the DNS server.	dnscmd <server> /Restart
Clear the existing DNS cache.	dnscmd <server> /ClearCache

Services (WINS) system in some cases. WINS does for NetBIOS/TCP what DNS does for TCP/IP; it maintains a list of NetBIOS names that map onto IP host addresses on a dynamic basis. Although NetBIOS can run over other protocols, WINS works only with NetBIOS/TCP.

The old NetBIOS name server method of hierarchical text files containing this address information in the LMHOSTS file was used from the time of LAN Manager until NT4. Although there is no hierarchy in NetBIOS names, you can manage them per domain and assign one or more WINS servers to handle the name resolution. WINS allows any domain client trying to access other nodes to do the translations from a server rather than attempting to do the NetBIOS node discovery each time. Windows clients are configured to use a particular WINS server as part of their TCP/IP properties, alongside other configurations such as DNS. Windows clients designate which are their primary and secondary WINS servers by ordering them in their list. The Windows client will use the secondary server only if the primary is offline.

The database and log files for WINS are stored under \Winnt\System32\WINS. The database itself is stored in a Microsoft Jet database called *Wins.mdb*. There are a number of log files and other data files stored in this directory that should never be touched manually.

WINS servers replicate their information in pushes and pulls. There is no difference between the primary and secondary WINS servers themselves, unlike DNS. They both contain the same information. However, to replicate information, the servers have to be set up to push local updates to other servers and pull remote updates to their own database. When the records are pushed, each record has an associated version number so as to state its most recent information. The receiving end of the push will check its database and update it if its version number is lower. If not, it ignores it. Push updates occur when address information changes. Pull updates occur at fixed intervals. There are some counterparts to WINS servers running on UNIX systems as well (see last section in this chapter and Chapter 12).

Routing and Remote Access Services

Routing and Remote Access (RRAS) for Win 2000 are combined into a single component since they have so much in common. Win 2000 supports multiprotocol RRAS services for TCP/IP, IPX, and AppleTalk, as well as virtual private networking built on top of these protocols.

RRAS is not installed, by default, and you have to go to the section under **Networking**, **Routing, or Remote Access** in the Win 2000 server configuration application. This will launch the RRAS console, from which you have to select your server, right-click for the menu, and choose the **Install Routing and Remote Access** option. The RRAS installation wizard requires input at several steps to determine which network interfaces RRAS will be enabled on and which protocol-level security options should be enabled.

Setting Up Routing Services

Using Win 2000 as a router can be practical since it supports a number of different network and routing protocols. Hardware-based routers from Cisco, 3Com, and so on, would better serve the needs of high-volume routers for the backbone or server clusters, but Win 2000 routers can work well within the smaller LANs. It comes in most handy for those developers who design network protocols and communications systems for a living, giving them a defined programmable environment on which to write their code, rather than designing for embedded operating systems in hardware routers.

Win 2000 supports static and dynamic as well as unicast and multicast routing services directly through a Win 2000 server. Static routes work for all the protocols between any two interfaces on the machine. Dynamic routing for IP includes support for the Routing Information Protocol (RIP) versions 1 and 2 and the open shortest path first (OSPF) protocol. For IPX, dynamic routing includes the RIP for IPX, and the service advertising protocol (SAP). All these are intradomain dynamic routing protocols as opposed to interdomain routing, which would set up routing between two different companies using a protocol such as the Border Gateway Protocol (BGP). Win 2000 does not support BGP routing. For multicast IP traffic, Win 2000 supports the Internet Group Management Protocol (IGMP) both as a router and as a proxy server.

Planning for Multiplatform Routing

Routing traffic is the main purpose of networks. Within single LANs, routing is not really an issue, since in most cases all the hosts in the LAN can see each other. However, this form of broadcast communication becomes inefficient beyond a hundred machines in a LAN. Therefore, you set up separate LANs that contain a smaller number of machines that can all talk to each other within their domain (their LAN). For machines to communicate from one LAN to another, there needs to be a route between them, a job handled by a device known as the *router*.

Each LAN needs its own router to communicate with the others. With a handful of LANs, all it involves is to directly point to the others. This method creates a *static route* that always points from one LAN to the other. Each router maintains a list or *route table* that contains these routes to the other networks. Each router is manually configured with its route table, which is stored in permanent memory.

Routers can be implemented directly in a server platform like UNIX or Windows, although they are most commonly available in hardware platforms. These hardware routers have very fast network interfaces designed to handle the functions of routing. Some even have the code for processing particular protocols like TCP/IP directly implemented in hardware circuits, making them magnitudes faster than software. Still, for regular LAN networks running between 10 and 100 Mbps, UNIX and Windows platforms make decent routers if you can't spend the extra cash to get a hardware router.

As the internetwork of LANs grows in size, static routes become too complicated to keep track, hence, the birth of dynamic routing protocols. These protocols allow routers to advertise to each other the routes they contain. This way, the system automatically sends routing information across the internetwork. Each router still has to be configured with its own routes, but they do not need an entry for each and every route to other networks. Dynamic routing protocols are the mainstay of most corporate networks.

Routing itself normally occurs purely on the protocol level, independent of the operating system. Thus IP routing is the same for Win 2000 and UNIX systems. However, routing protocols have different features and versions that sometimes vary depending upon the implementation. Thus the basic components of most IP routing is the same across platforms, but each may support a slightly different set of features.

Designing dynamic routing across the internetwork involves dividing the various LANs into routing domains. Each area contains one or more LANs served by one or more routers. Depending upon scale, these domains can then be directly connected to each other through a *backbone network* that is dedicated just for the routers and running at the highest speeds available. In some cases, there are even backbones for these backbones. For example, in a university or college; each building has its own internal network backbone connecting the various floors, each of which can have several LANs. The building itself will most likely have a router that connects to other buildings and to the campus IT center. At larger universities, the campus may even be broken up into several areas, each with its own interbuilding backbone, all connecting to a central backbone at the IT center. The terminology used in different routing technologies differs, but these concepts are similar to most.

Setting Up Static Routes

A small internetwork that has between two and five separate LANs to connect could work simply with static routes. This avoids any of the dynamic routing protocols and is simple to fix in case of a network outage. Static routed networks are point to point between one router and the next, and often simply rely on default routes out of one network to another.

Static routes are pretty much identical whichever type of host you go to, Windows or UNIX. Essentially, each machine indicates an outgoing route to a different IP address or network ID, and provides a subnet-mask indicating which addresses are to be put onto that outgoing route.

Installing a static route is fairly simple. Once you have RRAS installed, open it up and go to a particular protocol section, **IP Routing** or **IPX Routing**. There is a section on **Static Routes** that simply picks the interfaces and addresses that need to be routed. IP routing can be set up per address or network ID, with the appropriate netmask. IPX routing requires the IPX network number and the MAC address of the other end of the route, as well as the tick count and hop count IPX parameters, and finally the interface the route goes out through. For Static IPX services through SAP, there is a subsection titled **Static Services**, wherein you need to indicate the service type, name, network, and MAC address of the remote node, the socket address, the hop count, and the interface it goes out through.

Setting Up Routing Information Protocol

With a slightly larger corporate network, from 5 to 25 different LANs and networks, dynamic routing becomes necessary simply because of the overhead it would take to build static routes between each of these networks. It can also support several different paths between networks to allow for fault tolerance.

RIP is based upon transferring the local routing tables of each router to the adjacent routers on the network. This allows each of the routers to figure out how to deliver traffic from one endpoint to another. The downside of RIP is that it can result in a lot of traffic being passed around between routers but, more important, it supports only a certain number of hops (about 15).

RIP-routed networks should be planned before the networks are actually deployed or interconnected. Designing RIP networks is similar on both UNIX and Windows platforms, with small exceptions. The maximum number of hops—the number of routers between two networks—is 15, but Win 2000 decreases this to 14 since it counts any non-RIP routes, if there are static routes in some portion of the network, along the network path as two hops. Win 2000 can also support RIP routes over demand-dial connections such as an analog, DSL, or cable modem connecting to an Internet service provider. Some UNIX hosts still require you to manually install a static route over such connections.

With a topology map of your network ready, mark out each of the different LANs and the routers between them. The routers themselves should be interconnected either directly or into a backbone network. For each LAN, the router is normally assigned the first IP address—for example, 192.168.20.1—with an appropriate subnetmask for the number of hosts in the LAN. Some of these routers may be custom hardware, others UNIX or Win 2000 hosts with multiple interfaces. Their interface on the backbone side should be on a separate network, with each router its own unique address. Install RIP on the backbone interface of each router.

In the RRAS snap-in, go to your Win 2000 router, select **IP Routing**, then right-click on **General**, and select **New**, **Routing Protocol**. A dialog box of the various choices appears. RIPv1 will also show if you do not have a demand-dial interface set up on your computer (see the section on installing NAT services for an explanation).

Once the RIPv2 protocol is added, right-click on the new item named **RIP** that appears, click on **New**, **Interface**, and select the network interface that will be sending RIP information. First enable authentication and enter a password for communicating with your RIP routers. Then go to the **Security** tab, enter the address ranges that need to be routed at the very bottom, and click on **Add**. You can add multiple such address ranges or filters, so long as they don't overlap. You can indicate specific neighboring RIP routers in the **Neighbor** tab to propagate the routing information to other routing domains. The **Advanced** tab controls the timers for how often RIP messages should be sent out and for other options.

Once installed, you should allow 15 minutes for all the routes to propagate between the routers, and then check the Win 2000 router to determine whether it can see its neighbors. Go to **IP Routing**, right-click on **RIP**, then **All Tasks**, **Show neighbors**. Also, from the network within that router's area, try **ping** and **traceroute** nodes on the other networks.

Setting Up Open Shortest Path First Routing

OSPF can handle the kinds of networks that are beyond the limitations of RIP, to internetworks above 25 networks in size. Instead of individual routes, OSPF maintains a map of the network in its *link state database*, which is synchronized with all the participating routers. Should the routing topology at any subpart of the network change, the local router for that area sends updates to all the other routers for each to recalculate the map from its point of view.

OSPF routed networks are split into *areas* that cover one or more LANs connected to each other by *backbone areas*, normally reserved for the direct connections between the routers, or the network backbone. At the edge of each area going out to the backbone is the *area border router* (ABR). All these areas are contained within an *autonomous system* (AS) defining that corporate network. If your corporate internetwork should get to the size of hundreds of networks, it might be a good idea to split it up into separate ASs and install *autonomous system boundary routers* (ASBRs) in between them. Win 2000 does not implement ASBRs currently; this is primarily the domain of hardware-based routers.

To instate OSPF-based routing on your corporate network, you need to plan out where each of the areas will be and designate one or more backbone networks to interconnect them. The areas should cover as few LANs as possible. OSPF also allows the possibility that within each of its areas may be any number of LANs running RIP or static routes between themselves. The outgoing route from an area is an aggregate for all traffic coming from those LANs to the rest of the network. Win 2000 recommends that the areas it supports be less than a hundred networks each.

Each area has a different *area ID*, which is a 32-bit number. Although it looks very much like an IP address and the area can be assigned based upon it, the area ID is not related to IP addresses. This ID is used to define an area's routes to other areas. Each area can have one or more ABRs connecting it to the rest of the network, allowing for network redundancy, but both these ABRs should normally contain the same network map information. Having multiple ABRs to one area requires that they be assigned priorities and the ABR with the highest priority is the *designated router* (the primary router) for that area.

By defining a *cost* for using a specific route, the routers can create a more optimal map of all the routes through the network. This costing value is simply relative. For example, you might assign to a T1 connection at 1.544 Mbps a lower cost value than you would to an analog modem connection at 56 Kbps, to indicate a preference for using the T1.

ABRs can also have virtual neighbors, linking two networks that are separated by others. This allows traffic to be logically routed between the areas and leaves the ABRs to figure out how to do so according to the map. These *virtual interfaces* and *links* are efficient logically (easier to manage) but inefficient practically (cause a lot more traffic than is apparent), and so you should avoid them where you can.

To install OSPF on your Win 2000 router, in the RRAS snap-in select **IP Routing**, then right-click on **General**, select **New**, **Routing Protocol**, and choose **Open Shortest Path First**. You should then configure the global OSPF settings; right-click on the **OSPF**, then on **Properties**. Click on the **Areas** tab, **Add**, and enter the list of area IDs for your AS; for each area ID entered, also put in the IP address ranges within that area and the appropriate subnetmask. If this area is not connected through a virtual link and is not a backbone, it is a *stub area* and you should check the box appropriately. You can also configure *virtual interfaces* in this dialog box if you need to.

Once the global settings are in place, you need to assign OSPF routing to an interface on the Win 2000 machine. Right-click on **OSPF**, then on **New**, **Interface**, and select the network interface for sending routing information. When the **OSPF Interface Properties** dialog box appears, click on **Run OSPF over** and select the appropriate IP address of the interface; OSPF allows for multiple addresses on a single interface. Enter an OSPF **Area ID** that the Win 2000 router belongs to. If this is intended to be the designated router, assign a high **Priority** value to it, relative to the other ABRs for this area. By default, Win 2000 uses a password for the OSPF interface of *12345678*, so change the value of the **Password** field to something secure. You can designate a **Cost** for this interface as well.

The **Neighbors** tab is used if you designate this OSPF interface to use *nonbroadcast multipoint access* (NBMA) or multicasting, rather than broadcasting or unicasting (point-to-point) OSPF messages. Multicasting makes it more efficient to transmit information between the ABRs, but it requires you to add specific neighbor routers to each ABR to indicate whom to multicast to.

The **Advanced** tab contains timing properties for OSPF routing that are best left as defaults unless you have long experience with OSPF for your own network. The two primary values to set here are the intervals for **Hello**, which designates the time between contact between routers, and **Dead**, which indicates a timeout before another router is designated as not responding (dead) because of a crash or a network failure.

Installing NAT Services

Network address translation (NAT) and firewall services provide network security for the machines on your intranet as they connect to the public Internet. Both are now standard features of the RRAS system. They require that you have two separate network interfaces installed, most commonly a LAN connection to your intranet and a dial-up modem or WAN connection to the outside world.

Deploying a NAT system requires that you configure not just your Win 2000 system but also all the other machines on your network. The other computers have to point to the NAT as their gateway, and they *should* be using nonroutable Internet addresses. If you have your own assigned address block, but are extra-paranoid that people might know how your network is laid out, you can use those addresses on your other machines and have a NAT to cover them up. The NAT doesn't really care what the internal network addresses are.

We say *should* because, within the NAT domain, it really doesn't matter what addresses you use. However, NATs are not perfect and some protocols embed the IP address information in upper-level protocols as well as the IP network protocol that the NAT simply doesn't know of or can't get to. Thus, the machines should be set to the public addresses defined by the Internet Engineering Task Force (IETF) to be used only for testing purposes and not be routed on the public Internet. These addresses include the 169.254.0.0 Class B domain and the 192.168.0.0 Class C domain.

On the Win 2000 server that will act as an NAT, you need to configure the LAN interface to the internal network to one of these addresses. The default setting is for 169.254.0.1 and all other machines on the internal network should be in this domain, with a subnet mask of 255.255.0.0.

If you're using a dial-up analog or digital modem service, you have to set up the port to do *demand-dial routing*, where any traffic that is directed at the outside world causes the NAT to establish the dial-up connection, if it isn't already in place. Permanent connections, such as T1s, 56-Kbps DDS, or some DSL and cable services, do not need this enabled because the connection is always supposed to be up. In the RRAS snap-in, right-click on **Ports**, then on **Properties**. In the **RAS Device Configuration** tab, click on **Configure**, and then enable the **Demand-dial routing connections** option. Once enabled, you need to create a special interface for the demand routing device. If you have a dedicated link, your link device should already show up as an interface. To create the demand dial interface, in RRAS, right click on **Routing Interfaces** and select **New**, **Demand Dial Interface**; go through the steps of the wizard and pick the modem or adapter interface you will be using, the telephone number to dial, the various login options for the interface, and the account and password to use at the remote login site.

Now you need to set up a static route between the internal LAN and the external network port. Go into the RRAS snap-in, click on **IP Routing**, then right-click on **Static Routes**, and select **New**, **Static Route** to launch the route creation wizard. Select the demand dial interface or the interface of your dedicated link. For both the **Destination** and **Network mask** fields, simply enter 0.0.0.0.

Under **IP Routing**, right-click on **General**, select **New**, **Routing Protocol**, and then select **Connection Sharing (NAT)**. A new item called **Connection Sharing (NAT)**, will show up under **IP Routing**. Right-click on this, select the LAN interface, and choose the option **Allow clients to access shared networks**. Right-click on it again, select the demand dial interface, and choose the option **Enable translation across this interface**. There are additional tabs that allow you to control which client and destination addresses will require NAT services, if you need to add these.

Finally click on **IP Routing**, then right-click on **Connection Sharing (NAT)**, and bring up the **Properties** list. In the **Addressing** tab, choose the option to automatically assign addresses. In the **Name Resolution** tab, choose **Resolve names to addresses for TCP/IP clients**, and, if you need to, **Resolve names to addresses for Windows networking clients** for NetBIOS/IP or WINS clients.

Installing Packet Filtering

If you have routing enabled across interfaces, you can set up firewall-type services, such as packet filtering based upon protocol type, and source and destination addresses. This can be assigned as input or output filters per interface, so that each interface has a different set of filtering rules. An input filter works on incoming traffic through the interface, and an output filter works on the outgoing traffic.

To set up an input or output filter, go to the **IP Routing** section of your Win 2000 router, then select **General**; right-click on a specific interface and select its **Properties**. In the first tab called **General**, there are two buttons, for **Input Filter** and **Output Filter**. Choose the appropriate one, and you'll be presented with a dialog box. Click on **Add** and another box allows you to select the **Source Network** or **Destination Network** and enter specific **IP addresses** and **Subnet masks**. Below that is a pull-down list of the protocol it is to filter. If you do not see a protocol on the list, you can enter the protocol ID, but since TCP, UDP, and ICMP are the only protocols supported by most, you really won't need the **Other** option. For TCP and UDP you can then indicate the specific source and destination ports the packets are directed for. For ICMP, you can indicate a specific ICMP type and code.

Each filter is specific and separate per network or address to be filtered. Unfortunately, you cannot set up filters for whole ranges of addresses. Instead, you are allowed to choose whether you want to send or receive all packets except those listed in the filters or whether you deny everything except those listed in the filters.

Setting Up Remote Access Services

Setting up remote access services (RAS) for UNIX and Windows requires planning for user authentication, remote application use, and network encryption services. User authentication on the RAS server side can be directly done by a Windows or UNIX server, if the connectivity devices are directly attached to them. They can also be authenticated using the Remote Access Dial-In User Service (RADIUS) protocol, if you attach the devices to terminal servers, instead. In Win 2000, a RADIUS server is built into the Internet Authentication Service (IAS).

RADIUS provides a combination of centralized remote access authentication and an accounting of these connections. A RADIUS server typically sits on a UNIX or Windows machine that contains all the remote access accounts and passwords. The terminal servers then point to this server every time they need to authenticate a remote user. They take the remote user account and password, and pass it to the RADIUS server to check out. Once authenticated, the terminal server then sends a record of when the user logs in and out to the RADIUS server to keep track of remote access activity.

Microsoft's IAS software is provided as part of the Win 2000 servers. It supports the PAP, SPAP, CHAP, MS-CHAP, and MS-CHAPv2 authentication protocols (see Chapter 4), as well as AppleTalk Remote Access Protocol (ARAP) for Macintosh users and a new system known as the Extensible Authentication Protocol (EAP). This last protocol provides the framework for building other authentication protocols and systems to incorporate new technologies such as smartcards, certificates, and one-time passwords.

IAS, alongside RRAS, also has a snap-in for management through MMC, and service start-up and shutdown integrate with the Event log system. IAS keeps its own logs separate from those of RRAS and the Event log, since the login/logout activity of a RADIUS server can result in fairly extensive log files on a heavily populated server.

You can set up Win 2000 remote access machines as a RADIUS client and direct authentication and accounting to a RADIUS server elsewhere on the network, or you can install the IAS directly on the Win 2000 machine and have it run as a RADIUS server.

To configure a Win 2000 remote access machine as a RADIUS client, open the RRAS snap-in, right-click on the Win 2000 server on which you want to install RADIUS services, and select **Properties**. In the **Security** tab in the pull-down list for **Authentication Provider**, click on **RADIUS**, then click on the **Configure** button. In the dialog box that appears, click on **Add**, then enter the hostname or IP address of the RADIUS server, followed by a shared secret or password that the client and server will use.

To install the IAS RADIUS server, you first have to install the software component from your Win 2000 server CD. It installs IAS as a service that is started up at boot time for the server. It supports RADIUS authentication on ports 1812 and 1645 (both versions of RADIUS), and RADIUS accounting on 1813 and 1646.

By default, IAS status information goes into \Winnt\System32\LogFiles\lastlog.log. There are three groups of events that can be logged: the log start-up/shutdown, the authentication requests, and the periodic summaries. The information can be stored into a native format defined by IAS or it can go through an ODBC data format directly into a database table. As a warning, when first installed it allows for an unlimited file size of the log, so you should switch it over to the daily, weekly, monthly, or strict file size limited option. This will archive the old file and open a new log when the appropriate delimiter is reached.

IAS authentication in Win 2000 works slightly differently than NT. It supports the use of the domain to which the IAS server belongs rather than just the local user account database. Furthermore, it also uses the same access policies defined for RRAS, which it did not support in NT. Thus, anyone in the Active Directory domain with remote access privileges can log into the IAS/RAS server.

Once IAS is installed on the machine, you need to define a list of names of all the RAS servers that will access this RADIUS server for authentication or accounting. Each RAS server also needs to be configured as a RADIUS, as indicated earlier.

You can combine UNIX-based RADIUS clients (UNIX RAS servers) with Win 2000 IAS, just as well as Windows RADIUS clients for UNIX RADIUS servers; however, you do need to decide on one method or the other rather than a mix of UNIX and Windows RADIUS servers. The log files used by each server will be fairly different and thus difficult to compare when accounting for remote access traffic. Unless you have a decent commercial RADIUS server, choose the Win 2000 one that integrates with MMC, and thus take advantage of its management infrastructure as well as easier charting and graphing through the ODBC database tables.

Virtual Private Networks

Virtual Private Networks (VPNs) under Windows differs in operation from UNIX-based systems because of the protocols that Microsoft prefers to use. Even with the inclusion of the IPSec protocol in Windows 2000, there are still issues of incompatibility with Windows.

The main problem here is the Point-to-Point Tunneling Protocol (PPTP) and Layer-2 Tunneling Protocol (L2TP) discussed earlier in Chapter 4. Although some network router equipment support PPTP and L2TP, this is not yet supported on UNIX servers. With IPSec, Microsoft's implementation uses L2TP to encapsulate LAN protocols to be delivered to the other end. This is to support backward compatibility with other non-IP based LAN protocols such as IPX, and NetBEUI that can be tunneled to remote sites over the VPN. What you end up with is that you need a Microsoft compatible IPSec VPN device on each end to send the information securely.

The fact is that sites that do not plan to run VPNs that have any protocols other than IP (most UNIX sites), do not need this feature. Furthermore L2TP sends all LAN packets from one side to the other, and is a funky method of bridging network traffic by encapsulating it in routable IP packets. Additionally, there is the overhead of LAN headers and trailers such as Ethernet frames that need to be encapsulating it, chewing up more space. This means that there may be a lot of irrelevant LAN traffic that is transmitted to the other end of the VPN, causing greater and inefficient bandwidth usage.

At this point, the best advice would be not to use Windows 2000's internal IPSec mechanism but an external hardware box that performs the IPSec maneuvers. Several network hardware vendors offer IPSec tunneling boxes including CheckPoint Systems, and Cisco.

Windows Networking for UNIX Systems

Windows NT and 9x still run mostly over NetBIOS and thus cannot directly communicate with UNIX systems without the support of third-party tools. Even Win 2000, which relies less on NetBIOS, is still dependent upon this protocol and the associated services to be backward compatible with NT4 systems. Thus it is useful to take a look at some of the software packages available for UNIX systems that turn it into a NetBIOS . . . err . . . pumpkin carriage.

We will run through three such integration products: Samba, Syntax TotalNet Advanced Server, and Sun NetLink PC. AT&T's Advanced Server for UNIX is also just as popular, but the Sun NetLink product is based upon it and is very similar in operation.

There is usually little network protocol configuration needed for NetBIOS, since it is almost entirely autoconfiguring. Most of the actual configuration work is specific to user management, domain management, and file and printer sharing, and is thus covered in more detail in the following chapters. This section provides background information on these products.

Samba

The Samba package is an SMB network file sharing system for UNIX developed by the open source community and distributed under the GNU Public license. It is a very effective free software package that allows UNIX servers to export their file systems and printers to Windows clients using the native Windows Common Internet File System (CIFS) protocol.

The package includes not only the file sharing system but also the NetBIOS protocol that it needs. Samba runs as a user-mode process with SMB and NetBIOS running on top of TCP sockets created during the run of the application. Technically, this makes the NetBIOS implementation slower since it is not implemented as a kernel-mode driver.

 The package is downloadable from www.samba.org and the various international mirrors listed at this site. Originally developed in 1992 by an Australian programmer by the name of Andrew Tridgell, it is now still only in version 2 so many years later. Now that's what we call a package that's stable and to the point. It has been implemented on most popular UNIX systems, including AIX, HP-UX, IRIX, Digital UNIX, Solaris, and UNIXWare. Support for several different Linux systems is also available. Finally, the software has been ported to non-UNIX-like operating systems including OpenVMS, MVS, NetWare, OS/2, Stratus-VOS, and AmigaOS.

Samba does all that is needed on the UNIX server end to enable Windows file sharing and network printing. This includes the actual file and print sharing, Windows authentication, NetBIOS name resolution, and NetBIOS service announcement and network browsing. Samba can act as a PDC for an NT domain, but at the time of this writing only some of the basic domain controller functionality is implemented and should be considered experimental. In particular, it does not yet support the NT ACL system for files and directories. You should read the FAQ on setting up Samba as a domain controller ("Samba NT Domain FAQ") at their Web site, under the *Documentation* area.

Samba consists of several server and client application components. The main Samba server, known as *smbd*, does the work of file and print sharing, as well as authentication. It has a number of associated applications that control the server including *smbrun* (to start/stop/restart the server), *smbstatus* (to check its status), and *smbpasswd* (for creating Windows-style accounts and passwords). The Samba NetBIOS name and network browsing services are implemented in the *nmbd* server. This essentially does the same thing as the WINS server on NT, advertising NetBIOS computer names and service names. Other applications include nmblookup (similar to nslookup to find the NetBIOS name to IP address translation for a Windows machine), smbclient (allows you to transfer files between the platforms from the UNIX command line), and smbtar (allows you to archive SMB shared files and directories on the UNIX system).

The configuration for Samba is all done through the */etc/smb.conf* file. This includes all global and specific definitions describing the behavior of all shared objects. Details on how to configure Samba are available in Chapter 13. The other important data file is the *lmhosts* file. This is exactly the same format as that on NT systems and contains a static list of NetBIOS name mappings to IP addresses.

While Samba is a CIFS server, it does not allow UNIX systems to access Windows drives. The Samba project group, however, does have a separate SMB client for the Linux operating system, known as *smbfs*, that allows such systems to mount CIFS drives.

Further details on using Samba are available in Chapter 13.

Sun NetLink PC

Sun Microsystems' NetLink PC (once called Project Cascade) is a commercial implementation of the NT domain controller system and the CIFS sharing system that runs on Solaris machines. NetLink PC allows Solaris machines to act as a primary or backup domain controller to

Windows machines. It provides NT NetLogon authentication, CIFS, ACL support, and WINS, and the software can be managed from other NT servers through Server Manager, User Manager, and Event Viewer.

The software is implemented in several components. First of all, the Net-BIOS protocol is implemented as a kernel-mode STREAMS network protocol driver running above the TCP/IP protocol stack. With NetLink PC, it is thus not possible to run other NetBIOS packages such as Syntax TAS, which also provides AppleTalk services, at the same time, since this will cause a conflict at the NetBIOS level.

The SMB service runs as a user-mode system above the kernel-mode NetBIOS driver. The CIFS file system, which also uses SMB, runs as a layer above the standard UNIX virtual file system libraries, providing the mapping between the two file system types.

When you run the standard Sun **pkgadd** command, the software installs into the /opt/lanman directory. When the system boots, the NetBIOS driver and protocol services are started by the system init process through the /etc/init.d/netbios and /opt/lanman/bin/net commands. The latter command is nearly identical to the NET text commands on NT and can be used to perform other duties such as searching for computers, creating users and groups, and mounting drives and printers.

The WINS system in Netlink PC can work as a primary or secondary server to NT-based WINS servers. It supports full forward and reverse NetBIOS name mapping and updates between the servers. It runs in user mode as part of Netlink PC and communicates with the kernel-mode NetBIOS driver to access the network.

Syntax TotalNet Advanced Server

Syntax, Inc., offers a package known as TotalNet Advanced Server (TAS) that combines network protocol services for Windows, NetWare, and Macintoshes onto the Solaris, AIX, HP-UX, and IRIX operating systems. It stands out from these other packages in that it also supports the two other popular network operating systems. It provides protocol stack implementations for the NetBIOS over TCP, IPX/SPX, and AppleTalk, for the three PC platforms, respectively. Built on top of these protocols are application services for file and printer sharing and user authentication, all managed through a Web interface.

TAS implements NetBIOS and AppleTalk over IP as a user-mode application, much like the system in Sun Netlink PC. It adds IPX/SPX as a layer over the network device driver. Since NetWare can support both types of Ethernet (DIX and IEEE 802.3)—those of you old enough to remember that old geek argument, raise your hands—it can also support both the Ethernet II and IEEE 802.2 frame types. All the protocols are added with the installation of the TAS product.

For further details on using TAS, please see the corresponding sections in Chapters 12 and 13.

Summary

Network services suffer from slight protocol incompatibilities when it comes to working with Windows and other platforms. This is because Microsoft liberally enhances some system and application side services to add their own application protocol interfaces, and features to improve communications between Windows systems or to provide backward compatibility.

Still there is a lot to be said for the level of standardization it offers in the TCP/IP stack. Supporting Microsoft's higher level protocols for network file and printer sharing, user management, and resource location software, is now easier due to a variety of tools offered by Microsoft, UNIX, and third-party vendors alike. At the release time of Windows 2000, the number of fully supported and certified tools were still lacking but as this is a major niche business for a number of vendors, expect this to fill in pretty quickly.

With network services planned out, the next step is to find out how the very different user account models in the two platforms can work together, in our next chapter.

## CHAPTER 12

Managing Users and Domains

Managing user accounts is one of the first responsibilities of the sysadmin of a multiuser system. As systems grew larger, they gained more and more users. As they became more closely networked together, these accounts then had to work on multiple machines simultaneously. Sysadmins soon came to realize that it was too complex or unnecessarily problematic to handle separate accounts on each machine. This led to the development of network user accounts and directory services that each machine could check with to authenticate users.

Directory services are more complicated than just account names and passwords, and they contain not only information about the account such as which machines it can access, what user interface or environment it has, and when it can be accessed but also information about the person the account belongs to. The account is now often used as a unique identifier for individuals on the company network and is tied into other services such as e-mail, scheduling and calendaring, and roaming services.

Under UNIX, directory services are usually focused on a flat space of account names or a one-level hierarchy based upon which machines these accounts have access to. This works great for small networks of hundreds of accounts, but when you expand to thousands of users to maintain across hundreds or even thousands of machines, it becomes a nightmare to work with. New LDAP-based directory services for UNIX systems are just emerging to solve this problem.

Active Directory on Win 2000, however, employs a hierarchical model for accounts and allows them to be grouped together at multiple levels according to the structure of your company, thus making it much simpler to visualize and work with.

In this chapter we look at how to merge the directory services on each platform with one another. In particular, we will look at running NT domain controller services on UNIX systems, since this is the closest level of compatibility that the two platforms can have at this time.

Directory and User Account Services

Directory and user account services allow the administrator to integrate the user and OS information system between platforms. Rather than manage separate user accounts on each platform, they unite the user's account information such that the user can log in to either platform using the same account. There are many limitations to these services, primarily due to the differences between the account systems on UNIX and Windows machines.

Although the apparent benefit seems to be that the user has to use only a single account, it's the system administrator who actually benefits more. Maintaining multiple accounts on different machines can become an administrative nightmare on a large scale when there are many servers involved. There are account distribution services on the UNIX side (e.g., Network Information Service, the hosts.equiv file, Kerberos) that can manage a single set of accounts across multiple servers and workstations. Similarly, the NT domains and the Active Directory domains allow member workstations to check account information from a central domain controller or Active Directory server, respectively. However, what is needed is a mapping between the accounts on the UNIX system and that of the Windows systems.

It is possible to do such mapping or translation using three techniques: (1) You can translate account information from one format to another and import it into the other platform; (2) you can build the account information system of one platform into that of the other; or (3) you can use common information protocols to exchange account information.

Account Translation

Account translation is the process of converting information about an account from one platform to another. In our case, this means converting between UNIX-style accounts, passwords and groups, and NT domains or Active Directory domains. Much of the information stored on the two systems is similar. You have the account name, the password, the user's real name or description, a user identifier number, a primary group identifier number, and the user's home directory on the server.

On the UNIX side, however, you also have the shell user interface with which the user is allowed to access the system. The user's description can be split into multiple parts containing the user's last name, first name, office location, and address information. The /etc/group file shows secondary user groups and the accounts that are the group members. On some UNIX systems, there is an additional file indicating at what times of a day or week a particular user ID or group ID is allowed to log in to a system.

On the Windows side, the user identifier is part of a much more complicated security identifier, mapping a user to a specific machine or domain controller. The user account also has access rights and a default ACL, as described in Chapters 2 and 5. In addition, the system keeps a set of allowed login times on a per-user basis.

The account passwords are encrypted with different security algorithms on each system. Most UNIX systems use the DES (Data Encryption Standard) algorithm that uses the account name and password and creates an encrypted password. Windows 2000 uses Kerberos and public-key encryption.

An account translation system maps this kind of user information between the two systems by keeping additional files that contain the information relevant to the operating system. Some translation systems simply export the account information from one system to the format of the other. On any actively changing system, this means that the accounting information has to be exported on a regular basis, a possibly time-consuming process.

The account translation system in Microsoft's NT Services for UNIX product provides this form of simple account importing that takes NT account information and converts it into UNIX /etc/passwd and /etc/group files. This allows NT users to be recognized as UNIX accounts on the UNIX server.

Kerberos

With the Windows 2000 network authentication system, you can use the Kerberos protocol to maintain login information. The Win 2000 Kerberos implementation is compatible with the MIT Kerberos system version 5. You can use the same Kerberos Key Distribution server for both platforms. Essentially, this server maintains the user account and password mappings for both types of platform within its namespace, enabling you to create an enterprisewide single login system.

Kerberos, however, is only an authentication system. It does not contain account information other than account name and password mappings on a network. You still need the account databases that store the information for Kerberos to check against.

The Kerberos authentication system was first built on UNIX and is still available for the various platforms. However, the Win 2000 implementation is not compatible with that of the UNIX system on the authentication side; thus, you cannot use the Win2k Server Kerberos module to authenticate UNIX accounts and servers. The same goes for Win2k clients trying to authenticate on UNIX-based Kerberos servers.

Directory Services

Directory services under UNIX have long been either proprietary or nonexistent until the rise of the Lightweight Directory Access Protocol (LDAP) in 1997. Several UNIX systems have borrowed the model of sharing accounts and hostnames through Sun Microsystems' original Yellow Pages (yp) system. Now called Network Information Systems Plus (NIS+), it is still in active use on most Solaris-based workstations and servers. More vendors, however, are now moving toward implementing an LDAP system instead.

The NT4 domain controller provided the semblance of a network directory service using proprietary protocols developed by Microsoft for communications between the primary domain controller (PDC) and the backup domain controller (BDC). With Active Directory, the rules have changed completely. Although AD uses LDAP protocols, it bypasses the shortcomings of LDAP and implements its own access control system and replication methods. LDAP lacks these features at this time and a new protocol—the LDAP Duplication/Update Protocol (LDUP)—is promising to provide replication and synchronization when it is released.

Another standard also being developed at the time of writing of this book is the Directory Services Markup Language (DSML) a directory exchange schema for the Extensible Markup Language (XML). DSML creates a translation system between the different semi-compatible directory services. It uses the grammar and syntax of XML to create common elements that can be exchanged from one service to another. This allows a company to run separate directory services to support Net-Ware, Windows, and UNIX, if they should choose to, and still maintain coherence in the content between the services. Theoretically, this should allow UNIX accounts to recognize Windows accounts and vice versa. Microsoft, Novell, Sun, IBM, Oracle, Red Hat, and AOL Netscape division, are all contributors to this effort, showing support from most of the major directory product vendors.

As yet there are no products that allow a UNIX server to act as a full Active Directory server. However, AD can use LDAP version 2 or 3 to communicate with LDAP messaging servers. These servers can contain any type of information: user accounts, file information, application information, and so on. There are a variety of LDAP messaging servers from Netscape, IBM, and Sun that fill this role.

As mentioned in Chapter 4, Active Directory is a subset based upon the X.500 directory services standard. These directory servers use different protocols to distribute directory information. You cannot use X.500 directory servers with Active Directory unless they also support LDAP queries.

The system still requires a Win 2000 Active Directory server and administration tools to manage the information; the LDAP servers simply act as information storehouses in this respect. Client systems query first the Active Directory server to search for information within the directory information tree before they retrieve the actual information from an LDAP server.

NT Domain Services on UNIX

There are a few products that can provide the same or similar services to the NT domain controller on a UNIX server. This usually involves the use of native NetBIOS and Windows application protocols from the UNIX machine. Unlike UNIX, the NT authentication and security model is based upon special identifiers and complex access control lists. This means that the UNIX system has to implement mapping between NT SIDs and ACLs to the account and file permissions system that UNIX uses.

It sounds simple, doesn't it? Unfortunately, much of this code is proprietary to Microsoft and, although some attempts at reverse-engineering it have been tried, they have not been too successful. One good thing is that AT&T early on made a deal with Microsoft to license their code and port it to UNIX systems, which made it into a few commercial products.

There aren't really any packages that support UNIX account services on NT systems. The basic fact is that there really isn't a need for this. Almost every access control method in UNIX is based upon the account—in itself, a simple alphanumeric text identifier (the account name)—and file permissions. Thus it can be easily included onto NT systems, and the only real component needed is the authentication mechanism. The resource sharing packages, which we will talk about in Chapters 13, 14, and 15, usually include the basic plain-text authentication mechanism available for most UNIX systems. This means that with these resource sharing packages installed, a UNIX user can log onto and access network resources or even applications on the NT server directly.

Syntax TotalNet Advanced Server

Syntax Inc.'s *TotalNet Advanced Server* (TAS) product implements a NetBIOS file sharing system for several different UNIX systems (Solaris, AIX, IRIX, and HP-UX), in addition to other protocols such as NetWare and AppleTalk file sharing. TAS implements a NetBIOS stack on top of TCP/IP and implements the necessary parts of CIFS to perform file and printer sharing. (For more details on TAS's networking, see Chapter 11.)

TAS is managed through either a dedicated management Web site running on the UNIX server or through command line tools. Each network operating system service that it supports is delegated to a realm. Thus there is a CIFS realm (NetBIOS/TCP, NetBIOS/NetBEUI), a NetWare realm (IPX/SPX), and an AppleTalk realm (AppleTalk/TCP). To achieve this, it also implements each of these protocols in the UNIX environment, either at the driver level or as a user-mode application service.

For Windows services, TAS provides a nearly full implementation of CIFS, including file and printer sharing and network browsing. TAS also supports network authentication and some domain services for Windows systems, but it lacks support for access control lists, which prevent it from operating as a full domain controller. Although not complete in that sense, it is still the only product on the market that supports user authentication, file sharing, and printer sharing for all the major PC operating systems, on top of UNIX servers.

Solaris Easy Access Server and Netlink PC

Sun Microsystems' *Solaris Easy Access Server* is now included in all server models of Sun Microsystems hardware alongside the Solaris 7 operating system. It is a combination of several products designed to make it easier to integrate Windows clients and servers with Solaris-based servers, as well as support an enterprise application server system.

It integrates a Web server, an LDAP server, a RADIUS server, a mail server (IMAP4, POP, SMTP), and the *Netlink PC* server. This last component is of the most interest to our topic of cross-platform integration. Netlink PC, formerly known as Project Cascade, is an implementation of the NT domain controller system.

It is based upon code licensed from AT&T's Advanced Server for UNIX, which in turn is based upon the original Windows NT domain controller and CIFS code. Sun used to resell Syntax's TotalNet Advanced Server as SunLink PC, but has since replaced that with this software. It doesn't support the AppleTalk and NetWare services as SunLink PC, but does support NT domains and services much better.

Netlink PC implements the security authentication manager and its accompanying database as the domain controller. This includes support for security identifiers (SIDs) per machine and relative SIDs per user or network resource. There is a separate database component for the access control lists for each security and file system object.

Although Netlink PC does not support the use of NTFS on Solaris machines as a native file system, it does provide mapping between UNIX and NT file system types. This allows NT client stations to view the UNIX server drives as common CIFS-capable network drives.

Designing Cross-Platform Directory Services

Implementing useful directory services also involves more than just plugging information into the proper slots. It is an exercise in diplomacy, integration skills, system administration skills, and the limits of your sense of humor. In other words, stock up on ibuprofen pills and heartburn medicine.

To do this, you need to decide what kind of information each user will need to provide, how the information will be represented electronically, what kind of security each of the entries needs to have, how this information should be spread across multiple servers, and how to modify, access, or manage this information from the network. All this, before you even start collecting information.

Standards like LDAP or products like Active Directory do not magically handle all of these issues for you. LDAP is just a simple protocol that retrieves, adds, or modifies information on a directory server, and AD simply contains this information and replicates it. Any time you create a system of access to a resource, you must also create policies on who can access it, where it fits into your overall system, and how it will be managed. Much of this is independent of the protocols and tools that you use, and remains as the weight you must bear on your shoulders. The best we can do is show you how to shift that weight around so it's more bearable.

Directory Models

A modern directory infrastructure is based on six different models used to describe its information and operational state. Each of these models describes a facet of the directory and affects different groups of people.

The *naming model* describes how the tree of data is laid out. By organizing entries according to their respective positions in the enterprise infrastructure, you can build a treelike representation of your entire organization. Each entry can correspond to any type of real or abstract object (a file, a user account, a printer, a DNS resource record, a user's preference for their desktop environment, etc.). Unlike other tree hierarchies used in computing—such as the file system tree, the domain name service tree, and so on—each node in the directory tree can be of any type and can have any number of child nodes of different varieties. The naming model defines how each entry can be accessed within the context of the entire directory (or relative to other directories). Depending on where the entry is placed in the naming model, you derive the *distinguished name* (DN) or *relative distinguished name.*

The *information model* defines the attributes of each entry and the data types of these attributes. Thus, for each entry (i.e., a user account), there needs to be a definition of how the account name is represented (usually a string of characters, although even this can vary). Each entry also needs a definition of formats for user directory locations, profile information, and so on. The information model defines data types (strings, binary data, Boolean values, integers, floating-point values, etc.) and places constraints on what constitutes a valid range of information for that attribute.

The *functional model* defines how data is accessed from the directory system. This model basically specifies how the LDAP commands can be used. In some portions of the directory you may wish to allow some clients to only read the information and not change it. Other clients may be able to change the security and content of their own group but not those of other organizational units.

The *security model* defines how the directory is secured. This security could be established by subtree, by entry, or even by attribute within an entry. This also takes into account how directory access sessions are authenticated. By default, LDAP does not specify an access control system to define individual access rights. Since the access control methodology differs depending on the underlying operating system, LDAP leaves it to the implementation of the server software. Active Directory, Netscape's Directory server, and NetWare Directory Services all use access control lists to provide security down to the directory objects and their attributes.

The *replication model* is specific to a multiserver environment and defines how the DIT is subdivided or replicated across servers. This is not a function of LDAP, but many directory products implement a proprietary mechanism of their own design. A standardized protocol, LDUP, is still in the works by the Internet Engineering Task Force. Microsoft implemented their own mechanism for replication in Active Directory independently of the LDUP effort, although they provide similar features. The replication model for AD is thus technically, but not conceptually, different from that of other directory servers.

The *management model* defines how the tree is managed, either as a whole or in parts. The directory space can be fairly large in an enterprise network spanning tens or even hundreds of thousands of objects. Such scale can be next to impossible to manage from a single point. Subdividing management tasks across various locations and IT groups should logically follow the structure of the tree. The responsibility of sysadmins in this kind of scenario is to assist in keeping track of log files and events, to add or edit access control and security permissions, to troubleshoot application or directory errors, and to manually change or add entries to the tree when necessary. Active Directory allows you to delegate responsibility to directory administrators so that they do not interfere with each other's subtrees.

These models define how your directory behaves for all parties, users, administrators, and software developers. The users are the group most directly affected by the naming, information, and security models. Administrators are primarily concerned with naming, security, replication, and management. Developers need to know the naming, information, functional, and security models. If they also develop tools for directory server management, the replication and management models also become relevant for developers.

Goals of Your Directory

Any modern directory service requires careful planning before the execution. To begin, you will need to create a directory task force that is responsible for carrying through with the whole project. Select members mostly from the IT department and one or two persons from the human resources department to help make policy decisions. Make sure that you have the approval of the executive ranks to carry out the project at the level in the company that you are planning for.

Before you begin, you have to decide on the goals and the scope of the directory service. The goals define how the directory is going to be used. The scope defines who will use the directory. You will find that your task force will be faced with a number of questions, but a very basic set will keep popping up:

- Who will be allowed to use the directory?
- What or whose information will be stored in the directory?
- How will they be allowed to use this information?
- How and where can they access this information?
- How and when can this information be changed, and by whom?
- Who will be responsible for the security and management of this information?
- If similar systems exist, how does it impact their use?

The primary goal of the directory may be technical, such as creating a single enterprise login system; or administrative, such as an employee scheduling and calendaring system; or even informative, such as an open list of employees and their contact information. However, the preceding list of questions still stands, irrespective of the type of goal.

You will find that as you go through the project, other, secondary, objectives will also appear. This is mostly the result of talking to people who will be affected by the project and getting input on their needs. Take this input as advice and a request for services and evaluate it carefully before including it into your project. This is fine as long as you keep the goals and objectives of the project to a minimum and do not try to satisfy all of the people all of the time.

Be forewarned that a directory deployment project can get out of hand if you do not take precautions about controlling the decision process. Someone above you in the chain of command may decide that it would be a nifty idea to attach this project alongside another of theirs, especially if it involves a software development or company reorganization effort. Write down the formal goals of the project and keep it at eye level. If the project runs on for months, reassert the goals every few weeks so that everyone is in step with the project as intended. Do not be completely inflexible, but don't be a total rubber band, either. After all, when stretched too thin, rubber bands can suddenly snap.

Phases of Directory Deployment

Deciding upon the goals of your directory is a first step before design and deployment. In fact, you may even come to the assessment that the project is just too big to be handled on an enterprisewide basis and, rather, that each division or department of the company should attempt its own directory project. Nevertheless, once you have determined the goal and scope of the project, you can move on to the actual phases of implementation.

The *first phase* involves the process of collecting information about your company and your network. This could lead to a general census of everyone involved to get accurate information as the basis of your directory. This stage is complicated by the need to determine what kind of information to collect. Even with our general guidelines, you will probably need to make your own decisions on what to include.

The *second phase* involves assembling the pieces of the collected information to show how they interrelate on different levels. For example, you will need to overlay the way your company personnel are organized to the network map of the computers they use.

Once you have a general map of the organization of personnel and computers together, you need to decide how to partition the directory information appropriately. This *third phase* will create an analog of the map that can be represented in terms of directory objects. Based upon where most of these groups are located, you define partitions of the information space, each of which will be located on a server.

The *fourth phase* involves determining how the information on these servers can be distributed and replicated effectively so as to improve the performance of the system. This replication will depend upon the type of directory server product you will use. Although the information itself can probably be copied (synchronized) across platforms and products, replication involves keeping an active interaction between the various servers and mapping information much more closely. Thus you may have to decide if you want to replicate the directory across the same type of server product or synchronize it across platforms.

The *fifth phase* brings you to the process of how you manage the directory information, the servers, and the applications, and assign IT staff to handle such responsibilities. This is more of a process phase, indicating how you manage or change the information or change the methods to access the directories rather than the actual content itself.

The *sixth phase* involves promoting the use of the directory in the company and developing a training program for the end users of directory client software. You can only gauge how successful the directory is by the amount of use it gets; thus, this is just as important a step as getting your servers installed.

The *seventh* and final phase is ongoing maintenance and periodic reviews of the overall performance of the directory. This includes evaluating how the users like the system, what features it lacks that users want, the load on the directory servers, and how easy it has been to manage the directory. This is a long-term phase that will probably continue for the life of the directory.

Doing a Census for Your Directory

The roughest part of creating a directory service must surely be collecting and collating all of the information that needs to be put into the directory. This isn't always difficult to do, but it can be quite time consuming if you have lots of users. Collecting any form of data that crosses boundaries between groups or departments in your company is also affected by politics.

In essence, creating a directory service will most likely involve launching a census program within your organization. Although you may have the go-ahead from the top brass to put together a new directory, they may not realize how invasive it can be. All along the way, you are going to encounter obstacles. Individuals will question why you need the information, the legal and human resources departments will scan every questionnaire you create or collect, and sometimes people will not respond to repeated requests for information—for a variety of reasons.

Doing a company census to build a directory service is like hand-picking ripe peaches. You do it carefully and individually because the peaches can bruise easily. One good method is to get the cooperation of all the middle managers and supervisors in every group along the way and explain to them the need for the census and directory service. The middle managers and supervisors will have to field most of the questions from the employees directly, so by educating them you can win a valuable ally (and reduce the hundreds of calls and questions from individuals that you might otherwise have had to address yourself!).

Some companies prefer to ask their employees' opinions on what should go into the enterprise directory. Although this does make employees feel more involved in the decision, it usually results in a mass of diverse ideas that can be too much to handle. It is better to create a representative action group—consisting of system administrators, human resources staff, legal staff, directory programmers, and middle managers—whose job it is to determine what will go into the directory. Keep in mind that the larger the group, the longer it will take to come to a decision, but also that the decision reached in that case will be more representative of the general population's opinion.

Once the format for the namespace is decided and you have a list of attributes, you can create template-based forms that users or those who participate in the census can fill out. To aid in census taking, you should consider building a Web interface to a temporary database that will store most of the per-user attributes in a single file. This can be processed later, before it is formally entered into the directory. You might also consider hiring temporary staff to perform the census taking.

To create a new directory service system for your organization, you need to have a number of items at hand:

- An *asset list* of all computers that will use the directory, with brief details of the hardware and software configuration. This is the same thing we talked about in Chapter 10.

- A *network topology map* showing where the directory client machines will be physically located in the various rooms, buildings, and locations. A directory client can be an end user's desktop machine, a workgroup server, or any other computer that accesses the directory service for information. This is also covered in Chapter 10.

- A *directory software map* of all the applications that will use the directory, how they access it, what particular directory services they require, and where they are located on the map.

- A *list of directory programming projects* indicating all the software developer groups working on projects that interact with the direct services and where they are located on the map.

- A *hierarchy of your organization* showing how different workgroups are arranged into departments and how departments are organized into divisions.

- A *list of directory information candidates* indicating all users who will have some of their information stored in the directory for any purpose, and, if possible, where they are located on the map.

- A *list of end users* indicating all those who will access the directory service on a regular or semiregular basis to retrieve information and where they are located on the map.

- A *list of directory administrators* who will be responsible for managing the content, operation, and architecture of the directory services.

Details of Data Collection Items

This constitutes quite a volume of information that needs to be retrieved from many different sources. Each item requires a certain amount of detail that will be needed in later stages. To make things easier, start with just a name or identifying tag for each item—a client computer, a programmer, an end user, a job title—but also keep an entry indicating where you can get more information about that item for later use. Eventually, you will need to look at the details of these other attributes for each user in order to create the full database of directory entries. But to get started, you should be able to work with just their names.

To develop a network topology map (See Figure 12.1), look toward network management packages like Computer Associates Unicenter TNG,

Sun Solstice Manager, or Tivoli Enterprise Manager. They can help you collect data on the clients on your various LANs and on how the networks themselves interconnect. Another tool, Visio Professional, is designed to help you draw accurate, presentable diagrams of your network layout, although most of these network management packages can be used to do the same thing.

The software map (see Figure 12.2) is a logical view of how directory client and server applications communicate. If you are planning directory services for the first time, draw a generic layout of what you perceive will be the future system. If you have existing directory services, you should indicate which platforms they run on, the version of the directory software, how directory servers are replicated, and how they are being managed.

Directory programmers have different needs than do regular users. For the most part, a development project should have its own private directory server to work with rather than using live company data until the project is complete. Since the development effort can generate errors or even problems with the directory server, this will limit them to a testbed. Interview the leaders of each of these projects to inquire how they will affect the general behavior of the overall company directory should they be introduced into it.

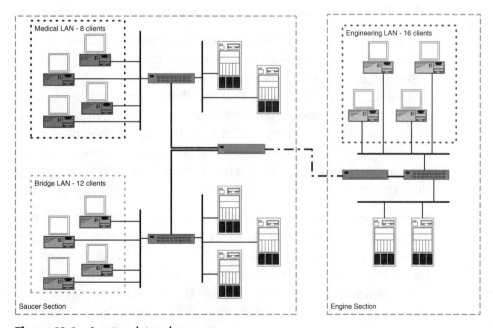

Figure 12.1   A network topology map.

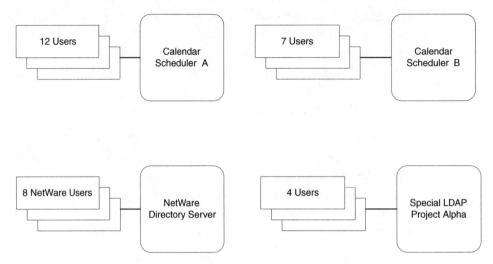

Figure 12.2 A directory software map.

The organizational hierarchy of your company (See Figure 12.3) can most likely be obtained from the human resources department or the chief operational officer's staff. It is likely that this could take a lot of time to develop on an individual employee level, if you have thousands of employees. In such a case, you can probably simply indicate workgroups of people at the lowest level. Visio also has a personnel organization template that allows you to generate such a visual hierarchy much more quickly.

For the list of directory information candidates, you have to be specific, since each candidate will be a separate entry in the directory. Human resource (HR) database packages, such as those available from Peoplesoft or Oracle, can provide you with the list of directory information candidates or, perhaps, the employee hierarchy of the organization. At this point of deployment, you do not need the full details per candidate. Rather, what you should find out is where you can get this information. Once the directory is complete, you may have to either reenter this information into your directory or tie it to a subset of the HR database that contains this info.

Not everyone in your organization may require the use of the directory. On the other hand, you may even have part of your directory available through a public Web site so that anyone outside the company can get in touch with the appropriate personnel directly. Of greater concern is the list of end users of the directory client applications. You should already have prepared the map of the client software. This step involves identifying who uses the software and what kind of training they have or need.

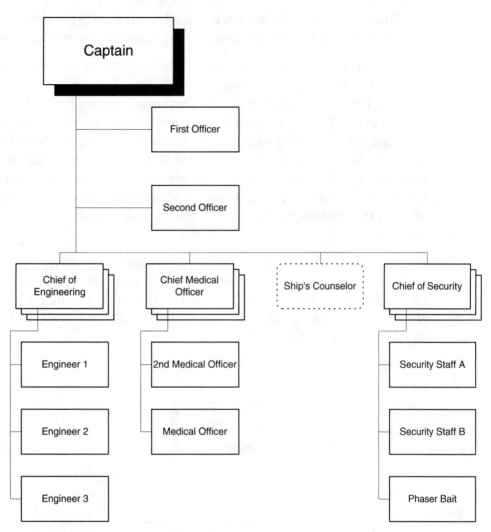

Figure 12.3 An organizational hierarchy.

This list needs to identify the employee, the computer(s) they use, the directory-related software they use, and how much they know about how to use the software properly.

Interrelating Your Organization and the Directory

Interrelation is the process of creating a namespace or naming model based upon the information you have about your company and users. Using the organizational hierarchy and the list of directory information candidates, you can map out a detail of who and what is to be contained in your directory and all the possible distinguished names in your directory.

The designs most companies use are fairly similar. At the very top is the domain for the entire company, which constitutes the directory space. One model creates subsets under this based upon identifiable object types such as users, computers, and network resources, which in turn contain the various divisions, departments, and workgroups of the organization. Another follows the hierarchical view of the company with divisions, departments, and workgroups containing the individual users, computers, and network resources. In either case, you can see that there are two dimensions to the space: organizational subdivision and directory object.

Figure 12.4 shows a design ordered by directory object type (Personnel and Computers), and then by organizational units (Bridge crew, Medical Crew, Engineering crew, etc.). In this example, all the individuals (not shown) in the organization are included in the directory; that is, they are all directory candidates.

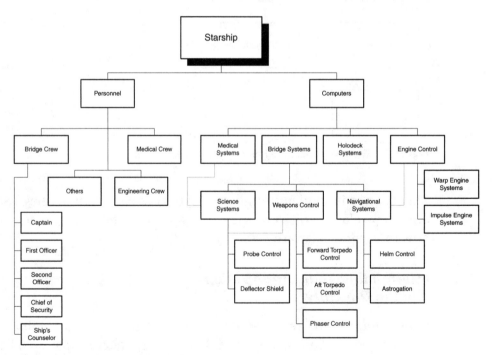

Figure 12.4 A namespace of all objects in our starship.

Directory Mapping, Information Distribution, and Replication

The second step is to create a map of the relevant computers that will use the directory services. If all your users will have access to the directory to look up phone numbers and other information, this could pretty well be all your client computers and many servers. Using the network map, software map, and list of directory programming projects, you can draw up a new directory services topology map specifically indicating the participant computers in the directory.

Our map in Figure 12.5 shows the four different directory groups spread across the three different LANs in the organization. The Medical LAN runs an existing NDS directory for the productivity applications of its members. The Engineering LAN has two of its own directory groups, one for the group calendar and work schedule and the other for a special application development project that works with its own directory. Finally, the Bridge LAN shows the major portion of the Commanding Officers directory group, indicating their schedules, meeting times, and allotted tasks. This group, however, also has members who access the information from the Medical and Engineering LANs (i.e., those for the Chief Medical Officer and the Chief of Engineering).

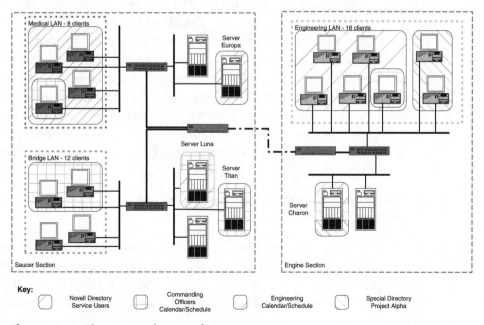

Figure 12.5   Directory services topology map.

From this directory services topology map, you can figure out where directory servers should fall into place, as it will always be near to the locus of the highest population of clients and applications.

There are four directory servers also represented on this map. The NDS directory server, named Europa, appears in red stripes for the Medical LAN. The Engineering directory server, named Charon, actually handles three different directory groups. There are the two directories within the Engineering LAN (the Engineering schedule and Special Project Alpha) and a cached replicated image of the Command Officers directory group. There are two servers on the Bridge LAN. The directory server Titan serves as the primary for the Command Officers group. The server named Luna contains replicated images of all the information in the directory servers for the Command Officers group, the Engineering group, and the Medical group.

The directory servers are placed where they can best serve the local group. In addition, there are replication services for those located remotely. Finally, one server (Luna) contains replicated information of all the other servers except that for Special Project Alpha. This last one is left out since it is a development project that is likely to test, reboot, or restructure its server often. For that matter, the project really does not need to be accessed from anywhere else.

The network map and software map can also combine to illustrate the traffic patterns for your directory. This does not give an exact idea of the amount of traffic that the servers will really encounter once it is running. Even when taken in combination with the list of end users and the predicted amount of requests they will be generating, this will still only be an educated guess at best. It will probably require a few months of operation to monitor actual network activity to figure out where to properly locate servers on the network so that they service the largest amount of requests and so that the information then travels the shortest distances.

Delegating Directory Administration and Marketing Your Directory

All directories are information repositories and thus must have someone responsible to take care of the information. Like a librarian, this person has to make sure that the information is cataloged properly and contains the proper information, and must control how the information is modified.

Since a directory space can be fairly huge, consisting of up to millions of entries, this is a lot of ground to cover for any one person. Furthermore, the information can be relevant to different locations and different departments. Thus you need to find a way to share this responsibility among a number of sysadmins locally or distributed around your company.

Delegating the control of the directory is also dependent upon the directory software you use. Some products offer a fine degree of control over what each administrator is allowed to do, while others just have a general group of admin accounts that are responsible for all areas of the directory. Some products provide an easy-to-learn Web interface, while others require cryptic hand-typed commands.

Whatever the degree of control available, you should subdivide the directory tree and assign specific sysadmins to take responsibility of the subtrees. This creates regions of responsibility, and each sysadmin can handle troubleshooting on a regional basis. The subdivisions can be along the lines of personnel groupings, computers and networks, or individual directory servers, or they can be according to commonly used directory applications.

Once the directory system is up and running and the technical administration details have been worked out, you have to get people actively using the system. This is more of an administrative step than a technical one. Nevertheless, one part of marketing the directory is developing the documentation on how to use it.

This documentation should be targeted toward users and the directory-related applications that they are allowed to use. After you install the directory system, you may need to reconfigure these applications so as to access the directory contents. If this changes the users' applications, they have to be briefed on how to use the modified system.

The good thing about directories is that they often fade into the background of applications. Since the applications that use the directory information often present it in their own interface, the user need only know how to use that application. In fact, they might not even know about the directory system behind it.

Directory Maintenance and Optimization

Maintenance is an ongoing responsibility for the directory that goes hand in hand with technical administration. All the usual server sysadmin tasks are part of the job: backups, system security, log file management, hardware management, and data management. In addition, depending upon the uses of your directory, the information will periodically get out of date and have to be modified by proper personnel. You should have a policy on who is allowed to do these modifications and how they should do them.

Maintenance involves not only keeping the information contents safe and up to date, but also periodically checking the usage and traffic patterns of the servers to determine how well the system is working. Using these traffic patterns, you can work to optimize the directory system and the client-to-server and server-to-server communications.

Looking at the traffic, you should attempt to classify the type of requests your directory service gets. One way is to classify them by the LDAP operation type. Another is to classify them by the groupings in your directory hierarchy. A third method would be to classify them based upon the origin of the requests, in other words, the client machines from which they come. Whichever method you use, the technique is similar.

The following is a description of the first method—operation type—on a per-server basis. In classification by operation type, the most basic class is the simple query for data based upon a complete or nearly complete distinguished name. Following this in popularity is the more complex compare query, in which a number of search parameters are used to match one or more data items. Then come the add, delete, and modify operations.

It's when you have multiple replicated servers in separate sites, which would require that such operations be propagated, that it becomes relatively more expensive. The most costly operation is likely to be the *rename* or *move* operation. This can radically restructure the entire directory and thus affect the namespace of many servers. A simple move of one endpoint data item isn't the problem here. The problem occurs when you have move operations that relocate a whole subtree. In this case, the entire directory may be affected. The use of the add, modify, delete, and move operations together may slow the whole system down considerably.

To avoid that and to help balance the load, you can build a weighting function for your servers. Start by classifying the requests and logging the number of executed operations of each class.

Then associate a simple numerical weight or factor with each class. Take a periodic log in which you multiply the weight of each class by the total number of requests of that type, and make a table of the values by class.

The total load on the server is the sum of these values. This is a relative number, and it should be used only for comparison between servers.

Then, based on the data you have recorded from these calculations having been performed over several time periods, you can monitor the overall distribution of requests and their distribution by server. This can help you to decide whether you need to move some of the information around or whether you need to change the replication rules and times.

One or Many Directories?

It may turn out that your organization is simply too large or too diverse to contemplate building a single enterprisewide directory service. There may be too many specific information attributes that are needed within individual groups and that simply do not make sense for everyone else in the company. In fact, a single enterprisewide directory often ends up containing only the lowest common denominator of information across the company.

A worse problem is found in a multinational or multidivisional company that has very different organizational structures within each location or division. This is a business model that exacerbates the already problematic implementation of directory services at the enterprise level. And, unfortunately, it can be hard to convince the company to reorganize simply to make putting together an organized directory easier!

Another problem with trying to make a single directory service is that different groups and departments may be running different types of directory server products. As we indicated earlier, this is a compatibility problem. But it can be a hard one to fix, given that each department is probably loath to switch operating systems. And so you might have no choice but to run several different types of directory server products.

Administration of a single large directory service can be a nightmare. The most common result of such administration is that the information in the directory itself becomes out of date. Although several directory services allow you to delegate the authority over subtrees of the directory to individual system administrators, this is not a standard feature of LDAP, which is just a protocol, after all.

You may end up questioning whether a single directory model is beneficial for you or whether you should try several separate directory services for different divisions instead—or even both! There is no simple if-then-else answer to this problem. It requires an analysis of your IT directory management group's capabilities to handle the various combinations of issues.

Implementing and Integrating Directory Services

Once you have designed the structure of your directory service, and decided upon which directory service products you want to use, you should be ready to construct your directory. If you plan to use multiple directories you should choose one of the systems for integrating them as described in the following sections. The complexity of implementing directory services currently lies more within Active Directory and thus we will focus specifically on this component first.

Implementing NT4 Domains

Implementing NT4 domains requires primary and backup domain controllers. These are special versions of the Windows NT server that have to be installed as domain controllers during the installation of the operating system. This is a long process, mostly due to the time it takes to install the NT server as it is.

Under the NT4 domain system, there is a primary domain controller (PDC), supported by one or more backup domain controllers. The PDC always has to exist, although the BDC itself is just a standby system in case the former fails. All updates to accounts and permissions go to the PDC. The BDC simply copies this information from it.

Once the PDC is installed, you need to start configuring each of the clients to point to it and start installing user accounts and access rights. With a BDC, you need to indicate the PDC it will support, and then you should be done.

Implementing Active Directory

Win 2000 does away with the need to install the operating system specifically as a domain controller. Instead, you can now use the *DCPromo* tool to promote and demote a Win 2000 server to and from Active Directory domain controller status, respectively.

In AD, there is no real difference in AD domain controllers, unlike the PDC/BDC system in NT4. Furthermore, there can be several domain controllers of equal status serving the same domain; in other words, the information is equally reflected in all the domain controllers.

Once the Win 2000 server operating system is installed, you can run the **dcpromo.exe** program from the WinNT directory to load the domain controller. This wizard takes you through a series of dialog boxes that inquire about the specifics for that domain.

First of all, it asks whether this is a new domain or if it will be part of another domain. If you're installing a new domain, it will act as the central repository for all objects in the domain. This can later be spread across other domain controllers as they are brought up. AD domains are based upon Internet domain names (e.g., straypackets.com), but they also have a counterpart NetBIOS name taken from the first 14 characters of the IP domain without the *.com* or *.org*.

It then requests the Domain Name System server that will be facilitating the AD domain controllers. This can be any type of DNS server running either on the same machine as the controller or on another platform. Microsoft even supports running this with the *bind* name server on UNIX systems, as long as it supports the Dynamic DNS services.

When you install a new AD controller, it creates the default first site. AD controllers replicate according to the sites they belong to.

Integrating NT4 Domains with Active Directory Domains

Active Directory is backward compatible with NT4 domains. At the domain controller installation time, the wizard gives an option to support older NT4 domains and clients that can authenticate with them.

Installing an Active Directory server to support NT4 domains is a simple procedure. It doesn't need any real changes to the domain clients unless you put it on a machine separate from the old domain controller. In such a case, you would have to rename the domain controller that all the clients point to, a time-consuming task for those with large numbers of stations.

A better method would be to stick your Win 2000 server CD on the NT4 PDC or BDC and upgrade the entire operating system. The installation tool is intelligent enough to recognize that the server is a domain controller and will run the appropriate wizard.

You should first begin upgrading the backup domain controllers and then move on to the primary, since this will affect the status of your network. This way the upgraded BDC, now an AD domain controller, can actually take over the role of the PDC when you move to upgrade it. After the PDC is upgraded, it does not really matter which one is in charge since they will be equals as AD domain controllers.

If this is the only type of domain controller on your network, you need to consider this carefully. For Win 9x and NT systems, this will work fine. However, what you end up sacrificing is some compatibility between the newer Win 2000 systems and the older Win 9x and NT systems. The new Win 2000 systems offer better management and system administration services such as Intellimirror and MMC. The Win 2000 servers really do need a full Win 2000-compatible domain controller.

Integrating with Other Directories

There are several approaches to integrating content from non-Active Directory servers such as NetWare Directory Services and LDAP-based servers. These usually involve the use of a third-party tool to combine, convert, or transfer the information from one directory to another. The four methods used for integrating directory services include:

- The *metadirectory* that creates an overarching superstructure over multiple directory types.

- The *directory translation* products that interpret and execute commands in the native format of each directory they serve.

- The *directory migration* products that permanently convert the content and structure of the directory to that of the new server.

- The *XML standard directory language* that provides a common language in which all directories can talk to each other to exchange information.

The metadirectory method envelops multiple directory server products into a new system with its own management tools. The information content from each of these directory servers is absorbed into the metadirectory. The individual directory servers still exist and run within their domains, but the metadirectory controls the overall system.

This can be very effective for the directory products it handles but provides little support for others not included in its list. It can also vary in terms of what features of each directory are implemented in the metadirectory. You may get full support of every feature or, more commonly, you can end up with the lowest common denominator in features. Furthermore, you have to use the tools to manage the directory that comes with the products rather than those per directory, or it can break the system. So if you prefer the features in one particular directory administration tool or another, you are pretty much out of luck.

Microsoft's (formerly Xoomit Corporation's) VIA product line and Net-Vision Inc.'s Synchronicity product offer metadirectory services for Active Directory, Novell Directory Services, Novell GroupWise, Lotus Notes, and Microsoft Exchange.

With translation systems, you get the benefit of using each directory exactly as you normally would and you can use the translation tools to exchange data and commands between the directory servers. The tools are normally scripting systems that enable you to perform functions specific to the platform and the directory server. With such a system you no longer have to worry about the lack of feature support, since each directory is still managed with its own tools. You can use the translation tools to organize sets of commands specific to each directory type and execute them separately.

The problem is right there. You still manage these directory servers separately, and having two completely separate systems doing the same thing has never been easy to manage. Although you can do many of the common tasks through the translation system, this is limited by what the vendor offers you. With scripting tools, you can extend the possibilities, but this can be time consuming and difficult to test on an enterprisewide scale.

Products in this class include FastLane Technology Inc.'s DM/Suite and Entevo Corporation's DirectAdmin and DirectScript products.

With directory migration tools, you effectively replace one directory server completely with another. The tools help to permanently translate the data and structure of the directory so that they are appropriate for the new server. Unlike the on-the-fly translation of information in the second method, this translation occurs only once and is permanent, making it faster.

By permanently converting the directory from one form to another, you effectively lose any or all of the benefits of the old system. In addition, if you have custom-developed software that interacts with the directory, you may have to redevelop this under the new platform and directory service.

Entevo Corporation also offers the DirectMigrate product line to convert Novell Directory Services and NT4 domain services to the new Active Directory system.

The newest method that is only barely starting to show is translators for directory servers written in the eXtensible Markup Language (XML). Unlike the earlier translation methods, the different directory servers in this scenario still exist within their own domains and are managed with their own tools, but they now communicate with each other using a specific XML definition.

Unlike HTML used in developing Web pages, XML allows the developer to designate data types and objects, and provides essentially a handbook (the definition document) for understanding these objects. Thus an object of type USER is the same whichever way you look at it on any platform or any server. Each directory server, in our case, has to translate this object into a native form for its platform, but the information about the object's type is given in the definition document.

The Directory Interoperability Forum created in July 1999 and led by IBM, Novell, and Oracle—three current leaders in the directory services area—has agreed on XML as the best path toward getting these different directory server products talking to each other. Novell has already demonstrated its DirXML solution at the recent Burton Group Catalyst Conference. A start-up, Bowstreet Software Inc., is working on XML definitions for directory services that may become the basis for a new standard known as the Directory Standard Markup Language (DSML). Vendors planning to participate in this work in progress include Cisco, IBM, Microsoft, Netscape, Novell, and Oracle.

Summary

Active Directory is a crucial part of Windows 2000. Although directory services are becoming more important in UNIX systems, they are not as strongly tied with system services as yet. Applications and application developers are the biggest beneficiaries of a directory service, allowing them to access system information in a uniform manner, from any managed system on the network.

Designing a successful directory service lies in approaching the problem in a logical manner according to the needs of your organization. Sometimes, trying to do too much will only result in late projects and unsuccessful deployment. Thus before you jump from zero to implement a directory service for thousands of computers and users, test out the service on a select pilot project. Then focus on the issues of user and application access to the directory, platform and service incompatibility issues, and integration issues with your management system.

You will find that Active Directory will make Windows administration easier for medium to large networks. It will help create better access and distribution of resources such as disk space and printer sharing across the network, which is the subject of the next chapter.

## CHAPTER 13

Disk and Printer Sharing

I n the beginning there was disk sharing . . .

That is pretty much how the whole thing started with UNIX-Windows integration. The one-time need to share expensive disk-drive storage resources with low-cost PC systems led to the development of one of the earliest PC-Windows integration packages, PC-NFS from SunSelect (part of Sun Microsystems) and FTP and Telnet from FTP Software, Inc. From there it went on to printer sharing, application sharing, and so on.

These early beginnings gave life to an entire industry based on TCP/IP for the Windows world. The primary protocol of the UNIX industry, TCP/IP later became the favored network protocol once popular applications like Mosaic and Netscape started taking over the desktops of most users.

However, at the core, disk and printer sharing remains one of the most useful aspects of UNIX-Windows integration, not for the reasons of yesteryear (i.e., access to high-capacity disk systems), but to achieve new goals in reducing the total cost of ownership (there, I said it). Although there have been some changes to the way file systems work both in UNIX and Windows since the early 1980s, the basic protocols remain similar enough that there has not been significant variance in the features supported by the early versions and those of today.

This chapter explores the various techniques, protocols, and applications used to share disk, printer, and backup services between UNIX and Windows.

Disk Sharing

Disk or secondary storage comes very cheap these days. That's probably a statement we will continue making for another 10 years or so, if we ever even stop to think about it again. Ten years ago, it was a fairly expensive part of the whole picture. Think about it—in 1989, a 1GB disk drive cost about $2000 to $3000. Ten years before that, about $20,000 to $30,000. Now they don't really even make them anymore, and a 10GB disk can be had for under $200.

In any case, when disk sharing between the platforms first came to light it was to provide the high-capacity storage that came with UNIX servers to low-end Windows PCs, which came with only floppy drives or 20MB hard drives. Users could then store their data files on a central file server that had the storage capacity, and system administrators could then manage all the user storage from one server. Today, with the price of drive storage so low, users can pretty much store all their data for years on a single local drive. However, that second benefit to system administrators—centrally managing storage—is still around and still significant.

The modern way of disk sharing is to keep a local hard drive that stores the operating system and some local data, while most applications and per-user data is stored on large high-reliability volumes on network file servers. These network volumes provide high reliability using technology such as redundant arrays of independent disks (RAIDs) and enhanced data availability and protection (EDAP) and are attached directly to the servers through storage area network (SAN) and network-attached storage (NAS) systems. In turn, these are tied to carefully groomed storage backup systems for long-term or crash-recovery storage. Basically, this all means that the things that most people rely on, such as having their data available at all times, and those they are apt to forget (or are too plain darn lazy to do) such as backing up data, are handled for them by the system administration crew, or even the automated computer systems themselves.

This, however, does not solve the very basic problem of allowing a Windows PC to access the contents of a UNIX server drive or vice versa. To get there, we can look at the three most common methods used for this: sharing a volume as a UNIX file system, sharing a volume as a Windows file system, or transferring files one at a time between both machines. These methods use some well-known protocols, such as the Network File System (NFS), the Windows Common Internet File System (CIFS), and the File Transfer Protocol (FTP). There are other ways of achieving the same effect, but these are the most popular.

Network File Sharing

Network file sharing provides a means of storing files on one machine and allowing other client machines to access those files over the network. File sharing can work either on the level of an entire file system or on a per-directory basis. Typically, file sharing is not done on an individual file basis since this is not very efficient over a network. For example, the Hypertext Transfer Protocol (HTTP), used for accessing files over the Web, is a terribly inefficient system that requires users to download an entire document before they can view it or work with it. Other protocols, like NFS, allow the user to retrieve only the needed portions of a file at a time, saving a lot of network bandwidth and user time.

As with most other client/server systems, the machine that contains the file system or drive is known as the *network file-sharing server*, and the machine accessing this file system or drive is known as a *file-sharing client*. The file server shares or *exports* or advertises its file system or drive as a *volume* on the network to a client, and the client browses the network for shared or exported volumes to *mount* or attach locally. A machine can be both a file-sharing client and a server, but typically it does not export the same file system that it mounts from another machine.

On Windows systems, a mounted network volume appears as additional drive devices. In addition to local drives C:, D:, and so on, you also see other drives F:, G:, and so on. The Windows client uses these files just as if they were on a physical drive attached locally. All the same function calls for accessing files work, although in reality they are being rerouted over the network to a server. The drives do exhibit some of the shortcomings of networks, however, in that file access to network volumes is typically much slower and susceptible to broken connections with the remote server. The client software simply responds with a failed access report or, worse, if written improperly, locks up the client system.

With network drives being shared, there is often a case in which multiple client systems must access the same volume. With such a resource contention problem, the file server system needs to implement a locking mechanism so that multiple users do not try to modify the same file at the same time on the volume. This sort of file-locking mechanism is implemented on most file systems on multiuser systems but introduces the additional problem of remote connections and network delays.

Typically, most clients keep their operating systems on a local physical drive since they need fast access to them; the user data is stored on the network server. However, some products take network file sharing to the extreme by allowing clients to store not only their user data on a network server but also their operating system. These clients essentially need not have a local physical drive at all, and boot their operating system and access all their data from the network server. Under the NFS system, a client machine that stores all user data on a network server is often called a *dataless client*. A machine that mounts its operating system and user data from a network server is called a *diskless client*. In more recent times, this kind of client has been referred to as a *network client* or a *network computer*.

The benefit of network file sharing is that you can locate storage on a central server. Network file sharing was a necessity originally to save on the cost of large-capacity disk-drive systems. Since the price of disk storage is no longer a worry, the other side of network file sharing—the security, reliability, and manageability of locating data on central servers—has become more important. At the same time, the network clients are dependent upon the server for their data storage. Should the server fail, all users may be left in limbo until it is fixed. However, this is less of a hassle than running around trying to fix problems on individual machines that could potentially be spread across multiple buildings or locations.

The (PC)NFS System

(PC)NFS implements the NFS protocol on top of UDP/IP or TCP/IP on Windows PC system. To use NFS sharing, each PC has to have a TCP/IP protocol stack and an NFS client stack, neither of which was native to the Windows networking environment. At one time, a small group of companies such as FTP Software, NetManage, and Beame & Whiteside had a very profitable business selling such stacks for several hundred dollars per Windows machine. Microsoft then offered Windows for Workgroups at a higher price that included a basic TCP/IP stack. Since Windows 95, the TCP/IP protocol stack has become a standard part of the operating system. Unfortunately, Microsoft kept its older NetBIOS file-sharing mechanism, and thus NFS is still a third-party product that has to be added to your Windows machine for remote mounting of UNIX file systems and printers.

(PC)NFS implements an NFS client on a Windows system so that it can browse the network for shared NFS drives and mount them. First of all, its name is spelled with the parentheses to differentiate the product category (an NFS client for PCs) from a specific product from Sun Microsystems called *PC-NFS* (which, incidentally, originated the category). It's simply a politically correct way of referring to it in writing.

The difference between a (PC)NFS client and a standard UNIX NFS client is that the former also implements a second protocol for communicating with the server. This protocol is used for authenticating users on PC clients, which do not normally have password files like those on UNIX systems, and for controlling and sending print jobs. Hence, on the server, you have to run not only NFS server daemons (often showing on the process table as *nfsiod* or *biod*) but also (PC)NFS server daemons (shown as *pcnfsd* or *in.pcnfsd*). This additional daemon process maps PC user accounts and passwords to those in */etc/passwd* and */etc/group*. It uses this information to check remote file system access rights.

(PC)NFS is purely a client-side software for accessing remote UNIX drives. For a UNIX system to mount a PC drive you need the reverse, an NFS server for the PC. Since this is a function of a file server, NFS server products for Windows machines come at a higher price.

(PC)NFS Packages

Chapter 9 discusses the beginnings and present implementation of (PC)NFS. We will now look at actual applications and packages that provide (PC)NFS services. From the point of view of Windows, this means introducing a foreign file system, or at least a translation between the two, which is what (PC)NFS provides.

Some of the leading (PC)NFS packages include Sun PC-NFS, Microsoft NT Services for UNIX (SFU), NetManage Chameleon UNIXLink, and Hummingbird Maestro NFS. The first one is a client package; the next two have both client and server packages; and the last one comes in client, server, and gateway packages, with which a single NT server can mount NFS volumes and then reexport them as Windows volumes to PC clients. We look at MS NT SFU and Hummingbird Maestro in particular here.

From the client standpoint, the software installed on the PC allows it to mount a UNIX NFS exported volume. Keep in mind that the UNIX NFS server has to have a (PC)NFS server running, as described in Chapter 9. An NFS server for PCs, on the other hand, allows the PC to export its local drives to UNIX machines on the network using NFS [and not (PC)NFS].

Hummingbird is the leading vendor of PC-X and (PC)NFS software, through its Exceed and NFS Maestro product lines, respectively. Chapter 15 looks at Exceed but for now we put NFS Maestro into action. NFS Maestro is actually an amalgamation of products. It contains common TCP/IP client applications such as Telnet, FTP, Finger, and Mail but also provides server applications for these same services. On the file-sharing front, it provides NFS client and server software. NFS Maestro Client supports all the TCP/IP client and server applications but also includes a (PC)NFS client. NFS Maestro Server does the same except with an NFS server. Finally, NFS Maestro Gateway acts as a proxy service between the NFS and SMB protocols, allowing any client PC to mount NFS exported volumes without needing to have NFS software on itself.

Microsoft licensed a group of products from Intergraph and Mortice Kern Systems to create its product, NT Services for UNIX.

Cruising the Network and Picking Up NFS Volumes

Browsing the network for NFS volumes is very much like mounting any Windows network drive. You start **Explorer**, then go to **My Network Places**, **Entire Network**, **NFS Network**, and look through the domains or workgroups that the machine is part of.

To mount the drive, right click and select **Map Network Drive**. If you happen to know exactly where it is located, you can simply click on the **Tools** menu in Explorer and select **Map Network Drive**. With Hummingbird NFS Maestro, you can go through the same procedure and accept all the default settings or use the **NFS Network Access** application to mount the drive with specific NFS settings (see Figure 13.1).

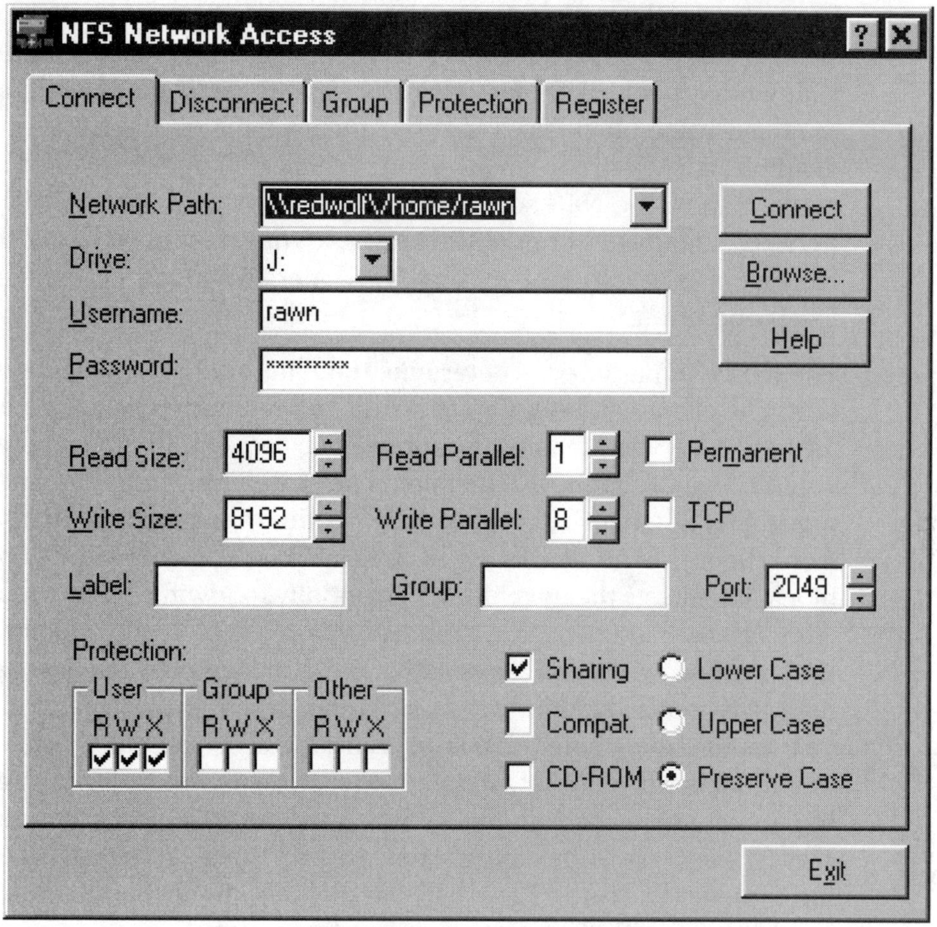

Figure 13.1 Mounting an NFS volume with Hummingbird NFS Maestro.

NFS Network Access shows a number of simple and advanced NFS options that you may or may not be familiar with. At the very top it shows the network path of the remote NFS volume, followed by the drive letter that it should be assigned to and the username and password to use to connect to the volume. The two parameters *Read Size* and *Write Size* indicate the maximum packet size (headers and payload) for each NFS read and write operation. The smallest this can be is 512 bytes, and the largest, 32KB. The default sizes are 4KB for read and 8KB for write operations. The lower the read size, the smoother the download of data from the file server; the higher the read size, the less overhead for the network, but processing is often slower. The same goes for write operations. The larger the write size, the more that can be delivered with less overhead, but the slower the operation. Writing itself is usually slower than read operations as it is, so having a larger size does not slow it down as much. You may wish to resize these if you have particular read and write block sizes for your file systems on the NFS server; for example, a RAID drive can have settings for read and write blocks which could map to the NFS server block sizes. However, since RAID operations are local and not over the network, they should be larger than the NFS block sizes so that several NFS operations can be executed per RAID operation.

The next two parameters determine the *read and write parallelism* factors. The client can be set up to send read and write operations in parallel to the server. Reading is normally a sequential event for an NFS volume, even though NFS maintains no state information. A single read request to a network server usually results in a stream of data coming from the server in blocks up to 32KB. When it reaches the end of the block, it requests the next block sequentially following. Thus, a read operation is mostly sequential. A write operation can be sequential or random. For example, when you are editing a file, small autosave updates are normally just nonsequential writes, although when you decide to save and exit the file, the whole thing is written to disk sequentially. Since a write operation is slower, it is normally better to send several write operations in parallel and leave it to the server to arrange the operations as necessary. The server can best decide how to write the data to disk based on its file system structure. The Read Parallel and Write Parallel options go hand in hand with the read and write block sizes.

NFS Maestro allows users to select if they want to run the NFS protocol over TCP rather than the default UDP transport protocol. UDP works well within the LAN environment since it is also stateless like NFS and requires much less overhead to maintain. TCP is more reliable and is appropriate for larger campus networks or WANs.

The option called *Permanent* simply indicates that this drive is to be mounted every time the system is booted. The *Label* field allows you to define a name label for the network drive, which is sometimes required for compatibility with DOS or Windows disk management applications. The *Group* field defines the default group that any files created will belong to. The *Port* field indicates the default port to look for a NFS server on the remote system. The *Protection* field should be familiar to UNIX sysadmins as the default file permissions (reverse of the umask).

There are other fields to indicate filename preservation, whether the system should use DOS sharing function calls, which lock manager it should use (the proprietary hclnfsd or the default rpc.lockd), and whether the drive is a CD-ROM device.

With NT Services for UNIX, the process is fairly similar. You can either browse the network for NFS volumes or use the Show Mounts tool to examine shared drives on particular servers. The tool works exactly like the **showmount** command on any UNIX system, except that it is presented in a little Windows application. The three options **-a**, **-d**, and **-e** display the NFS clients that have mounted the volumes exported by that server, the exported volumes that have been mounted, and the volumes that are being exported by the server, respectively.

Disconnecting from a drive is done through the Windows Explorer or the tools supplied by the vendors. You select the drive and click on *Disconnect*. It can't be any simpler.

Putting Out an NFS Volume

NT Services for UNIX also allow your NT servers to export drives as NFS volumes on the network. There are two components associated with this, the DiskShare Configuration tool and the User/Group Mapping Configuration tool. The first tool defines how drives are to be exported and the associated parameters. The tool is basically a dialog box with five tabs for **Share Options**, **Server Options**, **NFS Client Groups**, **NFS File Locking**, and **Security Permissions**.

Windows NetBIOS Disk Sharing

NetBIOS over NetBEUI or TCP is still one of the primary protocols used for Windows file sharing. As indicated in Chapter 4, it was the basis of Microsoft's LAN Manager system for file sharing and printing and is still used within Windows 2000.

NetBIOS and LAN Manager sharing are a peer-to-peer system that uses computer names to identify a shared resource. Unlike the Domain Name System, this is fairly nonhierarchical, with only one level of grouping—that of *workgroups* or *domains*, which all computers are equal members of. When a computer needs to locate a resource, it broadcasts the request to all other machines within its workgroup, using the mailslot IPC mechanism, until one machine responds. The remote machine then checks its internal settings to see if any network client is allowed access to the resource; it does not keep records of separate network user accounts or passwords, only whether they are allowed access and the access password.

Under LAN Manager this was improved partially by keeping a static table of mapping between a NetBIOS name and its machine address. The LAN Manager server indicates to the requesting client which machine to look for. In addition, the LAN Manager server can keep an account and password list for all users within a particular domain or workgroup. This same system exists in the NT domain model, where domain controllers serve the role of the LAN Manager server.

Under the Windows 2000 Active Directory domain model, some of this has changed. In particular, the hierarchical system of DNS now better serves the partitioning of computers on a network. Also, rather than broadcasting a request, the client now asks the nearest Active Directory server for the mapping information. The user account information is no longer just by the one-level hierarchy of NT domains, and access to resources can have a per-user or per-group ACL.

Once the remote machine has been mapped, the client machine accesses the full path to a particular file. When the client mounts a remote network drive, it keeps an internal table mapping all calls to files on that network drive volume to its full NetBIOS path. For example, on a network drive F:, a call to file *myfile.txt* actually translates from F:\directory\myfile.txt to the full NetBIOS name \\OtherComputer\F\directory\myfile.txt. All accesses to that file are sent over an established NetBIOS session between the two computers.

In spite of the better resource access and account administration features of Active Directory, Win 2000 still uses NetBIOS sessions to transfer data between machines. On a nonprogramming level, there is no significant advantage to using NetBIOS instead of Windows Sockets, but the latter provides a protocol-neutral system that is more powerful. Getting more programmers to use Winsock will help standardize applications development on more modern networking systems.

Windows Common Internet File System

The Windows Common Internet File System (CIFS) protocol provides the means for current Windows desktops to share drives over the network. It is now built into all the versions of Windows, so there is always the ability to share drives. CIFS is actually a fancy name for the same SMB-based file sharing that was introduced with LAN Manager.

Windows can share both drives or folders within drives with other hosts, if sharing is enabled for the system. This is a property that is set in the *Network and Dial-up Connections* control panel. For each network interface you can assign different network protocols. To provide CIFS services, you must have NetBIOS or TCP/IP installed as a network protocol, and you must also have the *File and Printer Sharing for Microsoft Networks* service protocol installed.

The procedures for mounting and unmounting drives or directories is identical, so we just take a look at one side here. To mount a drive over an SMB/CIFS session, you launch the Windows Explorer, go to the icon **My Network Places**, then into **Entire Network**, and look for the remote machine that is exporting the drive either under the domain or in **Microsoft Windows Networks**. When you find the remote machine, click on it, and it will show all volumes that it shares or exports. At this point you can either open the volume up within an Explorer window or mount the network drive to a local drive letter. To mount the drive, right-click on the network volume and select **Map Network Drive**. By default, it will attempt to remount this volume each time you log in, which you can select with an option. It also uses the next available alphabetic character to assign the drive letter for the device. You can also use a different user name to connect to the remote drive, if the remote machine does not recognize your current user and password on your local machine. This will create a new drive letter that you can see under **My Computer** in Explorer.

While mounted the drive can be used as any other local disk volume that you have permissions to. If the network volume is exported as providing per-user share level access, then only those folders that your user account owns can be manipulated. This per-user sharing is based on your account in the domain. If it is exported read-only, it cannot be modified by anyone.

To unmount the drive simply go to Explorer, look under **My Computer** for the network-mounted volume (it will say something like *NetVolumeName on 'RemoteMachine'*), right-click on it, and select the **Disconnect** option.

Exporting a volume to be shared through CIFS differs depending on the Windows system you use. Right-clicking on a folder or drive in Explorer and selecting the **Sharing** option will bring up this feature.

On Win 9x machines, the system simply asks for the *sname, comment* or description, the *share access type*, and any *passwords*. The share name is a short description of the drive that defaults to the drive letter for the device on that machine. It can be up to 14 characters long. The comment provides a slot to enter a brief description about the drive. The access type comes in two forms, *read-only* and *full*. The former allows remote machines to mount the volume and see the files not to change any of the contents. The latter allows full manipulation of the contents based on a valid user account for the domain. You can also specify passwords for each of these share access types that are used only for network volume mounting.

Sharing on NT and Win 2000 systems is slightly different. The system still asks for a share name and comment, but allows you to define a limit on the number of users who are allowed to connect, and allows you to define caching behavior for the contents of the volume. The access restrictions are also based on NT security identifiers and provide an access control list of who is allowed to connect to the remote machine. As with all ACLs on NT, you can change who is allowed to access the service by selecting user names and icons.

Windows 2000 Distributed File System

The new Distributed File System (DFS) under Windows 2000 now brings the ability to create a single file tree from separate volumes on the network. Similar to NFS, this allows one or more servers to mount network volumes into a tree hierarchy that they have specified and then export this entire tree to remote clients.

DFS client software is available for Win 9x and NT 4 systems. NT 4 machines can also install a DFS server component so that they can participate as DFS file servers on the network. However, they cannot take full advantage of DFS since it requires volumes that are formatted in the new NTFS 5 version, which is not available for NT 4 yet. Unfortunately, this DFS has very little in common with the DFS in the System V version of UNIX. Aside from the name and concept similarity, the protocols are completely incompatible.

DFS relies on the Domain Name System and Active Directory to locate and communicate with multiple file servers. It brings together all the storage from various sources on the network and creates a single tree (see Figure 13.2) that is advertised by Active Directory, from which it can then be accessed by remote clients. User applications can thus refer

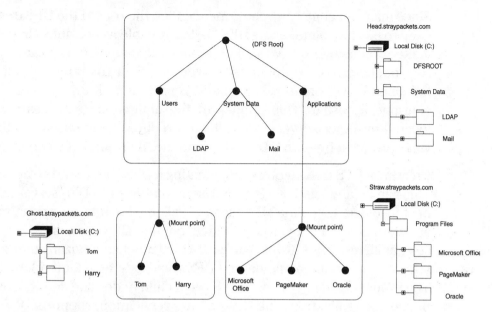

Figure 13.2 A Distributed File System tree.

to the same storage location for a file or directory irrespective of the machine they are logged into. This solves a lot of trouble for sysadmins when they need to assign every client desktop to mount a network volume to the same drive letter. Since there aren't any drive letters any more, it becomes irrelevant. All locations within the DFS tree point to the same location, even if the actual underlying structure has been rearranged and the data contents have been moved to a different server. This allows sysadmins to adjust the topology of the network file sharing system independently of how users access files.

Building a DFS tree, like designing an Active Directory service, requires some forethought. You can take the simple approach of storing all contents onto one server and exporting this file tree to the clients. A more nontrivial scenario involves several child nodes running on separate servers that connect to the DFS tree, as shown in Figure 13.2. You can see that mapping a DFS tree from the local file system on each server does not have to match the hierarchy of directories within the drives. For example, the Applications node in the DFS tree attaches to the Program Files subdirectory on the server straw.straypackets.com, while the directories Tom and Harry on ghost.straypackets.com map independently under the Users node on the main tree.

Since many machines may be dependent on the root of the DFS tree, you need to be able to make this DFS host as reliable as possible. Or, you can make it fault tolerant. Win 2000 provides this service by balancing the root node across multiple host servers for fault tolerance. Should one fail, another will take over as the DFS root, and all drive accesses will continue as usual. This applies to the child node subtrees that are located on other servers, as well. DFS replication is based on the services provided by Active Directory and the file-replication service.

Creating a DFS tree involves first creating a DFS root node on one server. This can be any Win 2000 Server system that has the DFS server component installed. Using the MMC snap-in called *DFS Manager*, you first create the root node by right-clicking on the DFS icon in MMC, then selecting **New DFS Root Volume**. This launches a wizard that asks if you want to create a standalone DFS root node or a fault-tolerant one. The former is limited to only one level of child nodes and does not use AD or provide replication. The latter allows replication, supports DNS naming, and works with AD. The wizard then follows through to select the domain and the host, and to create the root node and the shared directory or drive in which the DFS root will be located. You then right-click on the DFS icon again and select **Connect to DFS Root Node** to attach control to the appropriate DFS tree; you can, after all, have a number of separate DFS trees within your domain to serve different user needs.

To add child nodes to the tree, right-click on the connected DFS root node and select **New DFS Child Node**. You can then either browse the network for a shared volume to add or enter the drive path name to a new volume to share.

To replicate any node, select the node icon, then right-click and select the **New DFS Replica Member** option. You can then either browse the network for an existing share or create a new one. Once the share is selected, you must then right-click and select **Join Replication**, which begins the process of replicating the contents of the share.

Clients connect to the DFS tree using the same methods described in the preceding section on Windows CIFS network file sharing.

Windows CIFS on UNIX with Samba

The Samba NetBIOS file- and print-sharing system for UNIX servers is configured in the *sbm.conf* file. A Web-based interface to configure this file, known as *swat*, is also available. The file is divided into sections for each shared object, succinctly referred to as *shares*, and three special sections for all objects. A section begins with the name of the share in brackets, followed by the options describing the behavior of the share. The three special sections labeled *[global]*, *[homes]*, and *[printers]* define the behavior for all shares, all user disk shares, and all printer shares, respectively.

Figure 13.3 gives an example of what the smb.conf file may look like. It illustrates only handful of options. A full list describing all options can be seen in the *smb.conf(5)* man page. It begins with a disk share called *[rawndata]* that can be mounted only by certain hosts, as the user account *rawn*. The second section, called *[hplaser]*, defines a printer share that is accessible by all hosts except those named as *bohr* and *ein-*

```
[rawndata]
        comment = Rawn's Data directory
        path = /home2/rawn/data
        writeable = true
        allow hosts = localhost, feynman, 192.168.0.0/255.255.0.0
        user = rawn

[hplaser]
        path = /var/spool/lp/hplaser
        read only = true
        printable = true
        deny hosts = bohr, einstein
        guest ok = true

[global]
        workgroup = GENIUSES
        case sensitive = yes
        change notify timeout = 180
        create mask = 0744
        deny hosts = firewall, crashbox2

[homes]
        writeable = yes

[printers]
        path = /var/spool/lp
        writeable = no
        printable = yes
        guest ok = yes
```

Figure 13.3 A sample Samba smb.conf configuration file.

stein. The three special sections then follow. The *[global]* section indicates that this server is part of the workgroup *GENIUSES*; it is always to use case-sensitive filenames; any changes to the sharing will be exported to other machines every 3 minutes; any file that is created will have a basic umask of 744; and the two machines named *firewall* and *crash-box2* will be disallowed all access. The *[homes]* section indicates that any valid user account on the UNIX system can be used to mount home directories from Windows clients. The *[printers]* section indicates that all printers that this UNIX host is aware of (configured in the /etc/printcap file) will be exported to the Windows machines.

Windows CIFS with Syntax TotalNet Advanced Server

Syntax Inc.'s TotalNet Advanced Server (TAS) product implements a NetBIOS file-sharing system for several different UNIX systems (Solaris, AIX, IRIX, and HP-UX), in addition to other protocols such as NetWare and AppleTalk file sharing. TAS implements a NetBIOS stack on top of the TCP/IP protocol and implements the necessary parts of CIFS to perform file and printer sharing. For a full description of the product please read *NT Domain Services on UNIX* in Chapter 12.

TAS's Web-site approach to administrating applications makes it simple to export volumes from the UNIX server. After logging on to the TAS administration site, you simply go to CIFS Realm and click on Manage CIFS File Services. This brings up a form page requesting the various parameters for the file service. You enter a 15-character name for the file service, pick the type of NetBIOS transport protocol to use, and pick the UNIX volume to be exported. There are a number of other parameters that map behavior of the file system across the platforms. You can predefine a umask, indicating how the user permissions on each newly created file are to be set.

Storage Area Networks and Network-Attached Storage

Storage area networks (SANs) and network-attached storage (NAS) are the next generation of storage systems for enterprise servers. Both are similar in concept, differing only in how they attach to servers. A SAN is a private network that is solely dedicated to storage system units and that runs storage communication protocols such as Fibre-Channel. They attach directly to servers through a storage controller card and can usually connect to more than one server at a time. In fact, Fibre-Channel switches and smart storage controllers now allow groups of servers to connect to multitudes of SAN storage units.

Network-attached storage, on the other hand, has a complete storage system directly connecting to the server's LAN network and communicates with various servers using network file-sharing protocols such as NFS or CIFS. NAS systems are simpler in design and are actually an evolution of the ordinary file server. Most modern NAS systems have their own specialized operating system that is optimized for file and disk activity only. Some even have specialized native file system formats that are optimized for working over networks. Since they connect to standard LAN networks such as Ethernet, there is no need for an expensive storage controller, only the standard Ethernet NIC the server already has. Table 13.1 compares the similarities and differences between SAN- and NAS-based systems.

Figure 13.4 shows the two systems running in an enterprise network. Both types of advanced network storage are available for NT systems. SANs are available using either SCSI or Fibre-Channel, although the latter is more popular since it can support a much larger number of storage devices and supports faster network interfaces that can go over longer distances using optical fibers.

Each SAN has a controller, switches or hubs, and one or more storage units, most of which can be purchased as separate units. A NAS system also has similar components, but they are normally all part of the same package offered by the vendor and not separate units. Within each storage unit, whether in a SAN or a NAS, you can have several sets or racks of storage subsystems. Each of these subsystems can be connected to its own internal controller, and each contains a number of individual, usually hot-swappable, disk drives. Several racks and their internal controllers then connect to the external controller interfaces, which eventually go out to the servers.

The servers can connect directly to the storage units but normally go through a switch or a hub. This allows the servers to communicate with multiple storage units using the same controller. A Fibre-Channel SAN switch works very much like an Ethernet switch; however, instead of Ethernet packets, it directs channels of traffic using Fibre-Channel com-

Table 13.1 Comparison of SAN- and NAS-Based Systems

SAN	NAS
Large storage capacities (in the terabyte range).	Large storage capacities (in the terabyte range).
Storage system may have internal RAID.	Storage system may have internal RAID.
Supports hot-swap disks.	Supports hot-swap disks.
Provides access to multiple servers.	Provides access to multiple servers.
Can be a hierarchical storage system with tapes, optical drives, etc.	Can be a hierarchical storage system with tapes, optical drives, etc.
Can have hubs, switches, and routers between storage system and host connection (with SCSI or FC).	Can have hubs, switches, and routers between storage system and host connection (with Ethernet, WAN lines, etc.).
Can provide failover at storage system level.	Can provide failover at storage system level.
Can provide failover at switch/router level.	Can provide failover at switch/router level with some networks.
Can provide failover at host bus adapter level.	Can provide failover at host bus adapter level with some cards.
Can provide high-bandwidth connections (up to 2Gbps in duplex Fibre Channel).	Can provide high-bandwidth connections (up to 1 Gbps in Gigabit Ethernet).
Each connection is dedicated per host (a full 2 Gbps to a host).	Each connection is not normally dedicated to a host (1 Gbps is shared between hosts).
Requires host bus adapter card for connection (expensive).	Requires LAN network card for connection (cheaper).
Host bus adapter is intelligent and has large onboard cache (smarter and faster processing).	LAN adapter is simple and usually has no significant onboard RAM (not so smart).
Low overhead storage system communications protocol (SCSI or FC).	High overhead network and application protocols (NFS or CIFS over UDP or TCP over IP).
Always on separate storage network (no unnecessary network traffic).	Can be on same network as hosts or on separate private network (can have unnecessary network traffic).
Does not really have an internal operating system (less overhead).	Has its own internal operating system (more overhead but possibly smarter operation).
Does not have its own internal file systems (file system is host dependent).	Has its own internal file system (file system is NAS dependent).
Software security dependent upon host.	Internal software and system security.
High overhead to connect additional servers.	Low overhead to connect additional servers.

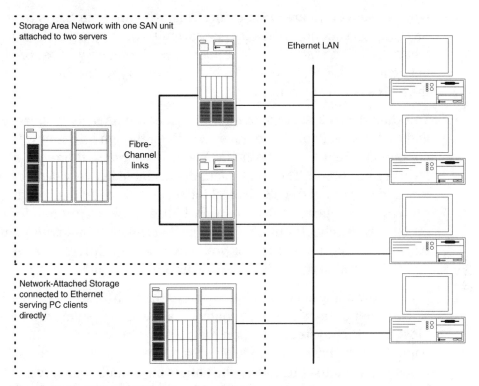

Figure 13.4 SAN and NAS systems in action.

munication standards. A hub is a shared network, while switches allow direct one-to-one communications independently of other connected devices.

Leading NAS vendors include Network Appliance, Inc. and Auspex, Inc. Both provide proprietary implementations intended for the high end of the storage market, although Network Appliance also caters to medium-sized networks and storage needs. Almost all the major PC and UNIX server vendors now offer a SAN product line, but the leader of the pack is still EMC, a company dedicated to high-end storage needs.

What to Look for in SANs and NASs

If you are contemplating whether you should get a SAN or NAS system, there are some things you should be aware of first. SANs involve direct connections to server platforms and often are specific to the server operating system. Even though the actual storage mechanism is independent of the server OS type, the storage management tools and network drivers often are OS specific. This can limit your SANs to your PC or UNIX servers only. Check very carefully with your SAN vendors on what operating systems they support *simultaneously*. Most SAN products can support different OSs, but only one type can be connected to the SAN system at a time.

You should check the type of interfaces that the SAN controllers support and that are available in your servers. Even though PCI is now the most common system bus in both UNIX and PC servers, there are different levels of PCI buses. The most common available in every desktop and in low-end servers is the 33 MHz 32-bit bus. Most midrange and high-end servers can support 33 MHz 64-bit PCI buses now (for more information on bus types, check out Chapter 8). Check which bus type your controller card is intended for, or you may see very different results from your SAN system than what is advertised by the vendor.

Check how many servers can connect to the SAN units at a time. This is often a limit of the number of controllers the SAN system will recognize. Most PC SAN systems support only two server nodes. This is good enough for the basic two-node Microsoft Cluster Server systems, but not when you want to consolidate the data from a number of servers. Also, if you are using any kind of clustering between your servers, check if your SAN system supports the data-sharing needs of the cluster system.

Finally, check the administrative tools that come with the SAN package. They should be able to configure different sets of drives into volumes that can be mounted by individual servers. The best tools are able to configure individual drives as separate volumes and pick and choose any collection of drives to be configured as a RAID volume. The tool should also have performance profiling features that examine the transfer statistics across the SAN at each connection point. This allows you to analyze the behavior of the storage traffic and reorganize it for better performance, if need be.

If you prefer using NAS systems, you can avoid many of the issues involving controllers that SANs have. However, expect lower performance because there are several layers of protocol information added to each packet. Look for NASs that support the fastest connections, such as Gigabit Ethernet or ATM. Almost all products these days support 100-Mbps Fast Ethernet. As with SANs, look for management tools that monitor and record performance behavior to help you improve the system.

Network Printer Sharing

Although disk storage is so cheap these days, the cost of fast printers is still high. Even with lowered prices, heavily used printers need a lot of technical and physical management. Hence, network printing has become a very common part of most organizations. Unlike earlier times, when network printers were fairly high-end devices connected to a large server, the printers of today come in a range of sizes, down to small 8 page-per-minute network printers.

All network printers need several features. They have to have a protocol stack and server system that communicates with the print client. They have to be able to store or spool and manage print jobs sent by multiple users and clients. They have to be manageable from elsewhere on the network. Depending on the network printing system, these features may be implemented within one device (the printer itself) or on multiple devices and machines.

A printer can have its own physical network connection, typically in the form of an Ethernet port, or it can be directly connected to a print server machine through a serial or parallel port connection. The print server, in this case, acts as a proxy for the printer by providing the Ethernet port and protocol stack. Most network printers with their own physical network port implement their own protocol stack with the device.

The job of the print spooler is to store print jobs until the printer can physically print them out. Since even the fastest printers take several seconds to print a document, compared to the milliseconds it takes to transfer the document to the printer, you need a temporary area to store the print jobs until the printer is ready. The print spooler that serves this purpose can be physically located within the printer, either in the form of a small internal disk drive or lots and lots of RAM, or it can be elsewhere on the work. Depending on the workload, a print spooler may need more storage space than that available in a printer's memory. Often it is possible to fill a printer with enough RAM to serve this purpose, but it is simply much cheaper to use disk drives.

Network printers, either within themselves or on a print server, can implement multiple network printing protocols. For example, a network printer can support UNIX lpr printing, Windows NetBIOS printing, AppleTalk printing, and so forth all in the same device. Each protocol has to be configured appropriately, and the printer has to be advertised on the network to the proper machines. Since the print spooler is responsible for accepting jobs, the network printing protocol is most often implemented where the spooler is.

Printers require a lot of attention. On a daily basis, you get paper jams, printing errors, print protocol errors, lost jobs, stuck print spoolers, and so forth, some of which can be fixed over the network, while others require direct hands-on operation. The UNIX lpstat or lpc commands can be used to perform some basic administrative tasks like stopping print jobs or resetting the print spooler. Whatever the protocol, most network printers have their own proprietary administrative tools that are particular to the printer and offer the full set of tasks that can be performed on it.

SMB Printer Sharing

Locally attached or network printers can be shared across the network among Windows machines. Windows server systems can export to the network the services of printers that are directly attached via serial or parallel cables. Printers that have their own network interface can directly export their services to clients but are normally assigned through a Windows server to provide better print management services.

From the **Start Menu**, go to **Settings** and then **Printers** to bring up the list of all local and network printers attached to the NT or Win 2000 system. Clicking on the **Add a New Printer** wizard, you must first define whether it is a local or network printer. A network printer can be attached using NetBIOS or the Internet Printing Protocol.

Under NT and Win 2000, printers can be strictly controlled as to who can access them and when. Win 9x machines support only a password mechanism that allows anyone with access to print any size job at any time. Thus, if you have locally connected printers on Win 9x machines that you want to share, it is better to export them first to an NT machine and then to the rest of the network. Assign the Win 9x printer a password that only the NT machine and sysadmins know, so that no one else on the network can directly access the printer.

(PC)NFS Printer Sharing

Printing is not a standard part of the NFS protocol. In fact, most UNIX systems use a separate protocol for sending remote print jobs, commonly through the *lp* or *lpr* command. However, since the ability to print from a PC to a UNIX network printer was such a highly demanded feature, they put it into the (PC)NFS protocol through some clever trickery.

(PC)NFS allows the PC to redirect print jobs normally sent to an LPT: port on the PC over the network to a UNIX printer. On the PC, the LPT: port is redirected to a file, so that when you attempt to print a document, it outputs the printer-ready version of the document (in Postscript, HPGL, etc.) directly into a file. With (PC)NFS, this file just happens to be sitting on a network-mounted volume on the UNIX server. What's more, the volume is actually the LPD server's queue for print jobs. The (PC)NFS software then signals LPD through the *pcnfsd* to print out the document.

All this is smooth and requires only that you export the file-spooling directory (e.g., /var/spool/lpd) on the UNIX server to the clients that intend to use the (PC)NFS-LPD system, and configure the pcnfsd server with the printing options necessary for using that printer. On the PC side, you need to indicate, through the (PC)NFS software, which UNIX server will house the network printer. Normally, you go through the same process of defining a local printer (not a network printer) for Windows described earlier. When you reach the point of picking the port, you must select the LPTn: port device that maps to the (PC)NFS package.

Using separate IP-based LPQ and LPRM tools that come with the (PC)NFS package, you can check the status of the print queue, and remove any print jobs as necessary.

Internet Printing Protocol

Windows 2000 is one of the few major platforms that supports the new Internet Printing Protocol (IPP). This system is intended to replace the aging LPD method commonly used in IP-based network printing. IPP restructures the system of how print jobs are created, rendered, distributed, logged, controlled, and output. IPP does not change the actual printing language such as PostScript, Printer Control Language (PCL), or Hewlett-Packard Graphics Language (HPGL), but rather the methods of how printing is handled.

Cross-Platform Backups

System backups are an important part of any system administrator's job. Its importance is often underemphasized due simply to unfounded optimism on the part of many administrators. The moment your disk crashes, however, you will be rushing for the backup tapes.

Most backup systems are specific to a file system or operating system type. Although simple tools like *tar* allow you to dump a file system to tape, they do not provide an adequate tracking mechanism for managing your backups. Cross-platform backups are complicated by the fact that the file systems are often very different. Furthermore, even the byte ordering of individual files may be different between the platforms. This means that you cannot simply copy all the files from one platform to another and do the backups on the second machine. Not only is this fairly inefficient, it can cause file error problems that you may not be aware of.

You have two options in a UNIX-Windows environment. You can create a backup system in which all the information goes onto one of the platforms, or you can deploy separate backup systems for each platform. Try to avoid the second option, since the whole point of integration is to not have to create such separate systems.

Of the commercial cross-platform backup packages, two stand out: Computer Associates ARCserveIT and Legato Networker. Both not only provide support for Windows and multiple UNIX platforms, but also feature powerful backup management and monitoring tools, and support a wide range of backup devices and media.

Backups with Hierarchical Storage Management

Hierarchical storage management (HSM) provides a system to maintain terabytes of data storage linked either directly to the server or indirectly over a network. HSM is a near-line storage system, indicating that some of the data is available directly on disk-based storage and other data has to be retrieved from tape.

A high-end HSM system combines all the elements into one device that contains hard-disk-based caches, tape or magneto-optical storage, and a network or direct-connect interface. You basically plunk down one of these units onto your LAN and direct your clients and servers to mount the file systems exported by the HSM unit. These file systems are actually stored on backup media, such as tape or magneto-optical disks, and are mounted with their contents cached to the hard disks so that they can be read and modified faster by the clients. The system automagically transfers this cache back to the media when the volume is idle. The disk system is much more responsive than slower tape media for random read and write operations, but is slower for sequential ones.

The HSM unit can export single or multiple tapes or magneto-optical disks as separate file system volumes. The clients to the HSM system mount these volumes either using native network file-sharing protocols or simply as raw devices directly attached. The transfer time is, of course, slower than that of just pure hard disks, but this method provides a means of storing massive amounts of data—tens or hundreds of terabytes. Such storage capacity directly on hard disks could cost many times more, and the larger pure disk-drive-based storage units can handle only up to around 10TB. In any case, HSM systems are mostly used for archival purposes due to their speed constraints.

It is possible to build an HSM system without such specialized hardware by simply using servers, hard drives, and backup systems. This is exactly the role that products such as Legato Networker and CA ARCserveIT fill. Using software agents running on client machines and an HSM software component running on the server, it is possible to automate the backups of all important data from your client stations directly to the server, and, in the case of these two products, do it independently of the platform or operating system types.

Both packages work very similarly. Each desktop system has a client backup agent installed on it that is configured to connect to the backup server and send data at given intervals. The tools use proprietary protocols to communicate. The server backup agent is configured with a list of all valid clients that require backups, instructions for how the backup rotation schedule is recorded, a search database of all data per backed-up volume to facilitate faster searches and retrievals, and a list of all backup devices that it can use.

Enterprise Storage Management

With data storage ranging in the terabytes in medium to large organizations, simply keeping track of shared volumes, user file access rights, and archived contents becomes an administrative nightmare. For example, if a desktop machine in one of the offices is about to run out of space, it is much easier to handle the problem if you can look up means of expanding its storage capability ahead of time—either by compressing volumes, deleting files, or adding new storage—rather than having an angry user waving and screaming at you. If you scale this problem to hundreds or thousands of desktops, you can understand how useful storage management products can be for the medium to large enterprise.

Storage management products take some of the pain out of keeping track of your total storage across the enterprise. Essentially, they manage the following elements:

- *Storage asset management.* Where storage is located, and what types of devices it uses.

- *Removable media library management.* What is contained in the various archive tapes or other media.

- *Distributed volume or file system management.* How file systems and volumes are created.

- *Network file sharing management.* How volumes are shared between machines.

- *Network user access management.* How users can access the network volumes.

- *Storage troubleshooting.* How to analyze and fix technical problems with storage on any of the managed systems.

- *Reporting, analysis, and planning tools.* How to analyze the behavior and performance of managed storage, and how to plan for increasing capacity.

Companies such as VERITAS (which merged with another leading vendor, Seagate Software), HighGround Systems, IBM, EMC, and Platinum offer products in this category. Most such products may be tied to other storage management tools such as those for HSM or backup management. Such storage management tools work on a cross-platform basis across clients and servers, since most of their function is primarily information management.

Summary

Disk and Printer sharing still form the most basic needs for integrating computing platforms. Although the reasons for this sharing have changed over the years, the need for centralized management of these services remains critical. Windows still supports CIFS as the common sharing system between Windows machines. However, a new, enterprise ready network file system known as DFS will become even more relevant in large networks with lots of shared storage systems.

Windows 2000 supports all the common printing standards for UNIX and Windows systems, as well as new protocols such as IPP. This means that it is now possible to send all printing through a Windows server system regardless of platform type.

Applications on both platforms can take advantage of these shared resources either from the Windows server standpoint or from a UNIX server. With this issue essentially solved, application access stems as the next important integration element, and the subject of the next chapter.

## CHAPTER 14

Integrating Server Applications

When you have different platforms that run almost the same applications, you first have to ask yourselves why, and then you must figure out how to integrate and manage them together. Web servers, for example, should perform the exact same task no matter which Web server software or system platform you run them on. However, each platform has its own slight variances or programming interfaces that have to be handled differently.

Server applications are where multiplatform integration most commonly comes into play. Often you need to run a server application on a particular platform to make use of its features. However, by itself this is not enough, and you need another server application of similar type on a different platform to support it. Again, with our Web server example, you might need a Windows-based Web server to handle all the incoming requests for HTML pages, but a separate e-commerce application that runs on a UNIX system to handle your online store. This takes advantage of the OS and hardware appropriately, using smaller, cheaper Windows boxes to handle the mass of traffic for simple HTML file serving and a larger, more powerful UNIX server to run a database and an online store that interacts with it.

Another example would be e-mail servers. You may need to use an enterprise-strength mail transfer agent such as Innosoft's PMDF mail server to handle the overall incoming corporate mail, but redirect this to smaller mail servers running Exchange on NT within each of the departments. Thus the overall mail rulesets that decide where to send incoming e-mail, how to process it, and what to allow get handled through one enterprise mail switching system, and the end users retrieve their mail from local servers that store their incoming mail passed through the switch.

To integrate server applications you need to consider common standards used in the industry for a given application. Although such standards are intended to work identically irrespective of the system they run on, in reality, the majority of vendors make it such that the standard interface is only a subset of the whole. This gives the impression that their product has a competitive edge in one feature or another. The standard interfaces themselves can sometimes work only through certain programming language interfaces. Thus, in some cases, you also have to learn how to program to get multiplatform server applications to work together.

In this chapter we consider several common server applications and their frameworks and what hurdles must be overcome to create a bridge between different implementations of the application type. We also take a look at some of the common scripting and programming systems available for the platforms that could allow you to build that bridge.

Integrating Server Applications

Integrating server applications is like juggling bowling balls. They are cumbersome, and a wrong step is likely to hurt you bad. Server applications fall into product types that perform similar tasks, but until the last decade or so, most have been fairly proprietary. Thank goodness for the Internet Age. The use of common standards on the Internet was an absolute necessity for the various platforms to work together and this has lessened the difficulties involved in getting server applications to work.

Server applications can be looked at in many ways but are most commonly categorized by the function they fulfill. There are e-mail servers, directory servers, authentication servers, file servers, database servers, and, certainly, Web servers. They all simply process information, but it is how they do it that makes them different.

What's more, server applications usually communicate with given types of client applications. This means of communication can be an openly defined standard or proprietary to a vendor's solution. An openly defined standard usually connotes that any application written to work on that standard should work perfectly with others made likewise. But, unfortunately, this is not 100 percent true all of the time. With Microsoft products this tends to be true much less of the time. Hence, you have to be careful and get hands-on and try to make two server applications work with each other rather than assuming that what they say on the packaging is accurate.

Server Communications

Most server applications these days talk with other clients or servers through *network ports*. A server application leaves a well-known network service port open so that clients can call up that port address and initiate a new session. These ports are usually particular to a network protocol but are usually independent of the operating system or server application type. Thus, a Windows Web server can open the TCP port 80 and wait for Web browser clients running on UNIX, Macs, or other platforms to request pages on that part.

It is these ports that are the fulcrum of communications for servers. They have to be left open or client systems simply will not be able to communicate with them. This means that any client has license to contact the server. Only after the client connects to the port can the server check other credentials to authenticate the server. Since these ports are an open invitation to any client, they constitute a security risk as well.

In client-to-server communications, there isn't any simple way to avoid interacting through open ports. There is sometimes an identification or authentication system built on top of the port so that client connections can be verified or recorded. This added security can then limit the interactions the client has with the server application.

Yet this is a level below the security precautions needed when two servers need to communicate to exchange data. The general premise is that servers only send messages to each other that are vital to their working in a distributed environment, thus server-to-server communications require a higher level of security.

When you use standard interfaces between server applications, you also have to decide upon the level of security in the communications between the servers. You simply don't want any Joe Schmoe server application sending commands to your own servers to execute operations. In some cases this may be harmless, but in almost every case it is still considered a security breach due to inadequate security measures on your part.

The most obvious way is to close off all your servers to a particular sub-network and guard it with a firewall. This prevents applications and users outside that subnet from sending commands to network ports reserved for server-to-server communications. It limits all internal traffic to the subnet as well, preventing others from seeing what commands are being issued between servers.

Multitier Server Systems

When planning to integrate across platforms you will always have a multitier system with at least three tiers: the user desktop tier, the platform A tier, and the platform B tier. In our case, A and B can be Windows and UNIX, or vice versa. With application services, the tiers can break down further, with each tier specializing in one activity or another.

By working in separate tiers it becomes possible to contain and limit problems. The idea is that each tier can be served by multiple servers of near identical setting, and one server can take over the workload of others in case of failures. Furthermore, each tier can be more optimized to its task. For example, with Web or FTP services, an initial tier just before the actual file servers (both FTP and Web are just file serving) could be a system that optimizes the incoming request and network traffic load.

Another way of looking at tiers is regionality. The enterprise is served with one group of application servers that handles the overall system and then passes on the work to smaller regional servers, each assisting a group of users. E-mail services in this way can first pass through the main corporate e-mail server that processes the incoming mail and then hand this mail off to local workgroup e-mail servers that users directly connect to and retrieve their mail from.

E-mail Services

E-mail is one of the earliest and most heavily used applications on networks. Even in this day of the Web, chat rooms, and virtual worlds, e-mail still ranks as one of the most commonly used applications. Although the face of e-mail has changed significantly over the years, most of the Internet still uses a protocol developed almost two decades ago to deliver mail.

In an intranet, proprietary mail protocols have since succumbed to the rampant growth of Internet applications. The dominant mail delivery protocol has thus also become the same as that for the Internet, the Simple Mail Transfer Protocol (SMTP). This allows a common standard for delivering messages between different platforms in a text format. With the development of the Multipurpose Internet Mail Extensions (MIME) system for encoding nontext data into a text format, Internet mail now contains binary documents, images, audio, and even video as attachments to the message.

Message Transfer Agents

The job of the message transfer agent (MTA) is to receive incoming or outgoing mail, process the mail headers, and direct it along the proper path to the destination point. MTAs speak mail protocols, such as SMTP, usually only with other MTAs. Some well-known MTA products include Sendmail on almost every UNIX system, Exchange on Windows, Lotus Mail/CC:Mail on Windows, and PMDF on OpenVMS, UNIX, and Windows.

For every message, there is an associated mail header that defines the source, destination, and intermediary points, as well as the time it was sent, the priority of the message, the content type, and so on. Based upon these mail headers, Internet e-mail is delivered from mail server to mail server. Typically, the MTA will look at the destination address, search for the mail exchanger (MX, really just another name for an MTA) that handles that particular Internet domain, contact the domain, and deliver the message. The Internet mail exchangers can support a single machine, a subdomain, or a whole domain of addresses, and are defined as part of the DNS information for the domain.

Mail Processing Rulesets

In addition to delivery, there may be other preprocessing mail rulesets that can translate or convert the source or destination address information as necessary. It is sometimes necessary to rewrite the source address so as to hide the actual machine it is delivered from. For example, if a user, Joe, sends e-mail from his account on the UNIX server *frosty.atollsw.com*, the MTA might want to rewrite the source address from joe@frosty.atollsw.com to the more simpler joe@atollsw.com. This way, when someone responds to an e-mail from Joe, it will go to the MX or MTA at atollsw.com, which may or may not be running on frosty.atollsw.com. This allows administrators to do various things: The machine frosty.atollsw.com may be allowed to send outbound messages to anyone but only receive incoming messages from the main MX for the domain atollsw.com; the administrator can move the MX service from one machine to another if that server needs to be taken down for maintenance; the administrator can hide the design of the internal network of atollsw.com from the outside world to increase security; or the administrator can concentrate the security on one server that is the sole machine capable of receiving incoming mail.

There can also be rewriting rules for the destination address. For example, Joe is trying to send mail to a list service that maintains a single alias for a whole group of mail addresses. The MTA takes a look at the destination address, recognizes the address as one of its own mail list service aliases, and expands the destination address to all the members of the alias. Thus the mail is delivered to a large group of people; and Joe has to remember only a single e-mail address for the entire list.

When a message is received, it needs to be processed through a common ruleset to determine how the message is to be passed on, which protocol to use, or how to translate the message contents. For example, an MX receives mail for joe@engineering.atollsw.com, indicating that there is a message for Joe Schmoe who works in the engineering department of atollsw.com. The host engineering.atollsw.com may not actually exist at all. It could simply be a DNS alias for a real host called frosty.atollsw.com. In such a case, the MX simply resolves the alias and passes the message on appropriately. On the other hand, joe@engineering.atollsw.com might be another mail exchanger, in which case, the first MX must look up the proper MX that handles the engineering domain, look up how to communicate with it, and then pass the message on to that MX. If the second MX speaks a mail protocol different from SMTP, then the first one has to know how to talk to it in the proper protocol tongue, as well as translate the message format accordingly. The first MX in this respect is acting as a *mail gateway* between the two different mail server protocols. This allows end users to send messages to others without needing to have special software that talks both mail protocols. The gateway handles all conversions as defined within its processing rulesets.

The ability to define complex preprocessing rulesets for e-mail addresses is what defines the power of the MTA. Different divisions in the company may be running different types of mail servers and clients. Some messages may need to be duplicated each time they are received and sent to multiple individuals. Others may need to be converted from text to a word processor document, and so forth. An e-mail service for a large corporation may need hundreds or thousands of such rules for different mail services. Although MTAs cannot be everything to everyone, they need to be extensible so that they can interface with other programs and applications that can handle such conversions as necessary.

End-User Mail Services

There are two commonly used protocols for retrieving e-mail over TCP/IP: the Post Office Protocol (POP, currently in version 3) and the Internet Message Access Protocol (IMAP, currently in version 4). POP, a fairly ancient protocol still in wide use, simply establishes a connection to the mail server, authenticates it based upon the user account on the server, and then downloads all the messages. It does not allow you to check the message headers first before downloading the e-mail, nor can you download only those messages you want. You can either leave all the messages on the server or download all of them and erase them for the server. Thus it is fairly inefficient and rudimentary. Still, POP servers are as common as daisies in a flower shop.

IMAP is a smarter mail download protocol designed for remote or roaming users. Using IMAP, you can select messages, download their headers or the entire message, store the messages on the server or locally, and maintain or manage access to your mailbox from multiple machines. IMAP can also be integrated with directory services such as LDAP to allow you to access or manage your e-mail address books from remote locations. Thus, you don't have to carry around a list of e-mail addresses of your friends; just look them up through the address book.

Web Services

Web information started out on a simple path with just one document definition language and one protocol for communications. Now there are a variety of language types, front-end scripting systems, back-end APIs, back-end application servers, and links that cross boundaries every which way.

If it was simply a matter of integrating Web servers anymore, we would see more cross-platform combinations, with each operating system handling what it is good at. It is possible to use Windows servers as the front-line Web server's feeding pages, and UNIX servers running back-end Web application servers and database, or vice versa. However, it comes about only with matching the right products together.

Microsoft Internet Information Server (IIS) is one of the most popular Web servers on the market. It comes free with the operating system and, together with other tools from Microsoft and third-party vendors, makes a fairly versatile Web server. Microsoft also offers a higher-end product known as Site Server Commerce Edition that implements additional services for setting up electronic storefronts. Aside from the MS products, there are a number of other leading commercial and noncommercial products for Windows such as Netscape Enterprise Server and even Apache (the number one Web server!).

Interfacing Web Pages with Applications

There are two main methods of integrating applications into the Web site. In the first method, you add in a component or applet, which is downloaded by the user and then executed on the user's machine as a client-side application. On the other hand, you could include script information directly into the Web page and allow users to enter information into forms. This is then sent to the server and processed as the application requires by the Web server or separately, as a server-side application.

Client-side applications are fairly familiar to most in the industry. Very few people have not heard of Java applets these days or, if you are a Microsoft developer, ActiveX. These are complete applications packaged and delivered over the network to your browser, which either run entirely within the desktop or communicate live with the server on the other end. The upside of client-side applications is that they can provide a lot of interactivity and are practically the same as any packaged application on a machine. The downside is that they can be big and take time to download. Not everyone is sold on the idea that they perform well or are bug-free, although this is generally more of a perception problem than a reality.

For the application developer, learning Java or C++ is time consuming and difficult. They are full programming languages and provide all the power available to them, but you need to know how to harness them properly or be condemned to that fourth layer of hell of constant application debugging. Building any good nontrivial application in a programming language takes years of experience and a programmer's mentality.

Server-side scripting is usually more limited than that for client-side applications. This is because most of the interactivity from a Web page is pure text or clicks onto buttons or options. This drastically reduces the interactive complexity of the application, but a lot can still be done simply with HTML output.

The most common means of interfacing applications with HTML pages from the server side still is the Common Gateway Interface (CGI). Almost all Web servers provide some way to pass information through the CGI. In almost all cases, this information is entered through HTML Forms and submitted to a URL that accepts the data through the CGI.

The CGI is simple in design, platform-independent, and simple to implement. However, it also has many shortcomings. It supports only two types of data: text and binary information. It provides no type checking or constraint checking at the front end and requires this to be processed by the back end application. It does not provide any means to identify a series of requests; every request sent is considered independent and it relies on the back-end application passing other information to determine whether it is independent or part of a series of forms. Some amazing things can be done with the CGI, but as with an API, it is lacking in many ways.

If you get more specific toward the Windows platforms, CGI is losing ground to more popular systems such as Active Server Pages (ASP). This system takes over the previous-generation interface known as ISAPI and is included in all Microsoft Web servers since IIS version 3.0. Basically, what ASP does is provide an interface for a Web page with front-end script (JScript or VBScript) to communicate with Windows components running as part of the Web server. The components themselves can be written in any language just as long as they support a COM interface. You write the Web page following the ASP syntax for command statements and save it as an *.asp* file. The Web server takes care of the rest, including compiling it, launching it upon request, and managing multiple instances of ASP applications.

Developing ASP pages is a cinch. I know a part-time graphics designer and full-time drummer in a band, with no programming experience, who picked it up in his spare time. It helps to know JavaScripting or Visual Basic, but neither of these is very difficult to learn, either. In fact, ASP-based applications are probably the most successful use of object technology to date, even if in only a simplistic manner.

Is ASP available for UNIX? Yes. One company in particular, ChiliSoft, is known for its ASP server products for various UNIX systems and Web servers.

To go the next step and integrate with a database requires the Open Database Connectivity (ODBC) interface under Windows. ODBC is a generic database API that works with every major Windows database product and most minor ones as well. On the UNIX side, applications that communicate with databases usually have to use the native API provided by the database vendor for their product. There is no loss to doing this, and, in fact, the native APIs per database are usually more powerful than ODBC. However, this makes integration a little more complicated.

To sidestep this issue of working with different database APIs as well as having to develop your own Web application system each and every time, a number of companies have stepped up and offered specialized Web application servers.

Web Application Servers

Many Web sites today do not simply push HTML pages to users. Many include online stores, search engines, database front ends, and even complete applications. To satisfy the needs of such demands, a number of product vendors have become fairly popular over the past few years.

These back-end products, commonly referred to as *Web application servers*, integrate HTML with databases and object services through common programming language interfaces or through special scripting languages of their own. The most common languages to develop such Web-based applications are C, C++, and Java, although some also use front-end (Web browser) scripting systems such as JavaScript, VBScript, and Dynamic HTML. To communicate with databases, they use database APIs such as ODBC or Java database connectivity (JDBC), or proprietary interfaces to Oracle, Sybase, or Informix. The really advanced ones can communicate with object systems such as CORBA or COM/DCOM.

Most of these products are designed to run independently of the Web server and almost all of them support IIS or Apache. Many use Web interfaces such as the Common Gateway Interface to communicate between the Web page, the Web server, and the Web application server. Thus, integrating these products with the Web server is easier than most people think. They usually include tools and directions on how to configure your Web server, running on either the local machine or over the network, to connect to the Web application server. Developing applications using any of these tools is fairly specific per product. Although they provide programming language interfaces, there is no standardization on class libraries or APIs to access these servers.

 A selection of Web application servers is available. Popular ones include Silver-Stream Application Server, Allaire ColdFusion, Apple WebObjects, Bluestone Sapphire, IBM WebSphere, and Oracle Application Server. Every one of these works with IIS and runs on NT. Most also work with Apache or Netscape Server and run on a number of different UNIX platforms. Please check the Web site for this book for further details on where to get these products.

Web Document Formatting and XML

The eXtensible Markup Language (XML) is hailed as the successor to HTML and is generally a much better system for building Web applications. What XML does is provide a way to indicate, in Web syntax, specific data type information in a neutral fashion. For example, by indicating that an item in an online store is specifically <MODEL AIRPLANE >Boeing B-52</MODEL AIRPLANE>, you indicate exactly the type of object it is. This can then be used by front-end or back-end languages for formatting or processing. When you connect to different XML-capable Web servers, the object type still remains the same. With HTML there is no way to accomplish this without having to program the data type into the back end.

By creating such data types, it is now possible to create much more complex applications with less work. What is more, there is a level of portability across servers and platforms. Each XML page refers to the definition file for the object, which can be used by the various servers to understand what the type is and how to work with it. Thus, the data type can travel with the object and the document. This makes communications between different Web applications, application servers, Web servers, and clients much simpler and more accurate.

There still is a problem with XML, though: How do you agree on data types? Sure, each Web programmer can create his or her own data types that they plan to use only on their own servers, but when you get to interfacing Web applications across groups, companies, and localities, this gets very complicated. XML is being considered as the next standard of electronic commerce and businesses are looking forward to directly interacting with each other through the Internet using Web servers and XML. XML will probably replace the electronic data interchange (EDI) standards currently used by large organizations for business-to-business electronic communications.

The good news is that several large and prominent organizations are working on developing such standards for various industries. Microsoft is leading one effort based upon its Distributed interNetwork Architecture and BizTalk systems. The Biztalk server system will allow Windows platform XML servers to communicate and exchange data according to defined XML data standards. Another group, Oasis, is a consortium of most of the leading UNIX vendors, Web software vendors, and several huge companies also working on similar standards. This will all take some time to work out so don't expect to see a working standard interface for XML for your industry for several years.

In the meantime, Web application server vendors are paying serious attention to XML. They include XML support in their products, which only enhances their existing system. Rather than the proprietary methods they use in scripting and interfacing, these products can also rely on XML to define and process Web pages.

Web Load-Balancing Systems

Large Web sites with millions of accesses a day need a way to balance out the load for processing HTTP requests effectively. By reducing the workload on the server, you can reduce the processing time, thus making the visitor happier. You can also use this to expand the capacity of the site without running into enormous expenses for high-end servers.

To achieve this serendipity, you can use load-balancing systems to distribute the requests across more servers. A load-balancing device is a software, or hardware and software, component that examines incoming Web requests and directs them to the server that can best handle the processing. It basically works by looking at the network traffic—in particular, the traffic intended for TCP port 80 (the default port for Web servers). The device either keeps track of the history of requests to the servers or communicates with an agent running on each Web server to determine the load of the respective servers. Based upon the load and, often, a weighting factor to indicate server preference, a new request is directed to an amicable server.

The balancing device keeps track of where incoming requests originate and sends all packets from that source to the same destination server. This helps maintain what are known as *Web sessions*, in which a user follows a series of pages in a semipredictable fashion such as when filling out forms. Other balancing devices look at the IP domain name or address of the source machine and will direct the request to the server that is "nearest" to it, based upon a topology map. These systems work best on a national or global scale to effectively direct traffic to, say, East Coast versus West Coast servers.

For more information on the technical side of how Web load balancing works, you should read Chapter 14 on this topic in *High-Performance Cluster Computing: Volume 1* (Prentice-Hall, 1999), edited by Rajkumar Buyya.

Microsoft has a product that also accomplishes this, with the earth-shatteringly surprising name of Windows Load Balancing Service (WLBS). This product works with any kind of TCP/IP network traffic, although the primary focus is on Web or HTTP traffic. Other products in this area include Cisco's LocalDirector and GlobalDirector, Alteon Web-systems' ACEdirector, RND Networks' Web Server Director, and Resonate's CentralDispatch and GlobalDispatch. All these products either work with NT and UNIX or are independent of the OS platform, just as long as they run TCP/IP.

Multi-tier Web Services

By splitting your Web services across multiple machines, you can improve the performance of the system and use the platform or the Web software package that is best suited for the task.

The solitary Web server is too trivial and even the scenario where several independent but identical Web servers all serve the same set of pages (see Figure 14.1) is not too complex. There really isn't an integration problem in such situations since each server works independently.

The first additional level we can add to the Web site is a separate device that optimizes the incoming requests so that they are handled more efficiently by the Web servers. This load-balancing device goes before the

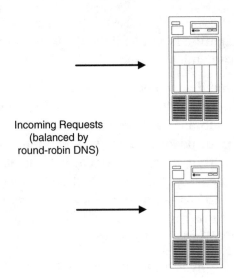

Incoming Requests
(balanced by
round-robin DNS)

Figure 14.1 A two-tier system with several independent identical Web servers.

front-end Web servers and directs the traffic to the nearest or least loaded server. It is an almost trivial integration step since most such devices work automatically and do not need to be configured.

The next level is to add an independent server that handles operations such as online stores, server-side scripts, and Web-based applications, as in Figure 14.2. This is a four-tier system, with the client desktop tier not being shown in the diagram. This separates the jobs of file serving, handled by the front-end Web servers, from the information processing, handled by the application server(s). The Web file servers either link to a page that is on the application server or contain forms that launch scripts on the application server.

Another way to look at this model would be such that the application server software is actually installed on each front-end Web server, and the actual information processing is handled by a database that the front-end Web server connects to. Or to look at it yet another way, the Web application server might even run on the same machine as the database and, in fact, be just an interface layer on top of the database (e.g., Oracle Application Server).

The final model separates all the server components into individual devices (see Figure 14.3). Thus there is a load balancer, the front-end Web servers, the Web application server(s), and the database server(s). Each component is thus optimized to perform only its function. Most of

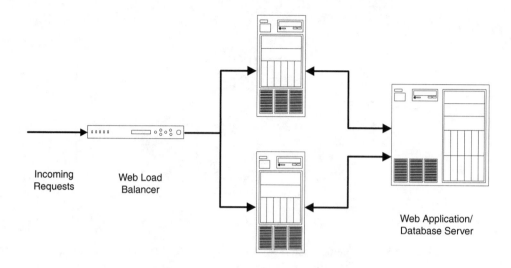

Front-End Web Servers

Figure 14.2 A four-tier system with a load balancer, front-end Web servers, and application servers (client desktops not shown).

these servers can interface with each other using accepted standard interfaces, although some products limit your choices with specific platform requirements or proprietary interfaces.

FTP Services

FTP is the longest-surviving application protocol in the TCP/IP family. In fact, its use was so ubiquitous that, before the coming of the Web, it generated the greatest amount of traffic on the Internet, significantly more than Telnet, e-mail, or any other protocol. FTP clients and servers exist for practically all major platforms that support TCP/IP, including, of course, Windows.

Unlike the NFS or CIFS services, FTP simply requires a small daemon or system service that is independent of the file system. This daemon reads local files and feeds them over the network to a requesting client. Similarly, an authorized client can feed a file to the server, which creates a local copy of the file. Simply said, FTP uses six basic operations: Read a file, Write a file, Create a File, Read a directory, Move to a different directory, and Delete a Directory. There actually are three or four times more actual commands in FTP that are listed in the standard but most of them are implemented, even in UNIX systems. Using the basic operations and

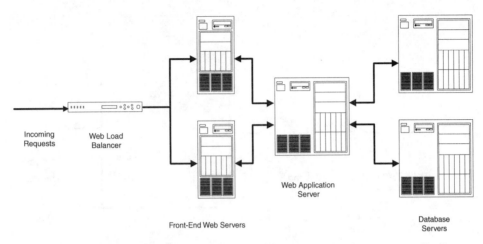

Figure 14.3 A five-tier system with a load balancer, front-end Web servers, application servers, and database servers (client desktops not shown).

predefined data encoding formats for ASCII characters and binary files, FTP sessions prove to be the workhorse of transferring applications or data files over the Internet.

On each system running an FTP server, you do need to create a special directory location that can act as the root directory for the FTP service. This limits anonymous connections to the FTP service to only a directory within the entire server's file tree and prevents guests from wandering around the tree looking at other people's files. Depending upon the FTP server, this is set up in /usr/local/ftp, /var/spool/ftp, or /home/ftp on UNIX systems. Within this area it re-creates part of the UNIX file system top-level directories to support the application. On Windows, there isn't a need for these directories. The FTP root directory on a Windows system running IIS is normally C:\inetpub\ftproot.

FTP services are available as part of the Internet Information Server system alongside the Web server system. If you start up the **Internet Services Manager**, there is a **Default FTP site** for the server. Right-clicking on the FTP site icon and selecting properties will bring up the configuration information for the server. The basic defaults for FTP include an anonymous ftp account (called Guest) that connects to the FTP root directory (C:\inetpub\ftproot, by default). You can adjust the maximum number of simultaneous incoming connections below the very high default limit of 100,000 to something more reasonable so as not to bog down your server with too much traffic. You can also configure which hosts or domains to specifically allow or deny access to your FTP site by providing the appropriate network addresses.

Wu-FTPD, one of the most popular FTP server packages for UNIX systems, created at Washington University, has control features similar to FTP in IIS. In addition, it also supports the full command set of FTP. For example, you can use its proxy FTP services to create a proxy connection from a client to an intermediary wu-ftpd server and then to a final FTP server. Unfortunately, few clients support this feature and few people know how to use it, so there is no burning need for it.

In any case, there is little to integrating FTP servers with each other. Since they do not communicate on a server-to-server level, each is independent of the other and accepts client connections separately. You really need an FTP server that can limit the number of connections and the length of time they can be connected. This defines how much you want to load down the server for the FTP service itself. This does not, however, limit how much data they can transfer to or from your site, a useful service if you need to be careful of your network bandwidth usage.

For heavily used sites, it is normally better to have several separate servers, each limiting up to a few hundred FTP connections at a time. This balances the file serving load across multiple machines. One method to balance an FTP load across several servers is by rotating through the list of DNS host names for the servers, a process known as round-robin DNS. You set up a common DNS alias for the FTP service (e.g., ftp.straypackets.com) and then name each of your servers in sequence (ftp1.straypackets.com, ftp2.straypackets.com, ftp3.straypackets.com, etc.). Using round-robin DNS, each new name service resolution request from a client will map to a different server each time. Thus, on average, the connection load is spread evenly across the servers.

Scripting Systems

Scripting systems provide a means to write tools that can be executed from the text-mode Command Line Interface (CLI). The text-mode shell is what many UNIX users are familiar with. In Windows, the Command shell still exists, providing a DOS-like interface, but it works fairly differently than do UNIX shells. The Command shell can be used to write shell scripts, but it is fairly limited in capabilities. Most Windows administrators have relied on other scripting systems such as Perl or VBScript.

There are distinct advantages to using the text-mode CLI rather than the graphical user interface. With GUIs you often have to click through a lot of dialog boxes to enter the parameters for a command; a text command is simply faster to type and execute. Writing scripts for text-mode tools is simpler and faster than developing a full GUI-based tool. Very often GUI tools work on a single item at a time; for example, you can create or modify a single user account at a time with the GUI administration tool. Although you could technically build a GUI tool that would allow you to modify or create a large number of accounts at a time, writing a script to simply repeat a set of functions for each user takes fewer steps.

The Windows system can be administered entirely through the various GUI tools, but it would be to your advantage as a system administrator to be able to write text-mode scripts using scripting systems such as Perl, VBScript, or shell scripts. Furthermore, you may be able to develop portable scripts that work on both your UNIX and Windows platforms that will save you time and mental energy.

Perl

Perl is well known in UNIX circles. It also has a steady following on Windows platforms since the release of Perl 5.0 and ports to Windows such as ActivePerl. The language began as a text processing and command line execution tool but soon found new value as a popular scripting system for server-side execution of Web pages through the Common Gateway Interface. This has given a significant boost to the use of Perl for most kinds of command scripting on multiple platforms. With Perl5, object-oriented features were introduced, allowing data structures to be created and manipulated that were more complex than simple strings and integers.

Perl on Windows is not very different from that on UNIX. Most of the added functions specific to the Windows platform are in a separate Perl5 class library simply called Win32. This provides most of the data structures and functions to deal with the DOS file system, Windows IPC mechanisms, domain controller functions, file sharing and mapping, managing Windows processes, managing the registry, and other system-level functions.

Perl is a fairly detailed programming language and it would be simply indecent of us to try to teach how to program in Perl within a few chapters in this book. For a better reference, look to the books from O'Reilly and Associates, written by the primary developers of Perl, such as *Learning Perl*, Randal L. Schwartz and Tom Christiansen (O'Reilly & Associates, 1997), *Programming Perl* by Larry Wall, Tom Christiansen, and Randall L. Schwartz (O'Reilly & Associates, 1996), and *Learning Perl on Win32 Systems* by Randall L. Schwartz, Erik Olson, and Tom Christiansen (O'Reilly & Associates, 1997). This last book provides all you need to learn Perl programming on Windows platforms.

Command Shell Scripts

The NT and Win 2000 Command shell is actually an emulation of the DOS 7.0 shell. However, the scripting system is identical to that of DOS. If you have ever looked into the Autoexec.bat file on a Windows system, you have seen what Windows shell scripts look like. Although NT and Win 2000 don't use the Autoexec.bat for the OS, many applications may depend upon it, and so it may or may not contain anything on a Windows 2000 system.

The Command shell has appropriate language constructs, but there simply aren't enough decent command line tools except for the administrator. To write decent Command shell scripts you really need the better selection of tools, available with the Windows Resource Kits. These are separately purchasable products from Microsoft that include a large number of useful commands that allow you to interact with the operating system administration features.

In our opinion, you can write some administration tools with Command shell scripts, but you will probably be better off learning Perl or VBScript. However, you should understand how the Command shell works and be able to read the scripts. We will explain any Windows command tools or Command shell scripts that we use in this book, but if you really want to learn how it all works, you should read *Windows NT Shell Scripting* by Tim Hill (Macmillan Technical Press, 1998).

UNIX Shells

As explained in a later section on UNIX emulators, several shells are available for the Windows platform. Shell scripting is a regular part of a UNIX administrator's job, but most Windows administrators are unfamiliar with it. Although the NT Command shell provides many similar features, it is pretty limited for use as a proper programming environment. UNIX shells like Korn and Bash, on the other hand, can compete on par with Perl by providing better programming constructs than the Command shell. UNIX shell scripts are often easier or faster to code than Perl, especially when it comes to file handling.

Most of these implement the Korn shell in various forms. An official implementation of KornShell (note the spelling difference) is available in the Global Technologies U/Win product and is 100 percent compatible with UNIX KornShell. The freely available GNU Bash shell is also 100 percent compatible with KornShell. Most of the other implementations contain small differences, especially when dealing with system controls and device files. The products from Softway, DataFocus, and MKS mentioned earlier all implement a derivative Korn Shell. Microsoft's NT Services for UNIX actually licenses the MKS Toolkit Korn Shell, which is not 100 percent compatible with standard KornShell.

VBScript

Visual Basic is a full compiled programming language available for the Windows environment. On the other hand, VBScript provides a simpler interpreted scripting system that allows users to write code that is just as powerful. VBScript is specific to the Windows environment but very popular nonetheless. You can use it to interface with other Windows user and system components such as the Windows Scripting Host and Active Server Pages.

The advantage of VBScript over Perl is that it is a little easier to understand and learn. Perl has many language constructs that can make the code fairly hard to decipher at a glance. VBScript is simply an interpreted version of the BASIC programming language, one of the easiest and simplest ones to learn. VBScript code can also be packaged and used as objects through Microsoft COM (Component Object Model), COM+, and DCOM (Distributed COM). This allows you to build distributed object-oriented applications in multiple programming and scripting languages and interface them together without too much difficulty. COM is a little beyond what most system administrators use to write administration tools, so we won't cover it in this book.

Remote Script Execution

Remote script execution provides an alternative to developing cross-platform code. The administrator is presented with a script interface, and the actual code to be executed on the remote machine is hidden from them.

You can set up Web pages that present these scripts to be executed by your less experienced administrators or operators. This also allows you to set up a secure administration interface to your server without actually creating a privileged account for every staff member.

The remote script can be executed through various interfaces. There are implementations of the UNIX *rexec* and *rcmd* servers on Windows systems that allow an administrator on the UNIX side to execute Windows CLI commands. Similarly, there are *rexec* and *rcmd* tools that allow Windows administrators to execute UNIX commands. These commands work on the simple security of the *.rhosts* file that lists other systems and accounts allowed command execution rights on the current system.

Web page script execution occurs primarily through the Common Gateway Interface. This system is a fairly simple command and parameter formatting language that can be specified together with HTML Forms. The Forms present a method for creating input boxes for a user to type in parameters and then sending the information to a CGI script. The actual script itself may be written in any language as long as it retrieves the parameter information through the CGI. This is where Perl is king. CGI scripts involve a lot of text processing, which Perl and shell scripts are good at.

Unfortunately, the CGI is a little inefficient when it comes to formatting data for exchange. On Windows, Active Server Pages provide a more detailed interface that can set up on a Web server. They exchange data with Windows scripting and programming languages—in particular, VBScript.

Summary

Integration of application services provide a means to uniformly support user needs. By integrating back-end services such as mail and Web, the user is shielded from the differences presented in their e-mail reader or Web browser. Unfortunately, this is often limited to the common application services. Although you would be able to integrate the lowest common denominator of services, Web, FTP, and e-mail, advanced features often get left out of the matter. Thus, it isn't easily possible to completely integrate address books from Microsoft Exchange, for example, with those on UNIX systems.

New application services that run through a Web server entirely aims to change this issue. They provide the user with applications through their Web browser and are neutral to the type of client platform or browser software used. You can go this route and replace your existing systems with new Web-based applications but it isn't necessarily easier than integrating current application services on different platforms.

At the same time, the client-side issues present different problems to system administrators, especially when the client application is specific to a desktop operating system platform. The next chapter deals with problems to such client application access issues.

## CHAPTER 15

Client Station Integration

Getting your desktop and workstation clients to cohabit a mixed environment isn't the sweetest deal in the world. You have client software that is intended to work with a specific type of server platform and either will not work at all or will start behaving strangely when you try to take it to a different platform. This gives purpose to an entire industry of integration software that takes clients abroad to where no clients have gone before.

The goal of client station integration from the user's point of view is to provide a means for them to perform their regular tasks independently of the platform infrastructure. In other words, the client desktops may never really know who's on the other end of the line as long as they can talk to them clearly. The ideal situation is where a user can work on any client platform and perform the same tasks without having to learn how to use different interfaces or applications. The reality is that they vary quite wildly between platforms such as UNIX and Windows, and we have to figure out a common ground between them.

From the sysadmin's point of view, having mixed clients, mixed servers, or both means trying to manage issues such as software deployment, help desk services, and troubleshooting with multiple platforms. Their goal is to unify the management environment or reduce the workload of managing separate systems. The goal of this chapter is to look at what is available for making the needs of both the user and the sysadmin a reality.

The Problem of Integrating Clients

The basic application problem of client systems is how to give users access to the applications they need on their platform. The hard way is to give each user the platform he or she needs to use and directly install the application by hand on each and every machine. What is the point of creating automated systems and computer networks if you do that?

There are much better ways than trolling around the office with disks in hand, taking over users' machines and installing new software for them individually. You can approach this problem from two angles: Either make it easier to access or run the application on the platform they already have, or make it easier to distribute the software out to the machines over the network.

The first method, *user interface access*, opens a window from one OS to another running on a different system. In this method, you keep the client that you already have and allow the user to access the environment that runs on a native platform elsewhere. Thus, users have full application compatibility on both sides. This method most certainly requires you to have a server system that users can access from remote locations and thus can be expensive to implement, depending upon the application and the number of users.

The second method is to emulate the other platform on the local system, either through software or assisted with hardware. This creates an emulation layer for the applications that varies in the level of compatibility with what the emulated platform would be like on a separate machine. For example, this allows UNIX users to run application code that is written natively for Windows, even if they use a non-PC platform.

To solve the problem of distributing software over networks, you have to deal with the problem of installing software remotely in a secure fashion, as well as accounting for it. Several application and software distribution tools perform just this function on several different levels.

User Interface Access

User interface access products allow a desktop user to access and run applications on a remote server, be it Win 2000 or UNIX. These usually have a client connectivity application that communicates in the native protocol of the server and present a user interface whereby the person can run applications remotely.

The four types discussed here include *terminal connectivity* (usually text- or character-based interfaces), *PC-X* (X Windows on PCs), *multiuser NT* (also called Windows Terminal Server), and *Webtop systems*. Terminal connectivity applications and PC-X allow PC-based clients to access UNIX applications and servers either on a LAN or over a WAN. Multiuser NT systems allow PC and UNIX desktops to access an NT server application. Webtop systems work similarly to X Windows or Windows Terminal Server, with the primary difference being that all applications can be accessed through a Web browser.

UI access applications are a *quick and direct* way of giving a user access to a remote application without having to deal with any sort of compatibility problems. Since the applications are actually running on their native platform, it does not suffer the problems that system emulators do. Furthermore, *little needs to be done to an application* to prepare it for access from an alternative client. The work lies more in installing the connectivity software on the client side. UI access provides direct *interactive access* to applications; users can work on the machine interactively and do not have to preprogram their actions or read files to see the results of their work.

The trouble with using UI access software is that you can suffer a *performance penalty* since the application is running over a network. The interface may become sluggish to the point of unusability if your network is extremely loaded down. To the user it appears that the remote server is extremely loaded down or even not responding. In truth, the applications on the server may be running fine, but somewhere along the network path there is a bottleneck that is slowing or blocking the interactive session.

Some UI access applications are *limited in their graphical capabilities*. For example, terminal connectivity applications commonly show only text characters and sometimes basic character graphics. Although you can perform a lot of tasks in character mode, most Windows applications are graphical and cannot be accessed this way. In multiuser NT, the client software is often limited in graphics resolution since a greater degree of graphical detail means heavier network traffic load.

One final problem with these methods is with the *burden of client configuration*. The client system has to be configured to access applications and hosts. If you change any applications or create new applications, you have to modify the settings of every client desktop, which could add up to a lot of work. Some client software can be configured from remote locations; although this helps to speed the process, it does not eliminate it.

Some products require the client to communicate with an intermediary access server that defines what each user has access to. Since the application definitions are contained on the server and not on the client desktop, there is no need to change every desktop. This creates a multitier system of clients, access servers, and application servers that distribute the workload and management system across the network. The burden of configuration is moved from the client to a tier of access servers, reducing much of the work.

Terminal Applications

UNIX has always been a character terminal access system and remains so to this day. Even when X Windows is used for the desktop, most users still pop up a UNIX shell window and type in commands. This, in fact, is one power of UNIX as well. Since a large number of commands can be accessed through the Command Line Interface, all you have to do is open a text terminal window to the server and you have access to a great number of applications and commands. We are talking about Telnet and rlogin, of course, as the terminal connectivity applications.

Such applications have been available for PCs to connect to UNIX servers since the late 1980s. The focus of terminal applications is in the type of screen standard or terminal type they will support. Since different character terminals have different features, these terminal types have their own definitions for text placement, color features, multiple windows, and even simple graphics. The terminal type definition must also be supported by the server so that it can interpret instructions from applications and display them properly.

A Telnet client requires a Telnet server application to connect to on the remote machine. A Telnet daemon comes with practically every UNIX system. On NT systems, however, where the model was intentionally different, vendors did not consider building Telnet servers until recent years. A Telnet server on an NT or Win 2000 box presents a Command window over the network to remote users. They can execute any text-based applications, DOS applications, or scripts, but will not be able to view a graphical application.

Telnet and rlogin client software has long been available for Windows. Although there is a basic Telnet application that comes with the Windows environment, it is pretty rudimentary, almost an afterthought when Microsoft originally released TCP/IP for Windows for Workgroups 3.11a. There are numerous freeware and shareware packages that work much better than this default program. However, the real utility comes from commercial packages from Attachmate, NetManage, WRQ, and Hummingbird. Telnet server software for NT is harder to come by. Pragma Systems, of Austin, Texas, makes just such a product.

Telnet is common to the UNIX environment. If you have mainframes or AS/400s, however, you will need a different terminal client application. The same commercial vendors previously mentioned provide IBM terminal emulation software for 3270 to connect to mainframes and 5250 for AS/400s.

PC-X

The X Windows protocol is a graphical user protocol and system for displaying a desktop and running graphical applications over a network. It began as the GUI for UNIX systems but has been implemented on other platforms as well, including PCs. X Windows has been running on PC systems since Windows 3.1 and is commonly referred to as PC-X.

X Windows functions by putting the desktop system to do the work of processing the graphics for display, while the server does the actual application processing. This is a model known as *thin-client computing*, where the client desktop does not need any application software or data installed locally except for the X Windows system. The X Windows system uses an apparently upside-down description of the components: The local desktop that displays the graphics is known as the X-server and the applications on the remote machine are known as X-clients. Normally we think of our desktop system as the client and the remote machine as the server. This apparently reverse logic is because of the role the software components are playing: The X-server manages multiple incoming applications for graphical processing; the X-client is simply a client application that is run by a user.

The X11 system defines separate layers for the *network protocol*, the *display manager*, and the *window manager*. The network protocol defines how graphical representations are transmitted over a network. A keystroke might set off one packet of data containing the alphanumeric value of the key, for example. Moving a mouse across the screen can send a whole number of packets. The X11 network protocol runs on top of TCP/IP, which in turn runs over an Ethernet or other network. The X11 protocol is fairly heavyweight, meaning that it uses a lot of network bandwidth for communications between the desktop displaying the application and the server the application is actually executing on.

The display manager deals with the issues of handling I/O from local desktop devices (the mouse, keyboard, and screen) and the creation and management of X11 client applications. It handles the requests to accept a connection from an X-client to communicate with the graphics card and display device on presenting the application. The display manager handles the core functions that constitute the X-server.

The window manager is the actual user interface that a person sees that creates and displays applications within a window. In the Microsoft Windows family of operating systems, the concepts of the window manager and the display manager are directly integrated into the operating system and cannot be separated. On UNIX systems, however, the X Windows GUI is just another application running on the system.

PC-X has to deal with the issue of multiple window managers running at the same time. Since you cannot replace the windows manager that is part of Windows, you have to build the X-server so that it either uses the Windows GUI or can share the display. With some PC-X applications, you can display Windows applications using the native GUI style while using familiar X Windows window managers to display X-client applications using that style. Aside from display, PC-X also has to handle cut-and-paste, drag-and-drop, and other GUI functions between the two windowing systems.

PC-X has also been available for many years. Popular packages include Hummingbird eXceed, SCO XVision, NCD PC-Xware, and NetManage ChameleonX. Most of these packages provide the same features but differentiate in the type of management and performance features they offer.

Multiuser NT and Windows Terminals

When NT was first built, it was designed as a network operating system with shared resources but really did not allow multiple users to directly run applications on the system the way that UNIX users can log into one machine and run applications independently. Users could access drives and resources and communicate with server applications on the system, but they did this through a separate desktop system running NT Workstation or Windows 95/98. What changed this role was the emergence of multiuser NT, typically a modified version of the NT operating system.

Multiuser NT first began with a product known as WinFrame by Citrix Systems, Inc. Microsoft licensed Citrix's code to build Windows NT Terminal Server Edition for version 4.0. This once-separate product is now a standard part of the Windows 2000 server products. Win 2000 incorporates the changes to the operating system to support multiple users.

One of the main problems with creating a multiuser Windows system is that there is no separation between the GUI and the operating system. In fact, even now this exists. What multiuser NT does is allow the Executive to run multiple copies of the GUI system, one for each user.

Terminal Server and Citrix WinFrame run on the server machine and communicate using proprietary protocols with client desktops. The client runs a connectivity application that displays the Windows GUI running on the server on the desktop. Citrix uses the ICA (Independent Console Architecture) protocol, which they designed themselves, while Microsoft Terminal Server uses RDP (Remote Desktop Protocol). Citrix also has a product that runs on top of Terminal Server known as MetaFrame that allows you to use ICA to connect to the Terminal Server system.

The protocols work similarly and send graphical screen updates and the I/O from mice and keyboards to the server for processing. Like X Windows, all application processing actually runs on the server, while graphical processing is done on the client. The client connectivity software that implements the protocol provides a more limited desktop view that supports smaller resolutions and fixed sets of colors. On screen it appears as a desktop within a desktop, as shown in Figure 15.1.

The two protocols differ in the platforms they support. Microsoft RDP is designed for and implemented only on Windows clients. Citrix ICA, however, will run on a number of different client platforms, including Macs, Windows PCs, and UNIX workstations. Citrix ICA can also transmit audio over the network, allowing the user to play audio clips off the server itself. The two protocols, although similar, are not compatible. You cannot use RDP software to connect to a Citrix WinFrame server;

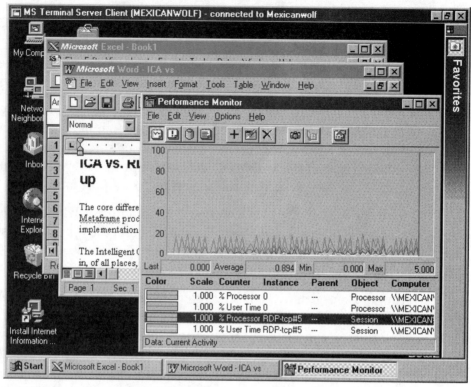

Figure 15.1 Remote connectivity through multiuser NT.

conversely, you cannot use ICA software to connect to a Windows Terminal Server, if MetaFrame is not installed. A server running Windows Terminal Server and MetaFrame will support clients of both types.

There are hardware equivalents whose sole function is to run the client connectivity application known as Windows Terminals. These are simplified desktops that run either a proprietary operating system or use the Microsoft Windows CE operating system and act as independent clients on a network. A Windows Terminal provides minimal graphical display resolutions up to 800×600 and up to 65,535 colors and can run on a small variety of processors including Intel Pentiums and several RISC processors from other vendors. When users log in, they are presented with the remote desktop that is downloaded using the ICA or RDP protocols. Any actions they perform at the Windows Terminal are directly passed to the remote server and executed. The devices are limited in capabilities but serve their purpose when it comes to application access. Vendors such as NCD, Boundless Technologies, NeoWare, Hitachi, and IBM make Windows Terminals that can access the servers using one protocol or the other.

Webtop Systems

A Webtop system allows access to an application system through a common Web browser. Webtop systems come in two major types: applications natively in a Web format using any number of competing programming standards for the Web, and those that interface to traditional applications through a Web browser. In this section, we will talk only about the latter kind, those that interface to UNIX and NT systems through a plug-in or applet in a Web browser.

Webtop applications combine the static HTML environment of the Web with an active element such as a plug-in, a Java Applet, or an ActiveX object. The active element provides the interactive session to a remote computer, which runs the specific applications. The benefit of this system is that any browser that supports the active element is able to access the remote application services. The administrator does not need to install any other client application or customized environment. There still is user authentication, but it takes the form of a direct login to the remote server through the browser.

It is possible to embed clients of other UI access applications into a browser, effectively creating a Webtop. In the current version of the X Windows system known as X11R6.3, there is support for the Web-enabled X-applications whereby an X-client is displayed within the browser window. Citrix provides a Java applet and native Windows ICA client that can access their WinFrame and MetaFrame servers through a Webtop as well.

There are other Webtop application systems that were built solely for use with the Web. SCO Tarantella (see Figure 15.2) and GraphOn jBridge & Go-Global provide alternative Webtop systems that can access applications from Windows or UNIX through the same software.

System Emulation

System emulation is the process of emulating the workings of an operating system or an API. This sort of emulation can work at several levels, from hardware-based coprocessor boards and cards to the emulation of a complete computer hardware platform purely in software. System emulation allows a user to run off-the-shelf software applications on a platform that it was not originally designed for.

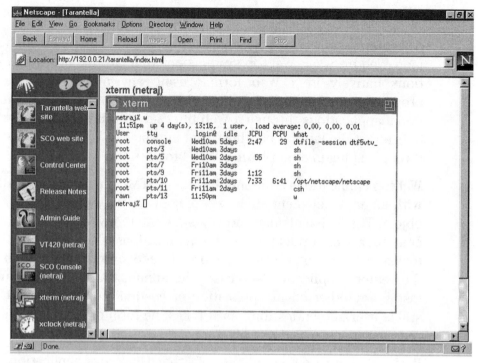

Figure 15.2 SCO Tarantella Webtop.

There are different levels of system emulation, as shown in Table 15.1. The simplest way is to provide emulation of the user interface. Packages such as U/Win provide a familiar UNIX shell for NT and Windows 2000 users that behaves just like the original.

Some emulation packages, such as WINE (WINdows Emulator), only create an intermediary binary layer that translates application function calls from the emulated OS to the native OS. This works well if the packages use standard function calls but fails when an application uses a function call improperly or uses an undocumented call.

Table 15.1 Levels of System Emulation

EMULATION LEVEL	PACKAGES
User interface emulation	U/Win
Application interface emulation	WINE, NuTCRACKER, CygWin
Operating system emulation	Interix
Hardware system emulation	SoftWindows, RealPC, coprocessing boards

Other packages rebuild or rewrite an operating system to run on a different platform and under another OS. These packages run into problems with potential incompatibilities between the rewritten OS and the original. Often these rewritten OSs have limited features or will run on only certain types of machines.

Still other packages, such as Insignia Solutions SoftWindows and RealPC, emulate an entire PC and its hardware architecture, which allows any off-the-shelf operating system to be installed on the machine. This last method is the slowest but has the least number of compatibility issues. Since the package emulates only the hardware and the OS installed comes straight from the original vendor, the only problems to arise are hardware issues.

Although this sounds like a wonderful technology, it has its limitations. System Emulation can be *slow* if done only in software. Since the software system has to emulate another operating system with different data structures and mechanisms and translate between the native and emulated OSs, running an application can be slow, especially if the CPU is not powerful enough to handle it. There are some exceptions; for example, NT on Alpha systems comes with a package called FX!32, which emulates Intel CPU-based systems so that NT/Alpha systems can execute NT/Intel packaged applications. The performance is so fast that the difference is not noticeable.

PC and Windows Emulators

There are only a handful of Windows or PC software emulators for the UNIX platform. Commercially, Insight Solutions provides the most functional version of Windows system emulation in software for most UNIX OSs. Another product, *Merge*, allows Windows applications to run on UNIX on Intel platforms. Noncommercially, there are a number of packages that run on specific UNIX on Intel platforms that can emulate the Win32 application environment, but one system, WINE, in particular has the largest following.

Insight Solutions SoftWindows and RealPC products emulate in software a Windows PC's software and hardware environment such that 32-bit Windows 9x or NT software can run on them. The products are similar in function but differ in implementation. SoftWindows is a reimplementation of the Windows 9x OS and the necessary PC hardware emulation that works on Intel- and non-Intel-based UNIX systems.

RealPC, on the other hand, implements a complete PC hardware platform and the Intel processor instruction set in software and a basic DOS system. It allows the user to install an original version of Windows 95, 98, NT, or 2000. Since it emulates the hardware platform in its entirety, the native Windows OS doesn't see the difference at all. Understandably, RealPC performs more slowly than SoftWindows on the same UNIX system since it works on a lower level. On the plus side, it also poses fewer compatibility problems for software. Both packages have to be purchased from Insight Solutions or one of their partners. Almost all UNIX vendors whose operating systems will run these products are partners.

Merge, or DOSMerge, is a commercially licensed package that runs on specific versions of UNIX that run on Intel hardware, in particular the SCO UNIX platform. It allows you to run 16-bit DOS or Windows 3.x, as well as 32-bit Windows 95. It can run 32-bit applications and enhanced-mode Windows 3.x software but will not run NT or Windows 2000 on the UNIX platform. SCO Merge is available for free for noncommercial use directly from their Web site at www.sco.com/offers/free_merge_faq.html.

On the freeware, opensource, and shareware side, there are a number of projects that implement Windows software emulation on UNIX systems. Wine (www.winehq.com) is the leading project in this area, with the most support. Wine emulates the Win16 and Win32 application call interface and implements them over X Windows and UNIX system libraries. It runs only on UNIX on Intel platforms, including Solaris, Linux, and FreeBSD. Unlike the SoftWindows system, it does not require the user to install a licensed copy of Windows. At the same time, this can introduce compatibility problems when running software. At this point there are over 600 Windows applications that will run on Wine with different levels of compatibility issues and at least 300 that will run with few problems. Although many commercial programs fall into this last category, any application running under Wine does not come with official support. As with other freeware applications, use at your own risk.

UNIX Emulators and Subsystems

UNIX emulators on NT have a head start, given NT's support for the POSIX environment. Although not truly UNIX, the POSIX subsystem on NT and Windows 2000 implements most of the system calls and many applications needed to build a proper UNIX environment. However, most agree that the default POSIX subsystem is brain-dead. Several vendors have built products that reimplement the POSIX subsystem or a similar user application system that provides a better UNIX emulation.

There are two levels of products: those that emulate the UNIX shell and those that emulate the UNIX system library. For UNIX shell emulation, several commercial applications are available. Softway Interix, DataFocus NuTCRACKER, MKS Toolkit, and Global Technologies U/Win products all emulate various UNIX shells. The U/Win product is also available for noncommercial use at no cost from AT&T. Noncommercially, there have been ports of the GNU *bash* shell to the NT system as well. At shell-level emulation, you can access the NT system through familiar shell commands and even write shell scripts that will work on both Windows and UNIX platforms. Products that provide this level of emulation implement not only the shell but also most popular UNIX commands such as *ls*, *rm*, *more*, *df*, and *cat*. Some even implement more complex applications such as *awk*, *sed*, and *perl*.

At the system library level, the package must support common UNIX system calls listed in at least one of the various UNIX standards. Both Softway Interix and DataFocus NuTCRACKER implement appropriate UNIX system libraries that can be used to port applications from the UNIX side to the Win32 platform. In fact, the Interix product does such a good job of it that a specific platform running Interix on NT 4.0 actually qualifies as a UNIX system according to The Open Group, responsible for the official UNIX standard.

An opensource project called CygWin, supported by Cygnus Solutions, Inc., has implemented a UNIX system call library that allows users to port UNIX applications to the Win32 environment. Under this project, many of the popular opensource UNIX applications, including *gcc*, *ghostscript*, *bash*, and *latex*, have been ported to Win32 and are freely available for download from the CygWin site.

Software-Based Hardware Emulation

It is also possible to emulate all the hardware components of a PC in software. This has traditionally been far too slow for it to be practical, but with the growing power of computing platforms, it may soon be just as fast as an independent machine. Since all the PC hardware components are emulated, the system has to be able to translate all the operations to the actual hardware platform. Two vendors, Insignia Solutions and VMware, have taken opposite positions on this topic.

Insignia Solutions' RealPC emulates an entire PC platform and the Intel x86 instruction set so that you can run a PC environment on other non-PC hardware platforms such as the Macintosh and Sun Solaris. RealPC installs a single virtual machine that boots up into a DOS or Windows environment and runs any DOS or Windows application. Since every element of the PC is emulated, it is 100 percent compatible with any Windows application. However, RealPC has to have device drivers that translate between the virtual PC-like devices and the actual Mac or Solaris hardware. The platform thus only supports a limited set of common devices and cards.

VMware on the other hand, makes a product that runs only on Intel PC hardware. With VMware it is possible to run several emulated PCs on top of a single PC system. This means that you can install Windows, Linux, Solaris, and so on, in separate virtual machines (VM) that all actually run on the same system. The underlying component that executes these virtual machines can be a native-mode VMware system, a Linux OS, or a Windows NT system. This underlying component, known as the *host OS*, provides the raw device driver, display interface, and execution environment that can then be multiplexed to support multiple *guest OSs*. The VMware system is essentially a multiplexing system that translates any real hardware commands between the guest OS that is currently in focus. Each guest OS runs in its own separate VM and has no contact with the other VMs. In fact, each VM is considered a separate machine and has to talk through a virtual network interface to communicate with any of the other VMs. All the guest OSs, however, can display their screens through the visual interface of the host OS. This means that you can open a window from the host OS to any of the guest OSs to see the command line prompt or desktop of that guest OS. At the driver level, the host OS multiplexes calls to the real hardware from each guest OS. Technically, VMware only emulates and multiplexes the raw PC hardware; you can install any kind of Intel-based operating system as a guest OS and it will still be able to access the hardware as relayed through the VM to the host OS's drivers and then to the actual hardware.

Hardware Coprocessing

Hardware coprocessing offers the fastest and, often, the most compatible way of emulating the Windows system on UNIX. In this method, you add a special board into your UNIX system, which is, in fact, a single-board computer, complete with its own separate Intel-compatible microprocessor. These kinds of boards are available for a number of non-Intel-based UNIX platforms, in particular, the SPARC and MIPS systems. They provide a separate execution environment for running Windows applications, emulating a complete PC hardware platform within the board. The PC board can have its own graphics card, network interface, and even drive system. However, in most cases, it uses the resources already available on the UNIX hardware with the help of special device drivers. In some cases, the Windows and UNIX environments run in completely separate screens, displayed either on the same monitor or on separate monitors. The user can switch between the two environments through a special keystroke.

Sun Microsystems, for example, makes the SunPCi board, which is an almost complete single-board PC with an AMD microprocessor and RAM. The board still uses the graphics, network, and disk components of the main SPARC system board but provides native PC-hardware emulation for them. Thus, the graphics, network, and disks look like real PC hardware to the Windows system. You still have to purchase and install Windows on the system, either as a separate partition on the drive or on a separate drive entirely for the PC side.

Distributing Software to Clients

A major nuisance of the client/server environment is having to figure out how to install application software on hundreds or thousands of client desktops. Each user has to have the application configured to his or her personal environment. Each application has its own installation procedures as specific to the operating system. Each operating system has to be installed slightly differently, depending upon the client hardware. Putting all this together has been next to impossible.

This is one of the big reasons that there has been such interest in developing a common application environment such as Java or XML. It makes large-scale deployment a much easier task since it reduces the number of different platforms that have to be supported. Unfortunately, these are fairly new technologies and it will still be some time before they have the same application base as existing Windows and UNIX software. The lack of proper software distribution tools is also one of the reasons that the industry seems to be circling back to server-based applications. With such a system, the client does not need to have the software installed, just the server access mechanism. The user then launches the application, from a remote location, that displays on the client but actually runs on a server. This was the basis of the X Windows platform and is the basis for Windows Terminal Server as well. However, such environments have problems of their own, such as not scaling too well or requiring server equipment that is too expensive. Thus we come back to the original problem.

With UNIX systems, application distribution has been a little easier since administrators can directly log into a remote system, download the package, and install it directly. Most Windows systems do not have that kind of benefit. Unfortunately, doing manual installations on a per-machine basis is time consuming and inefficient. Imagine having to deploy one application to 10,000 clients over the weekend. Sound impossible? Very likely so if you have a hodgepodge of client hardware, OS versions, and custom environments. It is most likely insurmountable if you have only a handful of system administrators.

So into this mix we throw a software distribution server. Such software is usually specific to one OS application environment or another, but it can still help. The method through which these distribution servers work is using software agents, which reside on each client computer and communicate the status of the application and system environment to central servers. The agent is usually implemented in software (Microsoft Systems Management Server, Marimba Castanet, CA Unicenter TNG, etc.) or a combination of software and hardware (Intel LANDesk, On Technology Command CCM, etc.). It could be a part of the operating system such as the Windows 2000 Remote Installation Service or simply an application that acts as a proxy for administrator instructions.

Operating System Distribution

The ability to remotely install an operating system is a fairly sizable administrative power. It gives one the chance to completely redefine the system, redefine the storage system, and upgrade system components and, most likely, user accounts as well. At one time, OS installation was a fairly rare event and doing it manually was the accepted method. This takes too much of the administrator's time.

With UNIX systems, installing the OS should theoretically be a one-time thing, although even here we sometimes have to go back and reinstall the whole system when something occurs to corrupt the system files.

Windows systems don't fare as well, especially Win 9x machines. Loss or corruption of system files is simply too common an occurrence. Whatever the actual reason for failure, the end result is that you have to go back and reinstall the OS and all applications, and possibly save any of the remaining personal data files.

In any case, distributing an OS to multiple systems goes beyond simply being able to boot the system over the network. Activities such as upgrading the hardware BIOS, formatting disks, and setting boot parameters are fairly low level and at one time were only possible manually. New tools make remote installation a real charm, offering an almost hands-off approach to doing OS installation anywhere on the network, even across the Internet if you are so minded.

Before we consider actual network-based OS distribution, we should look at a more down-to-earth mechanism that is still in popular use.

OS Distribution through Disk Duplication

The brute force method of distributing the OS onto lots of desktop clients is by directly copying an entire drive as many times as needed and then installing the physical drive units in remote machines. This isn't really network-based distribution unless you consider your administrators a physical part of your network. Still, it works and has been used successfully in large computing environments for some time.

The process is sometimes referred to as *disk imaging*, *cloning*, or *ghosting* (after a popular package that bears that name). You install a typical configuration for a desktop onto one computer, complete with all the necessary applications, and then make a direct copy of the drive onto other hard disks. Each drive is an exact duplicate image of the others. The process involves very little interaction by the administrator once the initial prototype has been installed. The work comes when you have to install the drives into each and every client, and this is mostly just physical monkey work (if only you could find that one trained monkey who knows how to do it).

There are three drawbacks to this method. First, this works great for Win 9x machines, but every NT system has a built-in security identifier (SID) that is normally generated during installation time and that has to be unique for each machine. This is a security precaution that prevents others from making raw copies of your system (exactly as in this method) to spoof or pretend to be the original machine, thus potentially breaking your network's security. Disk imaging tools normally include a separate tool that goes through and modifies this SID for each new drive it images so as to give them a separate identity. Unfortunately, this SID is sometimes also used by applications for their own security, which the imaging tools cannot anticipate.

When a company buys PCs from a vendor, they regularly come preinstalled with a Windows operating system (even if the client doesn't want one). The vendor does this in their factory to help reduce technical support calls from users who try to install the OS themselves and don't know what they are doing. This is great for the masses, but not every company needs a copy of Windows or all the default applications the vendor installs. In fact, most IT departments get them as such and then wipe the drives and do a fresh install with all the software approved by their company. With disk imaging, purchasing a large number of clients means taking out these preconfigured drives, wiping them, copying the image, and then reinstalling them into the client. The problem is that anytime you have to do any sort of hands-on hardware work, you waste time that could be spent better if the drives didn't have to be manually handled like that. The process is slow and, worse, it is dull.

Finally, disk imaging only copies a raw image from one drive to another. If you have to set up individual preferences per user, this has to be done in a separate step after the disk image is copied and the drive installed into the user's station. A few imaging tools also allow you to modify application preferences, but either this is limited to a few select applications or they require separate images of installed applications that must be put into place after the OS image is done.

So what's so great about disk imaging? It's cheap and relatively mindless. Enter our skilled monkeys.

OS Distribution through Remote Installation

Windows 2000 Server comes with a handy tool for remotely installing copies of Windows 2000 Professional onto clients. This remote installation system (RIS) is based upon the use of special remote-bootable network interface cards. Essentially, these NICs are the same as any regular Ethernet or other network cards but they also have a Boot PROM that contains a mini boot environment. These Boot PROMs (actually, they use FlashRAM technology rather than EEPROMs) contain the Portable Execution Environment (PXE) designed by the Distributed Management Task Force (DMTF). It comprises a small part of the Desktop Management Interface (DMI) hardware specification that allows Windows desktop clients to be remotely administered. By combining DMI with other network management protocols such as SNMP, RMON, or Web-Based Enterprise Management (WBEM), the DMTF has created a standard for any type of PC client to be remotely managed over the network at an operating systems and at a hardware level. Phew, that was a mouthful of acronyms.

The important thing to remember is that Windows 2000 RIS requires NICs that support PXE and have to be configured as such. The system works by loading a mini OS environment at boot time that installs a TCP/IP protocol stack. This network stack then sends out boot request messages using DHCP to look for the nearest RIS server. The server checks the requesting machine's hardware address (the 6-byte Ethernet address) against its table of configured clients and then proceeds to installation. If the client has been marked for an installation or system upgrade, the server begins by sending instructions on how to format the remote client's drives, then uploads the installation binaries to the client. Once prepped, the client runs the installation script, which loads the operating system onto the client.

Windows 2000 RIS currently only supports installation of Win 2000 Professional onto remote desktops from a Win 2000 Server. Microsoft may introduce other client installations such as Win 9x and perhaps even remote Win 2000 Server installations, but this won't go in until the next full upgrade of RIS, which has not yet been announced. Additionally, the server has to keep the entire copy of the installation files directly on its hard drives. A single copy of Win 2000 Professional takes up almost 650MB and that's when it's compressed.

For NT4, Win 9x, and even Win 3.x systems, there is at least one package out there that does nearly the same thing. A company called ON Technology produces a package called ON Command Client Connection Manager (CCM). This product runs with not only desktops but also laptop systems (which RIS does not yet support) and can also be used to install NT Server on remote systems. It uses a combination of tools: the PXE boot environment to format drives and install the OS, a remote control system that allows an administrator to take over visual control of a desktop to assist people from remote locations, an installation automation tool that records how you install a product so that it can be duplicated for other machines, and a database-driven method of configuring large numbers of clients from a single administrator interface.

The great part of these remote installation packages like RIS and CCM is that they are separate installations per client rather than the raw image copies that we described in the earlier method. Since each client is an automated fresh install, none of the inherent problems of disk imaging come into play. With mass clients, each can be configured with a different set of parameters that you would normally type in during a manual installation—the clients' hostnames, IP addresses, user preferences, account names, and so on.

Application Software Distribution

To automate the distribution of new software or upgrades to client machines around the network, you not only have to be able to run the install program from remote but must also be able to make sure that the following items conform to the specifications of the application and your company policy:

- Client desktop OS and system libraries version management
- Application version management per client desktop
- System preferences per client desktop
- User preferences per client desktop
- License management per application and per client desktop

First you need to check that the remote desktop has the correct OS version and system libraries needed for a fresh install or has an appropriate application version in place for an upgrade. These checks are performed by the application installation program, InstallShield, under Windows. User and system preferences are sometimes dictated by company or IT department policy. For example, everyone might have a special login window specific to the company; they might all have access to their own drives but be unable to mount just any network drive other than those allowed. It might also be safer to not allow users access or run registry control applications like RegEdit, since they have the potential for causing serious harm to the state of the OS. Finally, you have to be able to control licenses for applications installed on remote machines so that your company does not get into legal trouble with the product vendor or the Software Publishers Association.

The rules for distributing application software are somewhat different. The hardware or low-level dependence that is needed for OS distribution does not affect most application software installations. In fact, many applications can be installed while users still have sessions on the machine. Others require only the ability to reboot the server.

UNIX admins are often surprised to find that, for some Windows server applications, you not only have to kick everyone off the machine but you also have to reboot the machine after they are installed. With UNIX there are very few dependencies that affect the system operational status during software installations. So unless you are reconfiguring the UNIX kernel or installing new hardware, you almost never have to reboot. Extensions to the system are handled commonly through shared libraries that are loaded by applications.

Although Windows does have shared libraries, some of them have to be loaded before the user environment is started. Changes to the network interface or GUI properties also require reboots in most cases rather than simply restarting the interface. Almost any component that is implemented in a device driver requires a reboot. Reboot, reboot, reboot. A sad fact of life under Windows.

NT is well known for this bad habit, but Windows 2000 takes some steps to circumvent the need to reboot. Not all server installations require reboots of the whole OS, but installing server packages like Terminal Server, SQL Server, and Exchange still do. For client applications, installation does not affect the operational status as regularly.

With UNIX systems it is possible to create packages that install from prepared scripts. It is even possible to execute these scripts, taking the input from other scripts. Unfortunately, there is no unified system to distribute applications. Windows does not have such a correspondence between the interactive install program and a noninteractive scripting system. Windows Scripting Host can be used to create noninteractive batch programs but does not allow control of a dialog window-based interactive session with InstallShield.

Application Mirroring with Intellimirror

An interesting feature of Windows 2000 is the new Intellimirror data replication service. This system service replicates user data and applications to remote stations whenever and wherever they log on so that they can take their desktop environment with them. It mirrors the applications that person uses that are normally installed on their desktops by keeping a copy of all their personal data and their applications on the server.

Intellimirror is a server-based alternative to directly installing software on workstations or accessing them through Windows Terminal Server. This is the same concept once conceived for network computing and Java-based applications, whereby each user's workstation would be a basic computational engine with nothing but the user's GUI environment installed, and any application the user needs to run is downloaded from a server and then executed locally. Similarly, all the user's own personal data is housed on the server itself, so local hard drives become moot.

Microsoft was dead set against the idea of network computing proposed by Larry Ellison, CEO of their software competitor Oracle, back in 1996. In fact, they boldly declared that it would never work and even created alternate Windows-based boxes called NetPCs, which would sidestep the need for network computers. Ironic, isn't it, that this is exactly what they are building into this latest version of Windows?

Politics aside, Intellimirror serves a very useful purpose. By keeping data and applications off the local machine, there is less involved in managing remote desktops. However, Intellimirror does install the application onto the local desktop after it has been downloaded; it can remove the application after the user is done. This makes plenty of sense for small applications, but for large software suites such as Microsoft Office 97, it would simply take too long to install it every time. Office 2000 has been redesigned to allow server-based execution, a method that is more suited to the Intellimirror system.

What about Terminal Server? It's still there. Turning the Windows GUI into multiple interfaces, all running from a server, has proven to require a hefty server. TS can support over a hundred users at a time, but this requires a high-end server that is brimming with CPU and memory. TS doesn't distribute applications, either—just the visual interface as we described in an earlier section. The general single-user application model for Windows makes Intellimirror a more suitable system than TS when you need to support multiple users. Since Intellimirror does separate installations, which are each basically single-user systems, there is no need to implement any application compatibility scripts as you do with TS.

Remote Application Installers

Packages like Microsoft Systems Management Server, CA Unicenter TNG, and Tivoli Enterprise Manager allow you to distribute application packages to Windows and other platforms from central points. Compared to Intellimirror, these packages directly install the application software on the client permanently, rather than just for the user's session.

The remote agent that sits on each client accepts an order from a server to install an application package. The client receives the data files from the server and runs the installation program with the aid of a preprogrammed script per station. Since this is simply an automated version of a regular application installation, the process continues as normal. The script that it uses is either predefined by the vendor of the software distribution package or has to be developed by your sysadmin staff. The latter means that they may have to learn a new scripting method or a language specific to the distribution software.

License Management

License management in a distributed network environment handles the issuing of individual client licenses per application to each of the different desktop clients. It basically involves keeping an active database of where applications have been deployed, their user information, and the license number assigned to that station. It makes sure that the company does not violate software piracy laws by installing copies of the product without licenses. It also makes sure that products can be supported properly by the vendor, based upon the assigned license number per client. Such packages are also available as part of the major management packages (again Unicenter TNG, SMS, or Tivoli).

License management occurs at two or three levels and in various forms. There is normally a license for the operating system itself. There may be per-client licenses for the server OS for each client that connects to the server. Each client desktop itself must have a separate OS license (different from the per-client licenses on the server). For those of us who use Linux, there's nothing to say but, "Thank you, O Great Open Source gods!"

For Windows systems and other commercial OSs, a different, unprintable, exclamation might be more in order. Still, ours is not to wonder why, ours is but to do or die. At least on one front, there has been an alternative to paying for each and every license for every desktop.

Flat licensing requires you to pay one flat (and sometimes fat) fee for an unlimited number of access licenses. With flat licensing available for some server application packages such as Web servers and some database servers, you no longer have to worry about some users being locked out because of insufficient licenses. This practice is more common with application software than with operating systems (discounting noncommercial use or open source platforms). For example, Netscape Enterprise Server, Microsoft Internet Information Server, and Commerce Servers have removed their original per-user connection licensing and moved toward flat licenses. Database vendors are still with the per-user model in most cases, except when it comes to interfacing their database servers with Web servers, where they too are going the flat licensing way.

As a requirement of licensing, you also have to be able to uniquely identify computers on the network. This requires each desktop to maintain a separate identity on the network from other machines. Windows NT and 2000 use a globally unique identifier (GUID) during the installation time of the system that is used as a security identifier (SID) as well as a means to maintain licenses separately per host. Aside from uniquely identifying the OS, you may also need to uniquely identify the hardware unit that it is running on to keep tabs on hardware components in the system. This falls under the topic of asset management, which Chapter 10 discusses in more detail

Summary

Integrating client systems is a problem of managing access. Users have to be able to do their work without having to deal with complicated interfaces or application compatibility problems. The general approach for this is to provide some sort of connectivity application to a server, a form of application or system emulation that allows users to run their software on their machines, or distributing the software to the users' machines. Connectivity applications come in a variety of forms, ranging from simple text-based access to graphical access through Web browsers. Users may need to learn how to use the connectivity application, but it may be the only way to allow them access. System emulation is a little more risky since it is very difficult to become 100 percent compatible, thus always leaving that small chance that the users' applications may not work right. On the other hand, they are probably already familiar with the emulated environment and won't need to learn too many new things to work it. Distributing application software to the clients is probably the best method, but most distribution packages have to be designed to work with the software you intend to use. Furthermore, distributing the application to the clients is subject to the same pitfall as system emulation, where it becomes harder to manage since it is located on the numerous client stations rather than the much more closely watched servers. You also have to manage the use of any software on your network so as not to get into hot water with the law. Any sort of access will likely have a licensing agreement and, hopefully, a license management tool to help coordinate how they are distributed among the client machines. If not, there are handy third-party tools that can also help keep track.

## PART FOUR

Management Strategies

## CHAPTER 16

Establishing Integrated Management Policies

When you bring an operating system as different as Windows into your UNIX environment, you will need to think in a new light—not only because of the structural differences between the two operating systems but also to herd the new administrative needs of the integration between the two systems.

To manage this mixed environment, you have to develop a set of policies that covers both platforms for your users and your sysadmins. Although policies for usage and management may be the same across the multiple platforms, the actual procedures associated with the policies are usually particular to a platform. Therefore, it is often necessary to have one set of policies and two sets of procedures.

The mixed environment also means bringing the users and the system administration group up to speed on the new system through training or education programs and developing approved practices and processes for all users under the new system—what they should do, what they shouldn't do, and how they should do it.

Policies and Procedures

Policies is a nicer way of saying *the law*. Essentially, policies tell people what is allowed and what is not, within the computing environment of the business. The idea of policies is not to run a police state on your network and use your sysadmins as a secret police force, but to tell users what the company thinks is appropriate for the business environment and to protect users and the network from inadvertent harm through action or inaction in some respect.

Every policy usually has one or more associated procedures that describe how to carry it out. *Procedures* describe step-by-step operations to carry out a policy when necessary. They can be simple, such as "In case of a sudden implosion of your computer, contact technical support," or they can be as detailed as who to contact, what security authorization code to provide, how to explain the issue, how to approach the issue, how to handle the issue, and how to report on the issue (in case you happen to be running an international espionage operation). Procedures need not be technical and can involve administrative tasks, as well.

These policies and procedures are grouped according to who will use them—the sysadmins or the general user population. The sysadmins who are involved in most of the management (and sometimes menial) tasks of keeping the systems and network running need policies and procedures associated with these management tasks. Users, on the other hand, need a list of policies that define how they are allowed to use the computing resources to do their jobs.

Policy Handbooks

A policy handbook outlines the standard policies and procedures of your network. There are usually two handbooks, one for users and one for system administrators. The contents of each are fairly different because of the needs of each side.

The sysadmin handbook should also include copies of the user policies within, but in addition, they may also have procedures that explain what to do if a user breaks those policies for whatever reason.

The handbooks should be well identified and be kept in a prominent location, physically and online. Many sysadmins have the opinion that handbooks belong in the circular filing cabinet (the trash can), but when they hit a pinch they realize just how helpful handbooks can be—when they are done right, of course.

The last thing you need is a hefty tome fit for a scribal monk in some remote medieval monastery. System administrators should be given a small folder that outlines the policies and procedures intended for them. A few pages is all the users may need. Nothing is more overwhelming (not to mention boring) than having to read through pages and pages of policies that explain every single thing that a user or sysadmin can or cannot do. The longer it is, the less likely that people will pay attention to it or use it. Succinctness is crucial.

As mentioned, a policy is a statement of fact about what is acceptable use of the computing environment. With this in mind, here are a few words about writing policies:

- At the start, specify when, where, how, and to whom a policy is applicable.
- Keep sentences short, and do not use too many clauses in a single statement.
- Use examples to illustrate the point, but do not be superfluous or wild.
- Do not use legalese. Most people find it hard to understand.
- Do not make vague, hypothetical, or impractical statements.
- Do not use words that sound accusing, or try to place blame.
- Try to keep the total number of policies low.
- Give information on who to contact with further questions.
- Give information on who to contact in case of emergencies or inadvertent actions.

Procedures are instructions on what to do when something outlined in the handbook occurs. When developing documentation on procedures, keep the following in mind:

- Give short step-by-step instructions on exactly what to do.
- Do not skip any steps to make it brief.
- Give examples of what to expect as a response when a step is performed.
- Do not assume that the person will know what something means; explain it if necessary or tell them when it is not necessary to know it.
- Explain what to do when encountering errors while performing the procedures.
- Give information on who to contact in case of emergencies, inadvertent actions, or failure of the procedures.

When it comes to an integrated computing environment, the policy handbook may outline ways to perform particular instructions on operating systems the person may not be familiar with. For example, if the only tech-support person who comes across a problem on the UNIX side happens to be familiar with the Windows environment only, a step-by-step procedure sheet might help stem the tide of calls for help from the users, not to mention possibly save the company money due to lost productivity.

Policies for the System Administrators

System administrators have to work together to get things done around the network. You could have a small enough network that one person can handle it all, but even in such cases, a written explanation of all policies and procedures will help others in the event of a failure.

Server Task Log

The server task log or administrator's log contains records of all major activities or procedures that have been performed by any of the sysadmins on that server. The purpose of the log is to keep track of when a sysadmin performed an activity and what exactly was done. It is really just a notebook for the server that can be analyzed in the future if something else goes wrong. It can help another sysadmin track down a problem or repeat a procedure that they are not familiar with. The log is best kept in written form near the server or in a common location. The IT manager or server group manager should keep track of who has the log at all times and make sure that they check the log back in after they are done.

Although it is not possible to record every single event or activity, the log should be kept to a certain level of accuracy. There is no point to a log if the information is imprecise or incorrect. Each record should contain the time and date, the name of the sysadmin, a simple description of the activity, and any details on important system commands that are executed. When the operation is complete, the sysadmin should write down the end time, whether the activity was completed successfully, and any status report about the system that others should be aware of following this activity.

A more advanced form of the log is a *trouble-ticketing system*, in which the sysadmin uses special software to keep the log entries. This system

Excuses, Excuses, Excuses

We can hear the groans already. "Policies?! (Whine) Procedures??!!? (Whine again) Why??" Nothing is worse than excuses for the lack of policies and procedures. They basically amount to justifications for being lazy. They sound silly when we list them, but in truth, these are fairly common in many IT shops. Here are some that have little ground to stand on:

EXCUSES FOR THE LACK OF SECURITY POLICIES

1. What's a security policy?
2. We don't have any security problems, so we don't need a security policy.
3. We set our security policies when a problem arises.
4. We can throw together a security policy; just give us a day.
5. Everything changes so often that we can't keep track of the security issues.
6. We have a very tight security system. Our vendor assured us so.
7. We keep log files.
8. Our CIO/COO/IT manager never asked us to do it.
9. Our users are smart and trustworthy, so we don't really need policies.
10. We don't really have any important data, so we don't really need a policy.
11. We don't have the time or the staff to handle security policies.
12. We can't afford it.
13. We have them, but no one uses them.
14. I think someone here knows what the policy is.
15. That's all legal mumbo-jumbo and a waste of my time.

EXCUSES FOR THE LACK OF SYSADMIN PROCEDURES

1. What's a procedures file for?
2. Our sysadmins know what they're doing, so we just leave it to them.
3. We only have a few machines to deal with, so we don't need such procedures.
4. The changes or fixes are fairly minor, so we don't need to document them or follow strict procedures.
5. Someone else will handle the procedures while I fix the actual problem.
6. I followed some of the procedures, at least.
7. Who has the time for following procedures?
8. We can't afford it.
9. We have a very stable system. Our vendor assured us so.
10. The operating system logs some of the sysadmin activity, so we don't need any other procedures.

automatically records all the documentation regarding the procedure or problem. Essentially, each activity is assigned a ticket that is kept open until the procedure is complete. The system records the sysadmin who opened the ticket and the person who is handling it. The sysadmin enters the nature of the event or problem and a description of how it is resolved. The name does not imply that you use it only to handle your problem situations. Any event can be an opportunity to open a ticket, including regularly scheduled events such as backups or periodic performance data collection.

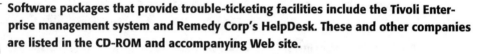

Software packages that provide trouble-ticketing facilities include the Tivoli Enterprise management system and Remedy Corp's HelpDesk. These and other companies are listed in the CD-ROM and accompanying Web site.

Environmental Emergencies

Environmental emergencies are those that pertain to the physical environment that the systems are in. There are a number of possibilities for such emergencies, including power failure, air-conditioning system failure, fire, water damage, theft, and physical damage. These are physical risks to the computing environment that may also be harmful to personnel. Procedures for handling these emergencies should be among the first and foremost of those that you develop. The conditions and solutions can differ for each.

You can define at least three levels of threat when it comes to environmental emergencies, worded simply as *small incidents*, *big incidents*, and *dangerous incidents*. If someone spills a cup of coffee on a computer, that counts as a small incident since it can pretty much be handled by the user, a sysadmin, or the custodial engineer (the janitor). Big incidents are problems that take time or effort to clear up and may involve more than one person; however, the problem itself may not be harmful or dangerous to personnel. For example, the power to a room may go down because of a blown transformer, which requires the help of building services as well as sysadmins to take care of the problem on several sides. A dangerous incident is definitely something that individuals should avoid. Usually this involves calling the fire department, the paramedics, or the police, and getting out of the way.

The procedures should outline how to handle each level of threat, who to contact, and what to do immediately. Any witnesses should be asked to give a short statement for your own records if it is a big or dangerous incident. Procedures for a dangerous incident should also outline what to do to get out of harm's way, such as a building evacuation plan.

Server rooms require particular attention when it comes to environmental emergencies; however, with just some basics it is possible to avert or at least limit the small incidents and even some of the big ones:

- Keep a working fire extinguisher in the server room at all times.
- Have a fire alarm installed just outside the room.
- Have smoke detectors installed inside the room.
- Keep a portable blow dryer or leaf blower in the server room. They come in handy to quickly dry off any wetness.
- Keep paper towels in the room, preferably inside a box or cabinet.
- Doors, windows, and other entryways should have alarm security.
- Keep a room thermometer and hygrometer (humidity meter) in the server room.
- Keep a first-aid box handy in the room, just in case.
- If you can, install an emergency power-off button for the transformer that feeds the power to the room.

In any case, you should never risk exposing yourself or others to personal injury when confronted with such a situation. We certainly hope you don't end up barbecued; your company surely doesn't either. Let others know that heroics are nice in theory but fairly painful in practice, and are strongly discouraged in your policies.

System Installation

Policies and procedures on new-system installation inform sysadmins on what they should do to bring a new hardware and operating system online on the network. These steps include following the requirements of hardware systems used by the company and requirements on where and how to connect to the network, how to install operating system software, where to get and how to assign OS licenses, how to tag the unit with an asset number and collect the asset information, how to add it to the list of systems to be backed up, and how to add it to the list of systems to be monitored and managed.

The policy should state when and where systems are allowed to be installed. The idea is that people should not indiscriminately toss another machine onto the network without the knowledge of the IT staff. Not only will this cause an unexpected load on the network and access resources not prescribed to it, but it is definitely a security threat. The people who have the knowledge and ability to install a new machine on your network are most likely in your sysadmin crew so, in a way, this is protection from their errors.

The procedures for this part are likely to be pretty long; after all, just installing a new machine can take some time, expertise, and tools. A step-by-step instruction guide for installing a system may be too complex to word, especially when you have a variety of types and configurations of systems to install. In the policy part, you can specify major tasks that need to be done and perhaps elaborate on the procedure a little.

Application Installation

Application installation policies and procedures inform the sysadmins on what they need to do to install a new package on a system. These steps include who can requisition the software, where to get the software, which systems it can be installed on, how to install it, how to get a software license number if needed, how to configure the software, how to add the software to the system asset sheet, and how to monitor or manage the software.

Like the system installation policy, the point of this is to prevent people from indiscriminately installing application software on any system. The good thing about this is that it can actually be enforced to some degree by securing the operating system environment against software installations. Basically, limit the access to system accounts that can perform the installation.

There should also be a policy on what to do when a sysadmin finds an application that has been installed without the knowledge of the IT group, either by another sysadmin or by a user. You should approach this as a potential threat to the network, a procedure discussed in a following section.

Crucial Systems Failures

When a crucial system such as a server goes down for any reason, the sysadmins should know how to respond. Since this is likely to cause a lot of people some worry and anxiety, it involves not only handling the technical problem with the server but also the administrative problems of the users.

Failures of this nature could be because of any number of reasons: hardware component failure, operating systems failure or crash, power failure, network failure, or application failure. Each of these needs its own set of procedures that sysadmins can follow to resolve the situation.

Basically, in the event of a crucial system failure, the procedures should include the following:

- Record when the failure occurred.
- Contact other sysadmin personnel assigned to handle a server failure situation.
- Assign an individual to answer the telephones and leave a message on the answering service informing others about the situation.
- Attempt to limit the problem to one system.
- Attempt to determine the nature of the problem.
- Describe the state of the component that caused the failure.
- Record what is being done to bring the system back online.
- Record the time and status when the system is brought back online.
- Inform all users that the system is back up.
- Return relevant telephone calls on the technical-support line answering service.

Once the immediate fix has been made, the sysadmins should go back and analyze what caused the problem so that they can learn from the event. In some cases, a quick scan will show that an important hardware component simply failed; there's no protection against that, really. Other cases might be more complex, such as a OS crash, which requires expertise in analyzing a crash dump and system applications to recreate the system status just before the crash.

Noncrucial Systems Failures

Other systems that are not as crucial to the operational status of your computing environment for your users can also experience failures. These include user workstation failures, printer failures, network end-point connectivity failure, and generally any other type of failure that does not affect more than a few individuals.

Although the problem is still significant to the users, you don't need to rush to gather a large group of sysadmins to attempt to solve the issue. The policies for these failures should state how to record them as a work order on a component, how to determine the nature of the problem, how to record the status of the failing component, how and where to get a replacement or fix, and how to record whether there are any changes to the asset description.

System Backup

The system backup policy defines how data from important servers and systems is to be saved to tape or other media. Backups are a regular part of any sysadmin's job. The policy and procedures define when and how they are to be done.

A simple backup policy includes a schedule of times when backups are to be performed, a roster of sysadmins whose duties are to perform the backups, a description of which systems and drives are to be backed up, a description of which tapes the backups are to be stored on, a description of how to perform the backup operation, a description of where the tapes are to be stored, and a description of how to log the backup activity.

Hand in hand with a backup policy is the *restore policy*, which defines when and how a data set can be restored from backup tapes. This policy and associated procedure defines who can request a restore operation, when it can be done, how to locate tapes that contain the appropriate backups, how to perform the restore operation, and how to log the restore activity.

Security Threat Management

The security threat management procedures inform the sysadmins what to do in case they detect a potential threat to the security of the computing environment. These procedures are necessary since not all sysadmins can be security specialists and know what to do when such a threat occurs.

Security threats can be an internal or external matter. Employees within a company are the primary source of internal security threats. These fall into two subcategories: the *malicious cracker* and the *accidental cracker*. The former includes disgruntled employees or ex-employees who purposely attempt to disrupt or destroy the company network by using resources within the company and their knowledge of the system. The worst kind is a disgruntled ex-sysadmin. The accidental cracker is a user who blindly runs a program obtained off the Internet or from a friend or stranger; the program can be a Trojan horse that attempts to break into the system in various ways or causes associated problems.

External attacks come over connections to the Internet or other networks. These are completely unpredictable and should always be considered malicious. To prevent most such attacks, you should definitely have a firewall in place.

The procedures on security threat management need to include how to monitor for suspicious behavior, how to record an incident and all its activities, who should be contacted immediately, which log files should be looked at and saved elsewhere, how to check the authenticity of an account, how to check the network connection for the account, how to determine the access and execution rights of the user, how to record the command execution history of the user during the incident, how to shut down the user or close off their access to other systems, how to shut down the systems that the user is on, and how to write up the complete incident report.

User Monitoring

The user monitoring policy is often left out of many policy handbooks because of its negative connotations. However, for legal purposes it can be a very useful guide. This policy often mirrors the policies intended for users.

People tend to forget that all computing resources within a company are normally considered the property of the company. This means *everything*—including the computer systems, the disks and their contents, online and printed documents, and even e-mail. Users should not be keeping personal files on the company network unless they have no reason to worry about sysadmins looking them over.

This policy defines what sysadmins can and cannot do when it comes to monitoring users. User monitoring does not mean that sysadmins have "god authority" to do anything. However, they can exercise the policy in the course of trying to neutralize a security threat.

The policy should contain such details as when it is appropriate to monitor the user's current screen or process activity from remote; stop user processes and jobs; log off a user forcibly; disable a user account for logins or specific activities; copy, modify, or delete a user's files; remove the user's rights to access their own files; cut off a user's network or Internet access; or cut off a user's access to network resources such as drives, printers, or applications.

Policies for the Users

User policies exist to assist users in receiving help for problems with the computing resources and to indemnify the company from improper use of the resources. A general set of computing services policies for all users should be included with every new-employee information packet. Others should be posted near common resource areas, such as near network printers, network faxes, the server room, or the company library.

Account or System Usage

The account or system usage policy defines how users are allowed to use their accounts and systems on the company network. Often this is the primary and only policy that is presented to users. It is often also referred to as an *acceptable usage policy*.

Limited strictly to accounts and systems, this policy defines who is allowed to use the account or system, whether the users are allowed to share it with others, when they are allowed to login to use it, what kind of usage is considered unacceptable behavior, whether they are allowed to install new hardware or software to the system on their own, whether they are allowed to take data from the computers off-site, and how often they should change their passwords.

Network and Internet Usage

The network usage policy defines when and how users are allowed to use the local network and access to the Internet. Local network usage is a fact of life. When it comes to the Internet, almost everybody needs it or wants it these days. Since the possibilities of what they can do are fairly huge, you should list what they are not allowed to do.

Depending on how strict your company's Internet policy is, you can limit the users from accessing news servers, personal chat rooms, and other non-work-related sites; uploading or downloading porn, illegal software, or other questionable material; downloading and executing software received over the Internet without running a virus check first; setting up personal Web pages not related to their work; sending or receiving large e-mail attachments or files over a certain size; setting up network server software within their own accounts or systems without sysadmin consent; and running snoop or other promiscuous-mode software to monitor traffic over the network.

You should also have a policy against internal or external e-mail spamming (mass mailing). Spamming can be an enormous waste of bandwidth and is annoying to most users. Spamming is usually intentional, although it does not necessarily have to be commercial. For example, chain letters are considered spamming by most. They serve little purpose and simply spread like a virus across your users' e-mail accounts, chewing up bandwidth, disk space, and system resources each time they are sent out. If a user needs to be able to send messages out to large groups of users, you should look into setting up group discussion databases, chat rooms, or e-mail list services.

Printer Usage

Printer usage policies are normally set for users of shared network printers. They describe what constitutes print output that is valid for business purposes, how many copies users may be allowed to print, when they are allowed to print large documents, what users should do when a printer jams or incurs a technical problem, what users should do when they send invalid or unwanted output to the printer, and what users should do when a print job comes out incorrectly from the printer.

The users should usually be provided with a set of the simpler procedures involved in printing, such as how to refill the printer with paper, how to clear the paper path after a paper jam, how to reset the printer, and how to cancel a print job. A sheet on these procedures will go a long way toward saving the sysadmins time.

Keep in mind that the need for printer paper kills more trees a year than most other kinds of pollution, so please do try to get your users to print less often.

Remote Access Policies

Remote access policies describe how users can access the corporate network from an off-site location. Any company that has remote access servers and provides these services to its users should have a well-defined policy and procedure set for its users. Remote access is one of the biggest sources of external security threats, and as such can be the cause of a lot of network and system management costs.

Remote access policies need to define which users will be allowed to access the system remote, when they can access it, where they can access it from, whether they should inform others before connecting in remotely, what accounts they can use, what software and hardware they can use, how they should configure the software for remote access, what tasks or operations they can perform, how long they can stay connected, and how they can reach technical support for further assistance.

Each user needs to have a set of procedures that shows how they can connect, disconnect, and access the company network from the outside. This may be several different sets of procedures, one each for every type of platform that you allow to connect from remote.

Telecommuting is becoming a favorite among many users these days, which makes remote access policies even more vital. Since these users are likely to be connected for long hours from home, they can often fall into the habit of leaving themselves logged in. Deciding on whether to install automatic logout after idle timeouts depends on how you support your users. It makes it safer for you but is an annoyance for your user. For telecommuting users, keep a record of the systems they use just as if they were an asset of the company. In fact, you should consider supplying the users with computing equipment for their home use, just so it is maintained under company regulations and warranties.

Training Development

Training your users in the newly integrated system and developing adequate training materials will contribute highly to the integration project's degree of success. After all, if no one uses or wants to use the system, it isn't likely to create too many benefits for the company now, is it? Developing a training program involves determining what needs to be taught, selecting a team of trainers, picking a style or format for training, developing training documentation and materials, planning training sessions and execution, and confirming the results of the training process. There are two types of people who need different training processes: the users and the sysadmins.

When a project has been implemented, there are likely to be many facets of the system that people may or may not directly use. It is up to the program developer to determine what users and sysadmins need to know and don't need to know about the system. Sysadmins need to know the technology behind the new system, how it works, and how it interfaces with the old system (see Table 16.1). They have to have at hand the details of the new configuration, either in a central record, if you have a nonhierarchical IT group where all tasks are almost evenly distributed, or distributed hierarchically to the respective sysadmins in charge of specific functions or systems. If the new system invokes some change in how technical support services are provided, then the sysadmins must be informed of their new responsibilities, who they will be supporting, and who they will be reporting to. Finally, they should have a diagram visualizing what the new system looks like and a quick list that they can use to answer the most basic or frequently asked questions about the new system. After they answer those questions a few times, the information will pretty much sink into long-term memory.

Users need to know what the new system looks like from their perspective (i.e., the user interface). If the system involves direct changes to a particular action or function that they are used to, they need to have a step-by-step description of the process (see Table 16.2). The quickest way is to draw up a document outlining most of the commonly used processes, complete with step-by-step instructions and screen snapshots of what the process may look like. Users should be informed on how to get more technical help and who to ask for it.

Selecting a training team and a style for training go hand in hand. The best way is to first get your IT staff up to par before moving to your users. In fact, some of your IT staff may become members of your training team. Training can be directly from a vendor or from a professional training organization. In the Microsoft world, there is a certified affiliate

Table 16.1 IT Staff Training Needs

INTEGRATION PROJECT	TRAINING REQUIRED
PC-X.	How X Windows works on top of Windows GUI.
	How to configure PC-X software.
	How to set up access to X-applications.
	How to set up network user authentication for X-applications.
	How to set up monitoring of X-application usage.
Telnet, TN3270 terminal applications.	How applications work between client and server.
	How to configure user authentication.
	How to configure clients to access servers.
	How to set up monitoring of application usage.
Web-based applications.	How applications integrate with the Web browser.
	How to configure applications for the system.
	How to configure user authentication and access.
	How to configure the application server system or protocol.
	How to set up monitoring of the Web application server.
New client hardware and OS system.	Familiarization with hardware (when and how to on/off, reset).
	How to boot up the system.
	How to log in and out.
	How to set up network resources on clients.
	How to set up the new OS.
	How to set up applications on the client OS.
	How to manage/monitor the new OS.
New multiplatform applications.	Familiarization with how the multiplatform application works on each platform.
	How to configure applications on each platform.
	How to provide user access to applications.

Table 16.1   *(Continued)*

INTEGRATION PROJECT	TRAINING REQUIRED
	How to access OS or network resources from applications for each platform.
File system integration.	Familiarization with how file systems integrate between multiple platforms.
	How to define volumes for export over network.
	How to mount/unmount volumes.
	How to define user authentication or access rights for volumes.
	How to monitor file system use.
Printer integration.	Familiarization with how network printers work with OS.
	How to export network printers to servers and clients.
	How to stop or cancel print jobs.
	How to monitor print activity.

training program known as the *Microsoft Certification* program that is provided in various training centers in major cities around the world. These programs are intended most for IT staff and software developers rather than end users of applications.

How the training is presented is just as important as who is teaching it. Training can come in various forms, such as direct live presentations, hands-on training and testing, computer-assisted training, and self-study documents. Live presentations take you back to the style of classes in college and high school. There is a strong dependence on the trainer to provide an interesting presentation to keep the attention of the trainees. They must also be supported with printed documentation on the same material. Hands-on testing implies that the classroom or training session will take place directly at a computer station so that the users can try out commands while being monitored and assisted by trainers. Finally, self-paced and self-study training require that all the material be presented in printed or online forms that the users can read and try out themselves. This last form is pretty much what most IT groups end up doing, since it does not require the more expensive training facilities and instructors setup.

Table 16.2   User Training Needs

INTEGRATION PROJECT	TRAINING REQUIRED
User-interface integration projects (PC-X, Terminal applications, Web-based applications).	Familiarization with the new user interface. How to log in and log out. How to access applications. How to locate resources. How to find online help.
New client hardware and OS system.	Familiarization with hardware (when and how to on/off, reset). How to boot up the system. How to log in and out. How to access applications. How to locate resources. How to find help online.
New multiplatform application.	Familiarization with the new application interface and any differences between platforms.
File system and printer integration projects.	How to access network volumes and files. How to transfer documents between network and local volumes. How to use network printers. How to stop or cancel print jobs.

Summary

No matter how bureaucratic it may seem, policy handbooks define the responsibilities of the user and the sysadmin to everyone involved. They determine what is and is not allowed and how to do the right thing. Defining policies is just "good egg" behavior. Some policies involve dire events that are not as likely to happen, but it is still better to have a plan than to plan on it never happening.

Once people have become familiar with the policies, you have to train them to understand how to use the system properly. The two groups—users and sysadmins—have different training needs but require an equal amount of attention. A good training program reduces the number of tech-support calls, so think of it as a strategic headache reliever. It may be enough to save you from snapping in two some day in the future!

## CHAPTER 17

System and Security Management

C omputers so advanced, they practically run themselves was a common sales pitch heard through the 1980s. The only proper response to that is "Hah!" Computers are nothing but a technical administration headache. Windows machines are twice the pain, and mixed Windows-UNIX environments are quadruple it.

The good news is that it is getting better. Windows 2000 has a solid, consistent management interface, which few other operating system vendors can brag about. The jumble of tools that were in NT have been rewritten to the new Microsoft Management Console API and now fit into a single easy-to-use interface. This covers all areas of server and system management on a single-node basis. You will still need an enterprise network management platform if you are serious about running a heterogeneous network environment, but the management console is ergonomically fit to monitor and fix machines on an individual basis.

Security management in Windows 2000 and UNIX network environments uses a combination of individual-node security and services available to the entire network. This chapter discusses the systems and security management of Windows 2000, as well as the tools that you should look into to keep your mixed-platform network safe and manageable.

System Management

System management is a Sisyphean labor of constant vigilance and repetitious operations. Although new software tools simplify the work, someone still has to put their hands on a keyboard to it. The mixed-environment problem is manageable, but it is still quite a job to keep three groups of systems going: the Windows-only systems, the UNIX-only systems, and the Windows-UNIX integrated systems. Only the first and last systems are discussed here.

Microsoft Management Console

The standardized system administration framework available with Microsoft Management Console (MMC) provides a centralized interface for all system and network services. The MMC can access any node within the domain that it is allowed access to. It is used in two different modes, *user* and *author*, to differentiate between the ability to simply access and use the console and the authority to create custom consoles for yourself or other users. These modes are set as options when the console is created.

The user mode comes in three versions: *full access, delegated access with multiple windows*, and *delegated access with a single window*. Full-access user-mode consoles allow the user full access to any aspect of the console, except for adding or removing MMC snap-ins, or changing the snap-in extensions available. Thus, a privileged user running a full-access user-mode console will be able to perform any of the tasks defined in the console. A delegated-access user-mode console allows the user to see only the portion of the console specific to their sysadmin duties. Thus, a sysadmin assigned to manage the DNS name space will have access only to the DNS Management snap-in, or even to only one specific domain within the snap-in. The difference between the multiple- and single-window versions is that the latter only allows the user to launch one instance of the console at a time.

The author mode allows privileged users to create new MMC consoles, defining the snap-ins and extensions appropriate for the sysadmin that the console is intended for. This mode is used more to create the delegated access. The author mode also allows the administrator to define which machine the console applies to, if the service is specific to a machine.

The MMC application itself can normally be run by anyone, but it does not actually show anything other than the framework. To use MMC, you have to have the proper access to the console file. A number of predefined user-mode consoles exist under the **Start Menu**, **Programs**, **Administrative Tools** menu. These normally include all aspects of management for one particular type of system service or component, such as DNS, Active Directory, and so on, and are usually assigned to the local node only.

Author-Mode MMC

You can also create your own console interface by launching a new instance directly from the command line, **mmc**. This allows you to create custom management controls that can be assigned to different system administrators and operators. You can then add the different management components presented in your MMC console by clicking on **Console**, **Add/Remove Snap-In**, **Add** and then selecting the components. Each of these components has its own set of extensions.

For example, the *Computer Management* console will normally contain all the elements needed to manage a specific node, including disk management, group policies, system services, and so on. By first deselecting the **Add all extensions** checkbox, you can focus the specific extensions that will go into this console. The MMC console files can then be saved in \Winnt\System32 with a *.msc* extension (also called a Microsoft Common Console Document).

An MMC file created for a user can be stored in their own personal folder area as well, but make sure that only that user or group is allowed access to the file, or others will be able to look into the details of the system. The administrator can define a group policy object for the **mmc.exe** application in the system directory to prevent nonsysadmins from running the tool, as well. This is just a security precaution. They may not be able to execute or change the status of the component, since it is checked when they run the program, but there is no need to make it easier for potential crackers to know the details of how the system is configured.

MMC and Active Directory

Active Directory allows administrators to delegate the management of the directory space to other sysadmins. This focuses the work to only the specific tasks that each sysadmin is allowed to perform. For example, some sysadmins may only be allowed to modify the information of user accounts within a given organizational unit (OU), while others may be allowed to create new OUs, add users or services, or back up the site-specific directory contents.

To perform such delegation, you need to use the group policy object system described later in this chapter. By defining a group policy, you can control the specific items that each sysadmin or operator is allowed to work with, and then apply this policy to a specific OU or node on the network.

Windows Service Packs

Service packs entered the Windows NT picture when Microsoft realized that it needed to send a large group of updates and bug fixes to users. Each service pack includes all the fixes and changes of previous service packs, as well. Thus, since NT 3.51, rather than issue version upgrades as most software companies do, Microsoft has released service packs. In truth, you should look at a new service pack as a minor upgrade (e.g., NT 4 with SP3 should really be thought of as NT 4.3). Microsoft's position is that it does not want to release them as version-number upgrades due to the confusion this can cause. Nonetheless, it still recommends that all users upgrade to the most recent service pack. The most recent one, but probably not the last, is Service Pack 6 for NT 4.

Windows 2000 will continue to have service packs after its formal release, but the new system makes it much simpler to deploy a service pack or backtrack from one. In previous versions, a service pack became part of the system and could not be uninstalled. The problem in this case was that some service packs could cause other applications or tools to break because the service packs made changes in the DLLs or replaced them all together. Most times, there was no way to know which components would break, and the poor sysadmin had to bite the bullet and do the installation. Previously, the only way to backtrack would have been to reinstall NT 4 straight from the CD-ROM and then reapply the earlier service pack.

With Win 2000 Service Pack Slipstreaming, it is now possible to add and remove a new service pack. Essentially, it keeps copies of the OS environment before the upgrade so that it can deinstall the upgrade if necessary. This goes hand in hand with the new DLL version conflict management system built into Win 2000. It reduces many of the headaches involved in installing system software.

Cross-Platform System and Network Management

Cross-platform system and network management is a beautiful dream of product managers and chief information officers. In reality, it rarely happens perfectly. A wide range of monitoring tools for cross-platform network environments is available. Some products even offer remote methods to change the configuration of systems, but only on a top level. In almost all cases, it is a lowest-common-denominator situation, and you will eventually end up going back to system management per platform at some level. The following subsections discuss some categories of system and network administration products.

 Further details on the products discussed in the following subsections are available on the Web site.

Enterprise Network Management Tools

Enterprise network management (ENM) tools are a supercategory or suite of products that collect and present statistics from each and every node on the network. They normally use a standardized network management protocol such as the Simple Network Management Protocol (SNMP), version 1, 2, or 3, and the Remote Monitoring (RMON) protocol, version 1 or 2. Each node runs an agent that collects this data, which can later be retrieved by a central network management workstation. Most ENMs are suites of products that combine the services of many of the other categories.

Leading packages in this category include IBM/Tivoli Systems' *Enterprise Management* system, Sun Microsystems' *Solstice Enterprise Manager*, HP's *OpenView*, Cabletron's *Spectrum*, and Computer Associates *Unicenter TNG*. Each provides about the same number of features and supports a large range of hardware and operating system platforms.

System Monitoring and Analysis Tools

These tools monitor the activity of the server operating system and can collate the information from any of the other managed systems on the network. For each managed system, the tool maintains a log of the machine's historical activity to determine trends in the usage of the system. It can also be used to track down recurring problems that are evident only under live-usage scenarios and cannot be replicated easily.

These tools are commonly subcomponents of ENM suites but are also available in separate packages. They include such packages as HP's *OpenView GlancePlus*, Platinum Technology's *ProVision* (now produced by Computer Associates), Tivoli Systems' *Distributed Monitoring*, and Boole and Babbage's *Command/Post*.

Network Monitoring Tools

These tools actively watch nodes on the network to detect if the nodes or any particular network services that they run go down. They usually provide an visual interface identifying each node or each service that is being monitored. In some cases, the packages also test the responsiveness of the node or service, to determine how well or poorly it is performing. When a monitored node or service starts behaving poorly, an event is triggered, which is indicated on the visual map and with sound alarms. These tools can also send notices to sysadmins by e-mail or directly to a personal pager, if a modem is attached to the workstation. Some of these tools may trigger a corrective action in an attempt to fix the problem, although in most cases, they simply attempt to restart the service.

Some of these packages include MediaHouse Software's *Enterprise Monitor*, Heroix's *Robomon*, Ipswitch's *WhatsUp Gold*, and VitalSigns Software's *VitalSuite*. Most of these packages run on Windows platforms. Most network management tools already include this capability as a subcomponent, although these tools are available separately.

Network Diagramming Tools

These are basically drawing programs that are geared toward creating maps of computer networks. Although any drawing program, such as Adobe Illustrator, can be used to create such maps, these tools make it significantly easier with actions that directly correspond to network concepts (e.g., Ethernet links, wireless lines, etc.). Furthermore, the icons and template images used to denote objects on the network are usually very accurate, thus allowing the sysadmin to create a professional-looking network map, suitable for presentation to the executive staff or customers.

The leader in this market is Visio, with several different packages for creating such technical diagrams. In particular, Visio's *Enterprise* is the most useful for network and system administrators. Other packages include NetFormx's *SE* and NetSuite's *Professional Series*. Some of these packages can interface with ENM tools to provide the network map that the ENM package will use.

Network Simulation and Performance Analysis Tools

These tools create simulations or generate test load factors for nodes on the network. They provide a means to stress test your network environment independently of the operating platform, so that you can determine how your network might perform under different situations. Network and application simulators either recreate your network environment completely in software or run tests on your existing network. A software-based simulation is nice since it does not require that you lock out your users from all the machines being tested, as you would with a real test environment, which is often not at all possible in large existing installations. On the other hand, it is only a simulation and may not accurately portray the capabilities of the machine hardware and operating systems in real-world conditions.

Popular network and application simulation packages include Make Systems' *NetMaker XA*, Bluecurve's *Dynameasure* (for Windows platforms), Compuware Corporation's *EcoScope*, MIL3's *IT DecisionGuru*, Analytical Engine's *NetRule*, and NetCracker Technology's *NetCracker Professional*.

Network performance and protocol analyzers can be software or hardware/software combination tools that test not just the low-level network hardware but also network and application protocol behavior. Protocol analyzers can also troubleshoot network problems by showing the exact contents of packets reaching a node or crossing the network at any point. If you have ever wondered what happened to the traffic flow you predicted, you can pop out a protocol analyzer and watch the traffic at different points on the network to see where it is getting mangled. The biggest benefit of protocol analyzers is that they are normally independent passive watchers that can be closely matched across several different sites.

By directly connecting several analyzers, you can test the exact performance of network transfers down to the millisecond. Network performance analyzers include Ganymede Software's *Chariot* (software), HP's *Internet Advisor*, and a number of software/hardware products from Wandel & Goltermann, Network Associates, and Network Instruments.

Security Management

Keeping in proper shape for security is not much different from a regular exercise program. If you slack off, eventually it will come around to hit you where it really hurts. Security requires a holistic approach to management involving users, software, computers, and the network. It is great that Windows 2000 now combines these concepts well through its intricately meshed directory system. Features such as Kerberos authentication, Extensible Authentication Protocol, group policies, and Active Directory domains not only increase the level of security but can be used to control the minutia of each system component.

However, this intricacy is exactly the thing that keeps it apart from UNIX and complicates the matter of security management. It will take some time for integrated security to catch up to the flexibility of the new system. In the meantime, the similarities to NT allow older software packages to work with Windows 2000, as well. This means the security component of an enterprise management system may still be valid under the new version, although you should still expect to upgrade to the Windows 2000 model in due course.

Security Management in Windows 2000

There are many security management components in Windows 2000 that have no equivalent in UNIX systems—in particular, the *group policy system* and the *security template*. The group policy system allows you to control many aspects of a user's environment when the user accesses a particular program or logs into a particular machine. The security template defines the access rights and limits on a particular machine for all users. The difference between the two is that group policies describe how the user's account is to react to the system environment, and security templates describe how the system is to react to the user's behavior. Thus, they complement each other.

Group Policies in Windows 2000

The group policy system replaces the older NT system of user and system policies. It is based on Active Directory's hierarchy of domains, groups, and users. Since every user belongs to one group or another, the easiest way to set policies per user is to define a group policy object (GPO) for a group of users, and then assign the user to that group. This policy is checked each time the user logs in, not only to authenticate the user but to also see what the user is allowed access to. The good thing about group policies is that they are independent of any individual users, applications, or machines and yet can still control access on a per-user or per-machine basis. Thus, sysadmins do not have to repeatedly create the GPO per server or workstation they manage. The GPO can still be specific to a machine if the sysadmin desires to define it as such.

Furthermore, the effects of policies are cumulative, and sysadmins can define restrictions at different levels for the domain, for the group, for a subgroup, or for the user. Policies at a higher level (the domain) can be overridden by policies at a lower level (the user) as the grouping becomes more and more specific to the individual.

The GPO is a complex object that can be applied to individual computers, groups of users, Active Directory organizational units, and Active Directory sites. For each GPO, there is a set of policies for the computer configuration and the user configuration, each of which, in turn has three types of settings: software settings, Windows settings, and administrative templates. These three settings are known as *group policy extensions* and are groupings of individual policy items.

The software settings extension includes policy items available for application software that have been packed with Windows Installer. The actual items vary according to the software but typically include items such as control of access of the software, permissions to reconfigure the software, and permissions to install or remove components of the software.

The Windows settings extension includes type subsets, the security settings and the Windows startup and shutdown scripts. These policy items control all security rights that affect the operation of the Windows environment, including user rights, account policies, system services, registry operation, file system services, IP security policies, and security certificate policies. The Windows startup and shutdown scripts are executed when a member of that group initiates a boot, reboot, or shutdown of the system.

The administrative templates extension defines policy items that control the administrative and performance behavior of the Windows system. This is further divided into system, network and printer subsections, which control the respective areas.

Security Templates in Windows 2000

The security template under Windows 2000 is a convenient method for looking at all the systemwide security aspects of a machine. It isn't really a separate OS component from the other security elements, just a more direct method of looking at all the security aspects. It is defined through the security template snap-in in MMC. You need to launch a new instance of MMC from the command line and add in the snap-in first.

Each security template consists of seven areas that span the security configuration of the entire operating system:

- *Account policies.* Shows all the policies concerning account lockout, allowed login times, password size and complexity, and Kerberos session policies.

- *Local policies.* Shows all the policies on auditing, user rights, and system operational behavior security.

- *Event log.* Shows the configuration settings for the event log files.

- *Restricted groups.* Identifies the local restricted groups (administrators, power users, domain administrators, server operators, etc.) of that machine.

- *System services.* Shows the startup mode and allowed users for any application running as a system service.

- *File system.* Shows how the security system is to react when any changes are applied to an important system file listed here.

- *Registry.* Shows how the system is to react to changes to any registry entry.

In addition, the file system and registry properties control the inheritance behavior of other objects derived or copied from the original items listed. This enhances the management of important files and registry objects that may change or evolve with updates to the operating system environment.

The security template specifically excludes IPSec and public key policies. All the information in the template is stored in a text file with a *.inf* extension, which allows the user to copy or paste information easily between the template and other programs. The security template can be attached to a group policy object in *Windows Settings* under the *Computer Configuration* section of the GPO. The GPO can then be assigned to a particular machine or organizational unit in Active Directory. Although not all the properties of the security template will apply to all organizational units in AD, this allows a means to assign or control the assignment of system security per machine across the domain.

Kerberos Authentication

Kerberos realms in Windows 2000 are associated with Active Directory domains. The domain controller is usually the domain's Key Distribution Center (KDC). This makes authentication simpler as it uses the domain-wide accounts defined in the controller. The relationship between the two goes beyond just the conceptual level. Some Windows 2000-based Kerberos services require the use of Active Directory to communicate between realms.

A company's network can span multiple Active Directory domains and sites, and, likewise, so can the Kerberos system. Since each domain is responsible for its own set of accounts, those users in one domain have to contact the KDC of the other domain and be authenticated before being allowed to use any resources in the other domain. The client sends a new authentication request to the local domain controller/KDC. The local KDC sees that the request is for another domain and sends a *referral ticket* to contact the remote KDC back to the client.

The trust relationships between Kerberos realms are similar to those of the old NT domain model and can occur either in the *direct* trust between two KDCs or in *transitive* trust, in which one KDC refers the client to another KDC, which then passes the client to the destination KDC. In Windows 2000 this is implemented with the Active Directory hierarchy model instead of with such one-on-one transitive trusts. The local KDC contacts the domain controller above it to pass the referral. It can thus span any domain or the entire forest.

Another issue with Kerberos is how to handle multitier authentication when a client needs to contact a front-end server and then a back-end server, in a three-way connection, to reach its final destination. This is particularly relevant to virtual private networks when users have to connect through a firewall to get to the other side.

One method is to use a *proxy ticket*, whereby the client is first authenticated for the back-end server and then passes this ticket to the front-end server. This, however, breaks the concept wherein the names or identities of back-end servers are hidden from the client by the front-end server. A second method is to use a *forwarded ticket*, whereby the client hands over a copy of its ticket-granting ticket (TGT) to the front-end server and allows it to send off its own authentication request to the KDC. Windows 2000 supports both these forms of multitier authentication.

Integrating Kerberos in Windows 2000 and UNIX

Integrating Kerberos between UNIX and Windows 2000 is a tricky proposition. First of all Windows 2000 Kerberos is based on Version 5 of the protocol, the latest version. This was available for most major UNIX platforms as of June 1999, but is too recent and thus not widely supported by UNIX vendors. Furthermore, Kerberos in Windows 2000 uses accounts specific to the Windows model, and you have to use the Windows 2000 Kerberos system for it to work with Active Directory properly.

Thus, what you have is a one-way system, whereby Windows and UNIX users can be authenticated on Windows 2000-based KDCs. Windows users can be authenticated on UNIX-based KDCs, but only on a single server, and not on the domain. For UNIX users to be authenticated on Windows, you need to set up matching accounts and passwords on both platforms. Thus, the Windows 2000 KDC will authenticate the user, then pass the approved authentication ticket to the UNIX user. This ticket will be valid for either UNIX or Windows 2000 servers to which the account is allowed login access. The UNIX systems must have Kerberos server software installed, and be configured to point to the Windows 2000-based KDC.

Fixing Security Holes and Bugs

It is both true and untrue that Windows has a lot of security holes and bugs. Any complex operating system will likely have these holes, but the fact is that the Windows environment has been around for a fairly short time; thus, not all the bugs have been worked out yet. What is worse is Microsoft's penchant for claiming that the operating system is totally solid when, in fact, it has had only a few years of life so far. With each new major version, Microsoft makes the same claim—that the system is extremely reliable—but inevitably, every few months, it has to release a service pack with fixes for all the bugs.

 If you have a formal support contract from Microsoft, you will probably see the announcements of new patches (Microsoft doesn't really announce that a new bug has been found). These are also available directly from Microsoft's TechNet site (www.microsoft.com/technet), or as Product Flash e-mails that you can sign up for. The periodic service packs are actually just packaged collections of the many necessary patches that are continuously released.

Windows gets a lot more press when a bug or hole is discovered, but UNIX systems are not without their own problems. These bugs and holes are regularly exposed by sysadmins and hackers everywhere, and sometimes are addressed by UNIX vendors who release patches to fix the problems. The server-application-related bugs are found more readily—in particular, those that deal with the network—as a direct result of incoming attacks.

 The CERT advisories (www.cert.org) are still the most common method of announcing the discovery of new bugs or holes in UNIX and the distribution of appropriate patches. Similarly, companies with support contracts with their UNIX vendors are regularly informed of available patches through technical support e-mail and CD-ROMs.

Cross-Platform Security Tools

The differences in the nature of each operating system make it difficult to create a complete platform-independent security system. For example, the file permission bits in UNIX are completely different from the ACLs and ownership privileges in Windows, not just in appearance but in internal structure and handling. Furthermore, in an attempt to increase the security of the system, Windows 2000 implements new policy concepts that are not available in most UNIX systems at all.

Thus, security tools that are intended for use in cross-platform environments usually come in separate modules for each operating system. Each module tests a particular environment, and the software collates this information to be presented in a common visual or data form across the systems. Other security tools test the platform for network vulnerability through entry through public network ports, misuse of valid network user accounts, and misconfiguration of server applications.

Security Auditing Tools

Security auditing tools examine the state of your system or network and worm out the holes and cracks. It automates the process of checking all aspects of the system by first checking all the common points of security breaches, then attempting different approaches to cracking the system. It collates the information on its break-in successes and failures and presents this information to the auditor, often with different grades or ratings for the security level of each system component.

These products include L-3 Network Security's *Retriever*, Internet Security System's *Internet Scanner* and *System Scanner*, and Network Associates' *CyberCop Scanner*.

Security Policy Management Tools

Keeping track of security is hard enough without having to build your own database of records on what the security policy is for each system on your network. Thus, the emergence of the security policy management and decision support tools is a real boon to the sysadmin. These products are adjuncts to the other categories, such as security auditing and intrusion detection, and help you locate or determine the security aspects of any single machine. Furthermore, some such products can also be used with software- or hardware-based policy routers for the network that route your traffic according to your clearly stated rules and policies.

Some fairly decent security policy management tools include Internet Security System's *SAFEsuite Decisions*, Network Associates' *Net Tools Secure*, and Securant Technologies' *ClearTrust SecureControl*.

Intrusion Detection Tools

Intrusion detection tools monitor incoming activity on the network or on a system. Certain ports on the network or areas of the system are well known as possible entry points for intruders. However, they have to remain open for the proper use of the system. By monitoring the activity of users attempting to access these entry points from both outside and inside the network, the software can identify malicious intruders. It watches for sequences of events that are well-known methods of cracking into systems. The software then triggers events that e-mail or page the sysadmins, alerting them to take a closer look.

These tools are very much like security auditing tools, except that they are always kept running on the system, continuously checking a number of different elements. In turn, the software is sometimes written differently, since you do not have the luxury of spending a large amount of processing power or time on analyzing the security of the system—you have to determine the nature of these events in real time.

Popular intrusion detection tools include Internet Security System's *RealSecure*, BindView's *HackerShield*, Axent Technologies' *ID-Trak*, and Network Associates' *CyberCop Intrusion Protection*.

Virus Management Tools

Virus-checkers are a regular feature of most desktop systems these days. However, in an enterprise network, it can be quite hard to maintain consistency among the independent virus-checkers on each individual machine. The problem is one of mass device management and update control rather than one of technical complexity. Of course, the virus-checkers on each desktop themselves have to work well, but part of working well means dealing with the fact that there are new viruses, Trojan horses, worms, and so on coming out all the time. Each desktop therefore has to be updated regularly so that it keeps up with the new horde of invaders in the never-ending information war. Furthermore, these updates have to be securely delivered to the desktop. After all, if you cannot verify that the update to a virus-checker is authentic, you cannot know that the update itself is not a virus, intended to disable the virus-checker.

Several products today can centrally manage and distribute virus management information to the various systems in your network. Since this is simply a software distribution issue, they work well for cross-platform environments. They includes products such as Network Associates' *McAfee Total Virus Defense* (a suite of products for portables, desktops, and servers) and Trend Micro's *Trend Virus Control System* (a management product that goes with its *InterScan* virus-checker).

Summary

System and security management together comprise the majority of a technical administrator's work. Therefore, you should familiarize yourself with every aspect of the Microsoft Management Console, because it is going to be your constant companion in managing Windows 2000 systems. It permeates all areas of the system, and most new server and application tools are being designed to fit to it. Both system and security management can be further improved by third-party software. For many enterprises, the most valuable network and security management tools come at additional cost.

With system management procedures and software in place, you have reached the end of the technical aspects of cross-platform integration. At this point it would be safe to look back and examine the success of the integration project in whole, the subject of the next chapter.

## CHAPTER 18

Success with Integration

S uccessful integration of UNIX and Windows systems is like trying to figure out the secrets of the pyramid and stone monument builders of the ancient world. Some believe that there is magic or technology that is secretly hidden and has to be sought out, like the quest of some adventurous explorer in a Spielberg movie. Others believe it is sheer hard work that makes it all come together. Both agree that knowing how to do it is the key to finding the answers.

If you have gone through most of this book, you should now have an understanding as to how to go about seeking your fortune in integration. It may turn out that new issues and travails will appear on your journey, and we look into that matter here. In the end, it comes down to actually realizing how the system is successful and proving it to your bosses, in terms of that magic substance known as *return on investment*.

Testing from End to End

With the integration system in place, the last step before turning it on for your users is testing the system in pieces and as a whole. In the best of all worlds, you could run a single test that would determine how well the new integration system will work under any kind of stress. Unfortunately, this isn't a reality, partly because of the two different platforms involved and also because the nature of the problem varies not just with the product but with the specific implementation.

It is relatively easy to measure traffic on the network given the right tools. It is also not that hard to measure how much the system has to work to run a specific program. What is difficult is measuring how multiple applications or uses of the integrated system will affect the load of the system. Since each user may be running the application differently, it causes the load to become asymmetric and thus skews the data, which makes it hard to make any sense of it. Another problem is that the testing software needs to run in a particular environment, and it may not be available for both UNIX and Windows. Finally, there is the situation in which you already have the system in place and in active use, and any testing of new components thus has to be done live rather than in a prepared test environment.

Bluecurve's *Dynameasure* is a network-based load generation and testing facility for Windows platforms that can also be used in an integrated environment for testing file sharing or Windows server-based access. Although Dynameasure will not run cross-platform, it can still be useful for measuring the load between your Windows systems. The product executes customizable load generators or *motors* from idle desktop systems and measures the status on the target Windows server, with testing commands issued from a separate control server. The test scheduling and the results are available from yet another software component that sits on the network manager's desk. Ganymede Software's *Chariot* product is popularly used for measuring network delivery performance between multiple systems and can also help in the testing process.

Web testing has become a rage of late, especially considering how important the Web server has become to the industry. There are several testing tools available for Web sites, as well as third-party service providers who offer nationwide or global testing of response time to your sites.

Mercury Interactive provides a Web site load-testing and site management tool for Windows systems in its *Astra* product line. *Astra LoadTest* emulates user access to Web sites to determine factors such as response time of Web transactions, bandwidth usage, and hits per second, and to identify bottlenecks. You can build tests by visually recording your button clicks, typing, and any other interaction with the Web page, using the tool's Virtual User Recorder. *Astra SiteManager* is used to track site content and to manage broken links and modified pages. It can also build a visual map of the site and develop usage patterns for your content flow. Finally, it can analyze and report on Web access log statistics.

Bluecurve also provides a similar service for measuring Web site performance known as *eMeasure*. The service uses Bluecurve's eMeasure agents distributed in locations across the Internet to measure response times to the customer's site in a manner conceptually similar to Keydata's. Bluecurve currently measures the response time to a set of popular user destinations, including Amazon.com, eBay, and barnesandnoble.com, and posts the results in a composite index every 30 minutes on its home page.

Dealing with Problems

The job of a network manager is a continual battle to maintain order. However, you may at times find yourself losing the battle. This may mean that you are just plain understaffed and overworked, or there could be a failure in the network somewhere. Perhaps the integrated network is not being used as you had expected it to be. It could also be a very stark drop-off in performance due to the integration itself.

Finding out what is causing a problem is the first step toward finding a solution for it. The source of the problem may turn out to be improper use of the integration software, or it may be a component on the network that is unrelated to the integration at all, but nevertheless has been affected by it. The problem itself may be easily identifiable by its symptoms, or it may be some esoteric bug that exhibits itself only on rare occasions.

For a complete investigation of the problem, you should begin with the users or those who report the problem. They may be able to explain the symptoms or processes that result in the problem. This may give an immediate tip-off as to where to look. A detailed written note describing the problem, no matter how silly it sounds, will help with the eventual solution.

The next stage is to look at the affected systems and the integration software installed therein. If the system or integration application stores log files, the errors may show up in them. The first step in this stage is to look at the current configuration of the problem systems and determine whether they contain immediately noticeable errors. Then make a list of the other machines that use the integration software to communicate with each problem system. This includes all servers and user stations on your network or elsewhere. If several machines exhibit the problem, you may be able to short-cut the procedure by identifying servers that they have in common and looking at them first.

You should prioritize the hunt by putting the machines that affect the most people or perform the most crucial business tasks at the top of the list, followed by the less crucial ones. These important machines are typically the major servers in your company. If the problem traces back to them, put your full attention on it. If the problem itself is a virus or other malicious threat, you need to stop it before it spreads to even more systems.

On each server, again check the logs to see if any errors are rampant. Then check to see how the server is configured to communicate with the problem machine. The problem could be in the configuration of the integration software, or in that of the system itself.

If the problem occurs during a network communication session between the machines, it may become an issue of checking the data exchanged between the two machines. Pull out the network sniffer and examine the packets. A sniffer is typically a self-contained computer that watches all the traffic that traverses a certain point on the network and stores a copy of it for analysis.

Sniffers can immediately point out problems of malformed packets or lost connections. They can also display the entire contents of each packet going from one machine to another, allowing you to watch the exchange closely while it happens. To make sense of the exchange, you do have to know how the software communicates between the two machines, the format of the packet, and what the exchange causes on each side.

The worst problems are the multitudinous kind where the problem exhibits itself only when a number of machines communicate with each other. Often this is an issue of application scaling and overloading one junction or another. Log files are absolutely crucial in this respect. If the application does not itself have a log file, use the sniffer to collect statistics going to the application itself over the network. The idea is to find the measure at which things start going haywire and start backtracking the chain of events from it.

If the problem is periodic or hard to catch in action but can be duplicated, then you might want to use a load-testing tool (described earlier in this chapter) to attempt resolve it. First, you should decide whether replicating the problem is going to seriously affect the other machines on the network in the short and long term. You do not want to aggravate the situation unnecessarily, after all.

Solving machine and application problems may be beyond your abilities. If it comes down to this, admit it to yourself and your boss quickly once you have done your own investigation. You may wish to hire an outside consultant to look into the situation further. As with hiring any outsider, clearly establish the nature of the problem, their expertise in the problem area, what you expect them to do, and your deadline for results. You cannot afford to leave a consultant on the payroll for months without measurable success. The more you document the problem, the faster the consultant may be able to solve it—and, hopefully, the lower the eventual bill will be.

Measuring User Acceptance

Will your users be happy with the new system, or will such changes cause a people's revolt? After all, if your users don't make use of the system as you thought they would, then the ROI could be thrown off balance, which would, in turn, make your boss unhappy, and possibly on and on up the chain. So if the users aren't content with the new system, your neck may be on the line.

There are basically four kinds of users when it comes to these kinds of changes: those who love the new system, those who couldn't care less one way or the other, those who are hesitant to accept the change but will take to it in time, and those who are adamantly against the change. You can see the increasing degrees of difficulty it will take to convince them to move over.

There are ways to take advantage of this. Those who love the new system can often help to convince those who don't care and the hesitant ones. You might want to ask them why they like it so much; you may come across new reasons for implementing the system that had not occurred to you. You should share this feedback with the general user community by e-mail to help convince the others.

Those who are adamantly against the new system are, of course, *les enfants terrible*. This group will be pretty vocal about not liking the new system and will share their opinions with anyone who will listen. Your best bet is to ask them directly what they don't like about the system. It may be the case that they do not know how to perform a task under the new system, and just need to be told how. It may also be the case that they are missing a key feature of the old system, which you perhaps could still provide under the new system with a little modification or programming of your own. Whatever help you can provide to assuage their fears and problems will be beneficial. You might be surprised to find that they can turn pretty rapidly once they know their problems are being addressed. As for the absolute die-hards, there is nothing you can do other than shut off the old system.

If you are transitioning the system gradually between the old and new, monitoring the number of users on both systems may provide a helpful indicator of user acceptance. Depending on how long this gradual transition will take, choose an appropriate interval, like a week or month, and measure the average number of users on both systems during that period. What you are looking for is an increase in the number of users on the new system, and a decrease on the old one.

It is likely that users will use both systems during the early stages, so do not be alarmed if the combined total of users on both systems seems to be higher than the actual number of physical users you have. You do need to make sure that there is an appreciable decrease on the old system since you want to wean the users off of it. If its use does not seem to be decreasing, you should investigate why your users are still on it. It may be that they are using a feature on the old system that is not available or is not clearly evident on the new one.

Return on Investment

Ahh, those three little words that every top-level executive wants to hear. Return on investment (ROI) is a measure of the amount of return—usually measured in dollars, in extra revenue generated, or in costs saved—resulting from an investment in a new technology. These investments can include the purchase or development of new hardware or software, maintenance contracts, technical administration processes, or business processes.

The actual calculation itself is simple:

$$ROI = \frac{Return}{Investment}$$

An ROI value greater than 1 indicates that the investment is well worth it, and that you will be making or saving more money in the long term than you will be spending on the initial investment. An ROI between 0 and 1 may still be a good option for you in the long run, although not in the next year or in the immediate future. A negative ROI value is always bad. You don't want to be making less money than before because of an investment, after all. However, in some cases, especially when the situation calls for modernization of your computer systems, it may be the only choice aside from eventual business extinction.

The catch is in figuring out what the return may be in the first place, and it all comes down to making educated guesses. When upgrading software from one version to another, it is easier to calculate the return because you know the costs of operating the older version of the software. It is also likely that a vendor can advise you on how the software will save on time and support costs.

However, with integration, the situation is more complex. In the first scenario, you are implementing a cross-platform integration where there was previously no system for interaction between the two platforms. It is also possible that this integration can provide a new service that was previously performed manually, rather than through the computing system. In this case, the key is to outline the benefits to the users in terms of accessibility and increased productivity. If users are able to perform a new task, measure the value of the task in terms of increased revenues or reduced costs for that side of the business. For example, if a business can now run an application 1.5 times faster than it did before, measure the potential increase in revenues relevant to that task or application, and multiply it by 1.5. If the increased speed results in cost savings, divide the reduction in cost by 1.5.

In the second scenario, you are integrating the platforms to replace an existing system that runs either specifically on one platform, or in the same cross-platform environment using a different technology. This is not really an upgrade but a transformation, but it behaves very similarly to the upgrade. What you should do in this case is measure the costs of operating the older platform, including annual licenses, periodic upgrade costs, annual depreciation, and support and maintenance costs, and compare them against the costs of operating the new platform. The support costs are the determining variable here, and hopefully they should be lower for the new platform. Next, you should measure the increase in revenues generated by the group that uses the integrated system, as relevant to the integration.

You do need to specifically exclude natural annual growth of revenues. If you have kept track of that group's revenue growth in the past, you can extrapolate what the natural growth will be for the coming year. You also need to exclude growth due to the introduction of a new service or product, unless it is a direct outcome of the integration project itself.

In terms of measuring investment, you need to include all costs that you perceive will be incurred to transform to the new integrated environment, as well as all costs of operating the new environment for one year. Also normally included in this are the often-forgotten costs of discarding or deinterfacing the older systems or processes. If you plan to use a gradual transformation between the old and new systems, you need to keep including the operational costs of the older system in the measurement, reducing it as necessary, as you remove portions of it over time.

Another cost that you need to determine is how much it costs to deploy this new system per user. This becomes a big factor when new system access software has to be installed on each user's desktop. Finally, you do, of course, need to include the cost of purchasing the new system in the investment cost.

Summary

The field of cross-platform integration changes every year or two. Although some of the same technologies have been here for a decade, new developments in other areas give rise to other software technologies. Some make it easier or cheaper to perform the tasks that you do now, while others introduce new services that you always wished you had or that you hadn't even conceived of before. The question is, how does one keep track of these changes?

If you have a solution that works amazingly well now and will probably do so for several years to come, you might not have to worry about this at all. Although you could read every new magazine article that describes all these emerging technologies, the ones that can help the most are articles with details on success stories at other companies. These explain, at a cursory level, the trials and tribulations of getting a system off the ground and report on how well it works. Then, if you are interested, you should look into the kinds of articles that explain the technology in detail to get an understanding of whether it applies to your situation. Finally, when you are really into it, find a book, an online site, or a person that can answer your questions.

I leave you with one thought on the matter. Alexander the Great of Macedonia managed to conquer a large portion of the Eurasian world by the age of 25. However, upon his death, the empire crumbled in a short time. The Roman Empire, on the other hand, took a much longer time to build, but it lasted in one form or another for almost two millennia, and managed to integrate the diverse cultures of many nations. We remember the Roman Empire not just because of its power, but because of its effect on the many cultures under its power, and the prosperity it brought, albeit by force, to so many different nations. A young Julius Caesar, according to legend, saw a statue of Alexander in Spain and wept at the thought that his predecessor had accomplished so much by so young an age. Caesar eventually became the ruler of the Roman Empire years later, but by that point he had built a dynasty that ultimately lasted. Alexander was a great figure by all accounts, even according to Caesar. It is, however, Caesar that we remember as the founder of one of the most successful empires.

What's on the CD-ROM?

The CD-ROM accompanying this book should be used as an information source for cross-platform integration. The contents include a look at application packages and program code that enable this integration. In addition, it is my hope that it will continue where the book leaves off as a continuing resource that keeps current with technology developments. To this end, the contents are also reflected and continued on the accompanying Web site to this book.

The contents follow the pattern of the table of contents for this book. Written in the form of HTML pages that describe and compare a wide range of products, it examines specific features of software available on the market. Each package has details on its platform support, availability, compatibility issues, and feature list.

A further section of the CD-ROM contains a Frequently Asked Questions list of common issues and problems related to such cross-platform integration. These range from the basic to the advanced in technical complexity. My advice to you is to check out the CD-ROM and then the Web site to read updated information about the topics discussed in this book.

What is Freeware/Shareware?

Most of the software included with this CD-ROM is freeware, although there may be some shareware or demonstration copies also included in the package. Since the CD-ROM is linked to the Web site, it may address additional software from sources located on the Web site.

Freeware is software that is distributed by disk, through BBS, and the Internet for free. There is no charge for using it, and can be distributed freely as long as the use it is put to follows the license agreement included with it.

Open source software is freeware that also includes the source code for the applications. As with freeware, it can be copied and distributed freely as long as the use it is put to follows the license agreement included with it. Open source software can be sold at a price by anyone wishing to distribute copies of it. However, any open source software included with this book is available at no charge.

Shareware is a means of distributing software created by individuals or companies too small to make inroads into the more conventional retail distribution networks. The authors of shareware retain all rights to the software under the copyright laws while still allowing free distribution. This gives the user the chance to freely obtain and try out software to see if it fits his needs. Shareware should not be confused with public domain software or freeware, even though they are often obtained from the same sources.

If you continue to use shareware after trying it out, you are expected to register your use with the author and pay a registration fee. What you get in return depends on the author, but may include a printed manual, free updates, telephone support, etc.

Installing the Software

Most of the CD-ROM is organized as a set of HTML files that do not require any installation. There are also a number of separate software programs, each with its own installation instructions on the CD-ROM. Please follow the instructions given along with the particular program through these HTML files. You should proceed to Using the Software to see how you can view the contents of the CD-ROM.

Using the Software

The software on this CD-ROM consists of HTML pages and applications. Using a Web browser such as Netscape Navigator or Microsoft Internet Explorer, you should open the file named **default.htm** that contains the *Table of Contents* for the CD-ROM.

To access the software from a Windows system:

1. Place the CD-ROM into your CD-ROM drive.
2. From your Web browser, select File, Open or Open Location, and type **X:\default.htm** (where X is the correct letter of your CD-ROM drive).
3. Follow the instructions on the Web page to access the software.

To access the software from a Linux system:

1. Place the CD-ROM into your CD-ROM drive.
2. Your Linux desktop may automatically mount the CD-ROM. If it does not, type the following command at the Linux prompt: **mount -t iso9660 /dev/cdrom /mnt/cdrom**.
3. From your Web browser, select File, Open or Open Location, and type **file://localhost/mnt/cdrom/default.htm**.
4. Follow the instructions on the Web page to access the software.

For other UNIX platforms, please follow the instructions in your user's manual for mounting the CD-ROM and using your Web browser to access the file.

The Table of Contents for the CD-ROM will contain links to all other documents, files, and software on the CD-ROM and instructions on how to use any programs contained within. Please refer to these instructions as required for such software.

User Assistance and Information

If you need help with any of the software provided with this CD-ROM, please refer to the Web site that accompanies this book for further instructions. This Web site is located at **www.wiley.com/compbooks/shah**, and **www.integration-toolkit.com**.

The software accompanying this book is being provided as is without warranty or support of any kind. Should you require basic installation assistance, or if your media is defective, please call our product support number at (212) 850-6194 weekdays between 9 am and 4 pm Eastern Standard Time. Or, we can be reached via e-mail at: **wprtusw@wiley.com**.

To place additional orders or to request information about other Wiley products, please call (800) 879-4539.